DENATIONALIZING IDENTITIES

DENATIONALIZING IDENTITIES

THE POLITICS OF PERFORMANCE IN THE CHINESE DIASPORA

Wᴀʜ Gᴜᴀɴ Lɪᴍ 林華源

CORNELL EAST ASIA SERIES
An imprint of

CORNELL UNIVERSITY PRESS
Ithaca and London

Number 220 in the Cornell East Asia Series

Copyright © 2024 by Cornell University

All rights reserved. Except for brief quotations in a review, this book, or parts thereof, must not be reproduced in any form without permission in writing from the publisher. For information, address Cornell University Press, Sage House, 512 East State Street, Ithaca, New York 14850. Visit our website at cornellpress.cornell.edu.

First published 2024 by Cornell University Press

Librarians: A CIP catalog record for this book is available from the Library of Congress.

9781501774393 (hardcover)
9781501776717 (paperback)
9781501774416 (epub)
9781501774409 (pdf)

For my parents, Lim Ah Bah 林亞峇 *and Soon Lily* 孫麗莉.

Contents

Acknowledgments ix
List of Abbreviations xvii
Note on Transliteration xix

    Introduction   1

1. Articulating an Alternative Cultural Identity: Kuo Pao Kun's Multilingual Theater Practice in Singapore   34

2. An Incomplete Break with the Past: The Remaking of Identity in Stan Lai's Taiwanese Theater   74

3. Theater of Rebellion: Danny Yung and Experimental Hong Kong Theater   117

4. Diaspora within China: Gao Xingjian and the Theater of Exile   159

    Conclusion   192

References 209
Index 239

Acknowledgments

It takes a village to raise a child. It has probably taken much more to help me finish this book and get me to where I am today! I owe a debt of gratitude to the many generous people who have accompanied me throughout my journey. Chief among them are the six members of my Special Committee—Edward Gunn, Petrus Liu, Sara Warner, Lorraine Paterson, Steven Sangren, and the late Donald Fredericksen—whose tireless advice, nurturing guidance, and wise counsel saw me through to completion. Their erudition, accomplished teaching, and mentorship—as displayed by their constant encouragement, ever-patient tolerance toward my shortcomings, emotional support, and advice to me on the different facets of academia and beyond—are attributes of the exemplary scholar-teacher to which I aspire but whose high standards I may never achieve.

My project has benefited immensely from formal in-class inquiries and casual interactions with other inspiring teachers at Cornell who have been equally concerned for my personal well-being as well as academic progress. To Nick Admussen, Shelley Sunn Wong, Brett de Bary, Naoki Sakai, Huang Hong, Eric Tagliacozzo, Yan Haiping, Stephanie Divo, Robert Sukle, Sherman Cochran, Ding Xiang Warner, Bruce Rusk, Janice Kanemitsu, Su Weiqing George, Frances Yufen Lee Mehta, TJ Hinrichs, Arnika Fuhrmann, Ellen Gainor, the late Mei Tsu-lin, Felicia Teng Qiuyun, Robin McNeal, Daniel Boucher, Sabine Haenni, Amy Villarejo, Ichikawa Sahoko, Pan An-Yi, Bruce Levitt, Nicholas Salvato, Magnus Fiskesjö, Andrew Mertha, Andrea Bachner, and Son Suyoung: I could not have asked for a more supportive and nurturing intellectual home than what you provided for me at Cornell.

My graduate school experience in the United States began at Princeton, where I was fortunate to study with teachers whose penetrating insights laid the cornerstone of my research project. I am eternally indebted to Perry Link, Jill Dolan, Chou Chih-p'ing, Andrew Plaks, Jerome Silbergeld, Stephen Teiser, David Bellos, Susan Naquin,

ACKNOWLEDGMENTS

Michael Cadden, Janet Chen, Anne Anlin Cheng, Joanne Chiang Yang Chiu, Steven Chung, Benjamin Elman, David Leheny, Matsui Kyoko Loetscher, Shibata Tomoko, Tokumasu Yukari, Wang Ping, and Stacy Wolf for demonstrating that the devotion to scholarship and teaching extends far beyond the classroom. Prior to my education in the United States, I had the privilege of studying at Oxford under the supervision of Liu Tao Tao and tutelage of the late Glen Dudbridge, my advisor at University College, who provided critical feedback on this book in its earliest incarnation and to whom I am gratefully indebted for their advice and encouragement.

Without the unflagging support and encouragement of friends from near and far, I would never have received a world-class education. At Cornell, extensive discussions about life within and outside academia with Wang Chun-yen, Yulianto Mohsin, Eno Chen Pei Jean, Chen Xiangjing, Jack Chia Meng-Tat, Daisy Cai Yiwen, and Chen Shiau-yun, often late into the night, have enriched my academic travels and made research—an otherwise solitary affair—fun, exciting, and memorable. My "BIGASS" (Beer Including Gossip of the Asian Studies Society) comrades, Annetta Fotopoulos, Park Jahyon, Christopher Ahn, Samson Lim, Kevin Carrico, Liu Xiaoyan, Tyran Grillo, Zachary Howlett, Lau Ting Hui, Eileen Vo, Christopher Jones, Matthew Erie, Fu Lin, Carter Higgins, Ai Baba, Huang Junliang, Akiko Ishii, Jason Kelly, Peter Lavelle, Wang Yuanchong, Erick White, Steven Wyatt, Yang Qilin, Song Misun, Thomas Patton, John Phan, Christopher Tang, Dexter Thomas, Tinn Honghong, Nguyet Tong, Tyson Vaughan, Courtney Work, Sophie Wu I-Fan, Yi We Jung, "Genie" Jin Yoo, Tyson Yost, and Zhou Taomo, as well as fellow teaching associates in Chinese-language instruction, Hao Mingming, Li Fangfang, Li Nan, Liao Chenlin, Liu Rui, Shao Wenteng, Shen Dongming De Angelis, and Xu Li, have been with me every step of the way. The routine of watching plays and films at the Schwartz Center for the Performing Arts, downtown Kitchen Theatre, and Williard Straight Theatre, followed by the sharing of meals together with folks in the Department of Theatre, Film and Dance, Aoise Stratford, Clare Hane, Ozum Hatipoglu, Teresa Knight, Lindsay Cummings, Walter Hsu Jen-hao, Karbi Chan Yuet, Nicholas Friedman, Claudia Gonzalez, Jimmy Noriega, Sarah Powers Norman, and Park Hyoin, proved to be some of my most enjoyable moments during graduate school. My housemates, orientation mates, and friends, Ronaldo Timm, Irene Ye Qingyun, Ruslan Abdulganiyev, Li Shiyi, Amrit Singh Pall, Ipshita Pall, Ashley Smith, Zhang Jipei, Matthew Schneider, James Li, Lindsay Wyatt,

Emily Fridlund, Mary Ann Krisa, Christine Mohsin, Brian Cuddy, Jayasri Srinivasan, and Bi Ran, have warmed my heart on the far-too-many snowy days in "gorges" Ithaca.

At Princeton, the loving friendship and support of classmates in East Asian Studies, Chong Ja Ian, Wayne Soon Shilun, Du Chunmei, Brigid Vance, Cao Dazhi, Ye Minlei, Evan Young, Ng Teng Kuan, James Bonk, Chu Pey-yi, Chung Young-Ah, Eno Compton, Maren Ehlers, Scott Gregory, April Hughes, Li Yaqin, Bryan Lowe, Mao Sheng, Chris Mayo, Margaret Ng Wee-Siang, Gregory Seiffert, and Jesse Sloane, were indispensable in getting me through the demands of graduate school. My friends Phyllis Sun Kit Yee, Jessica Pan Si Jia, Chiu Yen-ting, Tsai Yu-Cheng, Alice Chow Lai Kam, Sirhan "Bobby" Chaudry, Lee Cheng-hsien, Onaolapo "Wali" Akande, Jason Fitts, Wu Hau-tieng, Daniel Gonzalez, Julie Han, David Lennington, Wang Yin, Lin Ting-Jung, Tavi Meraud, Celine Tan Sze Ing, Elsie Pang, Chris Tan, and Amy Wu journeyed with me through my hardest as well as most celebratory moments in New Jersey.

I am eternally grateful to Bard College for my first job upon graduation. My time in Annandale-on-Hudson not only taught me from scratch how to be a professor, but also gave me invaluable pedagogical insights and illuminating self-knowledge. The late Ying Li-hua, Robert Culp, Éric Trudel, Nicole Caso, Marina van Zuylen, Stephanie Kufner, Bruce and Odile Chilton, Richard Suchenski, John Weinstein, Omar Cheta, Oleg and Denise Minin, Lauren Curtis, Robert Cioffi, Drew Thompson, Sanjib Baruah, Swapan Jain, Katherine Boivin, Justin Hulbert, Tatjana Myoko von Prittwitz und Gaffron, Jason Kavett, Tehseen Thaver, Thomas Bartscherer, Thomas Wild, Mika Endo, Maria Sonevytsky, Franco Baldasso, Ian Buruma, Richard Davis, Elizabeth Frank, Joseph Luzzi, Robert and Katherine Gould-Martin, Susan Merriam, the late William Mullen, Melanie Nicholson, Philip Pardi, Nathan Shockey, Yuka Suzuki, Olga Voronina, as well as my dear foreign language elective tutors (FLETs), Luo Yitong, Cui Qian, and Zhang Linlin, extended me the warmest generosity possible and created a most supportive and nurturing environment. The sonorous laughter emanating from our hearty conversations with the FDR (faculty dining room) luncheon group, the late Luis Garcia-Renart, Mario and Diana Brown, Alice Stroup, the late John Pruitt, and Joseph Ahern, are some of my fondest memories. When I felt lost and desolate, my peers, Luke Thompson, Scott Mehl, Junji Yoshida, Khondaker Salehin, and Susan Blake, went out of their way to take care of me. My advisees and students in Chinese theatre, cinema, language, and First-Year Seminar (FYSem) classes were my first readers as I explored potential ways to engage them in the new material of which I am making sense. Having the opportunity to interact with these bright young minds in close proximity in a liberal arts college setting renewed my conviction in the power of education, reminding me that what we do matters and makes a real difference.

After three years at Bard, I returned to my undergraduate alma mater, the University of New South Wales (UNSW), Sydney. My greatest intellectual debt is owed to Jon Kowallis, my undergraduate advisor, whose illustrious example first inspired me to become an academic. Former teachers who have now become senior colleagues, Meg Mumford, Barbara Hendrischke, Karyn Lai, Wang Ping, Mina Roces, Peter Slezak, and Nick Domanis, offered sagacious advice to help me transition into a full-fledged faculty member. The friendship, collegiality, and support of Wang Cheng-Wei, Li Yu-chieh, Jonathan Bollen, Anne Bartlett, Emma Christopher, Sun Yingli, Mengistu Amberber, Zheng Yi, Rue Yong-ju, Ayshe Eli, and Chen Huanghuang have been unfailing as I acclimatize back to life in Australia. I am thankful toward my mentor, Michael Pusey, for always believing in me.

Returning to my alma mater I have come full circle by being appointed as fellow at the postgraduate wing of my undergraduate residential college, New College. I thank the master, Bill Pierson, the deans of New College Postgraduate Village, Susan Bazanna and Edwina Hine, the assistant deans, Ben Staunton and Misako Morita, and deans of New College, Arend Bogg and Jonathan Billingham, for giving me free reign to build community across the two buildings. The privilege of living among and interacting daily with hundreds of talented young adults, especially the senior residents, academic tutors, residents in the English Conversation Group, Coffee Chat!, and Brian Udugama, made my return such a welcoming homecoming.

During my conference and research travels, I have had the good fortune of getting to know distinguished colleagues, some of whom became steadfast friends and whose unwavering support I have relied upon over the years. I have benefited from exchanges with Mabel Lee, Quah Sy Ren, Kevin Ip Ka-Wai, Wasana Wongsurawat, Grace Mak Yan-yan, Xu Lanjun, Gilbert Fong Chee Fun, Shelby Chan Kar-yan, Jessica Yeung Wai-yee, Rossella Ferrari, Kenny Ng Kwok-Kwan, Thomas Moran, Du Liping, Koh Keng We, Lim Song Hwee, Chu Huei-chu, Lee Ming-yen, Terence Lee, Du Wenwei, Emily Wilcox, Sai Siew Min, Lewis Mayo, and Chu Kiu-wai. Tang Siu-fu, Alexander Ehlers, Humphrey Ko,

Lin Pei-yin, Ruediger Ehlers, Lindsay Driediger, William Murphy, Tan Jia, Woo Yen Yen, and Colin Goh have helped me in more ways than I can ever thank them. Ng Tze Yong, Tan Wee Kwang, Angela Chng Koh Peishan, Ng Thian Lai, Rahul Joshi, Jodie Wong Hoi Yee, Ada Wong Tin Yan, Ho Su Jin, Deyana Goh, and Amber Chen have remained kindred spirits even after these many years.

The completion of this book would not have been possible without the support of several competitive grants and fellowships. Funding from Cornell's Asian Studies Department, East Asia Program, Mario Einaudi Center for International Studies, Graduate School, and Southeast Asia Program, and Bard's Research Start-up Budget enabled me to travel for conferences, library research, and conduct interviews. Cornell's Sage Fellowship, Hu Shih Fellowship in Chinese Studies, C.V. Starr Fellowship, and Princeton's Graduate School Fellowship released me from teaching responsibilities. UNSW's Writing Mentor Grant for Early Career Researchers culminated in the invitation of Colin Mackerras to work with me on my manuscript, on top of several Vice-Chancellor's Strategic Priorities Performance Funds (SPF02) that relieved me of marking duties. Two Taiwan Fellowships from the Taiwanese Ministry of Foreign Affairs, as well as the Yangmingshan Fellowship, provided me with uninterrupted writing time. I am indebted to Perng Ching-hsi for recommending my first affiliation with the National Taiwan University's Department of Drama and Theatre, Shen Shiao-ying for hosting my second affiliation with its Department of Foreign Languages and Literatures, and Peng Hsiao-yen for hosting my participation at Academia Sinica's Institute of Chinese Literature and Philosophy. In Taiwan, discussions with Wang An-chi, Li Huei-mian, Katherine Chou Hui-ling, Dai Jinhua, Hsu Ya-Hsiang, Ko Chia-cian, Lee Long-shien, Lin Ho-yi, Wang Pao-hsiang, and Yu Shan-lu helped nurture my project.

Research for this book was conducted across several countries and regions. I am immensely indebted to the librarians, archivists, and administrators of theatre companies, archives, and libraries for helping me to navigate the bureaucratic hurdles and unearth the rich treasures collected at these various sites. These unsung heroes, who work tirelessly behind the scenes to allow us access to materials we need to do our work, must be gratefully acknowledged: at Princeton, Hue Kim Su in the Department of East Asian Studies, Richard Chafey in the Program in East Asian Studies, Martin Heijdra and Gonul "Gail" Yurdakul in the East Asian Library, Paula Chow and Hannelore Hand in the International Center; at Cornell, Sheila Haddad, Kim Scott, and

Erin Knuutila in the Department of Asian Studies, Joshua Young, Ma Hongnan, and Doreen Silva in the East Asia Program, Donna Miller and Carolyn Palladino in the Department of Performing and Media Arts, Thamora Fishel in the Southeast Asia Program, and Jeffery Peterson, Teresa Mei, and Zheng Liren in the Olin and Kroch Libraries; at Bard, Lory Gray, Kimberly Bail, and Dxina Mannello in the Division of Languages and Literatures, and Leslie Melvin in Academic Technology Services; at UNSW Sydney, Kathryn Pintaric in the School of Humanities and Languages; Mark Gaal, Suzanne Osmond, and Julia Mant at the National Institute of Dramatic Art; at University of Hong Kong, Iris Chan, Vivian So, and Feebi Wong at the Hong Kong Special Collections; Bernice Chan Kwok-wai at the International Association of Theatre Critics (Hong Kong); at Zuni Icosahedron, Doris Kan, Cheuk Cheung, Nadia Lu, Kaya Lo, Wong Yue-wai, Cedric Chan, and Jacky Chan; at National Taiwan University, Judy Hung Yu-chu in the library, Fiona Liao Hsiu-ru and Liu Yilin in the Department of Drama and Theatre; Peter Chang, Melodie Wu, and Elaine Wu at the Center for Chinese Studies, National Central Library; Liu Ya Ya, Rebecca Chia Pei-hsuan, and Chia Ming-chang at Performance Workshop; at National University of Singapore, Lee Ching Seng and Chong Loy Yin in the Chinese Library; and Michelle Tan, Jasmine Lim, and Ronice Ho at The Theatre Practice. In addition, I thank the kind efforts of Koh Nguang How, Timothy Pwee at the National Library Board, Siew Kiang at Teochew Poit Ip Huay Kuan, Szan Tan at the National Gallery, Lynn Lee at the National Museum Singapore, Joanne Mok at Singapore Press Holdings, Lin Shu-chen and Huang Yu-chen at the National Taiwan Normal University's Gao Xingjian Center, and photographer Liu Chen Hsiang for sourcing pictures used in my book. At various stages of conceptualizing and writing this book, I had the privilege of meeting Stan Lai, Danny Yung, Gao Xingjian, and the late Kuo Pao Kun's family—Goh Lay Kuan and Kuo Jianhong—to whom I am grateful for granting me extended interviews.

Parts of chapter 1 were published in "The Changing Landscape of Politics and Language Use in Singaporean Theatre: Towards a Multilingual Praxis," in *Singapore: Negotiating State and Society, 1965–2015*, ed. Jason Lim and Terence Lee (London: Routledge, 2016), 76–93, and in Chinese "1980 niandai haiwai Huaren juchang de juhe yu zhangli: Yi Xinjiapo wei li" 1980 年代海外華人劇場的聚合與張力：以新加坡為例 (Tensions and convergences in 1980s Chinese diasporic theatre: The case of Singapore), in *Diversity and Singapore Ethnic Chinese Communities: International*

Conference, ed. Koh Khee Heong, Ong Chang Woei, Phua Chiew Pheng, Chong Ja Ian, and Yang Yan (Singapore: City Book Room, 2020), 87–94. A portion of chapter 4 was published in "Between Memory and Forgetting: Ten Years after Gao Xingjian's Winning of the Nobel," in *Polyphony Embodied: Freedom and Fate in Gao Xingjian's Writings*, ed. Michael Lackner and Nikola Chardonnens (Berlin: De Gruyter, 2014), 185–201. I thank these publishers for their permission to reuse these chapters, which have all been significantly revised for this book.

Working with Cornell University Press East Asia Series on this book project has been an enjoyable and heartening experience. The three anonymous reviewers whom the press sought are not just expert readers in my field but senior scholars whose genuine interest in the topic helped the book reach its full potential. The meticulous care they undertook to improve the quality of this book was evident in the thirty pages of copious notes they shared with me. I cannot thank them enough. Nor can I adequately express my gratitude for the superb CUP EAS editorial team, emeritus editor Siti Mai Shaikhanuar-Cota, editor Alexis Siemon and her team, India Miraglia, Ellen Labbate, Jackie Teoh, Kristen Gregg, and Alfredo Rios, for believing in this project, for their patience with me, and for their indefatigable efforts to shepherd this book to publication. Any errors remaining are mine.

My family's unconditional love and faith in my undertaking of this project was instrumental to its completion. My brothers and sisters-in-law Wah Fong, Wah Long, Jean, and Wei Kei relieved me of worries and financial responsibilities at home. My niece and nephews Yee Ning, Yee Zhi, Yee Yan, Yee Xing, and Yee Yuan are a constant source of joy to the family. Without them, I would never have been able to pursue my dreams of living and learning overseas during the past two decades. I am most grateful to my spouse Tiffany Lee Shuang-Ching and her family, Lin Chien-ling, the late Lee Shi-wen, Lin Ko-chung, Lisa Lee Shuang-Pai, and Daniel Bosch, for welcoming me into their lives and accepting me for who I am. My parents Lim Ah Bah and Soon Lily were my first teachers of literature. It is they who first inspired this project and gave roots to my identity, showing me with their everyday examples that we are natural polyglots in our part of the hybrid Chinese-speaking world. This book is dedicated to them.

Abbreviations

I have provided the year of birth for the important people I discuss in the book in parentheses after the named individual, such as Stan Lai (b. 1954). I have also provided the year of founding of theatre companies and arts institutions in parentheses, such as Hong Kong Repertory Theatre (f. 1977).

BPAT	Beijing People's Art Theatre
CCP	Chinese Communist Party
ETC	Experimental Theatre Club
HKAPA	Hong Kong Academy of Performing Arts
HKREP	Hong Kong Repertory Theatre
HDB	Housing and Development Board
KMT	Kuomintang
NIDA	National Institute of Dramatic Art
NIA	National Institute of the Arts
NUS	National University of Singapore
PAP	People's Action Party
PRC	People's Republic of China
PPAS	Practice Performing Arts School
ROC	Republic of China
SAP	Singapore Amateur Players
SPAS	Singapore Performing Arts Studio
SAR	special administrative region
TELA	Television and Entertainment Licensing Agency
TTP	The Theatre Practice

Note on Transliteration

My study across four sites has resulted in at least four different romanizations in this book. I use the preferred spelling of Chinese words, names, and phrases in their local settings (e.g., Kuomintang and Kowloon). Also, I follow the conventional ordering of Chinese names: for persons with well-known Anglicized forms of their names, Stan Lai is first name followed by surname, while Gao Xingjian is surname followed by first name.

Most names in mainland China after the 1950s are spelled in the standard Hanyu Pinyin. In Taiwan, names follow some variation of the Wade-Giles system. In Hong Kong, most names are spelled according to Cantonese pronunciation (although Danny Yung Ning Tsun's name betrays this convention; this romanization reflects his Shanghainese roots). The names of ethnic Chinese in Singapore are romanized according to the regional Chinese language group to which they belong. For instance, Goh Guat Kian 吳悅娟 is romanized in Hokkien, whereas Ng Sin Yue 吳倩如 is in Cantonese, although both share the surname Wu 吳 if romanized in Mandarin. My resistance against standardizing all romanizations according to Hanyu Pinyin is not meant to confuse the reader; rather, my purpose is to reflect the diversity of the map from which I draw my sources and allow the rich complexity of this mapping to illustrate the multiplicity of Chineseness. Unless otherwise stated, all translations in this book from the various forms of Chinese are my own.

DENATIONALIZING IDENTITIES

Introduction

Nearly 270 drama enthusiasts gathered in eager anticipation to participate in a drama camp in late 1987 in Singapore. Made up of high school students and teachers, undergraduate students, and members of local theater companies as well as the public, the participants were excited about meeting the guest lecturers, who had been invited from overseas to address the camp and were considered "some of the sharpest brains in Asian theatre today" (Chong 1988, 5). This year's drama camp was jointly organized by sixteen local Chinese-language theater groups between December 31, 1987, and January 3, 1988, and held at the Yi Nian Centre (Centre of activity and recreation for the elders). Aimed at expanding the horizons of local theater practitioners and lovers by providing them the opportunity to learn directly from foreign experts, the camp also intended to foster greater interaction and understanding among members of the organizing drama troupes, instill a deeper sense of appreciation for budding drama activities in local schools, as well as raise the general public's awareness on the importance of theater (Di'erjie 1988, 198).

Through day-long talks, training sessions, and workshops, the invited speakers at the camp drew in participants with their extensive knowledge of dramatic histories and praxis, lecturing on topics from theater aesthetics, arts creation and appreciation to Enlightenment dramatist Denis Diderot and Peking opera master Mei Lanfang 梅蘭芳 ("Huayu" 1987, 20). Using video recordings of play productions from their home regions, these foreign specialists illuminated the distinctive ways in which drama developed across the parallel Chinese-speaking worlds (Mo 1987, 28). Equally fascinating was the live demonstration of creative improvisation, where one guest speaker shared the methods with which he created his plays, laying bare the secrets of his playmaking from page to stage. Other activities in this four-day camp included answering a questionnaire that provoked participants to ponder if their theater-going experience was closest to "a meal, a session in the loo, a dream, a lesson, a trip, love making, brainwashing, getting sick or a church service" (Chong 1988, 5), a "Drama Criticism Session" that reviewed several recent local Singaporean theater productions, as well as discussions on the future of modern Chinese drama. In addition, these overseas guests gave three evening lectures to the public from January 4 to 6, 1988, at the Yi Nian Centre and the News Centre to share their "personal experiences in playwriting, directing and reviewing" (Goh 1987, 5).

Participants who were interviewed expressed different degrees of appreciation for the camp. While some were wowed away by these master classes, feeling like "a grade two piano player whose learning suddenly jumped to grade six," others had a deeper realization for the multiple potentialities and possibilities of the dramatic form beyond linear narrative expressions. Still others felt these lessons were theoretically heavy, too big of a jump from what they had been heretofore exposed, and more guidance should have been provided especially for amateur practitioners and school learners on how to apply them (Wang Yumin 1988). Nevertheless, this camp reignited the embers of drama across the field-at-large, revealing the exciting diverse range of happenings on the dramatic stages in the various locales of the contemporary Chinese-speaking world. The significance of this event goes beyond merely dispelling the critique of Singapore as a "cultural desert," but especially given the ebb in the prior decade's local Chinese-language theater scene, this assembly of the most promising avant-garde dramatists in the region was a huge morale booster to the artistic and humanities intellectual circles, and whose impact would be felt for decades to come. Several of the then student participants would go on to become eminent figures in the theater, literary, film, music, media, and broadcasting industries, demonstrating the camp's impact on the local arts scene and beyond.[1] Known as the Second Chinese-language Drama Camp 第二屆華語戲劇營, this historic meeting saw Malaysia's Krishen Jit (1939-2005), Beijing's Gao Xingjian 高行健 (b. 1940), Hong Kong's Danny Yung Ning Tsun 榮念曾 (b. 1943), Shanghai's Yu Qiuyu 余秋雨 (b. 1946), and Taiwan's Stan Lai Sheng-chuan 賴聲川 (b. 1954) being invited to guest lecture in Singapore and meeting as a group with their host and organizer Kuo Pao Kun 郭寶崑 (1939-2002).[2]

I will use this seminal congregation to launch *Denationalizing Identities: The Politics of Performance in the Chinese Diaspora*. Retrospectively, this assembly was considered a meeting among giants in the global contemporary Chinese-language drama scene. More importantly, the camp signifies the beginnings of the formation of a more integrated network of correspondence, collaboration, and exchange in the Chinese dramatic world. All of the major participants were on the brink of rising to become the most iconic figures and prime movers in their respective cultural scenes and beyond. Since the 1980s, Gao, Yung, Lai, and Kuo emerged as the most prominent artists from their respective localities. Not only were their dramatic works the most groundbreaking, commanding both a cutting-edge and critical reception, the four director-playwrights were also the most frequently translated and performed outside their home regions. As public intellectuals, they have been vocal about advocating greater spaces for cultural discourse, having organized conferences that brought together a rare mix of scholarly and artistic participants, and even policy makers, displaying a keen willingness to engage in intellectual debate as practitioners of the profession. As a result, academic symposia have been held in their honor and their artistic achievements have earned them the highest possible critical appraisals: Chevalier de l'Ordre des Arts et des Lettres by the French government (Gao and Kuo), "Asia's top theatre director"

---

1. Among the participants who would contribute in major ways to the Singapore Chinese-language arts industry were future leaders of the theater company The ETCeteras 海燕等人 (f. 1990) Lim Hai Yen 林海燕 and Choo Lip Sin 朱立新, head of the Singapore Press Holdings' Chinese Media Group Lee Huay Leng 李慧玲, singer and radio DJ Chye Lee Lian 蔡禮蓮, and journalist and television screenwriter-turned-filmmaker Eva Tang 鄧寶翠.

2. The list of master dramatists invited to this historic drama camp was also extended to the inaugural dean of drama at the Hong Kong Academy for Performing Arts, Chung King Fai 鍾景輝 (b. 1937), who did not turn up (Di'erjie 1988, 199). Although the organizing committee was made up of representatives from sixteen drama troupes, it was no secret that Kuo Pao Kun was the central figure behind this among other key organization events in the 1980s Singapore arts scene, which I will detail in chapter 1.

by *Asiaweek* (Lai), Merit Cross of the Order of Merit on Ribbon of the Federal Republic of Germany (Yung), and the Nobel Prize in Literature (Gao).[3] They have since nurtured numerous younger theater-makers and artists and inspired even more arts activists who have subsequently founded their own theater companies and institutions, thus amplifying their impact in other cultural fields and sectors.

This book presents a circuit of transnational Chinese creativity that differs substantially from that assumed by conventional literary history centered on the Chinese mainland. As a full-length comparative study of contemporary drama that seeks to reflect the diversity of the Chinese-speaking world, it investigates the issue of national identity formation that was prominent in the 1980s by examining the works of four important diasporic theater director-playwrights: Kuo Pao Kun, Stan Lai, Danny Yung, and Gao Xingjian.[4] In particular, I focus on the problem of "Chineseness," arguing that the aforementioned dramatists share an interest in problematizing essentialist notions of Chinese identity.

At the height of the Cold War, the "Bamboo Curtain" not only divided the "two Chinas" across the Taiwan Strait, but also impacted the two former British colonies in a way that resulted in a re-Sinification and eventual handover of Hong Kong to China, and a clampdown on Chinese education due to the "Red Scare" in Singapore. Consequently, the ethnic Chinese majorities of each state were forced to respond, on the one hand, to the accelerating emergence of China on the world economic and political scene, and on the other, to the ever-changing internal paradigms and differing circumstances within each site. Although

---

3. The symposia include the following: "When Petals Fall Like Snow—The World of Kuo Pao Kun, Playwright," Tokyo, New National Theatre (Oct. 25–Nov. 5, 2000); "International Conference on Lai Sheng-chuan's (Stan Lai) Works," Taipei National University of the Arts (Sep. 29–Oct. 1, 2006); "International Symposium: Gao Xingjian — a Writer for His Culture, a Writer against His Culture," Chinese University of Hong Kong (May 28-30, 2008); "Gao Xingjian: Freedom, Fate, and Prognostication Conference," Friedrich-Alexander-University of Erlangen-Nuremberg (Oct. 24–27, 2011); "Kuo Pao Kun International Conference," National Museum of Singapore (Sep. 14–15, 2012); "Hong Kong Theatre in Transnational Perspective: New Directions and Discourses Since 1997," School of Oriental and African Studies (SOAS), University of London (Sep. 8–10, 2017); and "International Symposium on Stan Lai's Theatre Studies: Dramatic Structure/Theatrical Expression/Historical Reflections," Nanjing University of the Arts (Sep. 23–25, 2022).

4. I have chosen not to pursue Krishen Jit and Yu Qiuyu as the subjects of my study even though they were also master dramatists in the Second Chinese-language Drama Camp because Jit does not contribute to the study of Chinese-language theater and the bulk of Yu's creative energies have focused on dramatic and cultural critique.

these states have very different aspirations to nationhood and different discourses of modernity, the cultural identities these dramatists were scripting not only provided an alternative to those sanctioned by their respective states, but also reacted against political forces beyond national borders.

Since the didactic function inherent in theater produces, reconstructs, and problematizes identities in ways that differ from other genres, my privileging of drama in the production of a global Chinese consciousness is uniquely positioned to address the complexities posed in the interweaving discourses of nationalism, identity politics, and cultural performance. Importantly, avant-garde drama was characterized by a political posture in opposition to prevailing values and an effective agent of change. The critical purchase of avant-garde drama, which these cultural producers shared, therefore, challenged their individual ideological state apparatuses to monopolize identity, while providing them a major inspiration and source of recognition at home and abroad. By mapping out the problem concretely and historically, this book challenges the notion of a unified Chineseness via a transnational perspective that underscores the question of identity construction.

Identities-of-Becoming in Four Chinese States

The development of drama across the various Chinese-speaking sites is anything but uniform. Intricately tied to the politics of culture, language, and identity of the particularities of their individual locales, their distinctive trajectories are as much a result of historical ruptures as their responses to local situations and geopolitics. Illustrating this difference, Gilbert Fong Chee Fun cites the linguistic variations across the communities in the region. He notes, for instance, the predominance of spoken Mandarin in mainland China and Taiwan differs from the situation in Singapore, which is comprised of three main ethnic groups (Chinese, Malay, and Indian) having four official spoken languages (English, Mandarin, Malay, and Tamil), and also from Hong Kong and Macau, which are biliterate and trilingual 兩文三語 (written literacy in Chinese and English, and spoken literacy in Cantonese, Mandarin, and English) (Fong 2000, 10). This linguistic variance is but one example to illustrate the complex and diverse sociohistorical development across the Chinese-speaking world. While the ethnic Chinese majority in these states may share "a common cultural heritage," each has "taken a distinct path towards modernity and globalization, responding to the specific imperatives of their respective cultural geography" (Tam, Yip, and Dissanayake 1999, xvii). My study aims to unpack their differences and demonstrate how drama participated in the making of these differentiations in identity and identification in the decade of the 1980s.

Since the "Chinese diasporas" are defined by what they are essentially not—grouped under the same rubric precisely because they are outside the geographical confines of the Chinese mainland—and not some kind of universal sameness, it is even more pertinent to historicize the unique geopolitical and social conditions in each site to account for the individual dramatist's rise to auteurism. Important too is that these intellectual artists span two generations, with Kuo, Gao, and Yung born around the 1940s, and Lai the mid-1950s, with their careers in different developmental phases when they met in 1987.[5] This book aims neither to elide their differences nor pretend that a selfsameness existed in all four locales, but instead problematize a multiplicity of Chineseness by examining how each performed a uniquely configured identity that responded to their particular sociohistorical condition.

Significantly, the 1980s was the period where the search for a local identity peaked in all four localities, which was in large part prompted by changes in regional geopolitics. China's reentry into the global order at the end of the Cultural Revolution in the late 1970s forced these states with an ethnic Chinese majority to each ask the question: Who am I? Because of the People's Republic of China's (PRC) isolation for most of the Cold War era, for instance, the Republic of China (ROC) regime continued to represent itself as the legitimate "China" on the international front, notwithstanding it had already lost control over the Chinese mainland since 1949, holding only the Taiwan, Penghu, Quemoy (Jinmen), and Ma-tzu (Mazu) islands. Now that the PRC has reasserted itself on the global front, replacing the ROC on the Chinese seat in the United Nations and on the Security Council since 1971, the Taiwanese were forced to reexamine their own identities vis-à-vis the new geopolitical reality of the contending "two Chinas." The bulk of Stan Lai's early work contemplates the epochal history of this cross-strait divide, such as his *xiangsheng* play 相聲劇 series *Nayiye, women shuo xiangsheng* 那一夜，我們說相聲 (The night we became cross-talk comedians, 1985) and *Zheyiye, sheilai shuo xiangsheng?* 這一夜，誰來說相聲？ (Look who's cross-talking tonight? 1989), as well as his most influential

---

5. I am indebted to Quah Sy Ren for sharing this insight with me.

play *Anlian taohuayuan* 暗戀桃花源 (Secret love in peach blossom land, 1986), providing critical reflection on the fragmented identity of the contemporary Taiwanese.[6]

Similarly, the identity of those residing in Hong Kong was immediately heightened after the official signing of the 1984 Sino-British Joint Declaration 中英聯合聲明 promising the territory's "return" to its "motherland" in 1997, thus sealing its fate. Hong Kong had by then developed into a bustling financial hub and commercial center in East Asia, with its gross domestic product ranked third globally only after New York and London. The territory's Canto-pop and film industries had also had immense influence in the region, especially on the neighboring Chinese communities in East and Southeast Asia, earning it the appellation "Hollywood of the East." Contrasted with the motherland that had newly emerged from the tumultuous ten-year Cultural Revolution, it was difficult for most Hongkongers to imagine a bleaker future than impending political merger with the Chinese mainland. An outpouring of emotional response flooded the entire society that resulted in a significant exodus from the territory, with Vancouver and Sydney being the primary migration sites; ironically, those who wanted to retain their sense of belonging had to exit the territory in order to do so. Of those who stayed, the question of identity was fervently discussed in all forms of literary and artistic productions. For the next fifteen years leading up to the handover, the abundance of dramatic works that emerged discussing the 1997 phobia, probing what being a Hongkonger during the Qing dynasty and colonial rule meant and in posthandover times might mean, were hence collectively termed "the '97 plays" 九七劇. Among his many works that examine this Hong Kong-British-Chinese nexus, Danny Yung's *Yapian zhanzheng: Zhi Deng Xiaoping de sifeng xin* 鴉片戰爭：致鄧小平的四封信 (Opium war: Four letters to Deng Xiaoping, 1984) was a pioneering work that spearheaded the '97 plays, seeking to foreground Hong Kong's subjectivity within this tripartite relationship.

Neither was the city-state of Singapore spared the rippling impact of the Cold War. Even though Singapore is a multiethnic nation, since the

---

6. Literally "face and voice," Perry Link suggests *xiangsheng* 相聲 might simply be rendered as "comedians' routines" instead of the commonly misconstrued term "cross talk." Dating several centuries old from China, the genre uses humor, especially satire, and may involve singing, imitation of sounds, and other kinds of oral antics that are most commonly performed by two comedians (Link 2007, 208).

Iron Curtain's partitioning of the communist bloc and the free world, Chinese education was deemed suspicious and highly susceptible to infiltration by communist insurgence. As a state with a three-quarter ethnic Chinese majority, becoming the "Third China" in Southeast Asia was not an option that would be tolerated in the free world (Chua 2009, 240). Consequently, the state clamped down on Chinese education and simultaneously elevated the status of English as the national working language. This linguistic change adversely affected social mobility, economic opportunities, as well as intergenerational communication across the entire country.

An avid theater practitioner who was originally only active in the Chinese-language sphere, Kuo Pao Kun proceeded in the 1980s to conduct workshops and write plays in the English language, as well as develop a multilingual theater praxis that henceforth became the definitive model of Singaporean theater. All the major artists in both the current local Chinese- and English-language drama circles have been nurtured under his influence as a result. In crossing the linguistic divide that governed Singaporean ethnic groups prior to the 1980s, Kuo was not only responding to the government's suppression of Chinese-language education, he was at the same time lending a voice to the Chinese-educated Singaporeans who had been disenfranchised by the 1979 language policy that was propelling the state into an English-speaking nation. Beginning with his magisterial *Xunzhao xiaomao de mama* 尋找小貓的媽媽 (Mama looking for her cat, 1988), Kuo's hybrid multilingual plays encapsulated a holistic Singaporean experience that revolutionized the hitherto monolingual dramatic tradition. His work could be seen as a space for articulating an alternative form of cultural identity in contradistinction to the government's multiracial model, positing dramatically new possibilities for rethinking Singaporean Chineseness amid a multiethnic, multicultural population.

In this regard, Gao Xingjian's avant-garde plays attempted to wrestle with the idea of an authentic Chineseness within China by arguing for multiple cultural roots in the 1980s "cultural fever" debate. The post-1978 "Reform and Opening Up" period ushered in a seemingly more relaxed political atmosphere in Chinese society, inviting criticism on the excesses of the Cultural Revolution from artists and writers who had since become disillusioned with the state. Innovative techniques in artistic expression such as "reform literature," "scar literature," "roots-seeking literature," and later "misty poetry," defined the period with experimental works reflecting on the turmoil caused by the ten-year upheaval that at the same time questioned state authority.

Like other forms of art and literature of the era, drama of the new period originated as a critical response to the Cultural Revolution (Yan 1998, ix). Experimental drama in the post–Cultural Revolution period had not achieved significant impact until Gao came onto the scene, which marked the emergence of China's "little theater movement" 小劇場運動. Gao has drawn his creative resources from the cultural peripheries of Chinese tradition as well as alternative forms of the Western avant-garde. More than critiquing the problems and excesses of the Cultural Revolution, however, his avant-garde *Chezhan* 車站 (Bus stop, 1983) employed novel forms of expression to contest the erstwhile dominant socialist realist mode of narration. In so doing, Gao posed a direct challenge to state authority by depicting a reality that differed from the status quo, and the play can be seen as his attempt to wrest the right of cultural definition and authority away from the political elites in Beijing. Therefore, an alternative Chineseness was not sought just across Singapore, Taiwan, and Hong Kong, but also within China. Just like how the PRC's emergence from the Cultural Revolution ignited an identity crisis in the other three regions with a majority of ethnic Chinese, within mainland China intellectual artists too were seeking what it means to be Chinese beyond the state's definition.

I have selected to analyze the aforementioned plays in the following chapters because I believe they best represent the critical interventions that took place at pivotal moments of historic change, where identity was vigorously contested and (re)constructed across the region. Weaving together native, foreign, and Chinese elements to give voice to the local, these original plays were breaking down barriers of form and structure, creating traditions anew, and producing many "firsts" that were highly innovative and monumental in global Chinese theater history. Needless to say, each dramatist achieved varying degrees of alterity in their work, as necessarily conditioned by their politics with the place and state; all were, to borrow the words of Diana Looser in her study of new Oceanic theater but applying to the Chinese context, "exposing new points of view and staging resistance to dominant narratives" (2014, 17).

Yet I do not make light of the significant innovations earlier dramatists had achieved in alternative practices well before the 1980s. Theater is constantly introducing innovations, and what "avant-garde" means can only be made sense of within their historical contexts. For instance, by revealing how the novelties of Tian Han 田漢 (1898–1968), Hong Shen 洪深 (1894–1955), and Ouyang Yuqian 歐陽予倩 (1889–1962) in scripting, directing, and acting are distinguished from their contemporaries, Chen Xiaomei's study demonstrates that the contributions of the "three founding fathers of modern Chinese spoken drama" go beyond pioneering "a socialist realist theater with lasting impact" (2016, 30), and can therefore be understood as avant-garde already from the 1920s. In this regard, the *xiqu gailiang* 戲曲改良 (reform to Chinese opera) that is traced even earlier to the late Qing, advocated by Liang Qichao 梁啓超 (1873–1929) "to free traditional operatic theater from its ancient rules" and allow the genre to "play a significant role in constructing a new nation" directly benefited modern Chinese drama's development and status (X. Chen 2010, 1–2), will count too. As will Huang Zuolin's 黃佐臨 (1906–94) experiments with the concepts of the German dramatist Bertolt Brecht in the late 1950s. The centuries-long history of modern Chinese drama is peppered with many such exploratory innovations, and Kuo, Gao, Yung, and Lai can certainly be considered as successors to the dynamic experimental traditions of their own theater histories from the early twentieth century. The focus of my book foregrounds their vital contributions to nonmainstream forms of theater-making at a crucial moment in the political and cultural history of the region in the 1980s context and whose impacts still resonate today.

Performing Chineseness in the Cold War

As part of a larger debate on Chinese identity, scholars have in recent years called for other ways of imagining "Chineseness" apart from that being fixated on nationality and locality. Attempts to delink culture, nation, and the political entity known as "China" began three decades ago with Tu Wei-ming's pioneering efforts to coin the term "Cultural China" 文化中國 (1991, 12) and Leo Lee Ou-fan's discussion of what it means to be a self-imposed Chinese exile in the diaspora (1991, 212). These early endeavors to privilege the periphery over the center saw debates, most notably by Rey Chow, Ien Ang, and Allen Chun among others, further echoing responses to de-center power from both the hegemony of the PRC as well as Western academia. While Ang's lived example as a cultural studies professor of Chinese descent who does not speak any form of the language questions the assumed normative relationship binding language to ethnicity (2001, 21), Chow deconstructs the conflation of power and language "suppressed under the myth of 'standard Chinese'" (2000, 12), and Chun exposes the concept as a political construct altogether, as nothing more than "just claims, or *representations*, that need to be constantly legitimized" (1996, 126). Therefore, Chow calls for Chineseness to be read as an "open signifier" that "can no longer be held as a monolithic given tied to the mythic homeland" and be spoken of henceforth "in the plural—as so many kinds of Chineseness-es, so many Chinese identities" (2000, 24). More recently, the emergence of "Sinophone studies"—as spearheaded by Shih Shu-mei (2007), David Wang Der-wei (2006), and Jing Tsu (2010)—erstwhile appropriated through the lenses of visuality, fiction, sound, and script, have been shifting the paradigm away from a focus on mainland China as the sole cultural producer. As Jing Tsu questions, "Is there no other way of inhabiting Chinese-language writing other than having either to surrender to—or to reject—its binding contract of nationality and nativity?" (2010, 203).

On top of these myriad voices from Western academe, scholars from other vantage positions were calling attention to a plurality of the literary productions in the various Chinese worlds that likewise resist a center-periphery or top-bottom hierarchy. While Yeo Song Nian, a Singaporean scholar who subsequently taught in Taiwan, terms this "World Chinese Literature" (Yeo and Jian 2004, i), Tam Kwok-kan, Terry Yip Siu-han, and Wimal Dissanayake in Hong Kong have called for a similar reexamination of the field's paradigm by underscoring the value of putting Chinese writings from China, Taiwan, Hong Kong, and Singapore on the same platform. Instead of positing a homology between state, nation, and culture, the most innovative artistic works from these four Chinese communities

> seek to *break out of the single state-national-culture boundary* by focusing on the *sub-nationalities* and *sub-cultures* on the one hand and the *supra-national* and *supra-cultural connections* on the other. . . . In this process of cultural transformation and diversification, it is interesting to *identify the global issues the Chinese self must face while striving to remain Chinese and local.*
>
> (Tam, Yip, and Dissanayake 1999, xvii; italics mine)

Already in his closing remarks at the 1986 Second International Conference on the Commonwealth of Chinese Literature, Chow Tse-tsung has proposed the concept of "multiple literary centers" (1989, 360), noting that Chinese literature in Southeast Asia always already possesses a unique "double tradition"—"Chinese literary tradition" and simultaneously "native literary tradition" (359). Echoing Chow's observation, Singapore and Malayan Chinese literature scholar Wong Yoon Wah surmises:

> The recent development of so many national forms of Chinese literature has changed our idea of Chinese literature. We can no longer assume that China is the only centre of Chinese literature. The Chinese *literatures* developed in Southeast Asia and elsewhere should *not* be seen as *tributaries* of the literature of China. Instead, each of these Chinese writings has become *another centre* of world Chinese literature.
>
> (1995, 361; italics mine)

Perhaps more than what David Wang would call "boundaries in flux" (2006, 4), it is these multifoci centers and "the way that citizens of these four communities seek to *make sense of being Chinese* in a rapidly changing world [making] *each place implicated in the density of others*" (Tam, Yip, and Dissanayake 1999, xvii; italics mine) that my book aims to illuminate, edifying insights through a comparative study of drama in these four contested sites. My research shares with these approaches similar pluralizing impulses and an increasingly globalized perspective that transcends national borders.

The field of theater and performance studies has taken a critical turn to focus on performance as a locus from which to contemplate and conduct challenges to authority, unmask operations of power, and rehearse new modes of being and belonging. As Jill Dolan suggests, "theatrical performance offers a temporary and usefully ephemeral site at which to think through various important questions about the representation not only of individual identities but of social relations within, across and among identity categories, and across communities and cultures" (2006, 510). Official historical narratives often carry a two-pronged approach: while illuminating the celebratory successes of the state, they simultaneously silence ways of identification that do not adhere to the state-sanctioned account. Peggy Phelan's *Unmarked*, for instance, explores the unspoken "assumptions about the connections between representational visibility and political power." In resisting the state's active erasure, she attempts "to revalue a belief in subjectivity and identity which is not visibly representable" (1993, 1). Although the phenomenon is common to many countries, I will unpack in greater depth the situation in the Chinese-speaking world and demonstrate how, to borrow the words of Elin Diamond, performances too are "negotiations with regimes of power" (1996, 2) and examine their political implications as well as impact on identity and cultural formation. In each of the following chapters, I will show how the critique of performance "can remind us of the unstable improvisations within our deep cultural performances" by exposing "the fissures, ruptures, and revisions that have settled into continuous reenactment" (E. Diamond 1996, 2) in the various Chinese states.

That performance is a synthesis of movements, sound, visuality, and narration, constituting the affective interaction of live bodies, words, and action in a shared space, uniquely situates it to suture, reconstruct, and challenge identities. As Diana Looser reiterates, after Marvin Carlson, "enabled by theater's ability ... to combine a number of different elements into a simultaneous spatiotemporal matrix," performance "generates a range of meanings that exceed the boundaries of the written text" (2014, 15). A principal feature of "theater's engagement with the past," she writes, "is its ability to imagine beyond existing records and established understandings.... For all its dynamic immediacy and ability to conjure memory, [theater] is a form inherently allied with illusion and make-believe" (17). These inherent qualities of performance, therefore, embed within it a unique variegated lens to view the multilayered constructions of identity. In Dolan's words:

> Because performance demonstrates the ways in which any reading is always multiple, and illustrates the undecidability of visual as well as written meanings, it provides a way of seeing identity as complex, as crossed with difference, and never as the static, innate, unchangeable thing it's described to be in other venues of social life.
>
> (2006, 510)

By attending to aspects in meaning and value making that are conveyed beyond the expression of the verbal language, the four Chinese dramatists I study all seek to challenge the fixity and stability of identity through strategies of constant *dis*identification, exposing identity as a construction that needs to be constantly legitimized and giving voice to those who are unmarked, unheard, or unseen.

In many countries worldwide, therefore, Looser asserts that "the theater—perhaps more than any other genre of creative expression—has operated as a powerful and persuasive locus for the construction, articulation, and questioning of national identity, both hegemonic and counter-hegemonic" (2014, 10). To this end, William Peterson's *Theater* and the Politics of Culture in Contemporary Singapore (2001), Quah Sy Ren's Gao Xingjian and Transcultural Chinese Theater (2004b), and Shelby Chan Kar-yan's Identity and Theatre Translation in Hong Kong (2015) are highly admirable works that have made significant headways in this direction. All three monographs unpack the complex political dimensions that define the tensions and convergences between state and their (trans)local theater scenes. Peterson's study of the Singaporean English-language theater judiciously maps out the difficult terrain Anglophonic drama practitioners have to navigate through the arts and cultural practices in order to inflect direct contentions with the regime. Quah's comprehensive account on the life of Gao Xingjian traversing the distance between mainland China and France details the transcultural processes in his dramatic praxis, which is a continuous dialogical discourse, fusing "Chinese and French, traditional and modern, literati and folk, mainstream and peripheral" cultures (2004b, 13). Synthesizing elements East and West and other seemingly diametrical opposites is not only indicative of Gao's tumultuous life trajectory and training, but also importantly a continued biopolitical tussle with the Chinese state's claim to culture, identity, and power. Chan's introspection of identity formation in the two-decade duration of Hong Kong translated theater examines the sociopolitical history that resulted in the rise of local identities in the city-state. Thanks to her insightful analysis, we now have a far better understanding of the productive role theater can perform in challenging the deep impact external politics have exerted on local policies. Whereas these commendable studies have focused on either single authors or singular sites, I seek to contribute to the discussion via a comparative transnational approach.

Of late, a small but growing interest in transnational Chinese and Asian theaters has enriched the study of the field. Staging China: New Theatres in the Twenty-First Century (R. Li 2016) and Routledge Handbook of Asian Theatre (S. Liu 2016) comprise collated thematic approaches by different scholars on the topic. Whereas the essays in these edited volumes are more commonly case studies of the disparate individual sites collected under a same theme, an increasing number of monographs has also contributed to this growing interest via cross-regional comparative study. All three of Daphne Lei Pi-Wei's monographs, for instance, probe the Chinese operatic genre transnationally. While her first (2006) details how Chineseness is imagined in the transregional East–West contact zones between the United States and China, and how the diasporic Chinese in the American West Coast use the genre to reify their identities in their everyday reality as a migrant community, her second (2011) examines "alternative Chinese opera" in Taiwan, Hong Kong, and the United States, and her third (2019) crosses national boundaries from the gender perspective. Alexa Alice Joubin's (2009) work on "Chinese Shakespeares" reveals how the Bard has been reformulated and used by artists across different Chinese-speaking states to fit their own agendas in their specific historicities. Amanda Rogers (2014) studies the transnational encounters across the Anglophonic British East Asian, Asian American, and Singaporean theaters to explore how identity is redefined in different contexts through border crossing. Jonathan Bollen's insightful thesis on how the expansion of international aviation led cabaret, stage entertainment, and other variety performances to traverse air spaces (Hong Kong, Manila, Melbourne, Sydney, Singapore, Tokyo, and Taipei) reveals "how the tension between national *containment* and international *mobility* was commercialised in entertainment on regional circuits during the 1950s and 1960s" (2020, 4).

Closer in scope to my study is Rossella Ferrari's *Transnational Chinese Theatres: Intercultural Performance Networks in East Asia* (2020). In her study, Ferrari traces "the transformative effects that the theaters of the region have wielded onto one another." In lieu of "monological narratives of distinct national traditions," she argues for "a generative pattern of inter-Chinese and inter-Asian allogamy" in reconceptualizing the history of Chinese-language "theatres as plural and intersecting *histories*" (15). Similarly, my book intends to make "further connections between different points on the global theatre maps" to illustrate the "significant glimpses in time(space) that can help interlock a chain of... parallel histories into a rhizomatic history of networks" (Ferrari 2020, 15). Indeed, the 1987 meeting in Singapore was a momentous event in gathering four of the most important dramatists in the same place and time to engage in an exchange of ideas. As will be unfolded in the following chapters, the impact of the dramatic work of one site became a significant feature on others as these dramatists drew continued inspiration by looking for creative resources and collaboration with other Chinese sites from beyond their immediate shores. Both our works draw on examples from across East Asia and the Southeast Asian site of Singapore. But our concerns, foci, topics addressed, and reading approaches of transnationality are entirely different. While Ferrari's excellent study explores the intercultural "transborder collaborations" between artists from cities of different origins that examine "the wounds of the territorial and affective fractures that have unsettled the region's geopolitics for decades" (2020, 3), my work unveils the politics of performance between both the state and its local actors as well as the transnational geopolitical influences on the region that accounted for the rise of identities in each site in the 1980s.

More than making individual case studies of four disparate sites, *Denationalizing Identities* draws our attention to the significant role the external impact of the Cold War played in narrating the various "identities-of-becoming" across these states in the same temporality, which transpired into very different sociopolitical local realities. At a time when the various governments attempted to impose state-sanctioned identities onto their people, these intellectual dramatists resisted unequivocally through their theater praxis by performing alternative cultural identities that affirmed local affinities. On the surface, these might appear to be local responses to local situations. However, one only has to remember how the Cold War ushered in the dawning of a new geopolitical sphere, wherein domestic affairs were increasingly imbricated in international relationships that forbade any state to remain in complete isolation, to realize that these dramatists were simultaneously responding to local as well as global conditions. Undoubtedly, the Cold War framework in the Sinophone world was very complicated during the 1970s and 1980s, and some of the political complexities these director-playwrights were addressing indeed stem from that major change. Principally, *Denationalizing Identities* historicizes the intricate political dynamics at play in the particular cases that are not just meaningful in relation to the Cold War epoch, but that have their own internal logic to them. My book aims to make a humble contribution to this growing body of literature on transnational Chinese theater.

Although its genre of study is drama and performance, *Denationalizing Identities* intervenes in a far broader conversation that goes beyond the immediate confines of the fields it engages. Theater was merely one of the many cultural forms that contested this identity issue; as will be made clear in the contextualization of my case studies, dance, film, fiction, music, and studio art among other literary and artistic genres were deeply engaged in this debate. More significantly, this discussion was not just relevant to the 1980s. Chineseness is one of the most urgent debates of our time, and there are gaps in our knowledge and conversations that this book can fill by conducting a uniquely transnational, multifocal project. Politics between language and ethnicity in Singapore, martial law and democratization in Taiwan, retrocession in Hong Kong, and the Cultural Revolution leading into the Reform period in China, are meaningful events not just in relation to the 1980s or the Cold War but also with significant impact that resonates perhaps even more strongly today. The Hong Kong "Umbrella Revolution" 遮打革命 and Anti-Extradition Bill demonstrations 「反送中」示威, the Taiwanese identity and Sunflower movements 太陽花運動, competing national interests and pride between Chinese migrants and local communities, global assertion of PRC's soft power, military might, and commercial aggression especially in Africa and Asia, the escalating US-China trade war, and the potential hostilities arising from the corona virus: none of these are contemporary affairs that stand in isolation. *Denationalizing Identities* contributes to our understanding of the historicity of these global events by providing a transnational perspective illustrating the vital role culture and the arts, and theater in particular, have played in this important narrative that accounted for the multiplicity of Chinese identities and loyalties. This in turn helps us make better sense of the increasingly rival affiliations and political complexities in our contemporary world.

Marginal Consciousness in the Chinese Diaspora

By highlighting the linkages between China and the diaspora, *Denationalizing Identities* reverses the traditional center-periphery cultural paradigm between the two entities, underscoring the role diasporic communities played in formulating different variations of Chinese identities. That the Second Chinese-language Drama Camp among other historically significant meetings took place well before communication channels between the two Chinas were officially opened and cross-strait relations yet to thaw demonstrates the Chinese diaspora's progressiveness and their proactive role in spearheading cultural exchange.[7] Simply put, I argue that the diasporic Chinese are anything but passive receivers of culture transmitted from the motherland; quite the contrary, their alternative formative examples not only debunked the notion of the Chinese mainland's inevitable communist outcome, but challenged an essentialist ethno-nationalist imagination

---

7. Another example was the "Asian Chinese Playwrights' Conference" 亞洲區域華人劇作家研討會 held by Chung Ying Theatre Company, the Hong Kong Arts Centre, and Hong Kong Institute for Promotion of Chinese Culture in Hong Kong 香港中華文化促進會 from April 30 to May 4, 1987. See "Experts" 1987, "Ying" 1987, and Lai 1994, 37.

by performing alternative cultural identities into being. Even though these four are the most important dramatists in their respective sites and beyond, that little has been published on them in the English language (with the exception of Nobel Prize–winning Gao) further indicates the telling lack of attention given to voices from the diaspora; *Denationalizing Identities* aims to address this imbalance.

Let me qualify my use of the term "Chinese diaspora." It could, on one level, refer to regions inhabited by ethnic Chinese beyond the geographical confines of mainland China (C. Tan 2013, 3). Even a seemingly clear-cut definition as such would incite contention on whether Hong Kong and Taiwan ought to be included. And the issue is compounded not just by the PRC's claim over Taiwan and Hong Kong, even though it has never been the government of Taiwan or pre-1997 Hong Kong, but that many *waishengren* 外省人 in Taiwan, southbound émigrés in Hong Kong, as well as first-generation overseas Chinese would not only consider China as their ancestral homeland, but also argue for Taiwan and Hong Kong's inclusion within China.[8] But even if we were to consider Taiwan and Hong Kong as diasporic, to talk about China *as* the diaspora would raise more than an eyebrow. I hope it has become apparent that my use of the term does not just refer to geographical location; rather, it is the sense of *marginal consciousness* one feels that I am attempting to further flesh out in this present book.[9] To put it differently, even while the works of Kuo, Lai, and Yung (which I discuss in chapters 1, 2, and 3) are performed outside mainland China and could hence be understood as Chinese diaspora in the conventional sense, Gao's *Bus Stop* (in chapter 4) attracted international attention during its premiere in Beijing when he was a resident playwright at the Beijing People's Art Theatre 北京人民藝術劇院 (BPAT)—the foremost theater company located in the nation's capital. In choosing to describe Gao also as diasporic, I am not merely foreshadowing his impending departure for France in 1987 where he has stayed since. I use the term

---

8. On the scholarly debates surrounding whether Taiwan ought to be considered part of the Chinese diaspora, see B. Chang 2015, 215-16n8. The *waishengren* 外省人 are ethnic Han Chinese from China who moved to Taiwan following the island's "return" to the mainland at the end of the Second World War, which I discuss in greater detail in chapter 2. Dominic Yang Meng-hsuan's (2020) study details the traumatic experiences that make up the historical memory of the *waishengren*.

9. Of late, historian Shelly Chan has developed an interesting thesis between homeland and diaspora in temporal terms, arguing how China and the Chinese diaspora mutually constitute each other in what she calls "diaspora moments" (2018, 10-12).

"diaspora within China" to underscore the state of consciousness Gao was deploying in his work, contending, like many of his contemporaries in mainland China, for the definition of being Chinese that contrasted from the governmental authorities. That even while Gao was in Beijing, he was writing with a cognizance that is detached from the political center. Clearly, this difficulty in labeling, to use the words of sociologist Tan Chee-Bing, has everything to do with the "politics of identity" (2013, 3), a key notion my book aims to unpack.

This *marginal consciousness* is a state of being I find the four dramatists in this present book share. As Ien Ang reminds us, the Chinese diaspora is "a concept of sameness-in-dispersal, not of togetherness-in-difference" (2001, 13). While these four sites have very different sociohistorical developments, these director-playwrights I study are connected by their sense of marginality. Each possesses a different (imagined) relationship with Chineseness and a different sense of diasporicity. In contrast to Letty Chen's suggestion that calling "oneself 'Chinese' can be a way of claiming cultural capital and thereby cultural authority or power" (2006, 6), none of these dramatists seems invested in being at the center of Chineseness. Similarly, the issues my dramatists probe depart from the questions Asian American playwright David Henry Hwang poses in his works: "which of us represents the 'real' China? Who is authentically Chinese?" (2001, 32). One of the aims of my book is therefore to plot four different trajectories of diaspora, united by the geopolitical circumstances impacting the region in the 1980s. Indeed, I agree with Wang Gungwu's observation that "if the past is anything to go by, it is doubtful if there will ever be *a single Chinese diaspora*. Much more likely is that the single word, Chinese, will be less and less able to convey a reality that continues to become more *pluralistic*" (1999, 169; italics mine).

Having spent a significant amount of time living in a country other than their own, these dramatists are not bound by any specific nation-state or culture. Their dramatic works display an unparalleled expansive, transcendental outlook that struggles against monolithic cultural paradigms. As Andrew Davidson and Kuah-Pearce Khun Eng point out, by their very nature diasporic communities suggest "an enduring albeit often ephemeral connection between the diasporic community and what is generally termed the country of origin and host country." They question if we can "still continue to speak of a diasporic community" when, given the time lapse, the migrant has become fully "integrated into the host society" (2008, 1–2). In this way, in contrast to other scholarly approaches, I am less interested in the expiration date (S. Shih 2007, 187) by which my dramatists assimilate into their host societies and end their diasporic status. These director-playwrights have always returned to Chinese culture as a creative resource and are dealing with issues of Chinese identity and Chineseness in their works, even if they do not display an overzealousness that can be misconstrued and attacked as cultural chauvinism. And unlike many of their peers, the works of these four director-playwrights have not indulged in what Rey Chow calls "the myth of consanguinity" (1993, 24) nor evinced in them a sense of cultural superiority or narcissism. Krishen Jit's observation on Kuo Pao Kun might similarly apply to the other three dramatists: "Separation from his birthland . . ., a rupture which was to prove almost permanent, [has] been partially responsible for Kuo's indifference to Chinese tradition and for his hard-won facility to live with an unusually creative ambivalence" (1990, 11). This could perhaps also explain why these director-playwrights ruminate on questions of identity and identification always from intellectual positions other than the mainstream.

Furthermore, the trajectories of these dramatists suggest there is more than a dualistic relation between China and Singapore, China and Hong Kong, or China and Taiwan. As I will demonstrate in the following chapters, whereas the journeys of their lived and professional experiences go beyond a simple China-Singapore, China-Hong Kong, and China-Taiwan binary, this book focuses on identity-suturing in the 1980s. Charlene Rajendran's discussion of the postcolonial Southeast Asian situation speaks aptly to the four sites I examine. She points out that contemporary theater artists in Indonesia, the Philippines, Malaysia, and Singapore "have repeatedly contested national imaginings of democratic identity, particularly in the second half of the 20th century when nation-building was pivotal to cultural production" in the region (2019, 329). Like the situation in Southeast Asia, "state-led notions of national identity" in East Asia were similarly "stipulated and singular." And hence, although Hong Kong and Taiwan are not recognized as nation-states in the same way as China and Singapore are, "Difference and disagreement with the state" were likewise "regarded as detrimental to national unity, and thus theatre that advocates criticality can be deemed disruptive" (Rajendran 2019, 329) and susceptible to intervention by state authorities. In this present study, therefore, "denationalizing" does not only mean debunking the PRC's claim to "one united Chineseness"; it really entails challenging the uncritical nationalist impulses applied across the four sites by their individual governments.

Specifically, for these dramatists, the flipside of denationalizing is *not* a reconstruction of an encompassing national identity and culture of the four distinct locales. By deconstructing identities advocated by their respective states, the dramatists do not claim their version to be representative of their individual site's identity but is merely one of many (proposals) that is alternative to the one their immediate governments endorsed. Again, to borrow Rajendran's words, the dramatists I study too "experimented with decentered and multi-perspectival frames" of resistance performances that were not only "contextually grounded" but "expressed the tensions of what it meant to be modern, plural, and different," envisioning "worlds where difficult issues could be openly deliberated" (Rajendran 2019, 329). Other artists who were their contemporaries were also advocating their own versions of local identity, be it via theater or other forms of artistic expression.

Subsequently, because the target of denationalizing is not the PRC, this book is not part of the Sinophone project. While the aim of most critics who employ the concept of the Sinophone is to unseat the centrality of mainland China (S. Shih 2013, 33), my project is a reexamination of Chinese cultural identity and politics through the examples of theater and performance framed around the debates on Chineseness in the 1980s as a Cold War legacy. But although my book explores the politics of culture and identity, its underlying concerns with the "identities-of-becoming" in these four sites with a majority of ethnic Chinese is historical rather than ideological and takes its inspiration, instead, from Leo Ching's *Becoming "Japanese": Colonial Taiwan and the Politics of Identity Formation* (2001). Ching's influential study reveals the psychological efficacy of colonial modernity: he plots the transformation processes of how the disparate groups of inhabitants on Japanese-occupied Taiwan came to identify themselves as Japanese subjects during the island's colonization period (1895–1945), while the "contradictory, conflicting, and complicitous desires and identities were projected, negotiated, and vanquished" amid the triangulation between colonial Taiwan, imperial Japan, and nationalist China (2001, 8). Similarly, my book focuses on the process of localization and hybridization of identity in the four sites. These localized and hybridized Chinese identities contrast and distinguish with that of China, but do not necessarily denounce or unseat it.

To varying degrees the lives of these dramatists that were anything but constant instilled in them a marginal consciousness. As I will flesh out in greater detail below, their early in-transit experiences traversing regional and national borders prevented them from seeing things from a static position. Moving across geographical locations confronted them with different cultures, pushed them to learn and adopt different languages, and provided them with comparative vantage points of reflection and conceptualization. On the one hand, adapting and adjusting to an unfamiliar daily experience was no enviable task; on the other, it piqued their curiosity for the unknown. From an early age they were already crossing from culture to culture, moving in between cultures, and exploring the marginal spaces in between cultures. This constant state of liminality forbade them the comfort of fixity; instead, these became spaces of creativity that made available for them different cultures and resources to mix and synthesize, immersing them in a constant state of hybridization and experimentation. As the child of a diplomat, Stan Lai was always changing environments, learning new languages, and observing different cultures. Thus, although this constant change in his surroundings has taught him to survive in any environment, he does not feel a sense of belonging to any one culture but is always "floating" in between cultures (Lee and Yu 2005). Returning to Hong Kong in 1979, Danny Yung felt overwhelmed by a sense of marginal consciousness after having been away for seventeen years. However, it dawned upon him that being on the margins has the conditions advantageous to discourse, observe, critique, and create from a reflective distance (Tian and Fong 2009, 410–11). Similarly, we find these qualities in Gao Xingjian's *Leng de wenxue* 冷的文學 (cold literature). The "coldness" in his literary expression is a peripheral position he has consciously adopted to distance himself from the center and "to engage society and to reflect on the problems faced by people in the modern era and, ultimately, the problems of humanity" (Quah 2004b, 187). Perhaps Kuo Pao Kun puts it best:

> Marginal in the sense that you are at the margins of different cultures, different communities. Some people stay with a mentality of a particular time and they don't change. But if you mix with different kinds of people you find yourself moving between the margins of different periods. . . . That kind of marginality, a fringe kind of existence, allows one to compare and reflect. Because you don't belong to any one of those times . . . sometimes you feel a sort of loneliness because you are different. But you also feel good because you are able to dialogue, to talk, to communicate with

very unique groups of people who think differently and have different experiences.

(1997a, 126)

The periphery was as much a space from which they were critiquing Chinese culture as they were borrowing other cultural resources to experiment with, enrich, and pluralize Chineseness. These dramatists were always learning, adapting, and changing; they were either overcoming limitations they have previously demarcated for themselves, or challenging existing (state) boundaries. When their individual states attempted to implement nationalist versions of identity and statehood onto their people, only through critical reflection afforded by the necessary distance on the margins could these dramatists stand apart from the fervor emanating from the political center. Adopting a reflective marginal consciousness allowed these dramatists to constantly *dis*identify with the state's definition of Chineseness; being on the diaspora of Chinese culture positioned them to destabilize constructed paradigms, unsettle power relations, and denationalize identities.

To say that the four dramatists' professional trajectories were not in the same phase in their 1987 meeting is to acknowledge the different stages of development in each individual site across the region. To begin with, Lai is approximately one generation younger than the other three artists. He was in his early thirties when the inaugural productions of his theater company Performance Workshop 表演工作坊, *The Night We Became Cross-Talk Comedians* (1985) and *Secret Love in Peach Blossom Land* (1986), became instant hits with the Taiwanese audience, solidifying the troupe's reputation and propelling him to fame soon after his return from the United States. What were these other dramatists doing in their early thirties? What was happening in these other sites that prevented the careers of these other dramatists from similarly taking off? Kuo had already returned from his studies in Australia and founded the first local professional integrated arts school, Singapore Performing Arts Studio 新加坡表演藝術學院 (SPAS), in 1965 to train actors and dancers, while actively writing and directing plays. However, his career as a budding director-playwright came to an abrupt halt when the state detained him without trial for four years and seven months (1976–80) on account of his leftist leanings. Only after his reemergence upon his release and contributions to revitalize the badly shaken Chinese-language theater scene through his efforts at building a transcultural Singaporean theater was Kuo hailed as the "Father of modern Singapore theater" (Ee 2000).

Similarly, the political circumstances of the times prevented Gao from pursuing his vocation publicly: he was twenty-six when the Cultural Revolution began and thirty-six when it ended (Moran 2013, 71). At the height of the ten-year upheaval, Gao even burned a suitcase of nearly forty kilograms of his unpublished manuscripts—including ten plays, an unfinished novel, and numerous poems and notes—to avoid persecution (Quah 2004b, 7). Only after the Cultural Revolution was Gao's vigor as a writer noticed when he was eventually posted to BPAT in 1980, becoming its resident playwright in 1982 (Fong 2005, xx). As for Danny Yung, he was in the United States pursuing his college and graduate degrees in his late teens and twenties. Upon graduation, he was involved in the Asian American movement, becoming a founding member of the Asian Counseling and Referral Service in Seattle in 1973—the year he turned thirty. His subsequent reputation as an avant-garde artist in Hong Kong was earned after his return to the then British colony in 1979 and the founding of his arts collective Zuni Icosahedron 進念・二十面體 that became his most important platform for artistic expression and exchange.

In tracing the genealogy of four disparate sites of performance, I am confronted with one of the big challenges encountered in studying theater and performance posed by the nature of the genre itself: How do you mark and record your feelings, thoughts, and reflections of the performance piece unless you are present in that particular live event? Compounded in this problem is that playscripts are not always published. For this reason, I have been unable to view and read all the plays whose titles I mention in this book, but reference and discuss them in my broader contextualization nevertheless because they have been frequently cited in my research. Funneling through the copious amount of information from play reviews in magazines, newspapers, and blogs, scholarly writings in monographs and academic journals, archived news reports, theater festival exhibitions, and play production program booklets, yearbooks published by national arts councils and individual theater groups from regional and university libraries, and repository archives of drama companies across the various sites I study as well as in the United States, I have attempted my best to reconstruct the historical contexts in which these plays were performed. Acknowledging the importance of documentation for critical analyses by scholars or play restagings by other drama companies in future (Kuo 2001,

120), the dramatists I study have either published their playscripts or archived their productions on recorded footage. The corpus of Kuo, Gao, and Lai's playscripts are published in Chinese and English. Yung, however, is skeptical that the essence of his works could be adequately represented by stage dialogue (Cheung and Lai 1997, xxvi), and instead of using playscripts in the traditional sense, he works with a blueprint with actors to collectively devise their piece in the rehearsal room. This is another way these dramatists distinguish themselves from their peers and artists of the previous generation in the attention paid to documenting their work and articulating a discourse for their creative praxis.[10]

In my reading of these plays, I follow Baz Kershaw's approach to "move beyond formalist analysis . . . and consider performance as a cultural construct and as a means of cultural production." I am similarly interested in investigating "how specific audiences might 'read' their performances" that are not "independent of [their] social and political environment" and hence "have to be seen in their full cultural milieu: in relation to the aesthetic movements of which they are a part; in relation to the institutional structures of the arts; in relation to the cultural formations which they inhabit" (1992, 5-6). Where possible, I have thus supplemented this research with viewings of play production recordings, as well as oral interviews of artists and scholars, situating my analyses in the particular sociohistorical moments of the inaugural productions of these performances. As Alexa Alice Joubin aptly reminds us in her study of *Chinese Shakespeares*, "textual fluidity is not a carte blanche for every reader to concoct his or her own meaning. Certain historical moments demand reading to be carried out in the reader's cultural context, while other historical junctures provoke interpretations that claim to depend on the 'text' itself" (2009, 24). Each of the main chapters in this book begins by narrating the individual sociohistorical context before analyzing the one particular play I have selected from each site that I consider best represents an identity shift in that important historical juncture and unpacking its cultural-political significance.

---

10. For one of these examples Yung provided in *An Oxford Anthology of Contemporary Chinese Drama*, see Yung 1997. Performance Workshop has made available most of their productions in DVD format, and Zuni Icosahedron has archived their past works in digital format, some of which are uploaded onto YouTube. Of the three Gao plays BPAT staged in the 1980s, only *Bus Stop*, the play I am analyzing, is not commercially available from the theater company.

My research suggests that it was external factors—China's reemergence onto the global order at the end of the Cultural Revolution—that propelled the discourse of Chineseness to take shape simultaneously in all four locales, giving rise to these artists' professional careers. In other words, in response to mainland China coming out of its lengthy isolation, different senses of Chineseness were beginning to form in Singapore, Hong Kong, Taiwan, and mainland China during the 1980s. In the exemplary works of these four dramatists one can discern these identities-of-becoming as an integrating theme. Contemporaneous with these developments was the economic growth and rise of a middle class that prompted broad cultural changes, crucial among which was support for modernist and postmodernist theaters.

These four pivotal figures are usually recognized as having acquired accomplished reputations in their respective homelands, yet the richness and complexity of their works are necessarily informed by their transnational and transcultural life experiences that constantly displaced them from their comfort zones. Despite their highly acclaimed statuses today, in the early phases of their professional careers they have in fact had multiple run-ins with their individual governments. Among the many qualities that distinguished them from their contemporaries, these four dramatists have not shied away from staging works that challenged the accepted norms of state and society, and their alternative theater praxis could be considered as a form of "cultural intervention" by Baz Kershaw. For Kershaw, alternative theater achieves three objectives. First, it belongs to "a much broader group of cultural activities which were all expressive of new ideologies, of new interpretations of existing social and political relations" and gives rise to "a new generational awareness." Second, since "there were no ready-made venues or audiences to begin with," alternative theater had to, by and large, "create its own context." And third,

> alternative theatre was expansionist. It sought to ... appeal to an ever-expanding audience. This populist impulse, when combined with the movement's oppositional ambitions, caused alternative theatre to develop exceptionally complex performative codes and strategies. Probably the most complicated practices evolved when alternative theatre mounted deliberate forays into alien territory, into contexts characterised by their likely resistance to oppositional ideologies.
>
> (Kershaw 1992, 6–7)

Being ahead of their times, Kuo, Gao, Yung, and Lai's works necessarily deviated from their socially conditioned norms to revolt against the mainstream representation onstage in a bid to combat the existing state-sanctioned representation of reality. Breaking away from the mainstream modes of performance that have dominated the stage across the various Chinese-speaking sites allowed these dramatists to stage new ways of seeing things, rehearse different possible modes of representation, and imagine alternative realities into being. Because this would immediately call into question the sense of identification delineated by the state, as such, even as these four dramatists tactically maneuvered to navigate the restrictions imposed by their censorship bureaus, some had very close calls with the authorities while others were less fortunate, spending time in prison; all were treading on thin ice as they continued to push against restrictions.

In chapter 1 of the book, I focus on Kuo Pao Kun. Born in 1939 in a poor village in Hebei, Kuo "witnessed natural disasters such as floods, droughts, locusts and ravages of banditry and Japanese aggression" as a young boy (Kuo 2000, 386). In 1947, at the age of eight, he moved to Beijing, acquiring his trademark Beijing-accented Mandarin in his early years there. Two years later, while being called to Singapore to reunite with his businessman father, he transited in Hong Kong for nine months where he was exposed to Cantonese. During the radical student movements in 1950s Singapore, his father changed schools for him as many as six times in six years, which included a short stint back to Hong Kong, to prevent him from getting into political trouble (Kuo 2001, 106). These included both Chinese- and English-medium schools that contributed to much of Kuo's early bilingual education (Lim and Tan 2012, 5). At least in part, this experience was instrumental in equipping him with the necessary bilingual literacy to work as a Chinese translator cum broadcaster with Radio Australia when he left Singapore for Melbourne at twenty years of age (Kuo 2001, 107).

Apart from visiting rural temple festivities and monthly village markets in Hebei and watching much street opera in Beijing as a young boy, Kuo's early exposure to theater was his introduction to radio drama at the local Rediffusion Mandarin Drama Group in 1955. Not until 1957, at the age of eighteen, did the young Kuo receive formal screen-acting training from Wang Qiutian 王秋田 (1905–1990), Low Ing Sing 劉仁心 (1924–2002), Lin Chen 林晨 (1919–2004), and Zhu Xu 朱緒 (1908–2007)—pioneers in Singapore Chinese drama—who introduced him to the concept of serious theater (Kuo 2000, 8). Subsequently, in

1959 Kuo went first to Melbourne, then in 1963 to Sydney to enroll in the National Institute of Dramatic Art (NIDA) to acquire formal training in contemporary theater and humanities in the European tradition. With his sense of theater professionalism solidified by the NIDA experience, Kuo returned at the age of twenty-six to Singapore in 1965 with his wife, dancer Goh Lay Kuan 吳麗娟 (b. 1939), and together cofounded the SPAS, devoting themselves to the training and making of drama and dance among other art forms, one month before the city-island was separated from its huge Malaysian hinterlands and declared independent.

Artists were responding excitedly in different ways to the nation-state's newfound independence. Kuo and his Chinese-educated peers naturally participated in this search for cultural expression that drew inspiration from a variety of sources to express their imagination of a new nation. For the leftist leanings in his works, Kuo was incarcerated for four-and-a-half years in the mid-1970s. His citizenship was revoked until 1992 by the same government that in 1989 granted him the Cultural Medallion—the highest accolade the state can bestow on an artist—because his achievements and leadership status in the artistic community had by then become impossible to be ignored. Incidentally, Kuo's mastery of the Malay language was acquired during this period of state detention, advancing another step closer to his vision of a multilingual theater praxis. In the 1980s, when the state-sanctioned identity pigeonholed its people into particular ethnic groupings, Kuo effectively resisted this by performing into being an alternative cultural identity that reflects on the problematic of multilingualism.

In chapter 2, I discuss how Stan Lai's works speak to a Taiwan that was struggling to find its voice with an emerging nativist sentiment and simultaneously declining global position displaced by the rise of China. Lai is unique among these four dramatists to be the only one not born in China, making him one of the few among his contemporaries (within and outside of Taiwan) to be first exposed to Western culture before going on to have an extended career creatively in the Chinese world (Patsalidis 2018). Born in 1954 to a *waisheng* family in diplomatic service in the Republic of China's embassy stationed in Washington, D.C., the young Lai left with his family for Taiwan at the age of twelve. Two years later, in 1968, he lost his father to cancer and was from then onward raised by his widowed mother. He went through his late elementary, middle school, and college education in martial law Taiwan (1949-87) before going back to the United States in 1978 to pursue a doctorate in dramatic art at the University of California, Berkeley. Losing all his savings soon after arrival, Lai had to work part-time as a waiter to make ends meet and balance his life as a young parent, yet he still managed to finish his five-year degree in record time and at the top of his cohort. The experience of living and schooling in Taiwan and the United States made Lai perfectly bilingual in Mandarin Chinese and English. In 1983, theater veteran Yao Yi-wei 姚一葦 (1922–97) invited Lai to return to Taipei upon his graduation to teach at the newly established National Institute of the Arts 國立藝術學院.

Like Kuo, Lai was one of the very few from his home country then who had acquired professional training in the theater. Armed with a PhD from the West and its associated cultural capital, Lai managed to assemble the ablest creative team of performing arts talents in Taiwan at the time to work with him. Although Taiwan was then nearing the final days of martial law, many topics were still taboo. In that era of high political volatility, creating works that might be misconstrued as invoking sympathy toward the mainland was a bold step. But this display of affection for the memories of Republican China was also one that touched the raw nerves of society, unlocking and stirring up the deeper recesses of its cultural memory. The *dis*identification strategies employed in Lai's works do not merely straddle across the Taiwan Strait; at the same time they also attempt to suture the rupture between the conflicting groups within Taiwanese society.

In 1949, when he was five, Danny Yung came on the last boat out of Shanghai with his family to Hong Kong. Brought up by extremely liberal parents who took him to nightclubs when he was only eight, he began to learn how to mambo and cha-cha with famous movie stars such as Teresa Lee Lai Wah 李麗華 (1924–2017) when other children of a similar age were doing their homework (Watson 2002). In 1961, at the age of seventeen, Yung left for the United States to pursue his tertiary education. Traversing both the American East and West Coasts, he was inspired by the anti–Vietnam War and Civil Rights Movement protests and stayed on to work to improve the lives of the Asian American community. Born with Shanghainese, Yung picked up Cantonese, Mandarin, and English in Hong Kong. Throughout his seventeen-year span in the United States, Yung said when I interviewed him, he had not used a word of Chinese to the extent that a sense of alienation arose in him that spiked a renewed interest in the language when he returned to Hong Kong. His arts collective Zuni Icosahedron was established in 1982—the same year that British prime minister Margaret Thatcher began meetings with Chinese leader Deng Xiaoping that concluded in the signing of the 1984 Sino-British Joint Declaration.

Yung had returned to a Hong Kong that was shortly to give up its British nationality for a Chinese one. A colossal wave of identity crisis surged across the territory when the blueprint for Hong Kong's return to China in 1997 was laid out with the ratification of the declaration, a document drawn up without the Hong Kong people's knowledge or consent that was presented as a fait accompli (Ooi 1995, 278). Hong Kong and China had developed under different systems for over a century and a half, and political events in recent decades had accentuated their differences in economic realities, civil liberties, and social values. Contrasted with Hong Kong's ascendance as a regional powerhouse of pop culture and global financial center in the early 1980s, China's recent emergence from the Cultural Revolution did not make the impending return seem an attractive option in the eyes of most inhabitants of the territory. On the dramatic stage, this epochal historic change erupted into debates over identity on an unprecedented scale, engulfing Hongkongers for the next decade and a half. In chapter 3, I contextualize the efforts of Yung and his artistic collaborators to spearhead works that seriously examined this sense of imminent loss by problematizing the power dynamics accompanying the state-sanctioned attitudes toward the triangulation of Hong Kong-British-Chinese identities.

In contrast, although Gao Xingjian had never traveled outside China until he was thirty-nine, his sojourn was no less capricious than his three Western-educated peers. Born in Ganzhou, Jiangxi, Gao spent his youth on the run from Japanese invaders (Sze-Lorrain 2007, 184). After the war and subsequent founding of the People's Republic, he moved to Nanjing to be schooled between 1950 and 1957, and then to Beijing for university and work. Gao is the only one among the four who did not receive formal academic instruction in the West, but he majored in French language and literature in the Beijing Foreign Languages Institute 北京外國語學院. As a ferocious reader in his college years Gao gave himself a comprehensive education through reading the world canon (M. Lee 2012, xi). Upon his graduation in 1962, Gao worked as a translator at the Foreign Languages Bureau of the Ministry of Culture. Working at the bureau exposed him to the latest Western literary trends coming into China then as he could read them in the original French, which was not as highly censored as works written in English (Quah 2004b, 6). During the Cultural Revolution he was sent to a reeducation camp in the rural areas of Jiangxi and Anhui, becoming trapped in an insular China. He resumed work as a translator in Beijing toward the end of the ten-year upheaval in 1975. Gao's first trip outside his home country was to France in 1979, when he accompanied a delegation of Chinese writers as an interpreter for the renowned writer Ba Jin 巴金 (1904–2005) (Lee and Dutrait 2001, 739).

After the Cultural Revolution, he was assigned to BPAT as a writer in 1980 and became a full-time playwright in 1982. There he teamed most frequently with the young avant-garde director Lin Zhaohua 林兆華 (b. 1936) to produce what was regarded at the time as the highly controversial plays *Juedui xinhao* 絕對信號 (Alarm signal, 1982), *Bus Stop* (1983), and *Yeren* 野人 (Wildman, 1985)—works that have now become classics in the history of contemporary Chinese drama in the Western academy.[11] Misdiagnosed with lung cancer and to avoid being arrested by the authorities for his "subversive" writings during the Anti-Spiritual Pollution Campaign 反精神污染運動, he traveled into the remote hinterlands of southwestern China for five months from late 1983 to early 1984, going "through eight provinces and seven nature reserves, covering fifteen thousand kilometers in the Yangtze region" (Quah 2004b, 10). There his interactions with ethnic minorities on the fringes of Han Chinese civilization became a prevalent theme in his magnum opus *Lingshan* 靈山 (Soul mountain, 1989) among other works. Knowing full well that his writings and dramas would never be tolerated nor openly staged in China again after the authorities disbanded the production team for his next play *Bi'an* 彼岸 (The other shore, 1986) during rehearsal stages and warned its cast not to collaborate again with him, Gao left for France in 1987 where he has continued to reside ever since. From then on, almost all the first versions of the plays he wrote were in French before he translated them himself into Chinese. In chapter 4, I situate Gao in the 1980s Chinese context where politics, state power, and censorship impinged on the artistic scene and depict the efforts of Gao and his contemporaries who struggled to champion ways of being Chinese other than that proffered by the state.

The 1980s make an interesting case for comparison because, in many respects, these auteurs were all filling artistic vacuums and creating

---

11. Gao Xingjian's works are considered classics of contemporary Chinese theater history in Western academia but not in the official discourse in mainland China. Gao left China in 1987, and his works have remained banned in China since 1989 when he tore up his Chinese passport in front of the international media in protest of the Tiananmen Square Incident, swearing that he would never return so long as the authoritarian regime remained in power (M. Lee 2006, 11).

FIGURE 1. Stan Lai, Danny Yung, and Kuo Pao Kun, three of the most important dramatists in the Chinese-speaking world, at the International Forum on Cultural Identity and Development, December 30, 1992, Hong Kong. Photo credit © Zuni Icosahedron.

cultural traditions anew. This decade is a consequential time frame as it accounts for identities-of-becoming in the various states that were responding to the Cold War legacy where China was newly emerging from the Cultural Revolution. From the identities of Gao Xingjian's diasporic position *within* the mainland, to the diasporic Chinese positionalities of Stan Lai, Danny Yung, and Kuo Pao Kun on its peripheries, what were they now that an Other China is (re)appearing? Or perhaps, now that the Original has (re)appeared, its authenticity was forcing these various locales to confront their own othered positions. I suggest that the 1980s saw a transition from a "Chinese in Singapore" to "Singaporean Chinese" identity, and so on, in varying configurations. Commenting on the Singaporean scene, Quah Sy Ren suggests, "the evolution of multilingual theatre since the mid-1980s is not only a result of innovative artistic representation, but it should also be perceived as a critical part of an identity searching process" (2002, 382). Similarly, while I am not trying to argue that a Hong Kong Chineseness or Taiwanese Chineseness did not predate the 1980s, I propose that since then a new type of consciousness was emerging due to the changing conditions in the international scene, forcing the ethnic Chinese across the region to reexamine their identities. By situating the work of four important contemporary ethnic Chinese dramatists from different *states* as a collective, I highlight how such comparative analyses might reveal significant but overlooked dynamics in the development of a pan-Chinese cultural consciousness outside the mainland especially in today's globalizing circumstances. Considered in the broadest sense, their work can be viewed as tacitly in competition for how to imagine the place and value of multiple facets of Chinese culture in contemporary experience.

CHAPTER 1

Articulating an Alternative Cultural Identity

Kuo Pao Kun's Multilingual Theater Practice in Singapore

On August 2, 2013, a headline in the Singaporean Chinese-language daily newspaper *Lianhe zaobao* 聯合早報 read, "After 23 years, ban lifted on Liang Wern Fook's song *Sparrow with Bamboo Twigs*" (Li Y. 2013). This song was part of a genre known as *xinyao* 新謠—literally "new ballads" or "Singaporean ballads"—created in the mid-1980s to celebrate the lives and vibrancy of the young nation, then eager to seek and shape its identity.[1] There was nothing seditious in the content of this particular *xinyao*, and its writer Dr. Liang Wern Fook 梁文福 (b. 1964), who was awarded the Cultural Medallion in 2010 by the state, has since become an icon of Singaporean popular music and synonymous with the *xinyao* movement.[2] The song was banned because the lyrics contained a line of Hokkien and two lines of Cantonese, as well as two intertextual lines from the Cantonese folksong incorporated into the background in the interlude.

---

1. Originally, *xinyao* 新謠 is short for *Xinjiapo nianqingren chuangzuo geyao* 新加坡年輕人創作歌謠, literally "ballads composed by young Singaporeans." This abbreviated term has come to take on the two extended meanings since the first character *xin* 新 could mean both "new" and "Singapore."

2. For a moving account of this incident by the songwriter, see Liang 2013. For its English translation, see C. Lai 2013.

With these exceptions, the rest of the song was sung in Mandarin—one of the four official languages the Singaporean government has adopted since the nation-state's independence in 1965. According to what has come to be called the multiracial model, governance is divided along ethnic lines. The recognized ethnic groups are Chinese, Indians, Malays, and Others (also known as the CIMO model), and the state's four official languages that represent these groups respectively are Mandarin, Tamil, Malay, and English. Regional variations of the Chinese language have not been permitted to air on public media since 1979, the year the Speak Mandarin Campaign 講華語運動 was launched,[3] with exceptions for a three-minute news-reporting segment in each of the six dialects to be aired daily at 8:00 p.m. over the radio (F. Chan 2008, 100).[4]

While the ban on dialects was only lifted in the music scene in 2013, the theater circle already overcame this barrier in 1988 with the play *Xunzhao xiaomao de mama* 尋找小貓的媽媽 (Mama looking for her cat) by Kuo Pao Kun 郭寶崑. In this devised ensemble piece, remarks founder of the Theater Studies Program at the National University of Singapore, K. K. Seet, Kuo has integrated "multiple languages and dialects (English, Mandarin, Tamil, Hokkien, Cantonese, and Teochew) in the same text to capture the cultural syncretism and linguistic pluralism of Singapore," and he "has come to epitomise the quintessential Singaporean in his increasingly instrumental role as a mediator between the hitherto polarised streams of Singapore theatre" (Seet 1994, 244). What were these different streams in Singapore theater that Seet refers to and why were they "hitherto polarised"? Quah Sy Ren, who usually presents his academic work in Chinese, has spoken in public and written on Kuo on several occasions in English. That Quah *has* to do so illustrates the extent of the bifurcation of the linguistic communities in Singapore: the artistic practitioners and academics in the English-language stream would otherwise be unaware of the many contributions Kuo

---

3. The Speak Mandarin Campaign was not aimed at increasing the Chinese cultural literacy of Singaporeans. Instead, it was targeted to discourage people from speaking dialects and adopt Mandarin. Coupled with the government's bilingual education policy that elevated the status of English taught alongside another native language, Chinese cultural literacy in the country has in fact declined significantly over the years (Y. Wong 1989a, 73).

4. Exceptions were made in 2003 and 2020–22 respectively with the outbreaks of severe acute respiratory syndrome (SARS) in Asia and the coronavirus globally, where the ban was temporarily lifted because the elderly—many of whom could only understand dialects—were the most prone to be affected and needed to be educated on precautionary measures through the mass media.

made to Chinese-language theater (Quah 2002, 377–78; 2010, 149; 2012). Indeed, theater in Singapore, as well as Singaporean society at large, before the 1980s was "noticeably divided into different language streams" (Quah 2002, 378). Chief among Kuo's many contributions to the arts scene in Singapore was perhaps his having become "the bridge-builder between the Mandarin and English streams" (Jit 2000, 92).

Kuo Pao Kun is widely regarded as Singapore's most important dramatist to date. As an avid theater practitioner who was originally only active in the Chinese-language stream, Kuo proceeded in the 1980s to conduct workshops and write plays in the English language, as well as develop a multilingual theater praxis that henceforth became the hallmark of contemporary Singaporean theater. As a result, all the major artists in both the current local Chinese- and English-language theater circles have been nurtured under his influence. By analyzing *Mama Looking for Her Cat*, this chapter addresses two questions: Why and how did Kuo cross the linguistic divide that so governed the ethnic groups prior to the 1980s? What did this transgression mean for the young Singaporean nation, which had by then achieved a decade of economic progress and was seeking to establish its own cultural identity? Quah Sy Ren's pioneering work on the play traced its evolution to the development of multilingual theater in the nation-state (2002) and has argued for the play's multicultural form to be a mode of resistance against the state's representation of multiethnic reality (2004a). Wong Souk Yee 黃淑儀 discusses the play through the context of the country's bilingual policy, racial otherness, and ethnic reification (2005, 82). In her reading, the Hokkien-only-speaking Mama as well as the Tamil-speaking Indian old man—and by extension, people of their age group, educational level, and social class—are "being pushed to the edge of the 'bilingual' society as she is increasingly isolated by the two languages that matter in the political economy of the country" (84), since the official policy that suppressed her language has also annihilated her history and her identity (83). Agreeing with this reading, E. K. Tan considers *Mama* "as a reaction to the limits of Singapore's language policies" (2013, 172–73). By building on the foundational work of these scholars, I examine the changing sociohistorical conditions that shaped the politics and language use in Singaporean society in general and theater in particular, from which multilingual theater evolved during the nation-state's search for a cultural identity. I also demonstrate how Kuo's response contributed to a different mapping of Chinese-language drama that stood the city-state apart from the theater scenes in Hong Kong, Taiwan, and China—regions with a majority of ethnic Chinese that were each reacting to the external pressures confronting them toward the end of the Cold War. In contradistinction to the government's multiracial model, I argue that Kuo's theater practice—beginning with his multilingual play *Mama Looking for Her Cat*—can be seen as a medium for articulating an alternative form of cultural identity.

Because correspondence between Singaporean theater cultural features and its government's official rhetoric and policy cannot be assumed, it is therefore necessary to discuss the government's formulation of the multiracial model briefly before reviewing the pre-1980s Singapore theater scene's response. Critics agree that Singaporean society before the 1980s was divided into "different language streams, namely, Chinese, English, Malay and Tamil ... as the result of the colonial governing authorities' 'separate-and-rule' policy" (Quah 2002, 378). When the People's Action Party (PAP) took over as Singapore's government in 1959, it sought to encourage the building of modern Singaporean society through "multiracialism," wherein the four major ethnic groups were given "separate-but-equal status" (Benjamin 1975, 12). Sociologist Geoffrey Benjamin exposes the paradoxical nature of this rationale: "In order to demonstrate the *distinctiveness* of each of the four cultures their *differences* have to be heightened, their similarities underplayed, and expressive forms have to be developed to display their separate-but-equal status." For instance, the vignette on the back of Singapore's ten-dollar currency note shows "four inter-linked but differently hued hands." By constantly reiterating "the Chinese-Malay-Indian-Eurasian categorisation" from national censuses and government reports to the schools, this "puts considerable pressure on people to see themselves as *ethnically defined*." According to Benjamin, the two institutions that have emerged to give expression to this idea are the cultural show and the organization of broadcasting:

> The cultural show consists of a series of dances or musical performances, almost always containing at least a Chinese, an Indian and a Malay item, the aim of which is to achieve *token representation* of each constituent "culture" rather than to provide an aesthetically satisfying evening's entertainment.
>
> (12; italics mine)

Benjamin's study emphasizes that the government's primary "concern for ethnic representation ... is also displayed by the locally produced dramas broadcast on the Republic's television service, which are almost always performed by 'racially' homogeneous casts appropriate to the language used" (13). To be sure, from its inception as Television Singapura in 1963 to today's Media Corporation of Singapore, the nation's television service has generally followed this ethos, with Channel 5 and Channel 8 screening programs primarily in English and Chinese respectively.

If what this multiracial model had intended was to promote "cultural interactions between different ethnic groups" (Quah 2004a, 35) and create a cohesive, integrated society as such, paradoxically the effects it generated were contrary to its aim. Take for instance, the Ethnic Integration policy for the Housing and Development Board (HDB), a state housing policy that promotes cultural interactions between different ethnic groups and ensures the percentages of residents occupying public housing reflect the representation of the national ethnic makeup. Before Singaporeans purchase their HDB apartments, therefore, their ethnicity becomes a primary concern, because they are otherwise not eligible to purchase an apartment if the racial quota in that housing estate has already been exceeded. In other words, when acquiring a property, Singaporeans—citizens of the same nationality—are required first to think of themselves as distinctively defined ethnic people in order to reside in a state-engineered multiracial residential environment. In all walks of their daily lives, Singaporeans are constantly reminded of the ethnic categories to which they are designated by the state each time these categorically marked differences are emphasized as they are performed. Further exacerbated by the seeming impossibility of transcending the governance of strict ethnic boundaries, Geoffrey Benjamin notes, "It is interesting in this regard to note a tendency for children of mixed Indian-Chinese marriages to become 'Eurasians,' and for Straits-born Chinese—the so-called 'Babas'—to resinicise to become Hokkien Chinese: these are convenient ways of maintaining ethnic boundaries while changing their content" (1975, 15).[5] Therefore, despite the state's attempts in "actively promoting cultural interactions between different ethnic groups since the 1960s," it might not come as

---

5. The Straits-born Chinese or Peranakans have lived in the region for three generations or more. They are English-educated, and many are offspring of intermarriages between Malays and Chinese in Singapore and Malaya and do not speak Mandarin even though they have retained Chinese customs. Unlike immigrants from China who have "strong emotional and family ties with China" and look "upon China as their homeland," most Peranakans perceive "themselves as loyal British subjects" (Quah 2010, 149-50). Male Peranakans are known as Babas and females Nonyas.

much of a surprise that "the search was still on, in the 1980s, to find a more effective and deeper form of interaction" (Quah 2004a, 35). As I demonstrate in this chapter, Kuo's multiculturalism aimed to transcend these linguistic and ethnic differences. His drama strove to be an "innovative artistic representation" on top of "a critical part of an identity searching process" (Quah 2002, 382).

Development of Local Consciousness in Pre-1980s Singapore Theater

In their reflections on pre-1980s Singaporean society-at-large, Kuo Pao Kun and Quah Sy Ren's accounts reveal the divisions between the different ethnic groups:

> Pre-1980s Chinese drama in Singapore was by far the most active, although it produced very few good original works. Until the 80s, English theatre had very little to show. . . . Before the 1980s, English drama had a very small audience. But when you talk about Singapore drama, you have to remember it's a very pluralistic situation.
>
> (Kuo 2001, 114)

> In the case of theater, practitioners strove along their own course and their works bore different characteristics—all well within their respective communities. . . . Practitioners and audiences of different language streams, however, were normally interested in and confined to their own community. . . . As such, before the 1980s, the development of theatre within each community was generally not known to members of the other communities.
>
> (Quah 2002, 378)

Of these separated language streams, the Chinese theater groups were the most vibrant prior to the mid-1970s, with local history going back to the early twentieth century.[6] Several scholars have pointed out that the development of early Chinese-language drama in Singapore, perhaps up until the 1960s, closely followed that of the dramatic scene in China. Very much influenced by the progressive intellectualism of the 1919 May Fourth Movement, the content of many serious Chinese-language

---

6. Quah Sy Ren's research traces Singapore Chinese-language drama to as early as 1913 (Quah 2013).

plays in Singapore reflected social concerns with sympathy for the masses, and their mode of presentation was very much in the naturalist realist tradition. Chinese drama's socially engaged role propelled it to educate and transform the masses, "based on the belief that theatre can help to make changes, to reach out to the uninitiated, and to educate and transform the less-educated" (Kok 2016, 44). Furthermore, the May Fourth Cultural Movement in China had historically strongly influenced the Chinese-educated intelligentsia in Singapore, and Kuo's "political awareness and inclination, which began to emerge in his theatre practice towards the late 1960s and early 1970s, were clearly influenced by this tradition" (Quah 2010, 150).

From prewar 1937 to postwar 1957, several artistic troupes arrived from China to try to influence Southeast Asia through drama (Tay et al. 1982, 18). Chinese-language plays staged in Singapore then were mostly scripted by playwrights from China or translations of Western classics—a phenomenon not unlike that of Chinese-language theater of the same period in the British colony of Hong Kong. Despite calls for writing plays with a stronger local consciousness, such playscripts were still lacking by the 1940s (Quah 1996, 95). Ironically perhaps, some of the plays that reflected local conditions were scripted by touring troupes from China, such as the Chinese Music, Dance, and Drama Society 中國歌舞劇藝社 that came to Singapore in 1947 and staged plays such as *Fengyu Niucheshui* 風雨牛車水 (Singapore's Chinatown: A changing scene) and *Fengyu Santiaoshi* 風雨三條石 (The fate of Three Miles Village) by the troupe's playwright Yue Ye 岳野 (1920–2001).[7] The troupe had been to Hong Kong before heading south to perform in Thailand and Malaya (Lai B. 1993, 145). According to Xu Lanjun (2012), although the group's official aim was to spread China's theatrical arts as well as impart dramatic techniques to troupes in Malaya, in reality it was attempting to spread communist ideology to the Chinese overseas. Given this ideological pursuit, therefore, it is not surprising to note that the language used in the plays is deliberately given a local taste. For instance, some of the characters are made to speak in a local dialect, and the names of local sites are used. Zhan Daoyu notes, in her study, that altogether Cantonese, Hokkien, Teochew, Hakka, and even Malay colloquialisms the ethnic

---

7. These two playscripts are anthologized in Xin she 1971. When *Fengyu Niucheshui* was later adapted into a film, its English rendition was *Rain Storm in Chinatown*. *Fengyu Santiaoshi* was also named *Fugui bianyuan wai* 富貴邊緣外 (Beyond the boundaries of riches) (Wong and Xu 2002, 198).

Chinese in Malaya frequently used are employed in these plays (2001, 49). Interestingly, some terms like "tea" and "coffee" are footnoted in the playscript to explain what they denote in local lingua franca. Why would a local audience or reader, however, require explanation of local terminology? I posit three possibilities: (1) these explanatory notes in the playscript were meant for the actors then newly arrived from China, and this script was subsequently collected verbatim in the anthology I consulted; (2) the footnotes were for the authorities in China to whom they were reporting back; and (3) in line with the international communist ideal, the publishers hoped that the play would also be performed by troupes outside of Malaya thus warranting the necessity of these explanatory notes. Nevertheless, these were deliberate efforts to appeal to local audiences for ideological ends and represent early examples of local language being written into plays. According to veteran dramatist Chen Zhenya 陳振亞 (1919–95), in spite of the group's short duration in Singapore, their impact on the local arts and literary scene that included music, dance, and theater was huge (Tay et al. 1982, 18). For instance, Zhan attributes the group's artistic training of locals to be fundamental to the spawning of theater practitioners and groups that vitalized the theater scene in the 1950s and 1960s (2001, 50).

Apart from troupes like the Chinese Music, Dance, and Drama Society, individuals from China also contributed, albeit unintentionally, to the development of overseas Chinese-language theater. Following a period of hiatus during the 1942–45 Japanese occupation, the Chung Cheng High School's drama activities, which began in 1939, restarted after the war by inviting renowned dramatists from China (Yang B. 1993, 20) such as Zhao Rulin 趙如琳 (1909–83), from Canton in the winter of 1946, to teach dramatic theory. Local dramatist Low Ing Sing, who was then teaching at the high school, was tasked to set up a drama club (Tay et al. 1982, 18; Lim S. 1995, 156n4). After performing the three-act play *Qundai feng* 裙帶風 (Nepotism) at Victoria Theatre in May 1947 to raise funds for the high school, the Chung Cheng High School Drama Club 中正中學戲劇研究會 was formed (Lim S. 1995, 147). The club's contributions to the development of Singapore drama from 1950 on are significant, and it is perhaps best remembered in theater history for its own spawning of the Singapore Amateur Players 藝術劇場 (SAP, later changing its name to Arts Theatre of Singapore)—the most influential Chinese-language theater company prior to the 1980s (before being superseded by Kuo's "Practice") and the longest surviving drama troupe in Singapore to date.

The pioneering historian of Malayan Chinese-language literature Fang Xiu points out two distinctive features in Chinese-language drama productions in the region in the years immediately following World War II. First, few recapped or were nostalgic about the past. Second, the immigrant mindset in which works prior to the war were beset was no longer as staunchly felt (Lim S. 1995, 150).[8] Significantly, the geopolitical situation of the time determined this consequence. The Malayan Emergency was declared in 1948 as a response to the heightened sense of anticolonialism and self-autonomy sweeping across the globe. Southeast Asia was not spared; white prestige had considerably declined in the region following the Europeans' inability to protect their colonies against the Japanese invasion. The promise of self-determination as symbolized by the newly established United Nations further undermined the legitimacy of the European powers to maintain colonies. It was now hard for Southeast Asians to accept reoccupation, especially after experiencing Japan's brutal subjugation. Thus, the British were returning to a different Malaya after the war. Many Chinese writers were consequently deported back to China during the Malayan Emergency: Zhao Rulin left for France (Y. Wong 1989b, 65–66n32) and groups such as the Chinese Music, Dance, and Drama Society were disbanded shortly after returning to the mainland (Lai B. 1993, 27).

As a result of the Chung Cheng High School Drama Club alumni's link to communist activities, the colonial government banned it from returning to its alma mater to participate in any form of literary or artistic activities (Quah 2012). In order to continue expressing their concerns for society through theater, therefore, members of the club's alumni, joined by alumni from other schools who too shared a common vision of building a professional theater company, formed the SAP in 1955. Unwilling to sacrifice its artistic pursuit for ideological affiliations, SAP's insistence as a cultural troupe with a serious position distinguished itself from its peers (Yang B. 1993, 23; Wong and Xu 2002, 201). As opposed to the commercial and entertainment approach represented by the outdoor vaudeville-like *getai* 歌台, SAP's socially conscious and serious approach to theater-making had a huge impact on the then young Kuo (Quah 2012): three of Kuo's four teachers who "introduced him to serious theatre" when he was selected for screen

---

8. This is quoted from Lim Soon Hock's study of Fang Xiu. For the originals, see Fang 1979.

acting training at Cathay Kris Studio in 1957 (Kuo 2000, 388) were heavily involved with SAP.

Although works ideological in nature often did not pass government censors, resulting in many to be abandoned during the rehearsal processes, the collective efforts by burgeoning drama groups in supporting local productions made the 1960s a fervent period for the staging of local works (Wong and Xu 2002, 201). This surge in local playscripts was the result of audiences growing tired of the repeatedly performed one-act plays that had gained popularity but were now passé and the unsuitability of playscripts from China due to the differing circumstances in Singapore, on top of the audience's demand to see their lives reflected on stage. Kuo considers this local consciousness developing around the 1950s to have been elicited by the increasing affluence and social stability that in turn prompted a search for a collective identity (Tay et al. 1982, 38). Apart from SAP, other notable groups that were active in the period included the Rediffusion Mandarin Play Group 麗的呼聲華語話劇研究組 (f. 1954), Singapore I-Lien Dramatic Society 藝聯劇團 (f. 1957), and Nanyang University (Nantah) Drama Club 南大戲劇會 (f. 1957), as well as Kuo's Singapore Performing Arts Studio 新加坡表演藝術學院 (SPAS, f. 1965), and Selantan Arts Ensemble 南方藝術團 (f. 1972, later renamed Southern Arts Society 南方藝術研究會) spawned by SPAS graduates. All these groups had distinct artistic visions (Wong and Xu 2002, 201). Significant original works these local groups staged then included Lin Chen's 林晨 (1919–2004) *Dapo jingzi de nüren* 打破鏡子的女人 (The woman who broke the mirror, 1965) by Singapore I-Lien Dramatic Society, Low Ing Sing's *Bainian shuren* 百年樹人 (The hundred years of cultivating people, 1966) by his Eastern Arts Company 東藝公司, Lim Beng Chew's 林明洲 (Shi Keyang 史可揚, 1937–2005) *Shenghuo de xuanlü* 生活的旋律 (Rhythm of life) by Recreation and Music Research Group 康樂音樂研究會 in 1966, and Tan Poh Han's 陳伯漢 (b. 1938) *Shengming de juedi* 生命的決堤 (The overflow of life) and Kuo Pao Kun's *Wei, xingxing!* 喂，醒醒！ (Hey, wake up!), both by SPAS in 1966 (Tay et al. 1982, 38).

Veteran dramatist Wang Qiutian 王秋田 (1905–1990) remarked that the modern Chinese drama that arrived in Nanyang emerged out of the 1919 Chinese May Fourth Movement's antifeudalist and anti-imperialist tradition and, like literature and the pictorial arts, was always part of a (social) movement (Tay et al. 1982, 18). From the late 1940s up to the early postindependence years in Singapore, as such, Chinese-language theater was always closely related to the social and political activism of Chinese-educated students, as evidenced in the significant overlap in membership between workers and Chinese-language theater participants (Quah 2010, 151). Before the 1980s, as Kuo recalls, audiences for Chinese theater were also the biggest among the four language groups:

> It had to do with the emerging affluence of Singapore. And drama had had a very big market. Between 1965 to 1975, the Chinese theatre at its height commanded as many as 20000 people per production.... Some of our original plays could sell out a season of 15 or even 20 performances two weeks before opening at the Singapore Victoria Theatre, which seats 900. The market was not really the problem when you have mass movements, and if drama is entrenched in those movements. You could have 30000 people per production.
>
> (Kuo 2001, 114)

While the works of this period were not always characterized by calling for a communist-styled revolution, the dramatists consciously attempted to effect social change through their plays. Moreover, "Although Chinese-language theatre seemed more related to political struggle," Quah is of the view "that the practitioners/activists' interest in local society and people demonstrated a strong sense of belonging to the place, and this inevitably led them to a reflection of their identity" (2002, 383n8).

The PAP government in Singapore made English the main working language after separation from Malaysia so as to establish "a common language of communication amongst its linguistically and culturally diverse people," as well as expedite "the young nation's post-independence entry into the world of international commerce" (F. Chan 2008, 99). The primacy of English was "put in place in the mid-1970s," which elevated it, de facto, to a higher status than the other three official languages (Chua 2009, 246). Postwar Southeast Asia was undergoing a volatile episode in the 1960s and 1970s, with the emergence of national self-rule on the one hand, and the threat of a communist insurrection on the other. Given that this period was in the midst of the international Cold War, "the geopolitical condition of Asia would not have permitted the ethnic-Chinese [in Singapore] to declare the new state a 'Chinese-majority' nation." As sociologist Chua Beng Huat observes:

> The fact that the communist and other leftist elements in Malaysia and Singapore were drawn from the ethnic-Chinese population,

in affiliation with the Chinese Communist Party of the People's Republic of China (PRC), would have rendered a "Chinese-majority" nation highly unstable at what was then the height of the Cold War in Asia. A "Third China" would not be tolerated regionally and internationally.

(2009, 240)

Since Chinese-language theater in Singapore had traditionally "always been active—[and] especially vibrant during the postwar-pre-independence period . . . with a strong social and political consciousness partly inherited from the Chinese May Fourth" Movement (Quah 2002, 378), like many of his contemporaries who were using the Chinese language as a mode of literary and artistic expression, Kuo trod "too close to politics" (Kuo 2001, 110) and was imprisoned in 1976 during a mass arrest that targeted left-leaning writers, intellectuals, and political figures. By the time of Kuo's release from prison four years and seven months later in 1980, the ground had tremendously shifted.[9] The government had implemented an "education policy of great consequence," elevating English as the national first language and relegating all the native tongues to secondary status. Consequently,

> almost overnight, dialects were taken off and mother tongues were not studied with so much literature, and even language input was cut down. In a matter of 10 years, within one generation . . . the supply of talent to the theatre changed radically. Because most kids would have been much better educated in English and few kids would come out fluent in Chinese, with a layer of literature, because now they only studied the functional Mandarin.
>
> (Kuo 1997b, 69)

This "education policy of great consequence" altered the social, and consequently economic, status of the different linguistic groups. Nanyang University 南洋大學, which was "widely regarded as the jewel of Chinese education in Southeast Asia and a bastion of resistance to the government in the field of Chinese education" (E. K. B. Tan 2003, 754),

---

9. Kuo has on several occasions mentioned the deep and thorough reflection he underwent during his incarceration (Devan 2000). It was also in detention that Kuo mastered the Malay language to the level where he could translate plays. For instance, Indonesian playwright Arifin C. Noer's *Kapai-Kapai* (The moths) was cotranslated into Chinese by Chan Maw Woh 陳妙華 and Kuo for the 1988 biannual Singapore Festival of Art.

was amalgamated into the English-medium University of Singapore 新加坡大學 in 1980. The renamed National University of Singapore (NUS) 新加坡國立大學—which used English as its language of instruction in all departments except Chinese Studies (which offered classes in both Chinese and English)—was "the final link in the homogenisation of a bilingual education system where English was the main medium of instruction" (Oon 2001, 100). The two leading Chinese newspapers—*Sin Chew Jit Poh* 星洲日報 and *Nanyang Siang Pau* 南洋商報—were to undergo a forced merger into *Lianhe zaobao* in 1983. Official decisions that were made during this "period, which resulted in the eventual disappearance of Chinese-language education, are now generally recognized as another major cause of the steep decline in Chinese-language standard and the shrinking of all fields related to the language" (Quah 2002, 383–84). In an interview, former head of Chinese at NUS Wong Yoon Wah expresses that when speaking "of the English-educated, there is a trace of disdain and not a little bitterness" among traditional Chinese-medium school graduates 華校生 and Chinese intellectuals who feel that they have "been shunted aside through no fault of their own" (A. Chen 1991). Wong explains:

> When English was emphasised, because Chinese intellectuals couldn't speak the language, they kept quiet. But this made it look like they had less ability. That's one thing that continues to irk the Chinese-educated—that English is still considered the superior language and most times, is the only language used.
>
> (A. Chen 1991)

This marginalized feeling is commonly reflected in Singaporean Chinese literature written in the 1970s, and one could certainly see *Mama* as an extension of that rancor. For the Chinese-language drama scene, the most direct consequences of these policies were that they effectively ended the supply of talent—both practitioners and potential audiences—going into Chinese-language theater (Kuo 1997b, 69). Chinese-language drama groups that had been "very active in the past" were now confronted with the common "problems of dwindling attendance and lack of artistic talent" (Quah 2002, 384).

To assume that Chinese dialects were never an important aspect in the lives and cultures of ordinary Chinese Singaporeans would be erroneous. In fact, performances in Chinese dialect were an ingrained part of traditional popular culture; one might even argue they were high art in Singapore's history. Chinese-speaking Singaporeans over fifty years of age today would recall fondly the traditions of *jianggu* 講古 (folklore storytelling) and *wuxia xiaoshuo* 武俠小說 (martial arts novels) orally narrated on Rediffusion—Singapore's first cable-transmitted, commercial radio station—by Ng Chia Kheng 黃正經 (Serious Ng, 1912-2003) in Teochew, Ong Toh 王道 (The way of the king, 1920-99) in Hokkien, and Lee Dai Sor 李大傻 (Big fool Lee, 1913-89) in Cantonese, from the 1950s to the 1970s (Chia and Loh 2012). The memorable epithets these radio broadcasters were known by demonstrate their popularity. Subscribers received a sound box that was fitted into many Singaporean households and coffee shops as a means of popular entertainment.[10] In its heyday, an estimated one hundred thousand listeners followed the programs these master storytellers hosted (Chia and Loh 2012). On the television, the comedic duo of Wang Sa 王沙 (1924-98) and Ye Fong 野峰 (1932-95)—who later became transnational celebrities in their own right by starring in films produced in Hong Kong such as the *A Niu rucheng ji* 阿牛入城記 (The crazy bumpkins) series (1974-76) and *Shuangxing banyue* 雙星伴月 (The happy trio, 1975)—were household TV celebrities in the 1960s and 1970s, famed for their Teochew and Cantonese interlinguistic comedic puns, peppered with Hokkien, Malay, English, and Mandarin among other languages and dialects.[11] With the PAP's rise to power came their standardization of all aspects of governance, including the area of language. Thus, the vibrant performativity represented by these grassroots artists came to an end. Ng, Ong, and Lee petered out, and Wang and Ye's show was later cleaned up to perform in Mandarin. It spelled the end of an era during which culture came to fruition organically among the grassroots and silenced the public voice of an entire generation of Singaporeans whose native tongue was a Chinese dialect.

While the ban on the use of dialects is enforced on television and FM radio, things are not as strict in live performances such as the theater. Street operas, for instance, are performed almost exclusively in regional

---

10. Rediffusion Singapore Pte. Ltd. is a commercial audio broadcasting station established in 1949. It provides direct sound broadcast via cable to subscribers on two networks (S. Koh 1999, 78). The use of dialects was more liberal on Rediffusion than on FM radio. While Liang Wern Fook's *Sparrow with Bamboo Twigs* "was silenced on FM radio, it could be heard on subscription radio station Rediffusion" (Boon 2013).

11. Wang Sa was invited to perform in Kuo's *Huanghun shangshan* 黃昏上山 (The evening climb) in 1992 with veteran local theater actress Margaret Chan and Ren Baoxian (1935-94), a seasoned actor with the Beijing People's Art Theatre whom Kuo invited to Singapore in the early 1990s for artistic collaboration, most notably to revive the folklore storytelling tradition. Wang declined the offer citing reasons of poor health (Kuo 1998).

languages. If the government fears that Chinese dialects will confuse the young and distract them from learning Mandarin properly, live performances arguably attract a smaller (and in some cases, more elderly) audience than television or radio, and therefore are blamed less for the detrimental effects of corrupting the linguistic abilities of the youth. Hence, Kuo's multilingual plays were not censored despite their use of regional Chinese languages.

After a long hiatus in the Chinese-language drama scene greatly weakened by the mass arrests of the 1970s, it took the collective efforts of fourteen drama groups to pull their resources together to stage a major production. This milestone in Singapore theater history was manifested in the play *Xiaobaichuan* 小白船 (The little white sailing boat, 1982). In a public forum recapping and projecting the development of Chinese theater held during the production's organizing phase, veteran dramatist Low Ing Sing expressed scant optimism that the bipolar language streams of the Singaporean education system would be dissolved. To Low, while nurturing theater practitioners with a sufficient command of the language and cultural literacy to be playwrights and actors in Chinese theater would be increasingly difficult, on the upside the traditional English-medium school graduates who did not comprehend any Chinese would now acquire at least a minimal grasp of aural Chinese, no matter how piecemeal. In Low's opinion, whether this group who had most likely never attended a Chinese-language play would now do so is difficult to say (Tay et al. 1982, 38). Nevertheless, without his explicitly stating so, I believe Low thought that they were the potential audience into which Chinese-language theater could tap. In more ways than one, Kuo's new turn in his artistic strategy after his release from detention was perhaps a response to his mentor's query—tapping into this new English-speaking community as a source of both collaboration and potential audience. In this way too we could thus say Kuo's conceptualization of a Singaporean identity has always been inclusive: to incorporate those who were different from his background (English-speaking Singaporeans) and, in so doing, make us bigger as a people (A. Tan 2012). This public forum was chaired by renowned theater performer Tay Bin Wee 鄭民威 (1926–2000), and in attendance were heavyweights in the theater scene then that included three of Kuo Pao Kun's teachers—Wang Qiutian, Zhu Xu, and Low Ing Sing—as well as Chen Zhenya, Fan Jing 范經, and Kuo himself as discussants. Except for Tay, all the speakers at the forum had come from China, in stark contrast to the theater practitioners under forty years of age of whom

90 percent were born and raised in Singapore. Increasingly, as Kuo pointed out, this bilingual generation would be the ones steering the future direction of Chinese theater development (Tay et al. 1982).

Importantly, Kuo's "Practice" single-handedly wielded the greatest influence on Singapore theater for over two decades beginning from the 1980s. Newly returned from Australia after completing their professional training in Sydney's National Institute of Dramatic Art and Melbourne's Victoria Ballet Guild respectively, Kuo and his dancer-choreographer wife Goh Lay Kuan had originally intended to go into professional theater and dance but could not find enough actors and dancers in the local scene with whom to work. Therefore, they established the SPAS in 1965 first to train performers. SPAS changed its name to Practice Theatre School 實踐藝術學院 in 1974 and again to Practice Performing Arts School 實踐表演藝術學院 (PPAS) in 1984. In 1986, the Practice Theatre Ensemble 實踐話劇團 was founded on the basis of the school, according to the plan worked out twenty-one years ago with Lim Kim Hiong 林錦雄, who served as the ensemble's president. In 1996, it changed its name to The Theatre Practice 實踐劇場 and was consolidated in 2010 with PPAS and reorganized as The Theatre Practice Ltd. under the leadership of Kuo's elder daughter Kuo Jian Hong 郭踐紅 (b. 1967), tracing the founding date of the company to 1965. Significant for being the city-state's first integrated arts school, "Practice" nurtured almost all the leaders of the drama groups in the contemporary Singapore theater scene.[12]

Localization of English-Language Theater before *Mama*

Compared to its Chinese-language counterpart, the English-language theater in Singapore was lagging behind in developing a local consciousness. Prior to the 1980s, the English-language drama scene was dominated by white expatriates mainly staging Euro-American classics for recreational purposes. This is the main reason that although Kuo Pao Kun was effectively bilingual, he did not participate in English-language theater after his return from Australia. In addition, since the 1930s, Chinese-language drama practitioners "had begun to emphasize the production of locally written plays as an imperative form of engaging local society and building local consciousness." To the young

---

12. See Kuo 2000, 386–404, and Quah 2010, 160n6; 2011, 74n5.

and enthusiastic Kuo, this "was certainly more appealing" (Quah 2002, 382–83).

Exceptions to the rule then were found in playwrights Lim Chor Pee 林楚平 (1936–2006), Goh Poh Seng 吳寶星 (1936–2010), and Robert Yeo Cheng Chuan 楊清泉 (b. 1940). Their efforts to nurture a sense of the local in their works when early English-language drama was still "shackled by a colonial consciousness and a colonial view of reality" (Le Blond 1986, 115) were truly laudable. While the Cambridge-educated lawyer Lim Chor Pee's *Mimi Fan* (1962) was widely accepted as Singapore's first English-language play, the Dublin-trained physician Goh Poh Seng's *Room with Paper Flowers* (1964) was the first to introduce Singlish (Yeo 2012) and his *When Smiles are Done* (1965) was the "first consistent attempt to use Singlish" (Life of Practice 2012–13). Following these plays was a seemingly decade-long hiatus in the emergence of English-language drama that discussed Singaporean identity. Commenting on the disparity between the various language streams in terms of developing a local consciousness through playwriting, Clarissa Oon opines:

> The state of English drama was unlike the Mandarin and Malay theatres at this time, where playwrights like Chen Bohan [Tan Poh Han], Kuo Pao Kun and Nadiputra were consistently turning out original works commenting on their time and place. . . . The problem was that the few English-language theatre directors had no concept of or desire to play dramaturg and help develop new scripts that might not have been very polished or did not translate immediately to the stage.
>
> (2001, 67)

While Lim and Goh's admirable efforts yielded little success, Robert Yeo's *Are You There Singapore?* (1974) and Li Lien Fung's 李廉鳳 (1923–2011) *The Sword Has Two Edges* (1977)—the only two original full-length plays produced in the 1970s—achieved more with their respective four- and three-night runs sold out (Oon 2001, 62). The greatest obstacle preventing a genuinely Singaporean experience from being represented on stage in English-language theater, according to director-academic Max Le Blond (b. 1950), was that "the characters initially *would not be themselves* . . . we are not yet at home on stage; at home, that is to say, with ourselves as Singaporeans" (1986, 117). Couched by "a colonial view of reality" (115), the local theater is "frightened of being itself," and the solution, Le Blond suggests, lies in confronting the "problem of theatrical *convention*" to get accustomed to colloquial language use and "Singaporean accents on the local stage" (119).

What followed was an "impetus to stage local adaptations of foreign plays" that some critics consider "an abortive attempt to find a Singaporean theater voice via foreign mouthpieces" (Sasitharan 1989) evinced in productions like Max Le Blond's *Nurse Angamuthu's Romance* (1981) and *The Samseng and the Chettiar's Daughter* (1982) (based respectively on Peter Nichol's *National Health* and John Gay's *Beggar Man Opera*) (A. Koh 2014), *Susan's Party* (1983), and TheatreWorks's debut *Be My Sushi Tonight* (1985). This "slew of localised adaptations" making "undirected use of Singlish" was credited with preparing the audience for the coming and eventual success of Stella Kon's 官星波 (b. 1944) *Emily of Emerald Hill* (1985) and Kuo Pao Kun's *Guancai taida dong taixiao* 棺材太大洞太小 (The coffin is too big for the hole, 1984), which was "due, in no small measure, to its assured use of stage language" (Oon 2001, 115–17). *Emily* and *Coffin* are milestones in Singapore theater history in opening the floodgates of local identity expression by homegrown playwrights. After the rave reviews that these two monodramas received, "suddenly, dramatists everywhere were holding a mirror to the Singaporean experience on stage" (Oon 2001, 109). Yet the use of multiple languages was not without resistance. The "undirected use of Singlish," in Clarissa Oon's observation, "was almost something to be exorcised from Singaporean drama, a parallel to Australian drama in the 1970s" (116). Quah's findings echo this view, highlighting that at the time, the use "of mixed languages would not escape attacks from 'serious' theatre audience[s] and practitioners" (2002, 382). Imagining a multilingual theater was difficult when the "apparent and approved choice" of the day was language purity: both actors and audiences were used to deliveries in British-style standardized English and standardized Mandarin (Le Blond 1986, 117; Quah 2002, 382).

Serious efforts by artists to create a national identity that reflects the multiracial makeup and multilingual reality of Singaporean society were apparent since the nation-state's independence, although none of these endeavors ever truly succeeded. Another way "Singaporeans had been attempting to creatively imagine their own versions of multiculturalism" (Quah 2002, 381) was through staging their work in more than one language. Some might have done it to establish cross-cultural dialogue while others tried to tap into new audiences whose changing tastes were a result of the emerging affluence and new language policy. Both the English-language Experimental Theatre Club (ETC) and

Communications Theatre, for instance, ventured to stage their plays in two language versions.[13] While Chandran K. Lingam directed a young cast for the English version of ETC's *The Lovers* (1986), director-academic Chua Soo Pong 蔡曙鵬 was invited to direct the play's Chinese version. The box office for the English and Chinese versions averaged 40–50 percent and a mere 10 percent respectively, losing a total of SG$4,000 for both runs (Ngui 1987). In the case of Communications Theatre, Helen Chia wrote the play *You Only Live Once* (1986), intending to have the same cast members perform the play in both language versions, but realized through open auditions that few Singaporean actors possessed the linguistic abilities to perform in the two languages. In the end, only one of their cast members performed in both. What derailed their expectations further was that none of the few bilingual audience members they knew attended both versions of the play, so dialogue regarding the differences experienced at each viewing never took place (Chia 1986, 46–47). Recalling this bilingual staging experiment, Chia recounted resignedly that "perhaps, despite the multi-lingual nature of our society, the need for staging bi-lingual plays was after all only a myth" (47). Attempts by other groups to stage multilingual productions have included the collaborative staging of Franz Lehar's opera *Land of Smiles* by the NUS Society and National Theatre Trust with some parts sung in English and others in Mandarin in December 1988, and the amateur group Arts & Acts, which has been staging plays in both Mandarin and English since its founding in 1986 (S. Lee 1989).

None of these endeavors, however, received as big a social response as those of *Emily of Emerald Hill* or *The Coffin Is Too Big for the Hole*. Directed by Max Le Blond and first performed by veteran theater actress Margaret Chan 陳美英 (b. 1950), *Emily* is a monologue detailing the rise of a Peranakan matriarch's wealth and status that sharply contrasts with the decline in her familial relations. Critics consider the play as the "turning point of Singapore English theatre" (Birch 1997, 41–42). Jacqueline Lo surmises that an important reason for the success of *Emily* "is the skilful use of the range of and registers that make up the

---

13. Lim Chor Pee founded the ETC in the 1960s and remained its artistic director from 1962 to 1967. Lim is not only attributed with having written the first English-language play in Singapore, he is also remembered as "one of the prime movers of Singapore's English-language theatre" by helming the theater company and distinguishing it from other groups such as the "expatriate-owned The Stage Club by pushing for experimental theatre" and not "drawing-room drama" (Maulod 2009).

spectrum of Singaporean English. Local audiences identified and celebrated the character's adroit switching of codes and accents to suit the dramatic context" (2004, 110–11). Indeed, Emily's code-switching "achieved a level of authenticity seldom seen before on the Singaporean stage" (Oon 2001, 117), which led critics and reviewers to hail the monodrama as "not only the Singaporean cultural landmark but also . . . the play's protagonist [to personify] Singapore itself" (Lo 2004, 111).

Whereas *Emily* focuses on a Peranakan household, *Coffin* is a comedic satire about the powerlessness of the individual's tussle with the state bureaucracy, poking fun at the state's dogmatic red tape against the heavy backdrop of an ancestral Chinese past. The play's title instantaneously sets up a paradox: how is the grandson supposed to fulfill his filial responsibility when his deceased grandfather's coffin is unable to fit the hole for which it is dug? The sarcasm could not have been more pointed when the official who was previously completely inflexible in making any "room for exceptions" for the grandfather's extra-large coffin, at one time even making the ludicrous suggestion of donating the coffin to the national heritage board, is at the end of the play awarded the title of "Most Humane Personality of the Year" for making the one-time exception of allowing the coffin to be buried in two grave plots (Kuo (1984) 1990, 45). Although the play was first written in English, marking Kuo's formal entry into English-language theater, its premiere staging was the Chinese-language version performed by Choo Woon Hock 鄒文學 on July 23, 1985. Lim Kay Tong 林繼堂 (b. 1954) performed the English version subsequently on November 11, 1985.[14] Like its twin piece, *Danri buke tingche* 單日不可停車 (No parking on odd days, 1986) also presents the helpless struggle of the individual against the state bureaucracy, this time describing a motorist's futile fight against an unjustly awarded parking fine. Significantly, these were the first two plays that Kuo wrote with distinct English and Chinese renditions. After staging them in both language versions, Kuo became the first professional bilingual Singaporean playwright, and members of different linguistic communities have come to view his works as important indexes representing and reflecting on the city-state's realities (Quah 2011, 90).

---

14. On the controversy surrounding the play's premiere staging in the Chinese language despite it being written first in English, see Kuo 1984b, de Souza 1985, and Jit 1990, 20–21.

Bridging Different Language Streams

Before the 1980s theater audiences in the Chinese- and English-language streams rarely overlapped (Quah 2004a, 35). Kuo Pao Kun's return to the theater scene in 1980 was the single most important factor in altering this configuration of audience by language affiliation. Kuo sought to invigorate the much-weakened Chinese-language theater scene by inviting foreign dramatists to lecture, workshop, teach, direct, and perform in plays, and at the same time introduce new concepts to Singapore theater. Kuo's rising leadership status in the 1980s saw him cement alliances among the different local Chinese theater groups that culminated in the formation of the Singapore Federation of Chinese Drama Associations 新加坡華語戲劇團體聯合會 in 1989, as well as develop extensive networks between local and foreign artists and groups. His move into English-language theater by writing and directing plays and teaching workshops in English attracted an entirely new group of potential practitioners who would otherwise not have come in touch with the Chinese-language theater scene due to the language barriers that traditionally separated these two groups. Owing to Kuo's efforts to work with practitioners in both language streams, he was able to adapt and introduce the resources of both groups to each other, opening up his vision of multilingual praxis that henceforth became a marked feature of the Singaporean theater.

The Singaporean government's mass arrests of left-leaning Chinese-educated citizens in the 1970s had shattered the vibrant Chinese-language drama scene. Coupled with the end of the Cultural Revolution that exposed the emptiness of this ideological fervor, by the mid-1980s those who belonged to this group either stopped doing art altogether or entered a time of deep reflection that saw them eventually abandon art as a means of promoting ideology; for them, art ceased to be subservient to political or social movements (Shenzhen shi 1993, 7–8). After this series of events, one of the core issues that confronted contemporary Singaporean theater practitioners, whether practicing in Chinese or English, was how an ethnic Chinese identifies with his/her ethnicity, whether s/he was Chinese or not. In an interview with Ronald Klein, Kuo expresses this view:

> I think when people begin to ask, "Who are we?" they begin this promotion of different cultures. But as an ethnic Chinese, you can't go back to China. As an ethnic Indian, you can't go back to

India. Even if you are a Malay here, where do you go? To Malaysia? Indonesia? Also, we have borrowed so much from the European civilization, but are we Europeans? We cannot be.

So, who are we? I mean, we are cut away. We are descendants of these people, but we are also orphans looking for a parentage, and that parentage can only be a multiple one. You can only recreate a parentage that cannot be any one of these, but an integration of all.

(Kuo 2001, 117)

Being "cultural orphans" 文化孤兒—a term Kuo famously coined—Singaporeans cannot return to their individual mother cultures (Kuo 1996). As a people who inherit from many cultures yet at the same time are cut off from all these parent cultures, Kuo prescribes that Singaporeans should tap into their own heritage and find their own expression through re-creating. In an interview he mentions:

In fact, we cannot actually do the art and call it our own without delving into our own tradition, our own history, our own experience. It is all really one. Different dimensions, different ways of seeing. How can you assert yourself without knowing who you are? What are you asserting? As you ask the question, you answer it. As you answer you ask more questions. As you question, you inherit. As you inherit, you create. Without creating, how can it become yours or your generation's?

(Kuo 1997a, 141)

As opined in the above critical reflection, Kuo's response to this conundrum was his multicultural theater praxis. When "the potential strength of this form (multilingual theatre) in constructing identity" was unleashed, the audiences and perhaps even more so the authorities were surprised to learn "that the most vital and critical reflective Singapore theatre was in the hybrid language-mixing variety." English might have become the "dominant language among various sectors of society," yet hybrid multilingual theater proved itself to be "a most powerful form of challenge to the mainstream consciousness and values" (Quah 2004a, 36).

At the same time throughout the 1980s, Kuo continued to reenergize and contribute to Chinese-language theater by inviting master practitioners from China, Taiwan, and Hong Kong to teach and train with the local Chinese-language practitioners, most of whom, unlike Kuo, had not had the experience of professional theater training. Prominent scholars and dramatists like China's Yu Qiuyu and Gao Xingjian, Taiwan's Wu Jing-jyi 吳靜吉 (b. 1939) and Stan Lai, and Hong Kong's Danny Yung and Daniel Yang Shih-peng 楊世彭 (b. 1936) were invited to guest lecture in Singapore at the First and Second Chinese-language Drama Camps that Kuo co-organized respectively in December 1983 and December 1987.[15] Kuo arranged for plays, such as Beijing People's Art Theatre's *Chaguan* 茶館 (Teahouse, 1957), Lan Ling Theatre Workshop's 蘭陵劇坊 *He Zhu xinpei* 荷珠新配 (He Zhu's new match, 1980), and Performance Workshop's *Look Who's Cross-Talking Tonight?*, works now considered canonical in global Chinese theater history, to be performed in Singapore. Furthermore, established Chinese directors and performers such Xia Chun 夏淳, Ren Baoxian 任寶賢, and Jiang Kun 姜昆 came to convene artistic collaborations with Kuo. In stark contrast to the cultural desert image that has so mired the city-state, Kuo's exceedingly proactive role in establishing networks within the disparate local arts community and among drama practitioners and academicians in the Chinese-speaking world at large turned 1980s Singapore into a focal landmark for a diverse array of cultural celebrities and events to conglomerate, interact, and exchange ideas (Quah 2006, 25).

The concepts he introduced to Singaporean theater circles included those of Bertolt Brecht and Jerzy Grotowski. Already in 1967, he had translated into Chinese and directed Brecht's *Caucasian Chalk Circle*. Introducing the Brechtian *Verfremdungseffekt* stirred much heated debate in the local Chinese drama scene erstwhile dominated by the Stanislavskian naturalist realist mode of presentation (Quah 2006, 23). This antecedent instantly turned Kuo "into a controversial figure" among both the "Stanislavski adherents" and the "more radical forces in Singapore Chinese theatre," so that "like Brecht himself, Kuo found himself to be in the uncomfortable position of being the man in the

---

15. Veteran Hong Kong dramatist Lee Woon-wah, the founding artistic director of the Hong Kong Repertory Theatre Daniel Yang Shih-peng, and the instructor of Taiwan's Lan Ling Theatre Workshop Wu Jing-jyi were among the master dramatists invited to conduct the First Chinese-language Drama Camp. They were joined by other expatriates then working in Singapore, including head of drama of the United World College in Singapore Thomas Ray, Hong Kong dramatist Chu Hak, who was a playwright in the state-run television station Singapore Broadcasting Corporation (SBC), and Lee Wing Shek 利永錫 and Xia Xiaoxin 夏曉辛 (Xia Chuan 夏川), both Shanghai Theatre Academy (STA) 上海戲劇學院 graduates and who were hired to train SBC actors. See Xinjiapo 1983, ("Ying" 1987), and (Di'erjie 1988).

middle" (Jit 1990, 15).¹⁶ He extended this in 1989 by co-organizing the Brecht symposium with the Goethe Institute, bringing distinguished dramatists and scholars of Brecht like Antony Tatlow from the United Kingdom and Huang Zuolin from Shanghai to Singapore. In 1987, Taiwan's Liu Ching-min 劉靜敏 (b. 1956) was invited by Kuo to direct his play *Sha guniang yu guai laoshu* 傻姑娘與怪老樹 (The silly little girl and the funny old tree, 1987), utilizing Grotowski's techniques and introducing the concept of the poor theater to the Singaporean drama scene. The production's significant impact on audiences and practitioners also rippled through to the English-language theater (Quah 1994, 120). As opposed to realist dramatic staging, *Silly Little Girl* adopted minimal staging that did away with elaborate costumes and backdrop, relying instead on the actors' bodies and movements for stage choreography and the audience's imagination to complete the mise-en-scène. The Grotowskian techniques used in this play were to again find their way into *Mama* a year later.

Kuo was perhaps the only artist to be involved as a core organizing figure in all four productions staged collaboratively by scores of Chinese-language theater groups in the biannual Singapore Festival of Art in the 1980s. He was tasked as executive director-playwright twice for both *The Little White Sailing Boat* (1982) and *Kopitiam* 咖啡店 (Coffee shop, 1986), involved in the directorial team in *Wula shijie* 烏拉世界 (The oolah world, 1984), and a cotranslator for *Kapai-Kapai* 喀湃喀湃 (The moths, 1988). The formation of the Singapore Federation of Chinese Drama Associations in 1989—of which Kuo was appointed advisor—was testament to the positive collaborative experiences formed among the various local Chinese theater groups in the 1980s. *The Little White Sailing Boat* was, on the one hand, a considerable event that helped cement alliances and promoted increased interactions among local Chinese-language theater groups for further collaborations, which was especially important after the deadened silence in the late 1970s. For its supporters, it "dispelled the myth that 'Chinese-language theatre cannot produce plays of quality'" (Han 1986, 130). On the other hand, that it took the collective strength of almost all the major groups then

---

16. Krishen Jit opines that Kuo's attempt might have been the first to introduce Brecht to Southeast Asia (1990, 17). Quah's latest research confirms that Kuo's translation and staging of *Caucasian Chalk Circle* in 1967 was the first time Brecht was introduced to Chinese-language audiences in Singapore (Kuo 2020, 195n8). However, the first time Brecht was performed in Singapore was probably an English-language staging of *The Good Woman of Szechuan* by the Dramatic Society of the University of Malaya in 1960. See Atticus 1960.

existing in order to mount these productions was perhaps more revealing of the extent to which the Chinese-language drama circle had been depleted. Hence, in a way, this marks a closing chapter for the era of the old Chinese-language theater scene.

The Little White Sailing Boat also signified an end to one phase of Kuo's writing. First, after *The Little White Sailing Boat*, Kuo no longer wrote playscripts only in Chinese. All his plays from then on (except *Coffee Shop*) were first written in Chinese or English, and translated by himself into the other language, or written in English for a multilingual staging.[17] Second, this was the last play that Kuo wrote in the realist tradition; from then on, his plays were defined by a complex multiplicity that defied a strict linear spatial-temporal progression. C. J. Wee Wan-ling notes that in this creative phase of Kuo's career, he was using his theater and intellectual work to emphasize the need for "diverse cultural and multi-lingual complexities" and the "historical memory of intertwined cultural connections" so as "to counter the homogenising cultural and other negative aspects of economic development" in Singapore (2012, xii). Be it his linguistic or dramatic form of presentation, Kuo entered a phase that was marked by a transcendental significance (Quah 2011, 80), moving from the realist to the allegorical. His creative works, which displayed a more confrontational stance in the 1960s and 1970s, entered the realm of the allegory wherein the bifurcation between enemy and hero was no longer apparent but the enemy was omnipresent and could even be the flipside of oneself. In Quah's observation, while Kuo's earlier works seem to directly confront "the political status quo, his post-1980 works did not retreat from the political but persists, albeit more obliquely, even allegorically, in provoking reflections on the relationship between the individual and the State and to interrogate the State's ideology" (2010, 148). This allegorical type of writing manifested a deeper reflection of humanitarian concerns that was signatory of Kuo's writing from the 1980s onward.

To cross this linguistic boundary and tap into the resources of the artistic practitioners whose lingua franca was not Chinese, alongside his own venturing into English-language playwriting, Kuo organized a series of bilingual directing workshops that attracted students from both language streams. In the 1980s Kuo held three seminal directing

---

17. Quah notes that *The Little White Sailing Boat* is a "collective production," and thus Kuo's "personal vision of society and culture was not clearly represented as it was clouded by a certain collective consciousness" (Quah 2004a, 35). The same might be said of *Coffee Shop*.

workshops. Entitled *Shiju shiti* 十駒試蹄 (10 new directors' works, 1983), the first directing workshop was held in Chinese over five months and culminated in presentations by Lim Jen Erh 林仁余 and Wong Souk Yee, among others, from June 27 to July 9, 1983. The second, *Xingzhe 12* 行者 12 (The 12 new directors), was taught bilingually to twelve out of ninety applicants, who included Ong Keng Sen 王景生 (b. 1964), William Teo 張家慶 (1957–2001), Chia Hong Chye 謝宏凱, Goh Guat Kian 吳悅娟, and Ng Sin Yue 吳倩如, which concluded with a public presentation held from April 15 to 25, 1986. Alvin Tan 陳崇慶 (b. 1963), Ekachai Uekrongtham 呂藝謀 (b. 1962), and Ivan Heng 王愛仁 (b. 1963), among others, participated in the third in 1989.[18] In the 1990s, Kuo further organized a series of playwriting workshops in Chinese to address the lack of locally produced Chinese playscripts, a gap that the English-language scene was filling themselves since they had by then come of age.[19] Therefore, in addition to the core members in Chinese theater, almost all the artistic directors in the major English-language theater companies—Wong Souk Yee of the Third Stage 第三舞台 (f. 1983), Ong Keng Sen of TheatreWorks 劇藝工作坊 (f. Feb. 1985), Alvin Tan at The Necessary Stage 必要劇場 (f. Dec. 1986), Ekachai Uekrongtham of Action Theatre 行動劇場 (f. Jan. 1987), William Teo at Asia in Theatre Research Circus 亞洲劇場研究團 (f. Sep. 1987, later renamed Asia in Theatre Research Centre), and Ivan Heng of W!ld Rice 野米劇團 (f. 2000)—have also been students of Kuo. Writing in 1989 on the efficacy of Kuo's "director training workshops, which was attended by all the new directors working in the scene today," Thirunalan Sasitharan (b. 1958) commented that they "were crucial both in providing the rudimentary skills of stagecraft and interpretation, and in opening up new vistas of performance" (1989). That almost all these major contemporary English-language theater companies were founded in the 1980s attests to the significance of the serious training they received from Kuo for their going professional.

---

18. A fourth, held in Chinese in 1998, was conducted by Szechuan Theatre's Zha Lifang 查麗芳, with participants including Kok Heng Leun 郭慶亮, Lim Hai Yen, and Koh Teng Liang 許聲亮 (Life of Practice 2012–13).

19. Beginning in 1991, Kuo organized the Chinese Playwriting Studio to address the small pool of local Chinese plays. He invited then Shanghai Theatre Academy's (STA) lecturer Yu Yun 余雲 (who subsequently became a longtime editor of the supplement section of Singaporean Chinese-language daily newspaper *Zaobao · Xianzai* 早報 · 現在) to conduct the playwriting studio for the first two batches of students while the third batch was taught by STA's head of the Drama Department Sun Zuping 孫祖平.

As one of Singapore's most representative playwrights, Kuo's continued exploration in different languages that eventually led to his crafting of a multilingual theater cannot be underestimated. Commenting on *No Parking*, Krishen Jit suggested:

> Kuo's real achievement in the play is his profound entrance into Singapore English. It is not quite Singlish . . . But it is very astute in catching the rhythms of Singapore English. It is also not quite BBC English either. But it is just as grammatical and lucid. What Kuo has done is to create a fictive Singapore English that feels like the local version but he has reconstructed it in such a way that it is eminently usable for drama. Remarkably, Kuo, hitherto a playwright in Mandarin, has created one of the most dynamic and useful forms of dramatic English for the English language theatre of Singapore.
>
> (2000, 96)

Even though Jit's comments are specifically on Kuo's achievements in English-language drama, Kuo is equally if not more successful in his Chinese-language plays. Kuo's language use in his theater praxis is precisely what I would call Chinese-language theater in Singapore becoming Singaporean Chinese-language theater. Quah argues that Kuo's *No Parking on Odd Days*, which Jit critiqued as being too colloquial and therefore lacking a universalist quality, precisely defines the uniqueness of Singaporean language use. Written primarily in Mandarin and interspersed with English, Malay, and Chinese dialects, the play's language use offers a convincing lifelike take on Singaporean society (Quah 2005, xxiv). Articulating his thoughts in a series of newspaper articles, Kuo continued to probe this lifelike language usage in Singapore and sought to transplant it onto the stage.[20] Finally, in 1988, Kuo created another milestone in Singapore theater history with his magnum opus *Mama Looking for Her Cat*, a play composed of seven languages and dialects, having an ensemble of actors of different ethnicities perform in their native tongues: English, Tamil, Malay, Mandarin, Hokkien, Teochew, and Cantonese. This was the first multilingual play in Singapore that drew audiences from different language streams into the same spectatorial space—a space where audiences assembled to watch what they have collectively come to identify as their *own* play. In Jit's words, Kuo's

---

20. See, for example, Kuo 1984a.

"influence reached a peak when he embarked on an experimental theater which was climaxed by his highly successful and inspiring performance piece called *Mama Looking for Her Cat*" (2000, 97).

Play Analysis: *Mama Looking for Her Cat*

Performed at the Singapore Conference Hall, Shenton Way, from August 10 to 15, 1988, *Mama Looking for Her Cat* dramatizes the increasing distance between an aged mother, Mama, and her children due to Singapore's changing language policies. The Chinese dialect Hokkien is the only language accessible to the monolingual Mama, and since dialects are discouraged from use in school and banned in the public media altogether, her children have only acquired a very weak grasp of the dialect. Their inability to communicate and impatience with their Mama has driven her to seek solace with her pet cat. One day, her cat goes missing and she goes out in search of it. Outside she meets an old Indian man who too is looking for his cat. Both being monolingual speakers, the Tamil-speaking man and Hokkien-speaking Mama are unable to understand each other's words. However, through physical enactments and the intent to communicate, they seem to establish camaraderie beyond the linguistic register, enacting what Max Le Blond describes as "possibly the single, most moving scene of human interaction in all of Singapore theatre" (2000, 142). Each understands the other is looking for their lost cat, and both realize that their cats are banished from their homes by their children. Once the Indian man's cat is found, he invites his new friend to play with his cat. Eventually, as they part ways unwillingly, they might have reached an understanding that they both are marginalized figures in this new language policy that enshrines the predominance of English speakers. Mama's children go out searching for her, blaming the cat for their Mama's disappearance. Turning into an angry mob as they proceed to hunt down the cat, the children end up in a heap trying to trap the cat, and from this pile of bodies Mama manages to lift her cat out. She sings in desperation to it the familiar lullaby that she sang for her children in the beginning of the play as she strokes the animal in her hand, while the audience remains uncertain whether it is still alive.

Two ideas reflecting on the effects of the language policy change germinated this multilingual play (Kuo 1988, 1996). The first was a student in the adult's drama class at PPAS stating her intention of taking up English lessons. When a surprised Kuo queried further, the

FIGURE 2. Scene in performance of *Mama Looking for Her Cat*, August 10–15, 1988, Singapore Conference Hall, Shenton Way. This is the first significant play that brought together performers from such a variety of different streams onto the same stage. Courtesy of The Theatre Practice.

soon-to-retire Chinese schoolteacher replied that she would otherwise be unable to communicate with her grandchildren. Kuo commented he had never heard a more poignant and painful account of how the language policy change had affected the older generation. The second encounter was during a rehearsal exercise where Kuo designated one actress to play a dialect-only speaking mother (Mama) and other actors to play her children, in which she orally dictates to them the content of a letter she intends to send another child currently studying overseas. As Mama spoke in Hokkien her children would repeat the message aloud in either Mandarin or English, symbolizing the words being penned and allowing the audience to audibly learn what was being communicated to their overseas sibling. As the dictation process progressed, the translated phrases shortened. What Kuo had not anticipated was that the younger actors no longer had a firm command of dialect compared to their older peers and were therefore abridging the mother's message, translating only the parts they could more fully comprehend. The standardization of all language streams into English did not just cut the supply of talent to Chinese-language theater, it also ruptured the intergenerational relationship for Singaporean families whose first language is not English. If we could take this rehearsal scene as a reliable microscopic view of life in society-at-large, it would essentially mean that communication between the first and third generation—or second and third generation—of Singaporeans was being severely disrupted, if not distorted. Under this new language policy, those who did not command the English language would feel increasingly distanced from their own children and grandchildren, and ever more alienated in society.[21] In the words of Wong Souk Yee, "Facility in English (or the lack of it) became the ostensibly neutral criterion for placing Singaporeans within a social hierarchy" (2005, 80).

The bilingual policy mandated that English and mother tongue are studied respectively as first and second languages in the public school

---

21. This explains in part why bilingual dramatists who founded their theater companies in the 1990s like Kok Heng Leun, Goh Boon Teck 吳文德, and Lim Hai Yen, artistic directors of Drama Box 戲劇盒 (f. 1990), Toy Factory Theatre Ensemble - Toy 肥料廠 (f. 1990), and ETCeteras respectively, all came from what would have been traditional Chinese-medium schools and Chinese-speaking families. Those who were good in Chinese also had to better their English in order to move up the social ladder; by contrast, those with a strong command of English only needed a passable grade in their mother tongue to get through the education system for admission into the local university. In 2004, even this requirement was flexed, resulting in an even sharper decline in Chinese cultural literacy standards nationally.

curriculum. The problematics of the term "mother tongue" is not within the scope of discussion of this chapter. Suffice it to say, however, that regardless of one's native language, so long as one is ethnic Chinese, one's *designated* mother tongue to be studied in school would be Mandarin, even if the first language one learns at birth or one's most commonly used language at home might be Cantonese or Teochew or another dialect. Cherian George puts it succinctly:

> Singaporeans of all ethnic groups have had to make painful compromises, [and] even Chinese Singaporeans were not spared the rationalising impulse of the state. Their greatest loss has probably been the government's suppression of dialects and the imposition of Mandarin as their "mother tongue." "For many Chinese Singaporeans, dialect is the real mother tongue and Mandarin a stepmother tongue," Lee Kwan Yew acknowledges in his memoirs, before adding with characteristic matter-of-factness: "However, in another two generations, Mandarin can become their mother tongue."
>
> (2000, 173)

Therefore, if the privileging of English displaced those who did not speak the language at home, then someone like Mama, whose native tongue is not one of the other three official languages, would feel twice removed under this policy.

Citing *Mama Looking for Her Cat* as the exemplary case in point representing the multicultural in Singapore theater, Quah Sy Ren suggests, "In multilingual hybrid theatre, the *majority* of the audience is unable to understand *all* the languages used." The multiple languages used in the play represent "Singapore as an ironic social space in which an official lingua franca exists amidst many other socially dynamic languages and yet effective communication is a perennial problem" (Quah 2004a, 37). Note that the play was performed entirely without surtitles. In this way, Kuo was intentionally not showing

> much concern whether the lines were fully intelligible to the audience.... *Mama* is a true reflection of Singapore's reality of language division among races as well as between generations, represented by the incommunicability of people using different languages.
>
> The use of different languages on stage without providing any kind of translation for the audience was a bold and untried experimentation. Kuo must have deliberated on the effects of alienating

the audience and inviting antagonistic responses. Paradoxically, it was also the same elements of theatrical representation of how languages divide the society in reality that brought issues with social, cultural and political significance into the artistic realm. Multilingual representation proved to be closer to the audience's heart; it struck a cord [sic] with the audience's search for social and cultural identity.

(Quah 2002, 385–86)

Quah's observation that the audience's sense of alienation might turn into antagonistic responses could, as a matter of fact, precisely be Kuo's intention. Employing such multiple languages potentially forces an effort on the part of the audience to translate and in turn be frustrated by it. This shared sense of alienation-and-frustration creates a very distinct otherness, which strangely enough unites the audience in a collective shared experience. Ironically perhaps, this sense of otherness is central to the paradoxical nature of the Singaporean artist's attempt to create an alternative cultural identity whose distinction from other states is one that lacks a unified national culture. Being or feeling equally alienated can also be a unifying experience and provide a point of identification.

In my viewing of the performance's video recording, feelings of angst and estrangement that encapsulated the audience's own viewing experience in the performance turned from an outpouring of collective anxiety and frustration into more critical insights during the dialogue session immediately following the play. Questions were raised in both Mandarin and English, by ethnic Chinese fluent in either language as well as Indians and white expatriates in the audience, with the discussion facilitated and interpreted in the two languages by Kuo between the audience and his cast. Kuo opens the postshow dialogue session by soliciting responses on whether the audience considers the performance contrived or if they feel they understand the play. Members of the audience nod in agreement; one points at a cast member and remarks, "I don't understand what he's saying exactly, but I understand him!" Another comments that Hokkien was more predominant twenty years ago, and hence the play's setting might have been more appropriate in the past. One cast member, William Teo, disagrees: he considers the play to be very contemporary, contemplating issues of language, communication, and intergenerational relationship, and he himself was very moved devising the play with the rest of the cast.

A middle-aged Chinese woman pours her heart out on how this play speaks to her situation at home. On the one hand, although she still speaks her mother's dialect, her education has molded her to speak in a different register. As a result, she often finds her mother to be too long-winded and abhors talking to her, much like the relationship between Mama and her children in the play. On the other hand, she bemoans her own daughter's inability to speak her grandmother's dialect and thus be unable to verbally communicate with her. Instead, on her grandmother's birthday she would buy her a cake, sing her a birthday song in English, and kiss her on her cheeks as an expression of love. This woman concluded that these are trendy things the young like doing for their elders but might not necessarily be what their elders desire. Veteran Singaporean Chinese-language playwright Han Lao Da 韓勞達 (b. 1947), who is among the audience, is particularly moved to see both the cast and audience being made up of members from different ethnicities and language streams, which he believes has henceforth launched a Singaporean type of communication.

These audience responses I gleaned from the recording suggest that the incomprehensibility of all the dialogue did not hinder the audience from connecting what they saw on stage with their own real-life experiences. Indeed, this supports Quah's observation that critics of hybrid multilingual theater "were not conscious of the potential strength of this form in constructing identity, nor were they aware of the necessity of theatre as the amalgamation of imagination and reality" (Quah 2004a, 36). Like the characters in the play, the audience too experiences the frustration and alienation of multilingual exchanges, assuming that no one person in the audience probably understands all the seven languages and dialects spoken. While the audience's feeling of alienation in the theater is deliberately created by the mode of performance, the larger implication is that this alienation extends into the everyday biopolitical reality. To be sure, as Kuo himself notes in the play's program:

> In Singapore, all our drama models have been mono-lingual. Is it odd making multiplicity in language the mainstay? "It is," said some. But what if when, as in our case, the reality has always been multi-lingual? *Mama Looking for Her Cat* is a new experience, registering our response to a very common phenomenon we have found very disturbing.
>
> (1988)

Kuo's strategy of constant *dis*identification is at work here. Using theater as a medium for intervention, Kuo calls on his audience to reflect on the possibilities and imaginings of the scenarios and outcomes by making them experience firsthand the characters' frustrations on the *other side* of the fence of the language policy. Notwithstanding that the language policy has been applied across the nation, it has impacted different sectors differently. A weak command of the English language might impede the social mobility of both the Chinese- and Malay-educated in dissimilar ways, but they might be unaware of others in more dire situations, like the uneducated, illiterate, or monolingual whose only language they command is not of the four designated official ones, such as Mama. Assuming that the majority of the audience has consisted of the middle-class, tertiary educated, and intellectuals, the bulk of whom have successfully risen through the social ladder, they would be invested in the continued success of the government's bilingual policy. The play's alienation strategy therefore has allowed them a chance to think and *feel* for those who are less empowered and occupied an even less privileged social position. Some must find this unique play-watching experience of sitting in the theater through languages they do not fully comprehend either emotionally unsettling or mildly uncomfortable at the very least. The affective discomfort that has arisen as a result must surely give them pause to critically reflect on their own privileged positions that distortedly mirrors the disenfranchised conditions of those on the other side of the language policy fence, leading them to *dis*identify with the policies of the powers-that-be that formulated such social structures.

Moreover, does the absence of translation of the various local languages suggest also, in the words of Naoki Sakai, the absence or avoidance of "a power relationship inherent in the translation of a language into another" (1997, 27)? In a language policy that makes English the working language in society, it would have seemed all too easy to provide surtitles as a solution to draw even more audiences into Kuo's multilingual plays. The difficulty in understanding the play posed by the multiplicity of languages would have been made obsolete, and the most fundamental of problems inherent in multilingual theater thus eliminated. And if so, why did Kuo not opt for this ready solution? I suggest that this was because, in the course of watching hybrid multilingual plays like *Mama*, "audiences experience a *critical space* arising out of a sense of alienation elicited from the unfamiliarity of certain languages represented in the performance" (Quah 2004a, 37–38; italics mine). In a forum on playwriting, Kuo warned of the dangers inherent in a highly affluent and materialist Singaporean lifestyle that is prone to numbing one's mind and emphasized the importance of developing a "critical sensibility" (1997b, 71). In a Brechtian way, Kuo's theater is a call to a halt, "cutting, interrupting, holding something up to the light, making us look again" (Brook 1996, 87), and an intellectual attempt to challenge this numbing effect through deconstructing the different layers that mask the problem. While the government's multiracial model presupposes four official languages providing equal representation to the four major ethnic groups, these languages have different hierarchical positions that translate into different realities in Singaporean society. Providing translation would only masquerade this difference inherent in the power structure and assume a selfsameness in power relations that is not an accurate actualization of the relationship among the different languages.

Furthermore, considered in terms of linguistic translation, like the copying in dictation, translation is a nonserious speech act, not necessarily enunciating what the translator him/herself wants to say, and thus an act that may be educated but not an act of properly constructed subjectivity. By not performing the act of translation, therefore, the playwright is making a conscious attempt at not coercing the characters to utter or translate what they do not think and feel themselves. Instead of claiming to speak *for* the characters, the act of withholding translation thereby emphasizes and reinforces the subjectivity of the characters created by the ensemble of actors through their workshop experience with Kuo. To put it differently, in contrast to Mama's children through whom she speaks to communicate with her child studying overseas and who censor her message when they verbalize the translation of her Hokkien dictation into letters written in Mandarin or English, the play empowers Mama and affirms her subjectivity by letting her address the audience directly in Hokkien.

Through this play, Kuo may have wanted to reflect what the language policy change meant to Singaporean society: economic growth at the expense of traditional values, especially those of family bonds. Yet Kuo's play suggests more by depicting that communication between Mama and the Indian man is achieved through transcending linguistic and ethnic boundaries, reversing the expectation that a bigger gap should exist between the mother and the Indian man than between she and her children. Wong Souk Yee argues that this is Kuo's attempt at transcending the official discourse of multiracialism, which "is based on the concept of the inviolable traditions and identity of the origin of each race" that resists compartmentalizing the populace into "essentialist" ethnic traits, and thus "stands this logic on its head" (2005, 86–87). But might this perhaps also suggest that Mama's language problem at home is less one of communication and more something else? By making the audience bear witness to the process of censorship Mama's children enact on her, which they might have neither intended nor necessarily been completely aware of but are nonetheless complicit in, Kuo is confronting them—and by extension, us—to reflect on this act in silencing Mama.

> MAMA: Write me another one. Tell him to be careful when making friends. You know a person's face, you don't know his heart. Must be very careful not to trust people too easily. But you must also be nice to other people. I know honesty very often makes you lose out on things, but still you must try your best to be honest and courteous to other people. Specially when you are not in our own country, you need more friends more often.
> JH: (*Already very impatient, in Hokkien*) Ok, I know *lah*, Mama. I know *lah*. (*Now in English*) "Mama ask you to make good friends but also beware of bad friends." Ok, finished.
> MAMA: Write me another one. Tell him don't spend so much money. You know our money never come easy. Every cent is very hard-earned. But if he really needs to spend money on something important, like when you want to buy books or what, you just go ahead and spend. If that is the case, then you know I will try every means to send you more money still. The important thing is for you to understand the importance of thrift. You must also be very careful when you deal in money with friends . . .
> W: (*Already very irritated, in Hokkien*) Ok *lah*, Mama, so big already, he knows what to do *lah*. (*Then in English*) "Mama tell you to be thrifty and be careful with friends." Finished!
> MAMA: Tell him: Your big maternal uncle has gone to live in what's that place? . . . Canada. Maybe I'll never see him again. I was so sad I didn't even want to go to the airport to see him off. I was scared I cannot control my tears. . . . And your maternal auntie also had problem lately. Very big problem. She fell one day and half her body cannot move anymore now. The right side. She can't even talk now, only cry. Every time I see her, she cries. Cannot say anything . . .

SB: (*Already very impatient*) OK, OK, OK *lah*! (*In Mandarin*) "Big maternal uncle immigrated to Canada. Maternal auntie paralysed by stroke." Ok, finished.

(Kuo (1988) 2012, 94)

One reason the children's translation of Mama's letter to their overseas sibling gets shortened is their weakened command of dialects, as a result of the language policy. Another, like the middle-aged woman in the audience, is that education and socialization have acculturated us to focus on upward social mobility, which has in turn numbed us increasingly to those who have been left out of the linguistic shift, carried out at the national level to connect the city-state to the international financial sector. As C. J. Wee Wan-ling reminds us: Kuo's "major object of critique in the 1980s and 1990s was the state-driven modernising process, with its impulse to standardise daily existence and its link to global capitalist development" (2012, xii). The mother has so lost any claim to a place in the social hierarchy on account of her language limitation and her children are so focused on upward mobility through English and Mandarin that they simply ignore her. Beyond critiquing the state's language policies, therefore, *Mama* is a stark reminder that we must take stock and reflect upon ourselves: whether we too have turned a blind eye to the needs of those who are less empowered and instead become perpetrators in further disenfranchising them. What have we lost, or traded, in exchange for greater efficiency and material benefits for our modern standards of living? Have we become complicitous with the system of which we are critical?

Aftermath of the Language Policy

In the article "Let the Banquet Begin, Who Needs the Cook?," Singaporean lawyer and writer Philip Jeyaretnam likens cultural (identity) construction to a banquet *without* a chef: unlike ingredients to add and methods of preparation in a banquet, the culture of a nation cannot be predetermined via a top-down approach; it always has to be bottom-up, a groundswell. A government who tries to steer—or worse, dictate—the directions of a national culture's development always warrants resistance. Kuo Pao Kun's work, he argues, is therefore an ideal representation of a culture of the people because it does not try to presuppose what that culture already is, and instead reacts and responds organically to how the ground was pulsating. In Jeyaretnam's words, Kuo's intervention was a "natural re-working of traditional values to meet a modern context" (1990).

In this chapter, I examined the sociohistorical, and especially the political, circumstances surrounding language policies in Singapore, which had a huge impact on its theater. In their individual quest for expression of local identity, each community was largely confined to their linguistic boundaries, although several attempts to transpose the city-state's multilingual, multiracial reality on stage have been made, albeit with little success. At a time when all fields related to the Chinese language have been steeply declining, Kuo incorporated and utilized resources from other language spheres and carved out an entirely new space for Chinese-language theater. Perhaps some might not agree that what Kuo was doing could still be considered Chinese-language drama. Significantly, it is owing to Kuo's timely intervention that theater in Singapore did not become wholly English-language, but instead multilingualism came to be accepted as a genuine reflection of Singaporeanness. In a place like Singapore where English has become the dominant language in most domains of society, it is hard to imagine a theater scene that would be otherwise. Indeed, as T. Sasitharan says, "*Mama* posed an implacable challenge to the hitherto entrenched assumption in the drama scene that a genuine national theater in Singapore, if and when it emerges, would be an English-language one" (1989). I would argue that Kuo's works reflect the sociopolitical conditions the ethnic Chinese were going through in 1980s Singapore and are what I would call Chinese-language theater in Singapore becoming Singaporean Chinese-language theater—one that distinguished itself from the theaters in other Chinese-speaking regions. Written by either Chinese or Singaporean playwrights, the former are Chinese-language plays that focus on issues addressing the Chinese community in Singapore; the latter are works written by Singaporean playwrights that reflect on the sociohistorical conditions that have given rise to the multilingual and multicultural reality encapsulating the contemporary Singaporean experience.

While I have highlighted attempts by dramatists in the Chinese- and English-language streams at building a local consciousness in their work prior to the 1980s, Kuo's effort distinguished itself, beginning with *Coffin*, by constructing social identification through critically appraising the state bureaucracy and national discourse instead of establishing affective belonging for its own sake (Quah 2011, 92). In other words, in contrast to the state's simplistic celebration of the diverse ethnic representations, Kuo's plays attempt to critically reflect on the issues surrounding the multiracial construct and deconstruct the hierarchies that veil such power structures.

On top of his critical hybrid multilingual plays, Kuo's efforts as a mentor to artists from the different language streams was crucial in opening up resources for and facilitating translingual, cross-cultural dialogue among the different artistic communities, in addition to nurturing a critical sensibility. Kuo's concerns can be poignantly identified in the works of younger Chinese-language theater practitioners, most of whom were brought up under the bilingual education policy. In a discussion on whether the Chinese-language theater had fallen behind their peers in the English-language scene, Kuo expressed this view:

> Most of the Chinese-language theater practitioners today, I think, are graduates of the Chinese-medium schools. But increasingly young theater practitioners are bilingual, like Lim Jen Erh, Ang Gey Pin 洪藝冰, Kuo Jian Hong, Drama Box, and Hwa Chong Alumni 華初校友會 . . . they are all bilingual, even though they mainly work in the Chinese language. This is becoming increasingly important. Because, if you know more Chinese, you will naturally know more Chinese culture, then you will become an embodiment or a vessel of cultures. And if you understand Chinese culture, you will understand that the turbulent development of its language—more like a downfall—has been embedded in the memories of Chinese-language theater practitioners. This has caused them to be concerned with how, in a cosmopolitan place like Singapore where English is the predominant language, they can rejuvenate their parent culture and make it relevant to the times. This type of concern, this type of struggle with dilemma—sometimes even a scar or a wound—is the hallmark of Chinese-language theater practitioners.
>
> (Fok 1993)

Indeed Kuo's works and those of the younger bilingual dramatists—in the footsteps of Kuo's critical hybrid multilingual plays—tend to represent "the pluralism of Singapore society" (Quah 2002, 386) in a way that while "reflecting on the problematics of the time . . . always displays a certain elevated marginalised consciousness" (Quah 2004a, 39). This articulation serves to provide an alternative view from that of mainstream discourse and remains an important feature of contemporary Singapore theater.

The consequences of the language policy change cannot be underestimated in the contemporary history of Singapore, which has had a tsunami of an impact on identification among other realms. While the government might have in part been prompted by the larger geopolitical Cold War conditions to implement this policy, the resultant effect was a huge identitarian shift such that even though the ethnic Chinese accounted for three quarters of the country's population, its identification with Chinese culture appears to be the most uprooted and relationship with Chineseness the furthest among the four sites I study. As has been demonstrated, the efficacy of how "Chinese" one feels about oneself exceeds well beyond the realm of cultural identity. Its implications are manifested in the altering of social hierarchy, economic prospects, and intergenerational communication, not to mention the immeasurable psychological pain it has caused, for an entire generation of Singaporeans who were raised in a language other than English. *Mama Looking for Her Cat* was a natural response to this phenomenon. The strength of the play lies in its ability to enact a role reversal on us: getting the audience to empathize with the plight of Mama by making us feel what the marginalized are going through. Indeed, as Sasitharan suggests, this was a theater that "gave voice to the voiceless, validated the consciousness of minorities and stood for the conscience of the people" (2017). In so doing, the play gets us to be reflective of our privileges and reminds us of the complicitous relationship we would otherwise be engaging in with the system if we are not more critically reflective of our thoughts, actions, and conditions.

Chapter 2

An Incomplete Break with the Past
The Remaking of Identity in Stan Lai's Taiwanese Theater

Performance Workshop 表演工作坊 (f. 1984) is Taiwan's best-known theater troupe internationally and among the most successful artistically and commercially today. Even during the period of the severe acute respiratory syndrome (SARS) outbreak in 2003, the company's box office recorded all performances sold at between 70 and 100 percent—at which every audience member had to wear a mask (Lai 2011). The group's inaugural production *The Night We Became Cross-Talk Comedians,* had an unprecedented twelve sold-out nights in a row—a stellar record that rocked the 1980s Taiwanese theatrical world (Li X. 1995, 52). The play was such a hit that newspapers noted, "*The Night We Became Cross-Talk Comedians* creates the highest ever record in box office revenue in the nation's theater scene, attesting to the commercial value of the dramatic arts" ("Naye" 1985). Subsequently over a million copies of the audiotapes of the performance were sold, with bootlegged copies perceived to number five times as much (Lai 2011). So successful are the company's critical reception and mass appeal that many television and film celebrities from Taiwan as well as mainland China—for instance, superstar Brigitte Lin Ching-hsia 林青霞 (b. 1954), Taiwan's top talk-show host Chang Hsiao-yen 張小燕 (b. 1948), and most recently China's "Super Girl" pop actress-singer Chris Lee 李宇春 (Li Yuchun) (b. 1984)—have chosen to turn down offers and block out several months of their schedules just so as to work in a stage play with the theater company and its artistic director Stan Lai Sheng-chuan 賴聲川.

By far the best-traveled and most renowned theater company from Taiwan, Performance Workshop has toured many locales with a significant Chinese-speaking demographic, such as New York, San Francisco, Los Angeles, Stanford, Irvine, Adelaide, Hong Kong, Singapore, and the mainland Chinese cities of Beijing, Shanghai, Xi'an, Shenzhen, Nanjing, Guangzhou, Chengdu, Chongqing, and Changsha. The group's ventures into the mainland have garnered several "firsts" artistically. *Hongse de tiankong* 紅色的天空 (Red sky, 1994) is the first Stan Lai play to be performed on the Chinese stage. Significantly, *Red Sky*'s restaging in December 1998 in Beijing, about the final journey of old age, essentially made Lai the first Taiwanese artist to have directed a drama in China with a primarily mainlander cast, comprised of actors from the Beijing People's Art Theatre and National Youth Theatre 中國青年藝術劇院, including the veteran Lin Liankun 林連昆 (1926–2004) (Lai 1999, 399).[1] In 2002, selections of Performance Workshop's *Qianxiye, women shuo xiangsheng* 千禧夜, 我們說相聲 (*Millennium teahouse, 2000*) became the first performance by a Taiwanese group to be showcased on China Central Television's annual Spring Festival gala 春節聯歡晚會 (Shui 2007, 140–41), a television variety program watched by millions of Chinese locally and internationally during Chinese New Year.

Lai is a multitalented artist, having experimented with and achieved success in various art forms and genres. His two full-length feature films, *Anlian taohuayuan* 暗戀桃花源 (Secret love in peach blossom land, 1992)—the cinematic version of his best-known play—and *Feixia A Da* 飛俠阿達 (Red lotus society, 1994), have earned him a deserving place in Taiwanese film history. Scholars have compared him to the Taiwanese New Cinema 台灣新電影 auteurs (Shen 1995) as well as positioned him among the most acclaimed filmmakers in the Chinese-speaking world (Wang Z. 2010).[2] Lai is the screenwriter and director of the television situation comedy *Women yijia doushi ren* 我們一家都是人

---

1. The first play staged in mainland China by a Taiwanese playwright was Yao Yi-wei's *Hong bizi* 紅鼻子 (Red nose, 1969) by China's National Youth Theatre in Beijing in February 1982 (Gao Y. 2006, 22). The first theater troupe from Taiwan to perform in mainland China was Hugh Lee Kuo-shiu's Ping-fong Acting Troupe, touring to Shanghai in 1994 with its *Shamuleite* 莎姆雷特 (Shamlet, 1992) (Chou 2016, 338).

2. For a discussion of Lai's feature films, see Kowallis 1997, 2013, 2018, Braester 2010, and Shen 2020.

(All in this family are human, 1995–1998), which satirizes politics and current affairs, experimenting with scripting, rehearsing, and performing live in a recording studio—all within a day. So popular was the production that the originally planned forty-episode TV series ran for six hundred episodes over three years, and Lai was subsequently invited to make a sequel *Women liangjia doushi ren* 我們兩家都是人 (All in two families are human, 2004). The state also appointed Lai as art director of the first Summer Deaflympics in Asia (2009) and tasked him to write and direct a rock-musical *Mengxiang jia* 夢想家 (Dreamers, 2011) to celebrate the Republic of China's centennial.[3] The oeuvre of his work extends to the operatic genre: *Xiyouji* 西遊記 (Journey to the west), which was commissioned for the opening of the National Theatre in Taipei (1987), and *Honglongmeng* 紅樓夢 (Dream of the red chamber) at the San Francisco Opera (2016), both of which are based on Chinese literary classics. Lai's most ambitious work to date might be the eight-hour epic *Rumeng zhi meng* 如夢之夢 (A dream like a dream, 2000), which traverses present day Taipei, Paris, Shanghai, Normandy, and Beiping in the early Republican era. By placing the audience in the dugout stage on individual swiveling chairs and viewing the performance that revolves around them, the play reverses the positions between audience and performance, bearing imprints of Lai's Buddhist teachings. On top of these, he is also a distinguished academic, having taught extensively at the Taipei National University of the Arts 國立臺北藝術大學 and served as the founding dean of its School of Theatre. Not only has Lai won the National Arts Award—Taiwan's highest award for the arts—an unprecedented two times for "the impact of his works on an entire era as well as his contribution to arts education" (National 2001), he was also hailed as "the best Chinese language playwright and director in the world" by the British Broadcasting Corporation (Renaud 2010). During modern Chinese drama's centennial in 2007, Lai was inducted into the Chinese Theatre Hall of Fame (Renaud 2010). Furthermore, in 2019, Lai became the first artist from the Chinese-speaking world to be bestowed with a star on the walk of fame at the

---

3. The heated controversy aroused in the production of *Dreamers* is not within the scope of discussion in this chapter. Wang Chun-yen (2014) discusses the musical together with the series of Lai's *xiangsheng* plays, and Jon Kowallis (2013, 137) suggests that *Dreamers* might be considered as the third of Lai's epic trilogy after his two feature films. While each scholar contextualizes *Dreamers* with a different set of works, both observe that Lai's corpus intervenes critically with Taiwan's identity discourse, distinguishing him from nonserious, noncritical playmakers.

Sibiu International Theatre Festival, Romania's preeminent performing arts event.

This chapter addresses the significance of Stan Lai's best-known work *Secret Love in Peach Blossom Land* (1986) vis-à-vis the sociopolitical situation impacting the region in Taiwan's search for a local identity in the 1980s. The play's title is made up by two separate plays, one *Anlian* (Secret love) and the other *Taohuayuan* (Peach blossom land), and these two halves of the play have invited interpretations as the two sides across the Taiwan Strait. Shen Shiao-ying suggests reading the utopic Peach Blossom Land in the play as Taiwan: the hospitable people there invite Old Tao "to stay on, yet he is unable to forget his past and therefore finds it difficult to feel totally at home in this 'utopia'" (1995, 100). In contrast, therefore, Old Tao's former home Wuling is interpreted as China, just as Old Tao's departure from home is construed as the Nationalists' forced and humiliated retreat from the motherland (Shen 1995, 100n27). Extending this reading to the diaspora, Jon Kowallis wonders if the metaphor of the Peach Blossom Land might not also extend to the United States, since America is "the 'new mainland' to which many mainlanders wandered from Taiwan in the later 1950s and 1960s and continue to end up now" (1997, 175). Joyce Liu Chi-hui suggests that Lai's theatrical productions, especially the intertextuality he employs "in dialogue with ancient Chinese texts," address "the archive and the repository of Chinese cultural memories shared by the audience" on the surface. On a deeper level, however, his plays reveal a conceptual interstice and "incongruity as well as an unsettling critique of the cultural past" (1997). While she argues that Lai underscores Taiwanese subjectivity by delinking the two entities, Wang Chun-yen is of the view that Lai has deliberately retained the ambiguity of the decoupling of the binary (2004, 162; 2014, 103–4). For Yomi Braester, the juxtaposition of these two halves represents Taiwan's "doubled identities" that are fragmented, incompatible, ambiguous, and dislocated (2008, 692). Indeed, Lai seems to suggest many such complementary opposites in this play, yet he does not allow an easy fixation of any one emblem as an unchanging identity. Building on the foundations of these scholarly insights, I argue that Lai encourages the audience to see the flexibility and constantly changing dichotomies he sets up, and it is this constant *dis*identification that I propose as a useful category with which to view his plays. In so doing, Lai works purposefully to destabilize the signifiers from the signified, allowing a multivalent postmodernist commentary of his play on contemporary Taiwanese society. In ways akin to Hong Kong, Taiwan's political reality lies outside its own making and is very much determined by the contestation of external powers with a vested interest in the region. What sets Lai's plays apart from previous dramatists' is that not only do they reflect characters who straddle affiliations across the Taiwan Strait, their commentary on the geopolitical situation of their times positions Taiwan as an ambiguous entity that has roots in premodern Chinese culture and is descended via the Republic of China's exodus to the island-state from 1949 onward. This exploration depicts Taiwan's identity always as indeterminate, uncertain, and irresolvable. The impossibility of Taiwan's self-determination might precisely be Lai's political comment: given the island-state's contested history and the current international geopolitical circumstances, its subjectivity can be neither self-proclaimed nor determined.

In a paper written for the panel discussion on "Tradition, Innovation, and Politics: Chinese and Overseas Chinese Theatre across the World," Lai suggests that the "Taiwanese independence movement" has provided another opportunity "of searching to *redefine who we are*":

> In Taiwan, the "independence movement" hasn't affected the way we work as much as the inner forces that this movement expresses. In my view, the movement is a struggle to be independent not from anyone else but from ourselves. This attempt to break away from ourselves constitutes another way of searching to *redefine who we are*.
>
> (1994, 37; italics mine)

Indeed, on many occasions Lai has mentioned Taiwan as an accident of history, a mixed entity of two contending forces that resulted in a strange offspring, whose genesis has not been replicated elsewhere in human history. Although Lai does not articulate as precisely as his detractors might have wanted him to on whether or not Taiwan is part of China—a question that intrigues historians and political scientists alike without conclusive results, and one that politicians endlessly milk for political cachet—he clearly demonstrates in his works the uniqueness of Taiwan's Chineseness through unpacking issues of identification and memory intertwined in its fragmented history. As I shall argue with my following examples, the complexity of the intellectual work of cultural producers like Lai is not easily reduced to political allegories, yet theatrical creativity occurs in a specific historical context. Art, however, has other manifestations that are not contained by narrow ideological differences and allows interpretations with contemporary relevance that goes beyond the China/Taiwan divide.

Political History

> YAN GUI: In his [dad's] entire life, he has never gone abroad. The first time he did so, was to return home.
> BAI TAN: What sort of logic is this?
> YAN GUI: What sort of world are we living in?
> (Lai (1989) 1999, 268)

In a special issue of *TDR*, featuring prominent director-playwrights in the Chinese-speaking world, Stan Lai writes:

> Taiwan in 1983, when I began creative work in the theatre, was pregnant with contradictions that were soon to evolve into political confrontations and acute social and cultural changes. Foremost among these contradictions was (and still is) the question of identity, not only the gross political questions, but the subtle questions of cultural identity and direction as well.
> (1994, 33–34)

The above lines in Performance Workshop's *Look Who's Cross-talking Tonight?* sum up the irony and dilemma of the Taiwanese subject: Where is home? As the character Yan Gui shares his father's homegoing experience, it is clear from the exchange that the senior Yan is leaving Taiwan for China: the first time he is going abroad (leaving Taiwan) is to return home (China). Evidently, in his mind, he identifies China as the home to which he is returning, of which Taiwan too is a part because he has to leave home in order to go abroad. Arriving in China only to realize his mother had already died two years ago, the guilt-stricken and overwrought Yan senior inadvertently blurts out: "[I'll] go home . . . to Taipei" (Lai (1989) 1999, 276). This psychological complexity, where "home is a foreign country," is perhaps most aptly suggested by Chang Bi-yu to describe the *waisheng* émigré mentality in Taiwan (2015, 155), which I will elaborate later in the section. Lai's plays are best at confronting such complicated questions of identity and identification, and mediating these contradictions through their strong plots, moving narratives, and intricate sensitivity to history (C. Wang 2021).

Given Taiwan's complex history, fraught with contentious factions asserting competing modes of identification from within and a mammoth neighbor constantly threatening to wage war from without, defining Chineseness on the island is an extremely difficult question. Even more so than mainland China itself, one might argue that Taiwan is the most Chinese of the four sites. After losing the Chinese Civil War (1945–49), the Kuomintang (KMT, or Nationalist Party) retreated to Taiwan with over two million military men and their families immediately following the Second World War. Moving its capital from Nanjing to Taipei, the Republic of China (ROC) considered Taiwan as merely a temporary site from which it would launch its attack to liberate its mainland compatriots from what it imagined must be the throes of communist insurgency. In contrast to the People's Republic of China's (PRC) rampant destruction of Chinese artifacts and eradication of traditional cultures during the Cultural Revolution among other man-made calamities, the KMT government honored the venerated status of traditional culture (just think of the fine collection at the National Palace Museum in Taipei, as an example) and utilized the Chinese Culture Renaissance Movement 中華文化復興運動 in the 1960s and 1970s to strengthen national spiritual education, promote Mandarin Chinese, and carry on Confucian traditions and culture (Lin G. 2011) to legitimize itself as a cultural inheritor and promoter, not destroyer.[4] As the self-appointed preserver of Chinese tradition, though, the KMT's iron-handed rule on the island was responsible for the silencing of Taiwanese and aboriginal voices, as well as heavy-handed censorship and suppression in the cultural-artistic discourse until the 1980s.

The ROC's deliberate attempt to distinguish itself from the PRC served specific ideological goals. Although the post-1949 ROC only exerted de facto control over the islands of Taiwan, Penghu, Quemoy (Jinmen), and Ma-tzu (Mazu), its continued assertion of being Chinese was made possible by the geopolitical structure during the Cold War. Since the United States and its allies were determined to keep the Soviet bloc (to which the PRC belonged) at bay, the ROC's continued representation of the Chinese seat in the United Nations Security Council after 1949 was welcomed and recognized by the international community as

---

4. Meanings are evidently stretched in such ideologically driven rhetorical wars. Chinese culture, for instance, when used for the purposes of the Chinese Cultural Renaissance Movement, took on meanings from "a culture of adhering to the Three Principles of the People" to "supporting combat missions," and extended even to "denouncing Mao Zedong and opposing communism" (Lin G. 2011).

Free China 自由中國. For many, the interest in Taiwan during the Cold War was thus clearly tied to the Chinese imagination. As Yvonne Chang Sung-sheng indicates (2007, 18–19), Taiwan has served either as a surrogate for China or as an alternative thought experiment: What would China have become if it did not turn communist? June Yip Chun goes even further to underscore that Taiwan's very existence "poses a fundamental challenge to the idea of a unified Chinese nation" (2004, 4).

Importantly, the geopolitical situation of the times ensured Taiwan's survival. Along with South Korea, Hong Kong, and Singapore, Taiwan experienced exceptionally high economic growth (in excess of 7 percent a year) and rapid industrialization between the early 1960s and 1990s. By the 1980s, all four had developed into advanced and high-income economies, known as the Four Mini Asian Dragons 亞洲四小龍—named thus because these four East and Southeast Asian states, located on the peripheries of mainland China, are heavily influenced by Confucianism. Dai Jinhua, however, contends that the rise of these Mini Asian Dragons has much less to do with converting Confucianist values of hard work and diligence into fiscal prowess than geopolitics. The Cold War's ideological divide served the interests of the free world to help these states advance quickly: since they did not want communism to succeed, the United States and Western Europe heavily invested in and transferred technical knowledge to these states to propel their rapid growth (Dai 2012). In contrast, the fact that China's material conditions paled in comparison to the region's improving living standards and thriving economies rendered communism materially ineffective and hence ideologically futile.

The Nationalist government's constant reiteration of ascribing Chinese identity onto the people of Taiwan before the 1980s reminds us of cultural theorist Stuart Hall's well-known dictum that identities are always "in the process of becoming rather than being" (1996, 4). "Recovering the mainland" was the slogan used that ensured the allegiance of those who retreated to Taiwan with the Nationalist regime and in turn kept the populace in check. Thus, Tu Wei-ming's now seminal observation of a "Cultural China" existing on the geographical peripheries of mainland China (1991, 12) was based on realpolitik: that Chinese culture was not merely retained but aggressively promoted in Taiwan to thwart the PRC's chances of *representing* China was, in essence, motivated by ideology, and not culture, explicitly to contend for the right of representation.

A series of domestic as well as external events beginning in the 1970s started to unsettle this identity formulation. Of greatest consequence is the PRC's replacement of ROC as the Chinese seat in the United Nations Security Council in 1971, a process that set off Taiwan's isolation, which was further exacerbated by the PRC's reemergence onto the international arena at the conclusion of the Cultural Revolution. Subsequently, following the One-China policy whereby members in the global community have to decide which "China" to recognize, an increasing number of countries ended their formal ties with the ROC in order to establish diplomatic relations with the PRC. Prior to this, Taiwan had always had the free world on its side. Embroiled in an unresolved ideological war with its mammoth neighbor, Taiwan still very much depends on American military presence in the Asia-Pacific region to ensure its sovereignty. Now that it had been booted out of the United Nations and its voice was gradually fading out of the international arena, how would the ROC government be able to ensure Taiwan's continued survival?

The complex question of Taiwanese identification is beset by the island's occupation by different regimes and particularly haunted by the ghost of KMT's authoritarian rule in its recent past. The imposition of martial law in May 1949 following the brutal suppression of public resentment in the "2.28 Incident" in 1947 where over twenty thousand Taiwanese were jailed and executed "marked a tragic beginning for KMT rule" when it had just succeeded as Taiwan's government after Japan's retreat at the end of World War II (Liou 2011, 680). The reign of White Terror continued until President Chiang Ching-kuo lifted it in 1987. Martial law was used to suppress political opposition in the intervening years when Taiwan was run like a police state. The many restrictions on freedom then included imposing curfews and media control, where all three television stations on the island were completely state run. Significantly, martial law was also the landmark event that determined the shift in the Chineseness vs. Taiwaneseness debate. The two million émigrés who moved to Taiwan following the KMT's defeat in the Chinese Civil War, composed of families of the party and military, were called the *waishengren*, literally those "(from) outside of the (Taiwan) province." Although making up only 15 percent of the population in 1949, these "mainlanders" occupied positions of power in the government and military and were hence seen as oppressors by the majority *benshengren* 本省人, "people of the province" or Taiwanese, whose families had been on the island for several hundred years. Identity politics between these two groups were to dominate Taiwan for the next few decades, with *bensheng* people vying for more power to articulate a nativist position against the *waisheng* people whom they consider as outsiders and oppressors. Added to all this internal strife was the island-state's equally uneasy relationship with mainland China. If the difficulty of completely identifying with any particular parent culture is one that plagued Singaporeans, especially after the 1979 language policy change, then the internal competing Taiwanese-Chinese loyalties coupled with the external geopolitical pressure of not being allowed to *be Chinese* are issues that beset the Taiwanese people. On top of trying to "bring the 'two China's closer" together (Kowallis 1997, 176), Stan Lai's plays, I propose, offer a perspective that highlights the sufferings the *waisheng* people had also undergone to acculturate to Taiwan and attempts to suture the rupture between these disparate groups.

Given how these internal contradictions are intertwined with geopolitics, the path to Taiwan's self-expression in the political, social, and artistic realms was no less fraught with competing interests and contestations on different fronts. Michelle Yeh Mi-hsi puts forward the dictum that interestingly twentieth-century Chinese-language literature is inextricably tied to the ideal of revolution:

> Ironically literary innovations often arise in reaction against political constraints. For example, modernism in postwar Taiwan flourished under the White Terror, and literature in mainland China in the early 1980s was a profound critique of the Cultural Revolution. In both cases, experimental works of lasting value were written, whether modernist poetry and fiction from Taiwan or "Misty Poetry" and "root-seeking" fiction from China.
>
> (2010, 132)

Considering Yeh's analysis, the literary and artistic scene was teeming with excitement just before the lifting of martial law. Creative energies from different sectors of society were coming together to push open the lid that had heretofore repressed these multilayered tensions.

To be sure, this search for a local identity was ongoing in all sectors of society. In the literary field, this was evidenced in the "Modernist literary movement" 現代文學運動 vs. the "Nativist literary movement" 鄉土文學運動 debate. Yvonne Chang's now classic study, *Modernism and the Nativist Resistance: Contemporary Chinese Fiction from Taiwan*, has well documented this debate:

> The elitist, Western-influenced Modernist literary movement of the sixties and the populist, nationalistic Hsiang-t'u wen-hsüeh yün-tung (Nativist literary movement) of the seventies may appropriately be regarded as "alternative" and "oppositional" cultural formations in Taiwan during this period. . . . As the Modernist adopted literary concepts developed in Western capitalist society, they simultaneously longed for an ideological transformation, taking such bourgeois social values as individualism, liberalism, and rationalism as correctives for oppressive social relations derived from a traditional system of values. . . .
>
> The Nativist literary movement, in contrast, with its use of literature as a pretext to challenge the dominant sociopolitical order, may be properly considered counterhegemonic. . . . The pronounced oppositional nature of this movement is evident in all three of its proclaimed goals: to destroy the political myth of the mainlander-controlled Nationalist government, to denounce bourgeois capitalist social values, and to combat Western cultural imperialism, which was thought to be exemplified by the Modernist literary movement.
>
> (1993, 2–3)

These literary movements reflect the larger competing forces maturing in Taiwanese society then. In the cinematic realm, the works of Hou Hsiao-hsien 侯孝賢 (b. 1947) and Edward Yang 楊德昌 (1947–2007) were maturing at this stage. Stan Lai's important dramatic productions in the 1980s were contemporaneous with the works of these iconic Taiwanese New Cinema filmmakers. One has often borrowed from and shared resources with another: for example, many of Hou's early works were subtitled by Lai (Wang Z. 2010, 270), and on the days when Yang was not filming he would sit in at Lai's rehearsal studio, probably to borrow ideas and at times even actors.[5] The qualities that film scholar Shen Shiao-ying attributes to the Taiwanese New Cinema—its radical experiments, critical challenges toward norms and regulations on top of casting a "space for rethinking a collective's history and its present condition" (1995, 1)—also fittingly describe Lai's dramatic praxis.

---

5. That the main actors in Lai's *Secret Love* ended up as the protagonists in Yang's *Kongbu fenzi* 恐怖份子 (The terrorizer, 1986) was therefore of no coincidence (Lai 2008, 3).

Taiwan Theater History

Lai's description of the local theater scene upon his return to Taiwan in the early 1980s depicts it as a barren desert:

> There wasn't any grammar to begin with. Because the choice I had in 1983 when I finished my studies here was to stay in the States, or to go back to sort of a desert, where nothing—there was no tradition of modern theater. . . . I started working in sort of a vacuum, where we didn't have anything to rebel against, we didn't have anything to make revolution against, because there wasn't anything.
>
> (Lai 2011)

But he shared in an interview that he had not only watched but also participated in plays as a student. And if so, what does he mean by Taiwan has no *huaju* 話劇 (spoken drama) tradition to speak of (Shenzhen shi 1993, 19)? In contrast to traditional Chinese opera, *xiqu* 戲曲, which had large singing parts, *huaju* is the new, modern form focused on the speech dialogues between characters. Plays were certainly performed in the island-state well before the 1980s, but most were either of low quality or heavily ideological in nature and failed to generate wider social attention. Playwright and professor of classical drama at the National Taiwan University Wang An-ch'i 王安祈 echoes Lai's views: because the *huaju* tradition existed in the mainland but not Taiwan, modern theater in Taiwan was basically empty until the "little theater movement" came onto the scene in the 1980s (2012). Wang and Lai are probably contrasting the local scene with master playwrights in China—such as Lao She 老舍 (1899-1966), Xia Yan 夏衍 (1900-95), and Cao Yu 曹禺 (1910-96)—and deploring that Taiwan did not have playwrights in equal measure and quantity. Significantly, when compendiums of Taiwanese literature were compiled in the 1970s, poet, essayist, and editor of the major newspaper *Lianhe bao* 聯合報 (Unitas) Ya Xian 瘂弦 (b. 1932) lamented that writings were collected from authors on fiction and poetry among others but not modern drama. The only quality plays locatable then were of veterans Li Man-kuei 李曼瑰 (1907-75) and Yao Yi-wei. Since compendiums require collections of works from more than two authors, drama unfortunately could not be included (Ma et al. 1988, 18).

The conclusion of the Second World War ended fifty years of Japanese occupation in Taiwan, "returning" the island to Chinese rule that witnessed a short period of artistic exchange across the Taiwan Strait. Between 1945 and 1949, three theater troupes traveled from the mainland to showcase the best of China's *huaju* to Taiwan, staging history plays that advocated patriotism and nationalism (Lü 1961, 365). These performances, however, had limited impact since the language these troupes employed was Mandarin, as opposed to Hokkien and Japanese that were most widely spoken on the island then (Lü 1961, 336). These attempts to re-Sinicize the island after its transfer of sovereignty to the ROC provoked ambivalent responses. Mandarin, the national language in China, was imposed on Taiwan and used in civil services, film, radio, and television, on top of modern theater, while Hokkien, which was considered a dialect and backward, was allowed in local traditional theater but prohibited in schools (Chou 2016, 335). The stage was set for a clash of differences between groups that identified with one language over the other. Simultaneously, during this transitional period, "a few Taiwanese performances attempted to address the issues dividing the natives and the newcomers, and present the Taiwanese side of the debate" (C. Diamond 1993, 6), but the outbreak of the 1947 "2.28 Incident" that ignited a heated clash between the *bensheng* and *waisheng* groups ended this prematurely.[6] After 1949, the antagonistic relationship across the Taiwan Strait stopped all exchanges, including the arts. Few playwrights followed the KMT regime's retreat to Taiwan as most were more sympathetic toward the communist cause (Shenzhen shi 1993, 10).

From the 1950s onward, the party, military, government, and schools were the primary promoters of spoken theater texts and performances (Lü 1961, 395), with the propagandistic "Fangong kang'e ju" 反共抗俄劇 (Anticommunist/Russian Resistance plays) dominating the theater scene that staunchly promoted nationalism and patriotism (Wu and Lan 2009, 212n105). Censorship was applied to all new works; plays without anticommunist themes could hardly pass the extensive bureaucratic examination (C. Diamond 1993, 7). Moreover, a ban was imposed on the works of playwrights who had chosen to remain on the mainland, and the few dramatists who followed the KMT government to Taiwan were absorbed by the state to produce works of such indoctrinating nature (Chung M. 1999, 15). Most of these were either

---

6. For a brief description of three such plays, *Bi* 壁 (The wall), *Luohan fuhui* 羅漢赴會 (The Arhat attends a meeting), and *Xiangjiao xiang* 香蕉香 (The scent of bananas), see C. Diamond 1993, 5–6. For a political analysis of *The Wall*, see Chou 2016, 335.

adaptations of old works or merely changed its antiwar sentiment to anticommunism and cannot, by any standards, be considered works of high quality (Lü 1961, 371). According to Chung Ming-der:

> From the 1950s on, modern theater in Taiwan differed greatly from *huaju* in mainland China . . . and in reality had nothing in common with anything beyond the "Anti-Communist/Russian Resistance" state doctrine. Coupled with the rise of film and television in the 1960s, Taiwan *huaju* eventually fell into a bad state. Before the rise of the little theater, from the 1960s to 1980s Taiwanese *huaju* was almost completely controlled by the KMT, limited within the confines of college campuses . . . and was boring.
>
> (1999, 15)

Perhaps for this reason, Chung, who is professor of theater at the Taipei National University of the Arts, quips amusingly that he had not heard of the art form until he entered college in 1971. In his growing up years, he said, bright students had no desire to watch *huaju* and would be sent by their school teachers to attend a *huaju* performance only as a form of punishment (Shenzhen shi 1993, 10–11). Reflecting on the quality of the theater works then, veteran actor Ku Pao-ming 顧寶明 (1950–2022) recalls that apart from the drama troupes established by the military, everyone else was an amateur and no sense of professionalism existed otherwise. Theater tickets were often handed out for free instead of being sold simply because no one would purchase them; while trying to hide from the rain some people stumbled into the theater and accidentally became audiences (Lee Y. 2013). As one could imagine, because theater had been subjugated as an ideological tool, plays "continued to have little relevance" to the everyday lives of the people (C. Diamond 1993, 8). For these reasons, almost no theater activities existed at the commercial or grassroots level (S. Ma 1991a, 16).

The ground began to shift in the late 1960s owing to the pioneering efforts of Li Man-kuei. Hailed posthumously as the "Mentor of Chinese drama" 中國戲劇導師, she was one of the earliest from Taiwan to be trained in theater from the West. Upon Li's return from the United States with an MFA in theater from the University of Michigan in 1967, she organized the first World Theater Exhibition 世界劇展 (S. Ma 1991a, 16) through her Chinese Drama Centre 中國戲劇中心 and Committee for Chinese Drama Appreciation 中國話劇欣賞委員會 to introduce university students to classic drama texts from the West. These included Anton Chekhov's *The Seagull* and Oscar Wilde's *Lady*

Windermere's Fan, which were staged by graduating seniors in the foreign languages departments in various universities (Zhang Liuzu 2010). Apart from Li, other forerunners in the 1970s who adopted Western theatrical conventions to create original works that laid the groundwork for the little theater movement of the 1980s included Chinese Culture University professor Hwang Mei-shu 黃美序 (1930–2013) who translated W. B. Yeats's verse dramas into Chinese and incorporated traditional Peking Opera elements, the Christian playwright Chang Hsiao-feng 張曉風 (b. 1941) who introduced Brecht's epic theater, and academics Yao Yi-wei and Ma Sen 馬森 (b. 1932) whose plays contained elements of the theater of the absurd (S. Ma 1991b, 259–71).

Undoubtedly while these early efforts were important, they did not generate as much societal attention as the second wave of the World Theater Exhibition series in the early to mid-1980s, now organized by Yao Yi-wei who had succeeded Li Man-kuei upon her demise. Significantly, Yao added an Experimental Theater Exhibition 實驗劇展 segment to the series, synthesizing drama with literature (Zhang Lixuan 2009), that was to generate works of significance in Taiwan theater history. The most notable play to emerge from the inaugural 1980 exhibition was Lan Ling Theatre Workshop's (f. 1980) *He Zhu's New Match*.[7] The group was spawned from Zhou Yu's 周渝 (b. 1945) T'ien Experimental Drama Club 耕莘實驗劇團 (f. 1976) (Chung M. 1999, 35), with Wu Jing-jyi as its instructor. Wu is an educational psychologist trained in the United States with an active interest in theater, having been involved with La MaMa Experimental Theatre Club (f. 1961) in New York's off-off-Broadway from 1968 to 1972. After returning to Taiwan, he imparted corporeal and voice training to Lan Ling members, with a focus on physical theater (Chou 2016, 337). The group also received training in Peking operatic techniques for a brief period by the prominent novelist Li Ang 李昂 (Shih Shu-tuan 施淑端, b. 1952), who had also newly returned to Taiwan with a master's degree in drama from the University of Oregon–Eugene.

Critics agree it was not until *He Zhu's New Match* that experimental drama and the little theater movement significantly impacted Taiwanese society (S. Ma 1996, 22). Adapted in part from *He Zhu pei* 荷珠配 (He Zhu's match), a traditional Peking opera play, *He Zhu's New Match* is widely accepted as the first modern drama in Taiwan. The comedy

---

7. For studies of the play in English, see C. Wang 2018 and S. Yu 2019.

plays on "role and identity reversal" that "implicitly touches upon an identity crisis issue." The hostess He Zhu accidentally realizes from Zhao Wang, a client who drinks at her wineshop, that she is of identical age to Jinfeng, the long-lost daughter of the president of the Qi Corporation. He Zhu therefore steals into the Qi household pretending to be Jinfeng to "reunite" with her "father." Zhao Wang, the Qi household's butler, sees through He Zhu's ploy and threatens to expose her until the two of them conspire to swindle the Qi household together. Written and directed by Chin Shih-chieh 金士傑 (b. 1951), the play's novel style of presentation, use of corporeal and psychodynamic elements, lifelike speech coupled with recognizable Peking opera stylization broke new ground. Many regarded the work to be paying tribute to the classical art form and hailed it simultaneously as "a rebirth of traditional Chinese heritage" and modernization of Chinese drama—"a perfect combination between modernity and nationality, progression and tradition" (C. Wang 2018, 571). Especially at a time when the theater environment remained inhibited and stagnant (Chung M. 1990, 64), Lan Ling's emergence denoted "that theatre could be connected with reality and real life" (B. Chang 2002, 356). The production's success inspired many to spawn their own groups to create works that boldly defied and challenged the aesthetic norms of the past, resulting in a period now known as the "little theater movement." Troupes that were established then included Chen Ling-ling's 陳玲玲 (Hong Zu-ling 洪祖玲) Fangyuan Theater 方圓劇場 (f. 1982), Tsai Ming-liang's 蔡明亮 (b. 1957) and Wang Yu-hui's 王友輝 (b. 1960) Xiao Wu Theater 小塢劇場 (f. 1982), Huang Ch'eng-huang's 黃承晃 (b. 1948) and Lao Chia-hua's 老嘉華 Notebook Theater 筆記劇場 (1985–88), Li Huan-hsiun's 黎煥雄 (b. 1962) Rive-Gauche Theater Group 河左岸劇團 formed by Tamkang University students in 1985, Circular Ruins Theater 環虛劇團 formed by National Taiwan University students in 1986, and Tian Chi-yuan's 田啟元 (1964–96) Critical Point Theater Phenomenon 臨界點劇象錄 (f. 1988). In their spirit of experimentation is a mode of alternative theater-making displaying an antiestablishment political stance (S. Ma 1996, 23). The movement acquired its name because many of these groups were truly little in terms of human and financial resources as well as audience sizes. As John Weinstein observes:

> In its initial incarnation in the 1980s, the little theater was closely linked to the western avant-garde, featuring troupes whose work was as likely to baffle the audience as it was to entertain them.

The troupes used an aesthetic based on political opposition [and] the breakdown of formal theatrical spaces.... Visual impact often took precedence over textual detail, and linear narrative and realistic dialogue were largely eschewed.

(2015, 11–12)

Despite its size, its deep concerns with the island's contemporary issues incited huge social ramifications (Ma et al. 1988, 28). Among the many new intellectual and artistic currents that emerged to reexamine existing social and political orders at the time (Y. Chang 1993, 1), the little theater movement certainly played an important role.

Hardly an independent phenomenon, the burgeoning of Taiwan's little theater movement grew in step with the state's political, economic, and cultural development (S. Ma 1996, 20). For instance, Chang Hsiao-feng had already been embarking on experimental theater from 1972 to 1978, but her efforts failed to gain wider social attention (Wang Yu-hui 1996, 71). What events of regional geopolitical significance took place that accounted for the definitive transition moment in Taiwanese theater to be attributed to *He Zhu's New Match* then? In 1980, the National Establishment Council 國建會 invited back from overseas many writers popular with the press, including Ma Sen and the celebrated novelist Pai Hsien-yung 白先勇 (b. 1937), to attend the Experimental Theater Exhibition. In part because they had been away from Taiwan for so long, their impressions of dramatic productions on the island might have remained with the Anticommunist/Russian Resistance plays of old. Hence, naturally they were bedazzled by the spectacle of experimental drama and wrote very positive reviews of the exhibition in the press. For *He Zhu's New Match* and its associated little theater movement to have become such a major cultural event, Wu Jing-jyi credits it to the convergence between media and the arts that links the development of theater to politics (1996, 31).

Undoubtedly, the movement's status was significantly elevated by the international artists and groups that were invited to perform in Taipei in the early 1980s, which were hosted by the spousal team of musicians Hsu Po-yun 許博允 (1944–2023) and Fan Man-nung's 樊曼儂 (b. 1946) now-legendary New Aspect Arts Centre 新象藝術中心 (f. 1978) (Wang M. 1996, 101; Chou 2016, 337). Pai Hsien-yong's *Youyuan jingmeng* 遊園驚夢 (Wandering in the garden, waking from a dream, 1982), Marcel Marceau (1983), and Merce Cunningham Dance Company and John Cage (1984) were among those invited by New Aspect to perform in Taiwan then. In particular, performances by the Hong Kong avant-garde Zuni Icosahedron 進念·二十面體 and the Japanese *butoh* troupe Byakko Sha 白虎社 (White tiger club), respectively in 1982 and 1986, were regarded to have directly inspired the little theater movement dramatists to explore their own corporeal expressions of antisocial experiential imageries (Wang M. 1996, 101; Hsu P. 2018, 359). Not many drama practitioners in Taiwan then had had overseas experiences, fewer had exposure to experimental productions, and hence in the International Theater Festival 國際藝術節 New Aspect hosted, many were watching foreign productions for the first time (Wang Yu-hui 2000, 202). Twice in the early 1980s was Zuni invited to perform in Taipei: *Longwu* 龍舞 (Dragon dance, March 8, directed by Gus Wong 王守謙) and *Zhongguo lücheng zhi wu: Xianggang–Taibei* 中國旅程之五：香港—台北 (Journey to the east part 5: Hong Kong–Taipei, March 9, directed by Danny Yung) at the First Asian Theatre Festival and Conference 第一屆亞洲戲劇節和會議 held in 1982, and *Bainian zhi guji di'ernian: Wangshi yu liuyan* 百年之孤寂第二年：往事與流言 (The second year of one hundred years of solitude: From a past event to prophecy, August 2–3, directed by Danny Yung) and *Lienü zhuan (Guoyu ban)* 列女傳（國語版） (Chronicle of three women [Taipei version], August 4–5, directed by Pia Ho 何秀萍) at the invitation of Cloud Gate Dance Theatre of Taiwan 雲門舞集 (f. 1973) in 1984.[8] The avant-garde groups that were established after being inspired by Zuni's performances in the 1980s is testament to the major impact the Hong Kong company had on the experimental drama scene in Taiwan (S. Ma 1985, 343; Wang M. (1987) 1992, 302; Huang Chien-yeh 1988). Viewing Zuni's productions during its 1984 visit stimulated Stan Lai's creative impulse that subsequently generated ideas for *Bianzou Baha* 變奏巴哈 (Bach variations, 1985) the following year (Lai 1990, 146). Discarding traditional linear narrative enabled Zuni's works to inspire reflection on the interaction between form and structure (Wang Yu-hui 2000, 202). The director-critic Wang Mo-lin 王墨林 (b. 1947) considers this movement as the burgeoning of a new "culture of the body" 身體文化, signifying the body's liberation from the KMT's incarceration and freeing oneself from the oppressive and authoritarian control of its White Terror regime. Wang's concept

---

8. Zuni was invited for a third time to perform in Taiwan in the 1980s. From August 23 to 28, 1988, Hugh Lee Kuo-shiu invited Zuni to collaborate with his Ping-fong Acting Troupe on *Shiyue/Shiritan (Taibei)* 拾月／拾日譚（台北） (October/Decameron).

expresses a desire to "create alternative perspectives and new cultural traditions through rethinking and (re-)presenting those bodies" (Y. Chen 2018, 273), which is a reflection of the movement at large.

More significantly perhaps, the reason the movement influenced an entire generation of theater practitioners, in the view of Wang Chun-yen, was because *He Zhu*'s performative aesthetics fitted the "anxiety discourse" of the Cold War schema, where "the national culture desires to become modern" (2018, 575). Most of the participants in the experimental theater exhibitions in the early half of the 1980s were either college students or fresh graduates who took an interest in theater and founded drama groups owing, in large part, to the training they received from their teachers. Remember that the aforementioned dramatists active in the 1960s–1970s, Yao Yi-wei, Chang Hsiao-feng, and Hwang Mei-shu, were themselves exposed to absurdist theater, poor theater, living theater, and environmental theater—which Ma Sen famously hails as the "second wave of modern Chinese drama from the west" 中國現代戲劇的兩度西潮—and thus influenced their students with a similar sense of modernist and postmodernist aesthetics (C. Wang 2004, 27). The geopolitical power relations during the Cold War doubly exposed the insecurity of Asian states, like Taiwan, for not being modern. And since being Western is akin to being modern, Asian nations therefore aspired to Western standards; this sense of "self-conscious need to modernize" was prevalent across society. The changing geopolitical context circumscribed artistic groups, like Lan Ling, to desire to become "a modern Chinese theater: a theater that is *both* Chinese and modern" (C. Wang 2018, 575).

Regardless of their fervor for eliciting new and creative ways of self-expression, most of these experimental drama groups—even Lan Ling itself—were short-lived. Why then was Performance Workshop able to outlast its peers of the little theater movement? Despite the similar circumstances of their founding, what accounted for Performance Workshop's continued trajectory but other groups' shorter lifespans? Assessing their differences, Wang Chun-yen suggests that Lai's rise is a result of the channeling and convergence of two forces: the 1960s elitist, Western-influenced Modernist literary movement and the 1970s populist, nationalistic Nativist literary movement (2004, 42–43). Going beyond the Modernist/Nativist contention at the turn of the 1970s, the Taiwanese intellectuals' growing consciousness of their endangered Chinese cultural identity incited the broadly defined "return to the native" 回歸鄉土 trend that manifested a sense of "cultural nostalgia"

(Y. Chang 1993, 179). Progressive intellectuals criticized their compatriots' "blind admiration and slavish imitation of Western cultural models" and exhorted them to "show more respect for their indigenous cultural heritage as well as greater concern for domestic social issues" (Y. Chang 1993, 148). Primarily responding to the social effects of Western capitalism, the concerns of the little theater movement drama groups were more aligned with the Modernists than the Nativists (C. Wang 2004, 27). While successive groups to the movement were still performing in informal spaces with minimal resources, their political consciousness was significantly "less apparent" and diluted considerably often "by a love of the hip and trendy." Although the ethos of the little theater was all but dead, "it had certainly been transformed" (Weinstein 2015, 12). Lacking the voice of the masses, the Modernist-oriented little theater groups had mostly run their course by the end of the 1990s and dissipated as quickly as they mushroomed.

Changes on the international front propelled the development of both hardware and software infrastructures in Taiwan, including the arts. Responding to an emergent Taiwanese nativism, a groundswell of pent-up societal frustrations was unleashed on the eve of the lifting of martial law. Drastic structural changes occurred at all levels of society: a political opposition party was recognized, the founding of new newspapers was no longer prohibited, and communication with mainland China at the civilian level was resumed (Y. Chang 1993, 1). Chiang Ching-kuo emphasized political, economic, and cultural reforms to discard the shackles of his father's anticommunist legacy. In the cultural realm, the Council for Cultural Affairs 文化建設委員會, the Cultural Centre auditoriums set up in different localities in Taiwan, Lin Hwai-min's 林懷民 (b. 1947) Cloud Gate Dance Theatre of Taiwan—the first contemporary dance troupe in the Chinese-speaking world—as well as Lan Ling were all established as models of this state-sponsored "New Taiwanese Culture" as a result (Wang M. 1996, 104). Furthermore, the state also contributed to building software infrastructures: on top of the two existing tertiary-level theater departments at the Chinese Culture University 中國文化大學 (f. 1962 as Far East Research Institute 中國文化研究所, received university status in 1980) and National Academy of Arts 國立臺灣藝術專科學校 (f. 1955, becoming National Taiwan University of Arts 國立臺灣藝術大學 in 2001), a third was added in the National Institute of the Arts (NIA, f. 1982, becoming Taipei National University of the Arts in 2001). In addition, Taiwanese trained abroad in the arts were invited to return to serve in the various tertiary arts institutions (S. Ma 1984a). Among such professorial faculty, three who would impact the Taiwanese theater scene beyond their academic contributions are Wang Chi-mei 汪其楣 (b. 1946), whose plays manifest a strong concern for the local environment and socially marginalized, especially children, the deaf, and aboriginals (Digital Collection); Ma Sen, who, on top of being a playwright, is among Taiwan's best known theater historians; and Stan Lai.

Lai was still pursuing his doctorate in Berkeley when *He Zhu's New Match* created a sensation. Upon his graduation in 1983, the founding chair of NIA's Drama and Theatre Department, Yao Yi-wei, invited Lai to assume a faculty position at the institution established just a year before, which he accepted (Lai et al. 2007, 118-19). On January 11, 1984, Lai marked his directorial debut in Taiwan with an improvisational piece he devised with the students in his inaugural production exercise class, titled *Women doushi zheyang zhangda de* 我們都是這樣長大的 (We all grew up this way), based on their experiences growing up under martial law. Just like Kuo Pao Kun's founding of "Practice" upon his return from Australia was due to a lack of local actors in Singapore, Lai had to devise his first play with college students because the Taiwan to which he returned had no drama industry of which to speak. Therefore, he had to put aside the professional training he acquired from the United States and start from scratch to work within these newfound limitations (Lai (1998) 1999, 11-12). Some Lan Ling members were among the audience of this college production and approached the newly returned PhD for future artistic collaboration. This became the second play Lai devised and directed in Taiwan: *Zhaixing* 摘星 (Plucking stars) in March 1984, about the intellectually disabled. An extremely talented team of theater performers had by now gathered at Lan Ling: Ku Pao-ming, Chin Shih-chieh, Hugh Lee Kuo-shiu 李國修 (1955-2013), and Liu Ching-min (later renamed Liu Ruoyu 劉若瑀, and who would found U-Theatre 優劇場劇團 in 1988, later renamed 優人神鼓 in 1993). Lai's collaboration with Lan Ling members allowed him the opportunity to tap into a deep reservoir of the most creative energies in the Taiwan dramatic scene then, which immensely synergized with his own subsequent dramatic works. Another, Lee Li-chun 李立群 (b. 1952), a seasoned performer at cabaret dinner shows, who often came to see the rehearsals of *Plucking Stars*, would go on to become another important artistic collaborator of Lai (Lai 1992a, 16). Collectively, these artists would become the mainstay in Taiwan theater in the following decades. The third theatrical piece Lai devised and directed in Taiwan, *Guoke* 過客 (The passerby), for the end-of-year NIA college students' production in June 1984, was about unstable psychological conditions among the Taiwanese youth.

Prior to the founding of Performance Workshop, these three plays by Lai were probably the earliest works of experimental drama in Taiwan that displayed a strong sense of realism and social consciousness, akin to the concerns of the Nativist school (C. Wang 2004, 28). In his review of *We All Grew Up This Way*, Ma Sen extols the work as "the birth of a new theater form on the Chinese stage" (1984b), clearly underscoring the play's distinctiveness from earlier works. Others share the view that the play's small audience did not deter it from generating a huge social impact (Lai 1992a, 28).[9] Armed with his recent training from the United States, Lai's creative aesthetics are clearly fashioned in the Modernist school. What distinguished his productions from other experimental works in the little theater movement was his forte to explore topical issues through his collaboration with both Lan Ling actors and NIA students, delving into a rich trove of stories about Taiwan by those residing on the island. Especially since this was the period of the "return to the native," Lai's "intellectual concern for society" fulfilled such a need, winning him the mass-based support that other experimental groups lacked (C. Wang 2004, 40). In Chung Ming-der's view, therefore, Performance Workshop built on Lan Ling's trailblazing path and expanded experimental theater's audience base from intellectual youths to common urban folks, raising production standards and solidifying the foundation for avant-garde drama (1999, 5).

Play Analysis: *Secret Love in Peach Blossom Land*

In the conceptualization stages of *The Night We Became Cross-Talk Comedians*, Lai was contemplating collaborating again with Lan Ling. Failing to secure a keen response from Wu Jing-jyi after approaching him several times pushed Lai to set up his own theater company with the two artistic collaborators of this play, Hugh Lee Kuo-shiu and Lee Li-chun (Wu M. 2008). When the trio cofounded Performance Workshop

---

9. In an interview, Lai discloses that although the theater exists for a small audience and even if Performance Workshop, which is considered a "mass-based theater," can only perform to tens of thousands of audience members—a miniscule number when compared to a television audience—the beauty of the art form lies in that when well executed, its impact on society can far exceed that of television's (Wu M. 2008).

in November 1984, Lai was asked to helm the company as artistic director because he held the highest academic qualifications among them, and subsequently his wife Ting Nai-chu 丁乃竺 (b. 1953) became the company's managing director.

Beginning with *The Night We Became Cross-Talk Comedians*, Lai's series of *xiangsheng* plays 相聲劇 investigates the fragmented Taiwanese/Chinese consciousness as he locates the Taiwan experience amid a greater Chinese cultural framework.[10] Lai's *xiangsheng* play is not the traditional *xiangsheng* 相聲 per se; rather it is a play performed in the mimicry style of the traditional Chinese performing art form. *The Night We Became Cross-Talk Comedians* was designed as a eulogy to *xiangsheng* because Lai had considered the art form to have died out in Taiwan (Tao and Hou 2003, 45). Unexpectedly, not only did the popularity of the inaugural *xiangsheng* play revive the *xiangsheng* form and save it from extinction in Taiwan, *xiangsheng* plays have since become a staple of Performance Workshop. A play meant to eulogize *xiangsheng* paradoxically revived the dying genre.

If *The Night We Became Cross-Talk Comedians* propelled Performance Workshop into the Taiwanese audience's popular consciousness, it was the company's second production, *Secret Love in Peach Blossom Land*, that planted an unshakable cornerstone for its repertoire (Lai 1992a, 16), cementing its niche position in the island-state's theater history. Indeed, Wang An-ch'i goes as far as to say, "Modern Taiwanese theater would not have existed without Stan Lai" (2012). For using a comical style of presentation to address such serious themes as identity, memory, and history in its first two works, Performance Workshop is hailed as "a milestone of the union between fine art and popular culture" (Chung M. 1999, 108). No wonder too, after the success of the inaugural staging of *Secret Love*, renowned Taiwanese novelist and screenwriter Chu Tien-wen 朱天文 (b. 1956) remarked that every Stan Lai production had become the talk of the town (1986, 13). For the next two decades, Performance Workshop along with Ping-fong Acting Troupe 屏風表演班 (f. 1986) and James Liang Chi-ming's 梁志民 (b. 1965) Godot Theatre Company 果陀劇場 (f. 1988) would earn the undisputed designation, in the words of veteran theater critic Gong Min 貢敏, as the "Big Three" 鐵三角 in contemporary Taiwan theater (1996, 27). All were established during the little theater movement, but

---

10. For a rare study on the corpus of Lai's *xiangsheng* play series, see C. Wang 2014.

each has developed into a major theater company with its own unique profile and largely professional staff, having achieved significant success commercially and artistically. Since becoming the mainstay in Taiwan theater by the mid-1990s, this trio has formed "the core of the mainstream national theater of Taiwan, a place simultaneously Taiwanese, Chinese, and international" (Weinstein 2015, 11).

The "collective improvisation" 集體即興 creation technique is Lai's now-signatory process of playmaking, a method he learned from Shireen Strooker of the Amsterdam Werkteater in the Netherlands who was visiting at Berkeley during Lai's graduate study (Kowallis 1997, 169). In this type of playmaking, Lai's role is more of a stimulator than a director, making "a series of judgement[s], all of which must be right" (Goh 1988, 3). This method inverts the traditional dramatic creative process: Lai and his artistic collaborators begin with an abstract central idea, typically a profound emotion or a strong guiding conviction, and work toward developing it organically and holistically. The entire play is anchored around this core idea, and the script, characters, stage design, and other elements evolve necessarily in the process, always growing together as an organic whole instead of taking shape individually (Lai (1986) 2014, 369). The creative process is undeniably collaborative: although Lai plays a stronger role in collating and revising the script, the plays reflect the personal obsessions and life stories of their cocreators (Joubin 2009, 205). Not only did this formula overcome the urgent lack of existing playscripts in Taiwan at the time (Lai 1990, 137), more importantly perhaps, the performers could input their creative impulses, hence supplying the Nativist content of the equation while Lai could shape the creative process with his Modernist concerns. The strength of such a collaborative process, according to Lai, is that

> improvisation as a creative tool has the possibility to filter out the deeper concerns within a performer bypassing the question of form while at the same time creating form. . . . We're really extracting the deeper concerns of the performer and we're not worried too much what the play is about. . . . We're just looking for truth, we're looking for real moments and real concerns within a performer. So it has a possibility to filter out the deeper concerns.
> (2011)

Danny Yung lauds Lai's ability to extract what is truly of value from his actor-collaborators through his collective improvisation, the method from which *Secret Love* was devised, as indeed extraordinary (Xu J. 2010, D08).

Secret Love in Peach Blossom Land is Lai's most widely performed piece and has been restaged the greatest number of times. To celebrate the twentieth anniversary of the play in 2006, Lai partnered with local Taiwanese opera group Ming Hwa Yuan 明華園 (f. 1929), wherein Performance Workshop actors played one half of the play, *Secret Love*, in Mandarin, while Ming Hwa Yuan actors enacted the other half, *Peach Blossom Land*, in traditional Taiwanese *gezai xi* 歌仔戲 opera style. At the end of 2006, Lai staged a Beijing version of the play that toured different cities in China. A year later, a Cantonese version was staged in Hong Kong and at the Beijing Capital Theatre 首都劇場, while Performance Workshop collaborated with the National Theatre of China 中國國家話劇院 and Hong Kong Repertory Theatre 香港話劇團 to stage a Taiwan-China-Hong Kong version 兩岸三地版. A Yue opera adaptation was created in 2010 in Hangzhou. Lai had also begun developing an English rendition with students at Stanford University (translated by himself) in 2007 and eventually mounted a full version with a multiethnic cast at the Oregon Shakespeare Festival in 2015.[11] Over the last two decades, as Lai increasingly moved his creative base to Shanghai, the play has undergone incarnations with an entirely Chinese cast. Altogether, including the 1992 film version, thirteen renditions of the play have been created with different artistic collaborators, with Lai remaining as its main director ("Lai" 2017). Unless otherwise stated, my quotations and analyses of the play are based on the version Lai has translated into English and included in *The Columbia Anthology of Modern Chinese Drama* (Lai (1986) 2010).

Secret Love in Peach Blossom Land consists of many diametrical opposites that are complementary in nature. Two theater troupes vie for the same stage to rehearse their plays: one, titled *Secret Love*, is a straight-faced, no-nonsense, serious, romantic tragedy, while the other, *Peach Blossom Land*, is a farcical comedy filled with elements of the theater of the absurd. The former is a script about recent historical ruptures: two star-crossed lovers, Jiang Binliu and Yun Zhifan, are separated in cosmopolitan Shanghai in 1948 due to the Chinese Civil War, not realizing that both have fled war-torn China and been in Taipei for the past forty years. Reunited at last in the economically thriving Taipei in the 1980s but already gray-haired having become parents and grandparents to their separate families, the lovelorn Jiang's final desires are crushed

---

11. A three-volume English translation of Lai's plays can be found in Lai 2021.

when he realizes Yun does not seem to share his nostalgic longing for the love they have had—and all that it represents. The latter script is a farcical adaptation of the fifth-century poet Tao Yuanming's 陶淵明 best known text, on a never-never land, allegorically representing a utopic timelessness. When put together, the names of the three protagonists, Old TAO, Chun HUA, and Master YUAN, in this half of the play are homonymous with "Tao-Hua-Yuan"—the Peach Blossom Land—the Chinese imaginary utopia (Kowallis 1997, 174). Their lives, however, are anything but utopic. The impotent boatman Old Tao, upon suspecting his wife Chun Hua of cheating on him with Master Yuan, departs his home Wuling, only to find himself traveling upstream and landing in the "Peach Blossom Land"—a place where people are hospitable and serene. When Old Tao returns to Wuling once more with the intention of fetching Chun Hua with him, he is disillusioned by the dystopic family Chun Hua and Master Yuan have established in his absence, and leaves yet again. Not knowing whether Tao manages to find his way back, the avid Chinese audience who is brought up reciting Tao Yuanming's *Taohuayuan ji* 桃花源記 (A chronicle of the peach blossom spring) will assume that he does not, as the protagonist in Tao Yuanming's fifth-century text did not. Each troupe's rehearsal process is constantly disrupted as the play progresses, either by the workings of the other troupe or by personnel external to the two groups, such as a Mysterious Woman seeking a man by the name of Liu Ziji. In Lai's own words: "Conflicts and interruptions served the basis for fragmenting both rehearsals, as the audience sees fragment pieces of the two plays in an order that is not necessarily sequential" (1990, 147).

How do we understand the two plays juxtaposed in *Secret Love in Peach Blossom Land*? The original title of the play in Chinese is *Anlian taohuayuan* 暗戀桃花源, where "Secret love" 暗戀 functions as a verb to the noun "Peach Blossom Land" 桃花源. Who is secretly in love with whom? And where is this utopic Peach Blossom Land? If this place is indeed so utopic, why is one allowed only to be in secret love with it and cannot openly do so? One is a comedy, the other a tragedy; one utopia, the other dystopia; one Taiwan, the other . . . China? However, which is which? Is Taiwan the utopia or the dystopia? The overt use of slapstick humor and comedic play in *Peach Blossom Land* depicts a very chaotic society: the marriage of the protagonist Old Tao is dysfunctional, and his wife Chun Hua has cheated on him; yet the new family of Chun Hua and the adulterer Master Yuan is equally ineffectual, and the relationships among the three are played out in an absurdly comedic fashion.

What comes to mind concerning the chaos depicted in this half of the play are portrayals of the disarrayed Taiwanese parliament where senators hurl verbal abuses and climb over podiums and chairs to exchange physical blows with one another; it is anything but orderly. Never having considered the island as home, the KMT had only intended Taiwan as a transitory base to reclaim the mainland. The resultant lack of central planning led to Taiwan's disorderliness and disorganized infrastructural state, even though the party has ruled the island for more than four decades. As the international political climate changed, the KMT increasingly realized they could no longer go back to China and have to permanently stay in Taiwan—the dystopia with which they have to settle. To many of the two million Nationalist Party cadres and their families who retreated to Taiwan with Chiang Kai-shek in 1949, the mainland still remained as the utopia to which they longed to return. As depicted in the character of Jiang Binliu in *Secret Love*, his last wish is either for his wife and children to visit his ancestral grave in China (in the inaugural 1986 version) or to take his ashes back to be buried in his hometown Manchuria (in subsequent versions). Or, is Taiwan the Peach Blossom Land to which mainlanders can flee from the oppression of communist China (reminding one of the Taiwanese media frequently reporting news of mainlanders risking their lives to swim illegally across the Taiwan strait)? Since Stan Lai himself proposes that Tao Yuanming's utopia is just a place in any part of Chinese traditional rural society where one plows for one's own keep, except for "not knowing history" (1992a, 19–21), in this sense then utopia can be anywhere.

If the two troupes vying for the same stage allegorizes Taiwan and China fighting for the international platform, each trying to represent the genuine China, then who does the constantly absent guy-in-charge of the theater allude to? To claim their lease of the theater, each troupe produces its own copy of the legal documentation, just as both the mainland and Taiwan have the word "China" in their official names: the Republic of China and the People's Republic of China. To sort out their differences then, they decide to turn to the guy-in-charge who has been absent the entire duration of the play. Who does he represent? The United States? The international community who will arbitrate on which China is genuine in the One-China policy? Jon Kowallis points out that the then American government had always turned a blind eye to this reality and "refused to recognize the division of" the two Chinas (1997, 184n11). Whenever it was called upon to clarify, the United States has constantly been deliberately ambiguous and would never state in explicit terms which China it acknowledges. The rhetoric has always been to maintain the status quo across the Taiwan Strait and support the One-China policy: but which one? Furthermore, if we identify the chaotic presentation of *Peach Blossom Land* as Taiwan, then Tao's purchase of different types of exotic animals' genitals to be cooked as a tonic to strengthen his virility might be read as the impotence of Taiwan's political leaders to articulate their position on the international stage. For, as Perry Anderson puts it: the future of Taiwan has always been determined within the Sino-American discourse of power (2004, 12). A possible indictment of Taiwan's inability to articulate its own discourse and determine its own future might be Lai's veiled criticism of the Chinese hegemony curtailing Taiwan's voice from being heard on the international front, as well as America's standing by and unwillingness to do more.

Just as Chun Hua and Master Yuan have never heard of the Peach Blossom Land, those in the Peach Blossom Land have never heard of Wuling or the outside world. Old Tao explains that the current inhabitants fled there in order to *biluan* 避亂 or "hide from the chaos." Kowallis points out that this is again suggestive of the Chinese who fled the mainland to Taiwan to "hide from the chaos" of the Chinese Civil War (1997, 184). Inhabitants in the Peach Blossom Land are unaware of the outside world, which to me is symptomatic of the Republican mentality: when the KMT retreated to Taiwan, for a long time they still maintained the façade that they were the real China and would one day recapture the mainland from the communist insurgents. Occupying the Chinese seat in the United Nations until 1971, the Nationalist government appeared to ignore the reality that mainland China was now under communist rule. For more than forty years under Nationalist rule, the Taiwanese school curriculum taught premodern Chinese history as its national history and studied Chinese maps in detail, but Taiwan geography was "kept to a minimum and simplified," implying its seeming unimportance and irrelevance (B. Chang 2015, 190).[12] Again, Lai's criticism of such mentality is implicit here: unless ignorance is bliss, then perhaps this Peach Blossom Land is not as utopic

---

12. Chang Bi-yu mentions that the *Guoli bianyiguan* 國立編譯館 (National institute for compilation and translation) produced textbooks that are supposed to teach students to understand Taiwan, but instead the lesson on Taiwan's geographical features made a disparaging comment about the island: when juxtaposed on a massive wall map of China, the size of our *jiaxiang* 家鄉 (hometown) "is so minute that it is even smaller than a soy bean" (2015, 190).

as it appears. Lai could therefore possibly be simultaneously criticizing the United States, the Chinese Communist Party, and the KMT.

I wish to now turn to two other sets of characters in the play. The caretaker of the theater attempts to lock up the space and is unwilling to concede to the troupe of *Secret Love* the ten more minutes they need to finish the play. As if too coincidentally, he arrives at the time when one play has just ended but not the next and requests that they stop the rehearsal. If these two plays allude to two separate narratives, then he is effectively preventing the other story from being told. If, however, we see the two performances as two sides of the same coin, each complementing and completing the other, then the exact timing of the caretaker's arrival is neither an accident nor coincidental: this deliberate attempt to censor the voice of the *other* side precisely underscores the importance of its being told.

The Mysterious Woman who is looming in the background of the entire play, at times coming in to interject saying she is looking for a certain Liu Ziji, is perhaps the oddest character in the play. Nobody knows who she is, no one in either troupe appears to know her, and it is unclear to the audience by the end of the play what her function really is. Equally puzzling is Liu Ziji: except for a vague reference to the last line in *A Chronicle of the Peach Blossom Spring*, of a Liu Ziji of Nanyang 南陽劉子驥, when the Mysterious Woman mentioned she had once eaten sour-and-spicy noodles with him in Nanyang Street for an entire year, we haven't a clue who he is. I posit three possible readings for this Mysterious Woman. First, she suggests a modern person of undefinable and unknown identity looking for fulfillment in something from the heritage of premodern Chinese culture, or something in the present understood or misunderstood through an allusion to the cultural past. This could certainly reflect Taiwan's current position: having roots in premodern Chinese culture, it has followed the Republic of China's exodus to the island-state from 1949 onward. Another possibility could be Lai's critique of the Republican mentality for holding on to the utopic past and refusing to come to terms with the contemporary reality, which I will further elaborate in the next section.

Second, in all the versions of the play and film I have encountered, the ending has consistently depicted the Mysterious Woman being left alone waiting onstage, who we assume is waiting for Liu. This immediately reminds me of the ending in *Waiting for Godot*. The common reading for Samuel Beckett's seminal piece is a tragedy because Godot does not eventually arrive, making futile any hope that might come as a result. However, in Kuo Pao Kun's view, there can be no greater hope than that found in *Godot*. Kuo singles out the ending in *Godot* to bear such optimism: even until the play's ending, the protagonists Vladimir and Estragon have not given up, but are instead still waiting ((1984) 2007, 14). Having been waiting endlessly for someone who does not show up, the act of continuing in anticipation signifies their hope in Godot to finally turn up. For Vladimir and Estragon, in other words, Godot is not someone who *does not* show up but someone who *has yet to*, and their persistence and belief in Godot's eventual arrival are their greatest hope. Similarly, when *Secret Love in Peach Blossom Land* comes to an end and the Mysterious Woman still does not give up on waiting for Liu Ziji, can she too not be an emblem of hope? One immediate take might perhaps be a signification that tensions along the Taiwan Strait will subside if we have hope and wait. A wider reading might imply that the play promotes hope and patience in waiting for resolutions for conflicts of any kind.

My third interpretation is that the Mysterious Woman (and by extension, Liu) represents some kind of overarching narrative that is constantly being othered. My analysis is built on Jon Kowallis's interpretation: the Mysterious Woman continually calls "the name of her boyfriend in Taiwan-accented Mandarin, which is not recognized by the actors of either troupe, *although each assumes him to belong to the other*" (1997, 174; italics mine). I emphasize this assumption made by both troupes here. More off- than onstage, the Mysterious Woman has been in the play from beginning to end and is a character whom no one takes seriously, although at times she seems to be speaking the truth to the two troupes that are breaking down in communication. Here, I highlight the moment just prior to both troupes agreeing to split the stage between them, and the two directors ridiculing each other's plays:

ACTOR PLAYING MASTER YUAN: A dying patient climbs out of bed, hums a song, and goes to play with a swing! If that's not enough, tell me how to portray a white camellia. Play a white camellia for me! Come on! You can do it!
DIRECTOR: Has he seen the play?
ACTRESS PLAYING YUN ZHIFAN: Stop arguing. Let's think of a solution.
ACTOR PLAYING MASTER YUAN: Solution? I'm out of time.
ACTRESS PLAYING YUN ZHIFAN: Well, we're out of time too!
MYSTERIOUS WOMAN (SUDDENLY): Everyone is out of time!

ACTOR PLAYING MASTER YUAN: Well that's tough luck.
MYSTERIOUS WOMAN: You have to find a way!
ACTOR PLAYING MASTER YUAN: There is no way!
MYSTERIOUS WOMAN: You have to find a way for me! For me!
(*The Actor Playing Master Yuan discovers that he is standing next to the Mysterious Woman. He moves away swiftly.*)
ACTOR PLAYING MASTER YUAN: Don't get excited, okay? (*To all*) How about this: Let's split the stage in half.

(Lai (1986) 2010, 1008)

In this exchange, the Mysterious Woman's lines cohere with those of the others. However, while the cast and crew from both troupes might have heard her, they do not listen and are unwilling to engage in dialogue with her; no one is particularly invested in her because they assume she must be from the other side. In a way, the Mysterious Woman brings to the fore the problem experienced by the two groups: because both troupes already see each other—and the Mysterious Woman—with tainted lenses, they have subconsciously already othered the other party, thus failing to hear what the other side has to say. If one of Lai's messages is that these are two competing theater troupes, each trying to tell its side of the narrative and needing the other to complete the picture, then the Mysterious Woman represents a figure from whom each must learn to see the other before one can be usefully complementary. After all, she responds (adequately) to both Actress Yun and Actor Yuan and, by extension, to both theater companies. To adequately put oneself in the shoes of the other or see things from an ambient perspective is often difficult. One is always blindsided or cocooned by one's limitations, and Lai might be using her to bring out the motif of the need to listen to both sides to form a more holistic narrative. If she represents an overarching viewpoint, then Lai is underscoring the importance of seeing things from the other side in a bid to find a winning solution for both parties.

Interestingly, the resolution of the two troupes does not come with sharing the same stage space; in fact, they are not sharing but partitioning and fighting with each other in the same space. Yomi Braester suggests, at about halfway through the play,

> the troupes have drawn a line in the middle of the stage and try to speak at the empty theater, each pretending that the other troupe does not exist. . . . Soon after, the dialogs break down completely, as actors from each troupe talk to those of the other, pretending

that they are still reciting their lines, to the effect of telling the other party to go away.

(2008, 691)

Pretending that the other troupe does not exist obviously leads nowhere. Fortunately, both parties eventually come to an agreement to allow each other the time and space to finish their own rehearsal. By giving in to the other side, they both win the space to stage their own plays, allegorically alluding to winning a space for each to tell their narrative. Notice toward the end of the play when the caretaker of the theater wants to lock up the place, the actors from *Peach Blossom Land* stand up for those in *Secret Love*, who are still in rehearsal. A sort of camaraderie begins to develop at a critical time when one of the narratives is threatened to end prematurely.

Lai's juxtaposition of two theater troupes, each telling a different story with multiple references of utopia and dystopia, yet competing for the same space, is not only emblematic of the historical period in which this piece was written, but also finds a broader relevance to the cross-strait situation. As earlier suggested, the signifiers in the play might take on more than one meaning, and this multivalent reading of the signified underscores the play's complexity. Above all, the juxtaposition of the two troupes on the same platform results in a dramatic staging of a play within a play—or, more accurately, two plays within a play—and I read these variations of meaning not as competing discourses but as complementary opposites. As Braester observes, different comic situations occur as the two plays contend for the same "stage space, first performing intermittently and later even sharing the stage . . . the two texts become hopelessly entangled in each other" (2008, 691). Old Tao's concluding remarks in the filmic version of *Peach Blossom Land* might indicate Lai's attitude. He says:

> In the past few years, I discovered that many things are not the way we've made them out to be. No more paths might seem to be ahead, but by changing your point of view, you might be able to find a direction, and sometimes you might not even know where you've positioned yourself.[13]

Perhaps boundaries do not necessarily have to cut one another off. If we approach things from a different angle, as Tao suggests, maybe

---

13. Tao's monologue is missing in the play. I have translated these lines directly from the film.

things can become complementary instead of competing, and accepting instead of excluding. Kuo Pao Kun proposes how exclusivity and inclusivity can be one fine line apart, a model illuminating a Stan Lai production:

> Stan Lai's theatrical work can't be pigeonholed.... It's an exceptional form of theater, being neither Chinese nor Taiwanese, neither Eastern nor Western, neither elegant nor vulgar, conforming neither to this rule nor that. Change all those neither-nors to both-ands and you might have a fitting description of it.
>
> (1999, 13)

The Utopia that Never Was?

At a time when Taiwan was seeking its own identity, Lai's intervention in the debate saw him straddling an undetermined Chinese-Taiwanese identification. In the play, he sets up binary opposites that do not lend themselves to easy determination, allowing each avid Taiwanese audience member of the 1980s enough ambiguity and openness to provide his/her own interpretation, and to choose with which side s/he wishes to identify. However, the difficult reality confronting the contemporary Taiwan that he depicts cannot be missed: fraught with fragments of history, the wreckage of a ghostly (Chinese) past will not go away just because one wishes it. Cultural critic Stephen Chan Ching-kiu's reading of *The Night We Became Cross-Talk Comedians* could serve as an insightful interpretation on these two inaugural Performance Workshop plays:

> And this tradition, as it gradually becomes clear for Lai's audience, signifies—by virtue of its textual inscription in the story and history...—not only an ensemble of past shows, past events and past values reminiscent of the history... but the collective unconscious of a Chinese people lost amid their ambivalent memory of what constitutes "modern history" for them.
>
> (1987–88, 25)

On the one hand, Lai is critical of the mainlander émigrés' mentality of refusing to accept the Taiwanese reality to which they are all bounded; on the other, he does not side with those who advocate severing with the past by reminding us of the impossibility of a complete rupture because a fragmented sense of history is always at work in the frustrations of everyday life in Taiwan. By suggesting that one should

FIGURE 3. Scene in performance of *Secret Love in Peach Blossom Land*, September 1991, National Theatre, Taipei. The male actors nearest downstage, Lee Li-chun, Chin Shih-chieh, and Ku Pao-ming—perhaps the most important performers on the Taiwan dramatic stage since the 1980s—reprise the protagonist roles in this 1991 production after the play's inaugural 1986 staging. Standing beside Chin Shih-chieh is superstar Brigitte Lin Ching-hsia. Photograph by Liu Chen Hsiang.

learn to view things from the other side—as represented by the Mysterious Woman—perhaps time might heal wounds and friction could be mended.

We might be able to glean Lai's stance from his treatment of Jiang Binliu in *Secret Love*. Lai himself considers the play's strength to lie in having its fingers on the pulse of the contemporary Taiwanese experience, which is messy and disruptive, yet from this chaos it somehow manages to find an order, thus satisfying the subconscious desires of many a people (1992a, 26). Nevertheless, is this play really about a utopia to which no one can return, or a dystopia in itself? Or both? Could this be Lai's message of saying there can be no utopia to which to return, and one (the mainlander émigré) has to settle for Taiwan no matter how chaotic it is? The obvious allusions to Sino-Taiwanese relations made this play dangerous at its inception in 1986 when martial law was still in place: not only was it a taboo subject then, what was more, the role of Mrs. Jiang could be interpreted as the neglected Taiwanese wife because Jiang Binliu was still secretly pining for his lover in mainland China (Lai 1992a, 27). The misconstrued yet "common reading of 1987 as the beginning of democratization in Taiwan," as Petrus Liu reminds us, is derived "in part from a perception that Taiwan was always and already liberal before the lifting of martial law" (2015, 18). It was not. Taiwan had to fight hard to achieve its liberalism that failed to arrive along with democracy. What Lai was propounding was extremely dangerous then and could be akin to political treason.[14]

The final scene of *Secret Love* shows Jiang Binliu, now in his old age, in a Taipei hospital bed. As his wife Mrs. Jiang plays the cassette tape he has just requested Nurse Wang to purchase, the "Golden Voice" 金嗓子 of the most renowned Chinese singer in the 1940s, Zhou Xuan 周璇 singing *Allow Me to Glance at You* 許我向你看 (1947), begins to fill the room. In a separate spatial-temporal sequence that represents Jiang's dreams and innate desires, he gets out of bed, wanders through the door of his hospital room, and into the park in 1948 Shanghai.

---

14. Stan Lai provides a chilling account of how two government censors coincidentally went out to smoke just before the most sensitive part of *The Night We Became Cross-Talk Comedians*. Lai followed them out of the theater and chatted with them to stall for time. He heard "For peace, to struggle, and save China" 和平、奮鬥、救中國, the dying words of the "Father of the nation" Dr. Sun Yat-sen—which the play made fun of—emanating from the theater, followed by the audience's laughter. When Lai saw that the line had gone unnoticed by the two men, who were still busy talking and did not seem to have caught it, he knew that the worst was over (Lai 1992a, 28; Lee and Yu 2005).

Everything in the park appears to be the same, even Yun Zhifan—his lover from more than forty years ago—who now shows up on stage right, crosses the door in the Taipei hospital and into the frozen time-space in the Shanghai park meeting Jiang. All this while, Mrs. Jiang is speaking in a mix of Taiwanese and Mandarin to Nurse Wang and later on the phone, possibly with a relative or a close friend who is trying to console her on mentally preparing herself in the event of Jiang's demise. Whether Jiang is entering a dream in his sleep in the hospital or going into his subconscious, this nostalgic imagery of old China is very much representative of the mindset of the mainlanders who fled China with Chiang Kai-shek for Taiwan at the end of the Chinese Civil War. The unfamiliarity with the reality of Taiwan, where they now have no choice but to stay, is represented by Jiang's dislike of his wife's Taiwanese cooking and his alienation by her use of Taiwanese, a language foreign to the ears of the majority of *waisheng* émigrés. Everything nostalgic is represented here in this frozen-in-time Shanghai, but little has Jiang—and the two million mainlanders—known that this is the utopia to which he could never return. Yun Zhifan reinforces this notion when she rejects the huge stacks of letters that Jiang has written to her all these years, none of which reached her. In desperation, he hands her these letters and remarks that these represent their aspirations, only to have her throw them up in the air and reply, "Ideals? If you had any ideals, you'd go out and accomplish them! Binliu, the New China has stagnated due to people like you! I can't accept these" (Lai (1986) 2010, 995)—symbolically destroying all hopes left in him that are clinging on to the past. Further reinforcing this is the actress playing Yun Zhifan who later breaks out of character and tells the director she cannot play the *real* Yun: if Yun Zhifan represents the symbolic love that Jiang and the Taiwanese mainlanders have of their nostalgic past, then this nostalgia is not only distanced further but completely shattered.

Five years after its inaugural production, the play had its second restaging in 1991, this time at Taiwan's National Theatre with Brigitte Lin Ching-hsia as the female protagonist. This restaging was in part a preparation to produce the film version the following year, with the main actors in the play reprising their same roles in the film. Taiwan's political circumstances witnessed more dramatic changes in these preceding five years: after martial law was ended and the ban on visiting relatives in mainland China subsequently lifted in 1987, ironically the play's theme became even more apparent. On the one hand, it goes deeper into the human condition; on the other, it probes the more permanent commonalities of the meaning of life. While the success of the inaugural version depended on the emotions attached to real(politik) events, the second version is connected to a larger schema, and its theme aims at an even broader perspective, no longer merely confined to cross-strait relations (Lai 1992b, 31). Shen Shiao-ying's observation of the differences between the inaugural stage version and film version presents an interesting anecdote. In the 1986 version performed during martial law "when visits to China were prohibited," the protagonist Jiang Binliu "instructs his Taiwanese wife to take their children to the mainland and visit his ancestral graves in the future when possible," whereas in the 1992 film version he insists his ashes be taken back to the mainland since his grave illness has prohibited his physical return to China. In Shen's opinion, the character of Jiang "is one who, in order not to lose the idealized past, insists on being a foreigner in what he considers as a foreign land" (1995, 100). I offer a slightly different reading in Jiang's unwillingness to revisit China even though cross-strait relations had thawed. If in the 1986 version of the play when Taiwan was still under martial law and Jiang could not go back to the mainland, and in the post-1987 versions of the play when martial law was lifted and yet Jiang still chooses not to do so, is this not critiquing the mentality of Jiang (and his ilk) for clinging onto the past and simultaneously foregrounding Taiwan's subjectivity? In a similar vein, Joyce Liu asks:

> What is the "Taohuayuan" to Stan Lai after all? "Taohuayuan" seems to suggest a land of unreality, in which Old Tao, Chunhua and Master Yuan, all dressed in white, with handkerchiefs covering their eyes, play hide-and-seek cheerfully and innocently in slow motion. Chunhua and Master Yuan in this "Taohuayuan" are played by the same actress and actor at Wuling, but they refuse to recognize Old Tao. The uncanny resemblance makes this dream land a mirror image of reality, an imaginary vision *projected by the subject*, while the persistent disavowal energetically maintained by the blind dream thoughts protects the gap from being bridged so that the dream can remain intact.
>
> (1997; italics mine)

Where Shen considers it the mainlander émigrés' choice to remain as foreigners in Taiwan, Liu regards it as "a land of unreality" that is "a mirror image of reality" that the mainlanders have "projected" and desire to keep "intact." Yomi Braester, too, agrees that the sentiment expressed in this play is that "a return to utopia is impossible" (2008, 697). Remarking that "the question of 'going back' is largely irrelevant" in the play, Jon Kowallis opines that on "a personal level, the moral dilemma of the diaspora is how we deal with others while coming to terms with our own displacement" (1997, 176–77).

While a return to the past is depicted as ridiculous and choosing to isolate oneself in that utopic memory is being scorned at, Lai is not about to become a spokesperson of the pro-independence movement either. At the same time, he is also critical of those who choose to willfully forget the past, or what Braester calls "Taiwan's amnesiac self-definition" (2008, 698). Liu Kuang-neng suggests that the endings in the two halves of the play are analogous to each other: Old Tao returning from Peach Blossom Land in the hope of fetching his wife to join him, only to realize how things have deteriorated at Wuling and hence disappointingly leave for the Peach Blossom Land yet again; after yearning for forty years, Jiang Binliu is finally able to meet his former sweetheart in Taipei, but realizes this longing is not reciprocated. Yun Zhifan, now a bespectacled, gray-haired granny, does not linger on the past to quite the same degree as Jiang. After a brief exchange, she leaves Jiang's hospital ward reassuring him that she is currently "well" and that her husband is "treating" her "very well" (Liu K. 1986, 21). In Liu's view, this is akin to many of the mainlanders who returned to visit China (perhaps through illegal channels before the cross-strait relations resumed in 1987?), only to be shocked at how much the place has changed—henceforth forever tarnishing the romanticized image of their motherland—and returning to Taiwan completely dismayed. Moreover, Liu also suggests that Jiang Binliu's dilemma is not between the two women of his life—Yun Zhifan and Mrs. Jiang—but rather, the Yun Zhifan of old Shanghai and the Mrs. Jiang of contemporary Taiwan. He cannot forget the Yun Zhifan of his memory—and everything that connects him to his memory of China before he fled to Taiwan; it is the clinging onto this memory and the failure for its realization that anguishes him (alas, it cannot *be* realized, as evidenced by Yun's visit in his hospital ward). Not uncommon to the *waisheng* émigrés in Taiwan, after having lived in the island-state for several decades, many still linger on the nostalgic memory of their hometown on the mainland (Liu K. 1986, 23). Again, this seems to support Lai's affirmation of a Taiwanese identity through constructing its subjectivity and sense of belonging to the Taiwanese soil. However, I propose that Lai is calling our attention to the acute painful history encountered by the mainland émigrés, and that a willful forgetting of the past might not be feasible because it is one of the components of the subject construction of the mainland émigré. This experience defines them as mainlanders in Taiwan and constitutes an important part of the collective Taiwanese experience—*waisheng and bensheng* people.

In the same light then, in seeking to establish Taiwan's identity, can it be done simply by rupturing with the (Chinese) past? Two scenes in this play suggest a critical tone toward this. The first is on the eve of Yun Zhifan's separation from Jiang Binliu in Shanghai to reunite with her family in Guilin for Chinese New Year in 1948.

> JIANG BINLIU: How nice to go home.
> YUN ZHIFAN: What's wrong? Thinking of home again? Binliu, there'll come the day when you can go home to Manchuria. Things won't always be like this. You must believe it!
> JIANG BINLIU: Manchuria isn't a stop where you can just hop on a train and go to.
> YUN ZHIFAN: One day you'll go home to Manchuria for New Year's. The war is over, Binliu. The situation in Manchuria will soon be resolved. We're blessed to even be alive! There are things you can't just keep thinking back on.
> JIANG BINLIU: *There are some things you can't just forget.*
> YUN ZHIFAN: But you must forget. Look around you. Is there anyone who's not been scarred with a thousand wounds?
> JIANG BINLIU: *There are sights, there are sounds that one can never forget.*
> YUN ZHIFAN: But you must forget! You must learn to forget!
> (Lai (1986) 2010, 970; italics mine)

If the word "Manchuria" is replaced with "China," the scene might have been taking place between a Taiwanese and a Taiwanese mainlander in mid-1980s Taiwan (or for that matter, even contemporary Taiwan) instead of two lovers in 1948 Shanghai. The political differences between the mainland and Taiwan resulted in a strained relationship where citizens across the Taiwan Strait were then not allowed visits from either side. When Yun attempts to comfort Jiang with "the war is over," yes, the Chinese Civil War is indeed over, but the ideological differences in the Cold War have kept the two Chinas separate still. Urging him to forget the past and move on, Yun must have been encouraging Jiang to forget about the pains of the Civil War—the war that the KMT lost—and accept the reality of Taiwan as their new permanent home. While this analysis is in line with our above discussion of Lai's critique of Jiang for holding on to the utopic past and refusing to come to terms with the contemporary reality, it also suggests the impossibility of a permanent break with the past. Jiang's painful sorrow is thoroughly expressed in his line "There are sights, there are sounds that one can never forget," suggesting that perhaps more than his unwillingness to let go, it is his inability to do so that allows the past always to project a ghostly presence in contemporary Taiwan.

The second example that might more clearly illustrate this point is Old Tao's entry into the Peach Blossom Land, when he meets the Man and Woman in White, performed by the actor and actress playing Master Yuan and Chun Hua, who try to explain to Tao the utopic life they currently live:

> MAN IN WHITE (GRANDLY): Our ancestors had a grand vision. It was they who brought us to this faraway land, so that this unending line of descendants could walk hand in hand, shoulder to shoulder.
>
> (Lai (1986) 2010, 1006)

The Man and Woman in White communicate to Tao that their ancestors have led them there to accomplish their aspirations and dreams. They also ask Tao to forget all about the past and stay forever with them there. Going with Shen's analysis that Chun Hua and Wuling represent China while the cuckolded and humiliated Tao (representing the KMT) has retreated to Taiwan (1995, 100n27), would this be Lai's message to the Taiwanese mainlander: that they should forget about the past and stay in Taiwan forever, thereby setting up the dichotomy of the utopian Taiwanese contemporary and the dystopian war-torn Chinese past? Using Joyce Liu's notion that the Peach Blossom Land "seems to suggest a land of unreality" and is merely "an imaginary vision projected by the subject" (1997), it is perhaps then not so much a letting go of a *lived* past experience, but a realization that this projection is based on one's *imagination* and might not after all be real.

Learning to View from the Other's Perspective

In tracing Taiwan's modern identity construction, this chapter has sought to illustrate theater's participation in the articulation of the state's contested notion of Chineseness. As Katherine Chou Hui-ling depicts: "Taiwan's constant state of conflict, negation and convergence along the path of modernization has played out on stage in a long battle over modernity and how to represent the shifting political and cultural status quo" (2016, 333). The most exciting modern theater in Taiwan arose as a response to its emerging identity, as it attempted to make sense of its contemporary fragmented history, declining international status, and competing interests among the two major groups who arrived on the island with very different memories of their home construct. When Lan Ling Theatre Workshop's *He Zhu's New Match* came onto the scene to announce the birth of modern Taiwan theater, Stan Lai was still completing his doctoral training in the United States. His subsequent return to Taiwan allowed him to succeed the trailblazing momentum started by Lan Ling, and his Performance Workshop created works that appealed to audiences of both fine art and popular culture, converging the dichotomous interests of the Modernists and Nativists that were reflective of the social division then.

To understand identity in Taiwan, one has to recognize the group identity of the *waisheng* émigrés who continue to be haunted by the ghost of their past directly linked to their connection with the ancestral homeland. Shen Shiao-ying shares the view that "different people in Taiwan have different pasts that define their being. And the past that Lai delineates is only one of them" (1995, 117). Just as Kuo Pao Kun's Chineseness speaks more for the Chinese-educated Singaporeans who are now more socially marginalized compared to their English-educated peers, Lai's Chineseness addresses more the concerns of the mainlanders—who form an inseparable part of the Taiwanese collective whole. On the one hand, he critiques their blind idolization of a utopic past; on the other, he appeals to a broader audience to give them room to reconcile with their internal displaced condition. The Peach Blossom Land in Tao Yuanming's fifth-century text is a place that was *never* to be found again. Extending that allusion to the play: the *waisheng* émigrés' imagery of their former homeland is one whose path cannot be retraced or relocated, and where they can never be again. Yet the mainland émigrés' insistence on clinging to a created past is a necessary condition that constructs their identity—an intricate part of Taiwanese history and identity that cannot be easily erased. Instead, therefore, Lai encourages his audience to view through different paradigms by creating room for various interpretations in his dramatic work. In his collective improvisation method of creation, Lai stresses the importance of listening:

> After I explain the situations, the actors are free to act. No one can predict what will happen. Much like jazz musicians riffing on

a theme or a set of chords, the actors develop a given situation. An outstanding jazz musician relies not only on techniques or inspiration, but more importantly on good ears. He or she has to listen well in order to transform the input from his or her partners into a music that is different from the original conceptualization but is even more brilliant. Our actors work in much the same way. Otherwise, improvisational theater will regress to a series of disconnected expressions of individual actors or abstract ideas. There will be no dramatic sparks, and theater will lose its life.

((1986) 2014, 370)

This emphasis on listening to the other party, attempting to see things from the other's perspective—as represented by the character of the Mysterious Woman—is Lai's proposal of diffusing tensions instead of inciting them. If only people slowed down, listened to the other side, and tried to consider things from the other's position, as suggested by Old Tao in *Peach Blossom Land*, perhaps things could be better and deteriorating situations improve.

In an interview with Phoenix Satellite Television on his play *Baodao yicun* 寶島一村 (The village, 2008), which was touring Chinese cities and eventually came to Beijing, Lai expresses his thoughts on roots:

So, what are roots? I consider *The Village* to be talking about a process, from assuming one is about to go home and then not being able to do so, to this place is home, Taiwan is home. Hence, I think I will stop here. Because what is this thing called "roots" is a very complicated question; in the evolution of history, this is a very complex question. I believe for most of the inhabitants of the *juancun*, their roots are in their hometowns in mainland China, but time changes many things. When you have been living somewhere, you might have left home at age seventeen, and then you stay in Taiwan for sixty years, so then where is home?

(2010)

The *juancun* 眷村, known as "dependent villages for military personnel" or "military dependents' compounds," were built in the 1950s for the families of Chiang Kai-shek's army that had retreated to Taiwan as sites of temporary dwelling. While *The Village* discusses exclusively the difficulty of the mainland émigrés' settlement in Taiwan—again in the spirit of encouraging one to view from the other side's perspective— might its intended audience not be China (and the play did after all tour many Chinese cities) as well as the pro-independence faction in contemporary Taiwan? I agree with Jon Kowallis that Lai "has continued to bring the 'two China's closer" (1997, 176), and I would add that his works have also contributed to bringing the different factions in Taiwan closer.

While unsettling the mainlanders from their seat of power has been a focus of contemporary Taiwanese politics, Lai portrays them as the underdogs—a generation who did not have a say in their chosen site of settlement, having to deal with the emasculation that must come with losing the war, and coping with the difficulty in their everyday displaced conditions. In narrating the mainlanders' story of sufferings and hardships, the message seems to suggest that in the course of building this place, we, the *waisheng* émigrés, suffered too, and by extension we are hence not that different from you. As mainlanders living on Taiwan for over forty years, many have found Taiwan to be their new home. And the political realities are as such: Even if they wanted to return to "China," where could they go? Many, military men as well as men of *lettres*, came with the Nationalists in 1949 precisely because they did not agree with the communist regime. Despite Lai's critique of the mainlander's holding on to a created past, it is also a condition that is necessary in the construction of the *waisheng* émigré's subjectivity: it is this past from mainland China, his previous experiences that followed and continued to haunt him in contemporary Taiwan that formulated his subjective self. Hence, a different type of Chineseness is being generated in Taiwan—one that is formed by its unique history and stands apart from the Hongkonger, Singaporean, or Chinese experience.

Chapter 3

Theater of Rebellion
Danny Yung and Experimental Hong Kong Theater

Two events of immense significance to Hong Kong took place in 1982. On September 24, Margaret Thatcher's infamous tripping and falling off the steps of the Great Hall of the People, the political hub of Beijing, seemingly prophesized Hong Kong's future. The then British prime minister had just exited from a secret meeting with China's paramount leader Deng Xiaoping. This series of meetings had begun behind closed doors in 1981 (Tang 2009, 131) and paved the way for the 1984 Sino-British Joint Declaration, a formal agreement between the two governments that the island of Hong Kong would be "returned" to the People's Republic of China (PRC) in 1997. As if as a response to these events, in March 1982, the arts collective Zuni Icosahedron 進念·二十面體 was formed. In the next few decades, Zuni would make headlines frequently, centering itself in controversies such as being the first troupe in the city to stage plays with nudity, discuss homosexual and overt political themes (such as Direct Elections and the Basic Law), and invite the audience onstage during performance, which provoked official intervention to end it prematurely, leading further to an island-wide public discussion on the issue of censorship. Zuni would become Hong Kong's most outspoken arts group, both within the city and on the international scene, constantly creating artworks that questioned and challenged the hegemonic powers-that-be that sealed Hong Kong's fate—a process that took place with no representatives from the territory to arbitrate on its own behalf. Coincidentally, these two events that took place in the same year were to have the greatest impact on Hong Kong politically and artistically for the next few decades, with Zuni's development intimately tied to Hong Kong's sociopolitical progress. Most importantly perhaps, Zuni's pursuit of a Hong Kong theater probably best reflects the commitment of the territory's residents to seek an identity for themselves (J. Wong 1982, 263). This chapter will discuss the significance of Zuni Icosahedron and its artistic director Danny Yung Ning Tsun 榮念曾 in the context of Hong Kong theater history by focusing on its 1984 production *Yapian zhanzheng: Zhi Deng Xiaoping de sifeng xin* 鴉片戰爭：致鄧小平的四封信 (Opium war: Four letters to Deng Xiaoping).

That Zuni Icosahedron has been the most influential cultural collective from Hong Kong on the global scene is of little doubt: its cultural impact has been compared to that of the Hong Kong film industry, which earned the territory the iconic appellation "Hollywood of the East" 東方好萊塢. On the group's twenty-fifth anniversary, *Haowai* 號外 (City magazine), an upscale magazine for white-collar readers among the first of its kind to introduce written Cantonese (Gunn 2006, 50), published a special commemorative issue on the arts group, commenting:

> Influenced by the 1960s French New Wave, a group of Hongkongers who coincidentally met in the Television Broadcasts Limited (TVB) training class in the late 70s—Patrick Tam Kar Ming 譚家明, Tsui Hark 徐克, Stanley Kwan 關錦鵬, Kam Kwok-leung 甘國亮, Ann Hui 許鞍華—enriched Hong Kong's film and television cultural industries by riding on the affluence of the 1980s decade. In the 1980s there was Zuni. Twenty-five years later, their members would permeate all sectors of society.
>
> (*Haowai* 2007b, 108)

Considering Hong Kong's preeminent global status both as an international financial center and as a filmmaking powerhouse, this speaks volumes to Zuni's significance in the territory. Up until 1997, the Hong Kong film industry had been the third largest in the world, after the United States and India (S. Lu 1997, 15). While Ann Hui (b. 1947), Tsui Hark (b. 1950), Stanley Kwan (b. 1957), and their contemporaries have since become iconic directors in the Hong Kong New Wave Cinema 香港新浪潮電影, whose standards for filmmaking are held as the yardstick in the region, Zuni has earned itself the reputation as an alternative vanguard of its theater scene, and its artistic director Danny Yung as "the 'Cultural Godfather' of Hong Kong" 香港的「文化教父」 (G. Tsoi 2012). By the same token, Zuni's impact on the artistic scene of the city through film should not be underestimated. In 1982, Yung was invited by Chinese American filmmaker Wayne Wang 王穎 (b. 1949) to be the producer and art director of *Dim Sum: A Little Bit of Heart* (1985). And Zuni has held independent film screenings for the public at the basement of its new headquarters for an entire decade since moving to Causeway Bay. Thus, the arts collective not only actively reached out to a wider audience beyond that of its theater productions, but it also literally created Hong Kong's first underground film season (Lam 2006, 26). In the company's forty-year history, the diverse range of people Yung has inspired and nurtured include cinematographer Kwan Pun Leung 關本良, filmmaker Susie Au 區雪兒, transmedia artist Craig Au-Yeung Ying Chai 歐陽應霽, comic artist Lai Tat Tat Wing 黎達達榮, lyricist Wyman Wong 黃偉文, and People Mountain People Sea 人山人海 in music, among others (*Haowai* 2007a, 105; 2007b, 108). Indebted to Yung for inspiring him to take up the critic's armchair (Chen Juan 2013), Leung Man-to 梁文道 even goes as far as to extol, "'Danny Yung is first of all a mode of thought,' a mode that has influenced many cultural thinkers of my generation" (2009, 91).

Born to an industrialist family in cosmopolitan Shanghai, at the age of five Yung left with his entire family to Hong Kong via Taiwan on the last boat out of Shanghai in 1949 before the arrival of the Chinese communists. He had his formative experience in Hong Kong and in 1961 departed for the United States at seventeen years of age to pursue degrees in mathematics at Pacific University, Forest Grove, Oregon, architecture at the University of California, Berkeley (1967), and computer science and urban planning at Columbia University (1969). His research at Columbia focused on ethnic minorities (Shih H. 1988). Upon graduation, Yung cofounded the first Asian American arts and cultural organization on the American East Coast, the Basement Workshop, along with Eleanor Yung, Peter Pan, Frank Ching, and Rocky Chin in New York City in 1971 (K. Wong 2006). Funded by the Ford Foundation with the first grant ever given to study Asian Americans, the Basement Workshop was involved in documenting the lives of the Asian American community by helping them overcome their psychological barriers as ethnic minorities and improve their living conditions (Shih H. 1988). These dedicated efforts eventuated in the founding of the Asian American Resource Center as well as the landmark publication *Bridge: The Magazine of Asians in America* (Bolling 2008). The United States in the 1960s was filled with an air of revolutionary liberation, championing the Civil Rights Movement and freedom of speech and opposing the Vietnam War (M. Leung 2009, 99). Collectively, these experiences had a lasting impact on the young Yung who was then based in Berkeley and New York—the two major sites of counterculture resistance (Chung Y. 2012, 49)—thus explaining his advocacy theater praxis later in life.

In contrast to Kuo and Lai, Yung was not trained in the dramatic arts but in architecture and urban planning. This might account for his intricate sensitivities to exploring concepts of time, space, and structure in his works, which depart from a reliance on linear narrative development in conventional theater. Yung's relationship with Chineseness is also unique among the dramatists I study: in my interview with him, he claims that he had not used a word of Chinese in all his seventeen years in the United States, such that he had a completely different experience when looking at written Chinese characters again after returning to Asia. These words that used to be part of his everyday life now appeared strange, strangely familiar, or familiar in a strange way. Perhaps this explains why he has a penchant to deconstruct and experiment with Chinese cultural elements: Chinese characters, idiomatic words, and phrases would be taken apart and rearranged to establish new meanings and relationships in his theatrical collage.

Prior to the founding of Zuni Icosahedron, Yung and his future artistic partners were already displaying an unconventional proclivity in their working styles and mannerisms. His inaugural theater piece and solo "Bubbles" Conceptual Comics exhibition was held at the then newly established Hong Kong Arts Centre 香港藝術中心 in 1979. On the exhibition's opening night, Yung staged *Pojilu yihao* 破紀錄一號 (Broken record # 1), which he had devised with John Sham 岑建勳 (b. 1952), introducing conceptual art and structuralist theater to the territory. An invitation for further collaboration by Shih Shu-ching 施叔青 (b. 1945),[1] then in charge of the performing arts at the Arts Centre, followed, which Yung expressed interest in only if he could do

---

1. The older sister of prominent writer Li Ang, mentioned in chapter 2, Shih Shu-ching is also an important writer from Taiwan who was based in Hong Kong from 1978 until its handover in 1997. She is most renowned for her *Xianggang sanbuqu* 香港三部曲 (Hong Kong trilogy) novels in the 1990s.

a series of works and not one-off productions. The *Zhongguo lücheng* 中國旅程 (Journey to the east) series, a discursive examination of the relationship between the observer and the observed, was thus sparked in 1980 as a series of four productions co-conceptualized with Gus Wong 王守謙, who would become a leading figure in the early days of Zuni.[2] Using the idea of Marco Polo and Michelangelo Antonioni's journeys to China and the impact these travels have had on global cultural communication, in this piece Yung and Wong placed China as the observed to reexamine both Hong Kong's position as the observer and how Hongkongers view their relationship with China. On and offstage, film, video, and projection slides are used to critique both stage and media: *Journey to the East* might have thus been Hong Kong's first ever transmedia theater production functioning simultaneously as a critical review of media itself (L. Yu 2006, 203). This was inspired by the Hong Kong University Drama Lab's 香港大學戲劇實驗室 *Jiamian—Sandao youjifu de gushi* 假面──三島由紀夫的故事 (Mishima 1979), directed by Gus Wong, which broke down the spatial division in the theater traditionally separating the audience from the performance, by which Yung was emotionally moved (Lee et al. 1988, 13). Two years later, in 1981, at the invitation of the newly established Hong Kong Repertory Theatre 香港話劇團 (HKREP, f. 1977) Wong and Yung codirected *Dalu* 大路 (The road), which reexamines the relationship between audience and actors by blending real life into theater ("Shenghuo" 1981, 7). Yung also designed sets for the Seals Theatre Company's 海豹劇團 (f. 1979) plays as well as Xiejin Drama Society's 協進劇團 1980 production of the David Hare play *Fanshen* 翻身 (1975), in exchange for their participation in at least one of the *Journey to the East* series productions (Yung 2005, 99; L. Yu 2006, 203).

Several factors contributed to the establishment of Zuni. Among the participants in these projects were a group of young people from the Rosary Hill School Drama Club alumni 玫瑰崗校友戲劇組 who, inspired by Yung's avant-garde theater praxis, asked him to lead them in future artistic collaborations. They formed half of Zuni's founding members; the other half consisted of artists like Pia Ho 何秀萍 who had worked with Yung during his collaboration with Seals. Other founding members of the company include Gus Wong, Edward Lam Yik-wah 林奕華 (b. 1959), Pun Tak Shu 潘德恕, David Yeung Wing-Tak 楊永德,

---

2. For a detailed study of the complete *Journey to the East* series, see Ferrari 2020, 71–137.

Jim Shum Sing-tak 沈聖德, and Jacob Wong Hing-cheung 黃慶鏘 (Yung 2005, 99). Only out of necessity and to organize publicity materials following an invitation by New Aspect Arts Centre to perform at the Asian Theatre Festival in Taiwan (Lilley 1998, 94) did these theater lovers register themselves as a group in March 1982 (Singerman 1983). The name of the arts collective combines "Zuni," a color between blue and green and also the name of a tribe of North American Indians famous for creative handicrafts in western New Mexico, and "Icosahedron," which can mean either a twenty-sided solid figure or an infectious virus (Chew 2008). From the outset, this self-styled cultural collective clearly defied strict categorizations and positioned itself instead on the margins of society. According to local practitioners, these early works by Zuni members before the company's founding already "had a major impact on the scene, because this was a kind of experimental theatre that no one had ever seen before here" (Tang 2009, 130).

Zuni has been hailed as "one of Hong Kong's—and perhaps Asia's—most cutting-edge grouping[s] of artistes" (Madhavan 2004), and their productions have since "become synonymous with the avant-garde theatre in Hong Kong" (Cheung 2005). From its inception, the group has been at the forefront of experimental drama; unlike conventional mainstream theater, their productions are distinguished by a lack of characters, plot, narrative, and dialogue. Often almost nothing happens onstage in the conventional Aristotelian understanding of dramatic progression: there are no characters who get into conflicts in need of resolutions; in fact, there are no characters per se. Actors merely play themselves, stemming from Yung's belief:

> Basically everyone can only play one character, that is him/herself. If we begin from this premise, the stage is precisely a place where we can learn about the collective and ourselves. The concept of performance then becomes a discussion of the process of honest expression and a clarification of views.
>
> (2009, 71)

Therefore, Zuni actors need neither immerse themselves in character in the Stanislavskian sense nor be trained in a theater school. Coming from all walks of life, they enrich the repertoire of the company by blurring "the distinction between amateurism and professionalism" (Abbas 1997, 144). Gilbert Fong Chee Fun and Shelby Chan Kar-yan suggest that even "dialogue was a dispensable element" in many Zuni productions, thus rendering their "presentation zen-like and relying on directness rather than mediation through words" (2016, 331). For instance, in *Bainian zhi guji* 百年之孤寂 (One hundred years of solitude, 1982), actors walk across the stage a hundred times without saying a line (Chew 2008). Instead, Zuni productions rely on objects, visual images, sound effects, improvisation, or an unrelated sequence of information and language that lack an interior cohesiveness (Hu 2007, 92)—traits akin to the works of contemporary experimental theater maestros Richard Foreman (b. 1937) and Robert Wilson (b. 1941), to whom Yung has often been compared (Yung 2009, 71). In postdramatic theater, Hans-Thies Lehmann notes, valorizing the performance dimension "does not imply that texts written for the theatre are no longer relevant" (2006, 6), but merely that they would "become just one element in the scenography and general 'performance writing' of theatre" (4). In other words, other components of the mise-en-scène are not simply subservient to the text. Indeed, in many of Yung's works, the text blends in with elements of dance, sculpture, and visual and audio arts to create a collage of images (Chow Y. 1983). Viewing a Zuni performance might pose challenges for the audience as these images appear unconnected without any meaningful association at first glance. However, given the lapse of time, Stan Lai suggests, the "blank" will allow every audience member to rearrange these images in ways in which s/he finds individual significance (Lai 1988).

Being so deviant from conventional theater, it is then not too difficult to comprehend why, despite its high standing, Zuni is not considered mainstream. The group, according to art critic David Clarke, "can be best described as a major feature of the Hong Kong Cultural Periphery" (1996, 146). For Yung, the system is always scrutinizing the actions of the periphery, because mainstream art is already part of the system. The system is wary of and yet wishes to absorb the periphery, knowing full well that the periphery is fluid, has the potential to incite, and is always an unknown. Historically, we see that the mainstream and the periphery are merely contending forces at work during systemic change (Yung 2009, 78–79). Using this peripheral position as a vantage point, Yung's stage becomes a laboratory for discourse and criticism. The dialectical relationship between the individual and the collective as well as the changing positionalities of how one scrutinizes and is being scrutinized are themes frequently explored in his works. Yung feels that Hong Kong is at a critical point where "the relationship between the individual and the collective is being put to the test." Emphasizing the urgency for "self-awareness, self-questioning, and a new identity," Yung believes "this is the first step to a collective identity" (2009, 72). In an interview conducted by Radio Television Hong Kong, he expresses most succinctly what his avant-garde dramas seek to examine:

> Playscripts are a frame, theater is also a frame; how do we understand this frame? (We) examine this frame, the meaning(s) of this frame, and the meaning of the theater. The audience responds by asking us many questions, because they are not used to this. When the audience enters the theater, they are used to being fed information by others.
>
> Normally audiences go to the theater for two reasons: (1) to relax, and (2) to be entertained. But we are discussing the meaning of the theater! Where is the frame or boundary of the theater? The entire society is a frame. Therefore, we have to understand this frame.
>
> (Yung 2013)

Little wonder that a journalist interviewing Yung would title her article: "Every Production of the 'Cultural Godfather of Hong Kong' Is a Critique on Society" (Chen Juan 2013).

One would not assume a uniform sense of identification across the spectrum of Hong Kong residents. Nor is identity itself stagnant (Dolan 2006, 510). As anthropologist Helen Siu observes, "Crucial historical junctures which have made Hong Kong culturally porous also pose problems of identity for its residents" (1996, 179). The city was composed of three major migration waves from China, each having varying degrees of identification with Chineseness, not only depending on their level of acculturation to Hong Kong or connections with the mainland, but also complicated by "the inward and outward pull of cultural and sociopolitical orientations" (Shelby Chan 2015, 40). The impact of two decades of Westernized education on the generation born after the war could not be underestimated. The university-educated among them, who "were most exposed to the social and political upheavals of the late 1960s worldwide" owing to their privileged access to Western-language media that provided progressive critique of governments, turned their focus to the particular social problems of their own society and demanded more responsive and accountable political leaders (Siu 1996, 183). At the same time, along with families that were "experiencing drastic social mobility within one generation or less," the indigenization of film and popular music spearheaded by Samuel Hui Koon-kit 許冠傑 (b. 1948) has "reinforced and made visible the outlooks, aspirations, and expressions of an increasingly distinctive culture of a generation made in Hong Kong" that cuts across class distinctions (184). Being "comfortable with a global cultural image of the territory" (191), this is likely the group who can most appreciate Zuni's postmodernist aesthetics. Indeed, Edward Lam opines that the majority of Zuni's audiences are made up of intellectuals, cultural workers, thinkers, as well as the young who find their works stimulating and attractive, but likely not the middle class who are uncomfortable discussing issues with which they are insecure (Lee et al. 1988, 13).

As observed by Chinese critic-director Lin Kehuan 林克歡, Zuni is not only contemporaneous with the development of Hong Kong theater, but is "in a very true sense" Hong Kong's first experimental drama group (2007a, 104). Their forte to shock, impact, and germinate was not confined within the territory's borders. Zuni performances have toured Taiwan, Singapore, China, Japan, Belgium, Britain, Germany, the Netherlands, Norway, Poland, and the United States—leading critics to hail the group as "a legendary fringe institution within Hong Kong's performing arts scene" that has received its "greatest critical accolades performing overseas" (Lilley 1998, 93). Zuni has other working styles apart from Yung's, who assumed the group's artistic directorship from 1985 onward (163). Most notable are the directorial styles of Edward Lam's personal and gender politics in the 1980s and 1990s, until he left the collective to form his company Edward Lam Dance Theater 非常林奕華 in 1991, and the more recent pure architectural images and popular culture series of Mathias Woo Yan Wai 胡恩威 (b. 1968), who is currently Zuni's co–artistic director (*Haowai* 2007a, 105). In this chapter, I focus mainly on Yung's creative aesthetics. As will be made clear in my examples later, Yung's method of constant *dis*identification pushes his audience to rethink the issue from different angles, confronting them to question their own assumptions in a bid to realign themselves and establish new relationships with the problem in context.

Like Singapore's The Theatre Practice and Taiwan's Performance Workshop, Zuni became the most internationally renowned cultural icon from Hong Kong because of the social impact of its plays. But even more so than its Singaporean and Taiwanese peers, Zuni also influenced culture and society through the activities it advocated offstage. The company has not shied away from being at the center of controversies, often using the censorship and taboos it has challenged to create platforms and spaces for dialogue. Through his decades-long negotiation with the authorities, Yung has become "an experienced tactician" adept at manipulating the media to Zuni's advantage whenever the company and the government are engaged in a tussle (Lilley 1998, 114). To challenge government restrictions, one of Zuni's strategies has been to force them into the open. For instance, the theater group has always printed in its performance programs the scenes it has been required to delete and the changes made in order to stage the production (115). Another example is *Lienü zhuan (Rouban · Ru ge de xingban / Kuaiban)* 列女傳(柔板 · 如歌的行板/快板) (Portraits of women [Adagio · Andante Cantabile · Allegro], 1983), which discusses the triangulated Sino-British-Hong Kong relationship from a feminized position. Although the play title is taken from *The Biographies of Exemplary Women*, a Western Han (206 BCE-9 CE) text considered a manual on teaching exemplary female behavior in ancient China, this play broke taboos by using language with overt sexual references and vulgarities onstage to showcase the highly volatile political atmosphere when the Sino-British Joint Declaration was still under discussion. The play's popular success, however, pushed the government to implement a vetting policy on all future theater productions. Yung reacted by contacting over forty Hong Kong theater groups to discuss this, of which twenty responded in the positive to hold collective discussions with the government for the next two years, concluding the event with the government eventually backing down (L. Yu 2006, 204). An unintended consequence of this series of meetings was the founding of the Hong Kong Federation of Drama Societies 香港戲劇協會 in 1984 (Yung 2007). Likewise, *Opium War: Four Letters to Deng Xiaoping* caused a huge stir, this time with the Hong Kong Arts Centre, which evolved into a discussion of the responsibilities between artists, bureaucrats, and society (Lam 2006, 26). No wonder Stephen Chan observes, "Zuni Icosahedron is one of the few most persistent artistic groups in Hong Kong to have attempted to speak politically in almost all of its creative endeavours made in the last decade" (1992, 36).

Increasing Sense of Localization

Recalling her days growing up in Hong Kong, Rey Chow poignantly expresses the territory's "diasporic reality" as a "marginalized position":

> What I retain from these memories is . . . the sense of immediacy of a particular diasporic reality—of Hong Kong caught, as it always has been since the end of the Second World War, between two dominant cultures, British colonial and Chinese Communist, neither of which takes the welfare of Hong Kong people into

account even though both would turn to Hong Kong for financial and other forms of assistance when they needed it.

(1993, 20–21)

Much like Taiwan's predicament caught in the jostling of power between China and the United States, Hong Kong's has been inseparable from the relationship between two external powers. Neighboring the southeastern province of Guangzhou, the Hong Kong Island was ceded to Britain in 1842 when it defeated the Qing government in the First Opium War. Subsequent to the Qing losing the Second Opium War in 1860, Britain acquired the Kowloon Peninsula. Finally, Britain seized the opportunity after China's defeat at the First Sino-Japanese War in 1898 to force a treaty onto the weakened Qing government to lease the New Territories to them for ninety-nine years. In a somewhat ironic twist of historical fate again similar to Taiwan, ninety-nine years after 1898, the Chinese government that negotiated for Hong Kong's return in 1997 was not the one that lost it: the Qing Empire was now defunct, and it was the PRC that wanted Hong Kong back under the so-called One Country, Two Systems policy, where the island would be integrated as a special administrative region (SAR) under PRC jurisdiction.

In the 150-year period under British administration, Hong Kong had developed from a backward fishing village into a highly successful global financial center, ranked third only after London and New York, with one of the highest per capita incomes in the world. Its relative social freedom and distinguished status as a filmmaking powerhouse in the region earned it the appellation "Pearl of the Orient." When contrasted with a communist China newly emerged from a ten-year socially and economically destructive Cultural Revolution in the early 1980s, therefore, it was hard for many to envisage a bleaker future than if Hong Kong were to be returned to China. From the early 1980s to 1997, the topic of the "1997 handover" therefore loomed large in the imaginary of the everyday Hongkonger and was vividly expressed in all kinds of literature and arts in the territory. As Rozanna Lilley puts it, "Contemporary discourse about 'Hong Kong identity' and contesting images of Hong Kong 'selves' can be partially seen as expressing the dilemmas of people interstitially placed between dominating powers—China and Britain" (1998, 49). In the field of theater, this theme found its way into the most important intellectual discussions and serious expressions of self-identity, which were thus termed the "1997 plays" 九七劇.

Apart from their social differences, Hong Kong played a historically complex role caught between the two Chinas. For instance, prior to 1984 before the Taiwanese authorities lifted their ban to allow citizens to visit the mainland, Hong Kong was the most important site for cross-strait secret communications where letters to and from Taiwan and China were sent covertly via Hong Kong (Fung 1988, 3). Most significantly perhaps, Hong Kong was a safe haven to where one escaped if their political stance differed with both the Taiwanese Nationalists and Chinese Communists. At the outbreak of the Chinese Civil War in 1945, the Chinese Communist Party had arranged for many leftists and progressive writers to enter Hong Kong, thus turning the territory into a leftist cultural center that functioned like a propaganda machine (Hong 1999, 8). Following the communist victory in 1949, a huge wave of these leftist writers returned to the mainland, only to have the ironic opposite effect of other writers who disagreed with the authoritarian communist regime simultaneously seek refuge in Hong Kong. Most of these "writers who came south" 南來作家 fled the mainland paradoxically because they "wanted to pursue a lifestyle of the past" (Liu Y. 1985, 13). Agreeing with neither political faction, these newly arrived writers made Hong Kong not only their refuge but also an indispensably important ground to continue articulating their thoughts and ideas on what it means to be Chinese. Among them were the Neo-Confucianist Tang Junyi 唐君毅 (1909–78), who actively promoted traditional culture in the territory (P. Leung 2011, 108); the great Sinologist Jao Tsung-yi 饒宗頤 (1917–2018); critic, editor, and founder of the journal *Xianggang wenxue* 香港文學 (Hong Kong literature monthly), Liu Yichang 劉以鬯 (1918–2018), who was credited with establishing modern literature in Hong Kong (Su 2018); novelist Eileen Chang Ai-ling 張愛玲 (1920–95); as well as Jin Yong 金庸 (1924–2018), whose "name is synonymous with *wuxia* fiction" in the popular imaginary (P. Liu 2011, 107).

In contrast to the anti-Chinese purges in several Southeast Asian countries, the British colonial administration in Hong Kong did not suppress Chinese education. And unlike the two Chinas, literary production in Hong Kong had never experienced a rupture since the May Fourth Movement (Liu Y. 1993). While the author in post-1949 China and Taiwan became a tool in the hands of either dictatorial regime to be punished "for diverging views with banishment or imprisonment" (Kubin 2009, 35–36), being in between the spaces of the two Chinas allowed Hong Kong an arbitrary openness that was prohibited on both sides of the Taiwan Strait. Precisely because of its peripheral and colonial status, innovation and experimentation in various genres such as photography, installation, documentary, and the performing arts thrived in the city from the 1960s, in effect making Hong Kong the freest among the Chinese societies in artistic and literary creativity from that time (Woo 2007, 106–7). David Clarke muses that the "very lack of established traditional culture" must necessarily be Hong Kong's "asset, freeing it from the kind of hang-ups Taiwan faces because of its self-imposed role as guardian of the Chinese heritage" (1996, 148). In this way, Hong Kong too became an important alternative site for the contestation of Chineseness, with some critics considering it the "Third China."

Hong Kong literature of the 1980s not only reflected this altering cross-strait relationship affecting the ever-changing and complex nature of the city's reality, but also expressed concerns for the sociopolitical circumstances that impacted the territory (Fung 1988, 2–3). After the communist takeover of the mainland, the border between Hong Kong and China was closed, restricting traffic between them from 1950 onward. At the same time, political conditions on the world stage summarily triggered the widening gulf between the two (Shelby Chan 2015, 42). Helen Siu summarizes this distinction most poignantly: while the "mainland remained mysteriously poor and hungry . . . the main business of corner stores in Hong Kong was to send care packages to China. As social contact between the two places shrank, ideology stood out" (1996, 182). However, even as China's Reform and Opening Up policy in the late 1970s precipitated free visits on both sides, the opposite of its intended effect was probably achieved. Rather than increasing the sense of affinity between the two peoples, the colonial government's abolition of the Touch Base policy in 1980, which had aimed at preventing illegal immigrants from China, seemed to estrange the locals further from the mainlanders (A. Hsu 2009, 9). While the island might have long been a city of immigrants, with most being migrants themselves in earlier decades and having family ties on the mainland, the locals' attitude toward the new immigrants, however, "became increasingly unfriendly, if not downright hostile" (Shelby Chan 2015, 44). Inadvertently, the disquietude that arose between the new immigrants and Hongkongers was displayed in the increasing sense of identification reflected in Hong Kong literature. The literary topics explored then included Hongkongers welcoming their newly arrived families from the mainland, the immigrants' inability to adjust to life in the city-state resulting in suicides, expression of sympathy toward new immigrants, and how youths who had experienced the student movements confront the impending arrival of 1997 (C. Lee 2009, 22). In each of these topics might be observed an apparent identity division growing between *us* and *them*, which in Shelby Chan's view, "was consequential for the emergence of a Hong Kong identity" (2015, 45). With 1997 fast approaching, many writers also dwelled on what they imagined were the soon-to-be-lost traditions (Fung 1988, 3). Indeed, "plans for a large-scale exodus" were in place "as pessimistic people planned to emigrate before the 'fall' of Hong Kong after the handover" (Ooi 2005, 28). Caught between an ever-changing Chinese mainland on the one hand and a Hong Kong that preferred to "maintain the status quo" on the other, the question that constantly plagued the minds of many was "whether to stay or to go" (Fung 1988, 4). These themes that Hong Kong writers and intellectuals of the times confronted were similarly reflected in the theater.

Gilbert Fong suggests that the development of modern Chinese-language drama in Hong Kong can be classified into four different waves of artists moving to the city (2006, 147–48). The second of these was during the Sino-Japanese War (1937–1945), where scores of artists entered Hong Kong along with the students they had trained in the aesthetic and ideological styles of the *huaju* arts from China, such as Lu Dun 盧敦 (1911–2000), Chu Hak 朱克 (1919–2012), Chan Yau-hau 陳有后 (1915–2010), and Baau Hon Lam 鮑漢琳 (1915–2007). Several of these dramatists taught in schools in the 1950s, and in their capacity as teachers encouraged their students to watch plays regularly. The curricula in those days were less regimentally regulated; thus these teachers used drama in their classroom teaching, such as getting students to write their own plays as a form of artistic expression. Essayist and literary historian Lo Wai-luen 盧瑋鑾 (Xiao Si 小思, b. 1939) is among those whose love for the theater was inculcated at this time (Poon 2012, 196–97). After the end of the Second World War, the third wave of dramatists arrived in Hong Kong. Yao Ke 姚克 (Yao Xinnong 姚莘農, 1905–91), the first Chinese student to graduate from the Yale School of Drama and who would be illustrious in playwrighting, screenwriting, and translation, and eminent scholar Liu Ts'un-yan 柳存仁 (1917–2009), the first ethnic Chinese to become professor of Chinese at the Australian National University, were among those who headed south to enrich the dramatic playwriting scene in Hong Kong. Finally, from the early 1960s onward was the fourth wave: Hongkongers returning from their study of the dramatic arts in the West, such as Lee Woon-wah 李援華 (1915–2006) and Chung King Fai 鍾景輝 (b. 1937) from the United

Kingdom and United States respectively, contributing actively to the nurturing and maturation of the local theater scene.

As with the cases in Singapore and Taiwan, drama was utilized as an important antiwar vehicle in Hong Kong. The surge in the arrival of dramatic troupes from the mainland, such as the Chinese Music, Dance, and Drama Society and China Traveling Theater Company 中國旅行劇團, created an opportunity for dramatists from Hong Kong and China to work together (Tian and Song 1997, 10). Of note were the latter group's outstanding performances of Cao Yu's *Leiyu* 雷雨 (Thunderstorm, 1933) and *Richu* 日出 (Sunrise, 1936) among other masterpieces, and together with the publication by renowned mainland playwrights such as Chen Baichen 陳白塵 (1908-94) and Xia Yan, they raised the level of modern drama productions and increased the genre's popularity in the territory (X. Chen 2010, 41). With China's declaration as a communist state, from 1949 onward the British government began to tighten its scrutiny of original plays produced in Hong Kong (Tian and Song 1997, 10-11). To avoid political persecution, therefore, some playwrights chose to write on material from the distant Chinese past, such as Yao Ke's *Xi Shi* 西施 (The beauty Xi Shi), Hsiung Shih-I's 熊式一 (1902-91) *Xixiang ji* 西廂記 (Romance of the western chamber), Lai Kok Bun's 黎覺奔 (1916-92) *Zhaoshi gu'er* 趙氏孤兒 (The orphan of Zhao), Liu Ts'un-yan's *Nie pan* 涅槃 (Nirvana), Lee Woon-wah's *Meng Chang jun* 孟嘗君 (Lord Meng Chang), among others (Tian and Song 1997, 11). This minor resurgence of historical plays in the 1950s Hong Kong theater scene, however, yielded lukewarm responses (X. Chen 2010, 41). To a certain extent, these southbound dramatists contributed to maintaining connections between Hong Kong and Chinese drama circles (Fong 1992a, 4), perhaps explaining why Hong Kong theater failed to take off in a different direction during this period. Importantly, the plays of these new arrivals from China were written for performance in Mandarin (a spoken language that was not native to Hongkongers), did not reflect local conditions on stage, and would increasingly differentiate the prewar arrivals from those born after the war.

Two events of significant consequence beginning in the 1960s prompted Hong Kong and Chinese drama to part ways. The development of Hong Kong theater had erstwhile been hindered by a dearth of original playscripts. Relying on Chinese spoken drama canons and adaptations from historical stories, classical literature, and Cantonese opera only resolved the problem partially; essentially, these traditional

Chinese themes did not appeal to a younger and more Westernized generation of audiences (Fong and Chan 2016, 330). Moreover, Hong Kong drama was divided along linguistic lines (Ingham 2005, 4), not unlike Singapore, which too was a British colony. Prior to the 1970s, the English-language theater in Hong Kong catered mainly to an elite audience consisting of expatriates among a small educated class. For instance, the amateur theater companies Garrison Players 卡里遜劇團 and Hong Kong Stage Club 香港戲劇學會, which grew from the military and civil service respectively, were "exclusively expatriate," reflective of a "British amateur dramatic ethos" (Ingham 2005, 1), and mainly staging works that had little to do with local conditions.[3] Indeed, as Dino Mahoney writes, "Before the 1990s English-language theatre in Hong Kong tended to ignore Hong Kong" (2005, vii). Among those who returned from the West in this phase, Chung King Fai was singled out for his efforts at translating works from Western classics. As the first Chinese to return with professional theater training with a master of fine art degree from the prestigious Yale School of Drama (Fong and Chan 2016, 330), Chung played "a very crucial role" in introducing the latest Western theater fads to the city, as well as staging absurdist plays and Broadway musicals in Cantonese. For instance, besides being credited as the forerunner who brought Thornton Wilder's *Our Town* to the Hong Kong dramatic stage in 1965 and subsequently adapting it as a television series in his capacity as Television Broadcasts Limited producer and director, Chung also staged Tennessee Williams's *The Glass Menagerie* among others in Cantonese (Tang 2009, 130). The impact of these works led other dramatists to also involve themselves in theater translation, such as Baau Hon Lam and Lee Woon-wah (Fong 1994, 20), resulting in a surge of translated plays in the territory that ultimately became the mainstream in the 1960s–1970s (Fong 1992a, 5). As such, Chung was hailed as a pioneer who broke with "the shackles of realism" that "had been dominating local productions" (Fong and Chan 2016, 330), as represented by the historical plays that mainly continued with the spoken drama tradition from the mainland. The outbreak of the Cultural Revolution in the 1960s negatively impacted China's image in the minds of Hongkongers (Fong 1992a, 5), prompting them hence to dissociate with things Chinese and accept more readily translated works from the West. Critics agree that "since

---

3. For an example of Hong Kong English-language plays, see Ingham and Xu 2005.

Chung, translated drama has become a staple in Hong Kong theatre" (Fong and Chan 2016, 330).

While some like Chung "insisted on a foreignization approach to staging Western plays, so as to retain their 'original flavour'" (Fong and Chan 2016, 330), others chose to rework foreign pieces to adapt them to the Hong Kong context (Fong 1992a, 7). One such group was the Seals Theatre Company. Founded in 1979, Seals was a major group dedicated to the ideal of translating Western works into demotic Cantonese for the local audience's consumption. Its artistic director was Penang-born Chinese Vicki Ooi Cheng-har 黃清霞, who left Malaysia for Hong Kong in 1962, completing her bachelor's degree in English at Hong Kong University and PhD in drama at the University of Bristol (1967–69). Upon her graduation, she returned to her alma mater in 1971 to teach English literature and drama. Beyond her role as a professor, she was choosing between two possible ways to facilitate the provision of drama in society: one was to continue her former professors' well-trodden path of directing plays in English with elite university students but limiting her impact to a small audience educated in the language; the other was to plot the uncharted terrain of translating overseas works into the local language for a larger consumption. Ooi chose the latter (Ooi 2005, 17–18), because, while she was inspired by the Garrison Players' performance of *Waiting for Godot*, she regretted that many Hongkongers had no access to this play due to the language barrier (Lai and Ooi 2017).

Like the *huaju* situation of a similar period in Singapore, both Hong Kong dramatists and audiences were increasingly dissatisfied with the standard Chinese translations coming from China. Ooi expressed frustration that "most Chinese directors and actors still preferred to work in the formal rather than the demotic Cantonese. But it seemed to me even then that you cannot act in a language that you do not use every day to quarrel in or make love in" (2005, 17). One need not agree entirely with Ooi to see her strong predilection in promoting local language on the dramatic stage. The bulk of Seals's works were translated into demotic Cantonese through the skillful pen of translation studies scholar Jane Lai Chui-chun 黎翠珍, who too was trained at Bristol. Lai provided the "important link" in the ensemble as "a translator who understood both Western and Chinese culture and who would use words with understanding and ease in both English and spoken Cantonese" (Ooi 2005, 23). The group's repertoire consisted mainly of translations of Western drama classics highly regarded in academia, such as works by Shakespeare, Anton Chekhov, Eugene O'Neill, Bertolt Brecht, Tennessee Williams, Edward Albee, and Harold Pinter (Shelby Chan 2015, 91), which significantly contributed to the audience's understanding of Western drama when such knowledge was extremely skeletal in Hong Kong. Into the 1980s, however, this no longer served its purpose when dramatists of a younger generation had come of age and were expressing their views and experiences in the stories they themselves wrote (Ooi 2005, 44). Considered thus, while on the one hand staging works translated into Cantonese nurtured a sense of localization, on the other the appetite for this sense of the local had outgrown what the Seals was offering: the company was after all enacting stories from foreign countries whereas the changing audience needs and tastes determined that *their own* stories be told.[4]

From the 1970s on into the 1980s, governmental efforts also contributed to the building of a local consciousness. The second generation of locally born residents who grew up in postwar Hong Kong's booming economy did not necessarily identify with their ancestral hometown in mainland China as their parent generation did. For the first time this postwar generation witnessed Hong Kong's stability threatened by the "1967 riots" 六七暴動: witnessing terrorist attacks, bombings, and murdering members of the press for voicing their opposition to the violence by leftist sympathizers in the territory. These spillover effects from the radical Cultural Revolution fervor that began in China the year before eradicated "whatever sympathies the Communist supporters had previously generated" (Shelby Chan 2015, 42–43). Responding to these aggravating attacks, the succeeding and longest serving Hong Kong governor, Sir Murray MacLehose (term: 1971–82), made attempts at cleaning up the colony to improve Britain's image. Narrowing the economic gap between rich and poor, replacing the old wooden houses from the 1950s–1960s with new housing, fighting corruption, promoting the Keep Hong Kong Clean campaign in 1972, and advocating family planning with the slogan "Two is enough" 兩個夠晒數 in 1975,[5] transformed the city-state into a home with a strong sense of belonging

---

4. For a rare study of the Seals in English-language scholarship, see Shelby Chan 2015, 91–95.

5. Written as a jingle in colloquial Cantonese, the slogan was sung and popularized by the copious and multitalented artist James Wong Jim 黃霑 (1941–2004). Families in Hong Kong tended to have more children before the 1970s. Parents then wanted to have more children because it was considered a sign of prosperity and fortune. Since male offspring were favored in traditional Chinese culture, married couples sometimes kept having babies until they had

(B. Lee 2006, 7). Developing the territory's modern infrastructure was a calculated political move: MacLehose packaged Hong Kong as an ideal Asian city to negotiate with China on extending Britain's lease. However, the plan failed and MacLehose returned to Britain after his term (Tsao 2008, 157). In this way too, Hong Kong's economic boom benefited from Britain's miscalculation.

A series of social movements and endeavors propelled the Hong Kong theater scene into the next phase of professionalization. Two of the most established local theater groups, the HKREP and Chung Ying Theatre Company 中英劇團, were formed, respectively, by the Urban Council in 1977 and the British Council in 1979. Daniel Yang Shih-peng, who distinguished himself as the first Chinese to become producing artistic director of the renowned Colorado Shakespeare Festival and concurrently the university of Colorado Boulder's professor of theater, was appointed as the founding artistic director for HKREP. Chung Ying's inaugural artistic director was Glen Walford, and it would not have an ethnic Chinese to helm the company until its fifth artistic director, Ko Tin Lung 古天農 (1953–2022) in 1993. Known for the quality of their original works by local playwrights as well as works in translation, both troupes have also been criticized "for being 'predictable'" (Lilley 1998, 67). Nevertheless, along with the founding of the semiprofessional Seals Theatre Company also in 1979, these three troupes signified the beginning of Hong Kong theater's going professional (Huawen 2007, 23). The government too demonstrated its commitment to professionalizing and elevating the status of the performing arts by establishing the Hong Kong Arts Centre in 1977, Council for the Performing Arts 香港演藝發展局 in 1982, and Hong Kong Academy for Performing Arts 香港演藝學院 (HKAPA) in 1984. To anticipate the "radical changes brewing with the coming of 1997," Kuo Pao Kun observed, only when the Urban Council poured millions of dollars into the arts "to capture the heart of the emergent new generation" did theater in Hong Kong finally "take off" (1985, 16).

The 1980s was a particularly fruitful decade for locally written theater works. The 1997 imaginary started to loom large in the literature of the 1980s when the signing of the Sino-British Joint Declaration set the territory's political direction (A. Hsu 2009, 8). To interrogate the deeper significance of home and identity, many plays probed the "'97

---

a boy. Thus, family planning was considered a way to improve the quality of living and reduce government burden on providing education and other social welfare.

complex" 九七情節 and "local consciousness" 本土意識 by using Hong Kong's history to discuss the anxieties caused by the 1997 handover (C. Lee 2009, 23). These included Yuen Lup-fun 袁立勳 and Gerald Tsang Chiu Chui's 曾昭柱 *Shi hai* 逝海 (Gone with the sea, 1984), Anthony Chan Kam-kuen's 陳敢權 *1841* (1984), Raymond To Kwok-Wai 杜國威 (b. 1946) and Hardy Tsoi Sik Cheong's 蔡錫昌 *Wo xi Xianggangren* 我係香港人 (I am Hong Kong, 1985), Seals Theatre Company's "Hong Kong trilogy" collectively titled *Xianggang wutaishang* 香港舞台上 (On the Hong Kong stage, 1986), James Cheung Yim-cheung 張棪祥 and Hardy Tsoi's *Xianggang meng* 香港夢 (Hong Kong dream, 1988), and Anthony Chan's *Dawu* 大屋 (American house, 1990), among others (H. Tsoi 1992, 78; Lin K. 2007b, 39). According to Shelby Chan, these works were mainly topical,

> particularly on the questions of sovereignty and identity, as Hongkongers tried to sort out their relationship with the territory and with China: In what sense were they both Hongkongers and Chinese? If there was an emerging feeling of dual identity in Hong Kong, merging Hongkonger and Chinese, then, were the people Hong Kong *Chinese* or *Hong Kong* Chinese? The difference between the so-called Hongkongness and Chineseness was predicated on the fact that the Hong Kong identity contained both Western and international aspects.
>
> (2015, 45)

On the quality and quantity of these plays, the Hong Kong Drama Project 香港戲劇工程 manager Hardy Tsoi cautioned that at best these numbers are on par with the translated plays being produced in the 1980s; and since the latter tended to be classic works, the quality of locally written plays had much catching up to do (1992, 79). One approach that affirmed Hong Kong's subjectivity in the plays of this period was adopting the strategy of "Da Xianggang, xiao Zhong Ying" 大香港, 小中英 (Fong 1992b, 109)—literally "Big Hong Kong, Little China and Britain," these dramas laud the former and belittle the latter. Yet these plays also betrayed a sense of loss, of being undecided about whether to stay or go, questioning if this was even their choice to be made (Tian and Fong 2009, 449). Highlighting the city's precariousness, sandwiched between two external powers that would decide its future, reminds us of Rey Chow's poignant observation on its "marginalized position, which is not one chosen by those from Hong Kong but one constructed by history" (1993, 21).

Although *I Am Hong Kong* is usually considered the most iconic work marking the watershed of a local identity in the territory, Tian Benxiang 田本相 and Gilbert Fong opine that rather *1984/1997* 一九八四／一九九七 and *Opium War: Four Letters to Deng Xiaoping*, both staged in 1984, were the pioneering works that spearheaded this movement (2009, 449). Staged by the bilingual Chung Ying Theatre Company and directed by Bernard Goss 高本納 and Hardy Tsoi, *I Am Hong Kong* enjoyed a record 114 performances in Hong Kong, Guangzhou, and the Cantonese diasporic communities in Australia. Adopting a Brechtian approach where actors not only switch between Cantonese and English but move in and out of character to intersperse the performance with querying the audience directly about their sense of identification, the play also blends "colonial and local cultures to reflect multiple identities" as well as the territory's "complex past." At the same time, the play also displays "profound anxieties" over the potential erosion of Hong Kong's unique culture as the impending handover approaches (X. Chen 2010, 42–43). In contrast, *1984/1997* was staged by Augustine Mok Chiu Yu 莫昭如 and Yuen Che Hung's 阮志雄 People's Theatre 民衆劇社 in the form of a street theater enacted in front of Hong Kong University's main library. The first half of the play's title references the year of the Sino-British Joint Declaration and simultaneously George Orwell's now-classic dystopian novel, and the latter half the handover. This political theater piece discusses Hong Kong's future, authoritarianism, alienation, as well as sexual repression and liberation. The following, an open invitation to the audience, is excerpted from the play's program notes:

> Who is Big Brother? He is a character in English novelist George Orwell's *1984*, the leader in a totalitarian society. But today, he is omnipresent.
>
> Big Brother is riding you, just as he has held the reins on your ancestors and parents, now he is controlling you and all those around you.
>
> At one time, not too long ago, he emerged in the east. His surname was Chiang, Mao, later changing it to Deng; he is also known as Reagan, Gandhi, Marcos, Amin, Gaddafi, Castro, Brezhnev, and MacLehose. His lackeys are everywhere: your father's work

manager, your sister's construction foreman, and celebrities appearing on television have all taken his bribes; their souls sold to him. Will you, the lucky undergraduate, perhaps become his minion in the future as well?

(Mok 1984)[6]

These words reflect the political direction and intensity of this production, as well as directly implicate the audience in the performance. Zuni's works were already raising eyebrows by challenging conventions then, but it was not until *Opium War* that the company was etched in the collective memory of Hong Kong theatergoers.

Play Analysis: *Opium War: Four Letters to Deng Xiaoping*

No topic in the history of contemporary Hong Kong theater has been given closer attention than the issue of the "1997 Handover" (Tian and Fong 2009, 449), since no other date has had a greater impact on the lives of Hongkongers in its recent past. As theater director Tang Shu Wing 鄧樹榮, who founded the company No Man's Land 無人地帶 (f. 1997, which became Tang Shu-wing Theatre Studio 鄧樹榮戲劇工作室 in 2011) as well as having served as former dean at HKAPA's School of Drama, remarked, "Were it not for 1997, I might still be a lawyer" (2009, 129). The Sino-British Declaration was the first time Tang and his generation were confronted with "the issue of Hong Kong's future head-on." Slighted by "a strong sense of grievance" that Hongkongers "had no say in the entire negotiation process," they began to reflect more deeply about the relationship between China and themselves. This sense of political awareness and concern was also then beginning to be reflected in Hong Kong theater (Tang 2009, 131–32), in which Zuni's *Opium War: Four Letters to Deng Xiaoping* played a pioneering role. Hailed by *Yazhou zhoukan* 亞洲週刊 as a watershed in the company's performance history, the production openly discussed Hong Kong's historical identity and its future relationship with China amid an intensely unsettling sociopolitical atmosphere on the eve of the Sino-British Joint Declaration's official ratification ("Jinnian" 1988, 37).

Opium War: Four Letters to Deng Xiaoping germinated as an exploration of Hong Kong's identity, which is inseparable from history and the Opium War, as well as the relationship between the individual, authority,

---

6. For scholarly research on Augustine Mok in the English-language, see Yeung 2021.

and censorship (Yung 2009, 25). The play was staged over four evenings, August 16-19, 1984, at the Hong Kong Arts Centre's four-hundred-seat Shouson Theatre 壽臣劇院, with a different performance held nightly between 11:30 p.m. and 12:30 a.m., each representing a different letter written to the Chinese paramount leader. The first was titled "On the Beach" 在海灘上, the second "In the Living Room" 在客廳裡, and the third "On the Road" 在路途上. The final evening, "Offstage" 在舞台下, was a consolidation of the three previous evenings' performances. Respectively addressed to God, Father, Lover, and the Self, the letters allude to one's relationship with each of them, with the final allowing oneself the opportunity to clarify what has been previously said (You 1984, 6). None of these letters, as a matter of fact, reached Deng Xiaoping—a point that Zuni was making about the "impotence in writing to someone 'up there.'" The play's controversial title was "meant as a takeoff to discuss some social and metaphysical problems," and as Danny Yung contends, "The idea is that if Mr Deng Xiaoping is so aloof, no effective communication can be established between him and us" (E. Chan 1984).

Controversy shrouded the production even before its opening night. The Hong Kong Arts Centre, which had traditionally been supportive of Zuni productions, withdrew its funding a month before the play's premiere stating "financial reasons," charging the theater group instead a token rental fee of HK$1 per night for the use of its premises. With the withdrawal of the Arts Centre, which had until then acted as a buffer between the two, Zuni was left to face the Television and Entertainment Licensing Agency (TELA) alone. A year earlier, in April 1983, TELA had mandated that all scripts be submitted for vetting before permitting performance licenses. Despite the official retraction of this ruling in May 1984, TELA still retained the right to vet scripts at random. Subsequently, Zuni was requested to submit the script for *Opium War* before its performance, but since the theater company does not use conventional scripts, they only provided a plan of the play. While Zuni was issued a performance license in the end, the Arts Centre would have been scapegoated as *Opium War*'s main organizer had it stayed on as the play's financial sponsor. By pulling out, the Arts Centre avoided having to deal with TELA. This eventually became the model of institutional bureaucracy, which would withhold support for works that were deemed politically sensitive (Ma B. 1988, 81).

The play's title makes no pretense of avoiding its political intent, drawing attention to the 1839–42 war that sealed Hong Kong's history for the next 150 years, and the paramount Chinese leader who would presumably determine the territory's future from 1997 onward. Like many Zuni play titles that reference an important historical precedent or classic text, such as *Shitou ji* 石頭記 (Romance of the rock, 1987) and *One Hundred Years of Solitude* that reenact neither Cao Xueqin's Chinese classic novel nor Gabriel García Márquez's literary masterpiece, this play only makes references to these important sources to discuss matters of contemporary relevance. As Rozanna Lilley suggests, "These productions are so torn from the original texts that we can hardly recognize their presence. Images and narratives are refigured and recontextualised for our allegorical interpretation" (1998, 98). For instance, in *Opium War*, the year the historic war began, 1839, was merely mentioned as part of the daily radio weather forecast, being referred to in the broadcast as "the nineteenth year of the Daoguang era" 道光十九年—Daoguang being the emperor reigning in the last imperial Chinese dynasty, which lost Hong Kong to the British.

In this play, the antiopium hero Lin Zexu 林則徐 (1785–1850) is reduced to two audio interviews. Historically, the imperial commissioner was vested with extraordinary powers by the emperor to eradicate opium, which was corrupting and poisoning China. Onstage, the role of Lin is not represented by any live actors, but rather by a voice-over, void of a body, soliciting his opinion on the following questions: the opium ban, his being championed as a hero, the "Taiwan question," and Hong Kong's being unrepresented at the Sino-British negotiations. More sarcastic is that the voice of Lin, the subject of the interview, is not heard throughout the entire play; during the interview, all we hear are the questions raised to Lin but not his responses. Hence, he has either chosen not to speak or his voice has been muted. I wonder if this isn't an allegorical reading of Hong Kong. Lin's persistent moralistic resistance to the opium trade was considered to have incited the war. Yet the Qing government, who had appointed Lin to lead the antiopium campaign, also scapegoated him for provoking the war and summarily exiled him after their defeat. Considered thus, the presentation of Lin as a character who is unseen and unheard in the play might be motivated by this historical treatment: despite his elevated status as a "people's hero" 民族英雄 for his courageous "resistance to foreign encroachments" (Welsh 1993, 81), he was cast out and silenced from the Opium War narrative in which he occupied a central position. In his sardonically titled essay, "A Hong Kong of the Hongkongers?" 香港人的香港？, Johnny Chan Koon-chung 陳冠中 asks matter-of-factly whether, in discussing Hong Kong's lease, ought we not include the (arguably, most important) element that has heretofore been ignored, the people of Hong Kong (2001, 60)? The parallel sarcasm here is hard to miss: the Hong Kong residents—the real protagonists of the Sino-British talks—have ironically been constantly absented from these negotiations about their own fate.

Correspondingly, the parody extends to the depiction of the British monarch. In the play, Queen Elizabeth II is similarly caricaturized as an imageless voice-over who repeats the same line thrice. When the radio announces—respectively in English, Mandarin, and Cantonese—that the British Broadcasting Corporation is going to transmit the queen's comments on the Opium War, we hear a caricatured woman's voice all three times in English saying only, "I am not a mute!" The monarch of the once largest colonial empire is now reduced to a rubber stamp, a yapping strawman.

Enacted on a minimally bare proscenium stage, *Opium War* has no traceable storyline or plot narrative. An ensemble of actors in everyday clothing moves horizontally across from stage right to stage left repeatedly, at different frequencies and speeds, throughout the entire play. From upstage right enters a lady with a wide brimmed boater hat, shades, and a long flowing dress, suggesting her well-to-do family background. Following two steps behind is someone carrying an umbrella over her—probably her maidservant—observing the same walking pace. A man pushes a bicycle casually across the stage in the same direction, passes them by without making any contact, and continues walking until he exits on upstage left. Another man in a trench coat carrying a large suitcase hurries in from centerstage left, appears to look for a hiding spot, fails, then dashes out immediately. Many others come in, quick-paced, either singly or in groups, holding laundry baskets, suitcases, and large boxes, also entering stage right and exiting stage left. They seem oblivious to one another and might not even be in the same temporal space. While some appear to be mere passers-by, signifying the flow of life, others take on more specific meanings, such as crowds running away from chaos attempting to seek a place of sanctuary. In the background at times are sounds of gentle waves and chirping crows playing to a relaxed ambience; at others the magnetic contralto of Mandopop singer Bai Guang's 白光 *Revisiting Old Dreams* 魂縈舊夢 (1940s) casts a reminiscent mood bemoaning a romantically beautiful past that ceases to return. At yet other times the stage is dimmed into complete darkness, filling the entire theater only with reverberating sounds of cannon fire and gunshots. This heightened atmosphere perhaps reminds one of the technologically superior British cannons blasting open the gates of Canton that forced China's entry onto the global stage on terms being dictated to them.

One of the recurrent motifs in Yung's plays is that of an empty chair, at times facing upstage at the mise-en-scène and at others facing downstage confronting the audience. This empty chair would be a visual sign for *absence* that marks *presence*. But whose absence do they mark and/or whose presence are they calling upon to fill? The Hong Kong Handover is the most obvious reference here. The inhabitants of the city-state are absent from the negotiations between Britain and China about their future. In addition, this staged absence is a direct appeal to the audience in calling for intervention by a corporeal presence akin to Augusto Boal's advocacy theater. In his "Theatre of the Oppressed," the Brazilian activist-dramatist states, "In every one of us there's an actor—someone who acts—and a spectator, who watches the actor acting. We have the ability to watch ourselves doing things" (1997, 32). Boal is convinced that "we aren't content . . . to be just actors and spectators of ourselves," secretly wishing also to be the playwrights, directors, wardrobe masters and mistresses. He proposes that "everyone can, and should, take part" to become playmakers of our own lives (32–33). In *Opium War*, actors continually bring in two chairs to be placed alongside each other at downstage left facing upstage. Actors who come in later remove these chairs, only to have other actors bring in another two to replace them in the same position. Similarly, actors walk in from stage right to stage left to take up these seats, then leave, and other actors again replenish these chairs. For most of the play's duration one of the chairs remains empty. Because the chairs face upstage toward the mise-en-scène, and the chairs are placed downstage, nearest to the audience, the actors in the seats are viewing the performance *just like* the audience. As David Clarke proposes, in lieu of specialized performance vocabulary, Zuni's works utilize everyday moments to demystify the stage. This deconstructivist impulse not only makes explicit the parameters within which they operate, it also widens access to the stage for performers who no longer are required to submerge their personalities, as well as "enables the audience to think of the stage as a place *which they too might occupy*" (1996, 146; italics mine). Therefore, the one seat that remains empty onstage most of the time, it seems to me, is an open invitation for the audience to fill it.

Yung's theater implicates his audience to become proactive decision-makers in the viewing process. Boal's "Forum Theatre" advocates the transformation of his spectators from passive onlookers to active "spect-actors": in using theater as a rehearsal process for social change, he unmasks the oppression in society thereby encouraging his spectators to take up an active revolutionary role in society (1979, 122). While Yung's empty chair did not literally invite the audience to perform onstage there and then (this would happen on the final evening of the production), it engages them to think together with his cast how best to continue the way forward for Hong Kong. Boal's and Yung's theaters are perhaps what Hans-Thies Lehmann would call "'open' or 'writerly' texts" in postdramatic theater as

> they require the spectators to become active co-writers of the (performance) text. The spectators are no longer just filling in the predictable gaps in a dramatic narrative but are asked to become active witnesses who reflect on their own meaning-making and who are also willing to tolerate gaps and suspend the assignment of meaning.
>
> (2006, 6)

Watching a Zuni play can make the audience uncomfortable because it calls upon us to make a decision: if we pick the dissenting option, avoid choosing, or choose not to pick, we will be guilt stricken; if we pick the affirmative option, however, we might not necessarily know what to do or how best to pursue this cause. Then, which course of action does Yung advocate in particular? Stephen Chan considers:

> This peculiar kind of theatrical engagement allows, indeed requires, the political intervention by the private individual at a level of experience that is closest to her ties with the changing sociohistorical realities. It is predicated therefore on the emergence of a very different kind of cultural-political consciousness among the community at large.... Its success would have to involve the radical re-ordering not only of the fundamental relationships between culture and politics for a metropolis like Hong Kong, but also of the respective fields of action/discourse delimited by the cultural and political practices of the Hong Kong people in the face of the difficult times ahead, towards and beyond 1997.
>
> (1992, 36)

This state of being undecided or hesitating to choose is also represented onstage. Throughout the entire play, actors approach the empty chair one after another in long intervals: many look on longingly at the chair, some stroke it but hesitate to sit down, and few eventually do so. My reading of this apprehension is addressed by the continuous replacement of the chairs after they are taken offstage, and the actors who have taken leave of the seat(s) replaced constantly by yet others. Here the message could read: some will leave the cause for various reasons, but this absence will unfailingly be filled by others to continue the journey ahead, presenting an optimism that there will always be advocates. One of the most poignant depictions has been having the sounds of cannon shots thundering in the pitch-black theater with only a soft spotlight cast on those two empty chairs: the audio impact of the bombardment thus confronts the audience's affect, reminding them simultaneously of their implication and responsibility.

Akin to Bertolt Brecht's "Epic Theatre," *Opium War* also turns "the spectator into an observer" yet arouses "his capacity for action," forcing him "to take decisions" (Brecht 1964, 37). In this sense Yung's plays are always already Brechtian: the actors, without immersing into character, are playing themselves performing critique onstage. Brecht's *Verfremdungseffekt* seeks to defamiliarize his audience's viewing experience through interrupting the play's progress by having his actors step out of the characters they are playing and, in their actors' persona, interject critique on the mise-en-scène that has just been previously enacted. In disrupting the flow of the narrative, the German director-playwright aims to prevent his audience from emotionally immersing in the storyline, defamiliarize them from the narrative, and thus engage them in critical reflection. Yung's stage has achieved *Verfremdungseffekt* even without employing the technique of having his actors step in and out of character to halt the performance. In the absence of a traceable storyline or plot structure, most audiences have already found it difficult to get emotionally absorbed in Yung's plays. That part of us that would wish "to surrender wholly to the tug on the heartstrings" and compel "the alienating device" to "keep us awake" (Brook 1996, 89) would hence have little risk in a Zuni production. Instead, by presenting a collage of visual images, movements, and audio references that lack a coherent narrative and therefore requires the audience to synthesize these various elements in order to make sense of them, Yung's theater is constantly engaging his emotionally distanced viewers to observe the mise-en-scène with a critical eye. Like the spectator in Brecht's epic theater who would stand outside of the narrative in order to study it (Brecht 1964, 37), the empty chair that is placed at the edge of Yung's stage then induces the critical audience to observe and critique the mise-en-scène from a distance.

The play has also attempted to consider the war and Hong Kong's history amid a broader context. In the theater, cannon shots are heard for the first time as the entire performance space is darkened. Flashed on the backdrop of the stage are the numbers "1492"—the year Christopher Columbus discovered the New World, beginning Europe's exploration and colonization of the Americas. The Italian explorer, however, was not originally on a quest for the Americas but for Asia. How would Hong Kong's history have been different if the place that Columbus discovered in 1492 was not the Americas but Asia or China, or even Hong Kong itself? Would it merely be a case of an earlier colonization of the territory? Would 1997 still be relevant? Apart from these imagined alternative scenarios, by connecting the 1492 expedition to the Americas with the 1839 Opium War—and by extension 1997—Yung is situating *Opium War* in a larger historical context, underscoring that like the Americas, Hong Kong had similarly been forcibly colonized without the consent of its inhabitants. Perhaps worse than the American Indians, Hongkongers had to go through this twice: they were not consulted when the sovereignty of the land on which they were residing was to change hands *both* in 1842 *and* in 1997.

And what historical lessons might we glean from this, if any? Might this be Yung's attempt at lightening the historical burdens weighing on the British and Chinese governments by underscoring that they are mere historical actors, and at the same time urging them to learn from the lessons of history? The Age of Discovery resulted in the founding of the Americas that prompted global colonialism—a genealogy to which the Opium War belonged. By the same token, China's responsibility for losing Hong Kong—even though it is the Qing and not the PRC that lost it—is also relieved. European colonial expansion into Africa and Asia through their superior firepower and China's relative military weakness and hence inability to prevent Hong Kong from being severed at the 1842 Treaty of Nanking are historical facts. Despite the fears many Hongkongers had toward the impending handover to China in 1997, this reminds us that China too was a victim during the Opium War. Therefore, in drawing parallels between these important historical events, Yung might, on the one hand, be lightening the responsibilities and blame on Margaret Thatcher and Deng Xiaoping if considering 1997 as but another historical occurrence. On the other, this serves as a stern warning to the British and Chinese leaders to reflect upon history and caution them against committing these travesties in the future. As we hear the sounds of cannon shots reverberating in the background and onstage people running hurriedly with their luggage appearing as though they are escaping from a calamity, one cannot tell if these are Hongkongers attempting to flee from the "'97 Doomsday" 九七大限, Chinese seeking refuge from the British in 1840, or the Native Americans taking cover from the Spaniards in 1492. What the Spanish conquistadors did to the American Indians—spreading diseases, killing them off, and milking their resources—must not be repeated in Hong Kong. The adage of George Santayana, "Those who cannot remember the past are condemned to repeat it" (1905, 284), finds adequate contemporary relevance here.

At the same time, this also raises the important question of *us* versus *them*. Are *we* Hongkongers versus *they* the British and Chinese? Or are *we* Hongkongers and the British versus *they* the Chinese? Or vice versa? Most Zuni productions in this phase explore Hong Kong's political development, questions of identification and positionalities, as well as "how some people dictate the lives of others" ("Jinnian" 1988, 37). To address this, I borrow from a scene analysis of *Lienü zhuan (xinban)—Sange nüren de yizhi shenhua* 列女傳 (新版)—三個女人的一隻神話 (Chronicle of three women [a revision of *Portraits of Women*], 1984), another major Zuni play series that premiered on July 25, three weeks before *Opium War*. Directed collectively by Danny Yung, Pia Ho, and Edward Lam, this 1984 version is a reworking of *Portraits of Women*, scripted and directed by Pia Ho the year before. On the same evening at the Hong Kong Arts Centre's Shouson Theatre, the play was performed by an all-female cast at 8:00 p.m. and an all-male cast at 10:00 p.m., with an additional alternative ending by a mixed cast. *Chronicle of Three Women* employs strategies of gender bending and gender reversal to discuss the power dynamics—traditionally a masculine topic—between Britain, China, and Hong Kong. Is Hong Kong like a traditional woman in old society who cannot decide her own fate? When two men fight over her, she does not have a strong view of what she wants, seemingly *shen buyou ji* 身不由己, literally "having no say over her own body." The directors also extended this inquiry to examine if this power relationship was analogous to other relationships on- and offstage: Are actors the traditional women in old society and the audience watching them the men? Is alternative theater the traditional woman in old society and mainstream theater the men looking on? Are theater practitioners the traditional women in old society and those outside the theater field either scrutinizing or ignoring them the men (Yung 2007)? In the play's final scene, in what appears to be a domestic squabble, two actors who are standing are fighting over the third, who is seated in bed in an agonizing manner with her head buried in her arms. Below I reproduce and translate the dialogue from a DVD of the play provided to me by Zuni:

> ACTOR B: I thought we had been discussing this? Even if you have her body, you won't have her heart!
> ACTOR C: She's already said she doesn't love you!
> ACTOR B: You made the decision? Have you ever asked her consent?
> ACTOR A: Listen to me!
> ACTOR B: See, see! Now, it's not that I don't want you. But you might not belong to me for long. Hence, if something happens, I can't protect you!
> ACTOR A: Can you all hear me out?
> ACTOR C: Stop frightening her!
> ACTOR B: Me scaring her? She's a woman, she's a scaredy cat! When did I ever need to depend on her? I have my own hands and feet, why do I have to depend on her? Speak for yourself!
> ACTOR C: So what if I depend on women? Why can't I? Why can't I?
> ACTOR A: Give me a chance to say something . . .
> (*Actors B and C move to sit with Actor A, sandwiching her between them, with their arms crossed looking like gangsters, and continue to speak over Actor A who is increasingly squelched by the two.*)
> ACTORS B & C: Speak lah! You keep saying you want to speak and now you don't?

Up to this moment, whether the person or entity Actors B and C are referring to is of the male or female gender has been impossible to tell, since the drama plays on gender reversal, and in the modern Chinese language (Mandarin as well as Cantonese) the third person pronoun of both sexes is pronounced with the exact same sound and intonation. In all the three versions of this play I watched, whether it is an all-female, all-male, or mixed cast (where the speaking roles would only be given to one particular sex at any one time), Hong Kong is always referred to as the female gender, even if the role is played by a male actor, hence occupying the subordinate power position among the three. In Jill Dolan's now-classic *The Feminist Spectator as Critic*, she points out that "gender is not innate" but instead "dictated through enculturation, as gender divisions are placed at the service of the dominant culture's ideology" (1988, 10). Drawing from Brechtian theory, she reminds us:

> By denaturalizing the illusionist forms of traditional theatre, the smooth operation of psychoanalytical processes is thwarted. Rather than being seduced by the narrative that offers a comfortable gender position, the spectator is asked to pay critical attention to the gender ideology the representational process historically produces and the oppressive social relations it legitimizes.
>
> (14)

Aimed at demystifying "the dominant ideology masked by conventional theatre" (Dolan 1988, 14), these strategies now deconstruct the "ideology in social formations influenced by gender, race, class, and categories of sexual preference," viewing "the power base in these relationships dialectically, as capable of change" (Dolan 1988, 16). In this play, to what extent has Yung been able to achieve these deconstructionist aims through adopting a same-sex cast performing different gendered roles—and the nations/states that were assigned these genders? At the very least, by masking gender identification within the same biological sex, it forces us to reexamine our assumptions of gender roles and the power relationships these roles inhabit. But how does the blurring of gender differences performed through same-sexed bodies provide us with a new lens with which to reexamine the "us/them" binary?

Here the allusion to Britain and China fighting over Hong Kong could not have been clearer. Negotiations over the Sino-British Joint Declaration—a document of such importance that would decide the livelihoods of the five million residents in Hong Kong—have been reduced to the imagery of a domestic squabble. In one version of the play, as Actor A breaks free from Actors B and C, she is pushed by them and falls flat on her back in bed. In other versions, as Actor A attempts to break out of the other two actors' physical confinement and opens her mouth to speak, she is immediately gagged by the other two actors. This climactic moment is interrupted by the playing of the Mandarin version of "The Internationale," as a fourth actor sitting on the stairs on downstage center screams repeatedly at the top of her lungs, "Give me a chance to speak!" while we see the gagged-and-bound Actor A being forcibly taken offstage amid the lyrics heard in the background "Stand up, prisoners of starvation; Stand up, damned of the Earth." No degree of sarcasm could have been more pointed than the juxtaposition of the nondiegetic music with the actions just enacted.

In Actors B and C's bicker, they are continuously engaged in a series of physical activities: pushing, shoving, hugging, and embracing. When an all-female cast reenacted the scene of Actor B hugging Actor C from behind with B wrapping his arms around C's chest, this version provided a more sexualized interpretation. In that same moment when Actress B hugged Actress C from behind, her hands were wrapped around C's breasts. The physical differences between male and female bodies inscribed on them different signs. Only upon seeing Actresses B and C enacting this corporeal act do I wonder if the directors are insinuating that Hong Kong has been sold out by two partners colluding in a complicit sexual affair. Or, is this the directors' way of sending a warning to the political actors that since the Sino-British Joint Declaration was still under discussion when *Chronicle of Three Women* premiered, this complicitous scenario that is alluded to must not be turned into reality?

Returning to our discussion of *Opium War*, toward the end of the performance on the first evening, a chorus of actors assembles upstage, then they exit one by one, leaving only three actors and two empty chairs onstage fading into darkness amid the sounds of cannon shots. We can see from the fading lights that the three actors have moved toward centerstage in the darkness, and when the lights come back on again, facing the audience now are the backs of the three actors and the open side of the empty chairs. Suddenly, the audience realizes that the stage has flipped. Or rather, the presentation of the performance has turned around 180 degrees so that the audience is now viewing from the opposite end of the original mise-en-scène. This visual flipping has surely thrown the audience off and challenged us to reexamine our positionalities from which to view and act. In this moment of epiphany, the open side of the empty chairs now squarely faces the audience and is visually even more confrontational and an immediate challenge to the audience to take up and stake a position. In keeping with Boal's aesthetics, this epiphanous moment creates the effect of demolishing the wall separating actors from spectators, making the "spectators feel that they can intervene in the action" (Boal 1979, 134).

At the end of the second evening's performance, four actors were prancing on and off of the stage, each holding up a huge placard inscribed with a different Chinese character. Their entrances onto the stage at different times form different pairings of the characters each person is holding. Finally, when all four reemerge onstage and stand in a horizontal line, we see two idioms being formed: the first, written in simplified characters in black print on white background, is *chubian bujing* 處變不驚 and when flipped around the placards reveal the second, written in traditional characters in white print on black background, *xin you yuji* 心有餘悸. Forming complementary opposites, the former of the two idioms asks one to "remain composed amid change," yet the latter suggests that one might still "have lingering fear" or "unforgotten trepidation." Which of the two attitudes should Hong Kong adopt to confront 1997? Are these two sides of the same coin? The performance on the second night concluded with actors running onto the stage and taking cover amid the sounds of an alarm siren and explosions.

On the final night of the performance, Zuni initiated the idea of changing the audience's positionality by inviting them up onstage to view the performance that would take place offstage in the auditorium. The Arts Centre authorities rejected this proposal for safety regulation violations: audience members were not insured under the Arts Centre's policies if they were not in seats that were bolted in a consecutive row of four. Just before the performance commenced, Zuni explained the situation to the audience and allowed them to choose between going onstage or remaining in their seats. About thirty audience members ascended the stage, prompting intervention by three of the Arts Centre staff, who made the "persistent threat of closing the theatre, calling in the fire brigade, and withholding future support" if Zuni did not get the audience offstage and return to their seats ("Row" 1984). Meanwhile Zuni actors began the performance by placing blown-up headshot pictures of Marx, Engels, Lenin, Stalin, and Chinese leaders Mao Zedong, Zhu De, and Zhou Enlai in the audience seats, and then moving into the auditorium space. One audience member, Vicky Leung, chairman of the Phoenix Cine Club, recounting the event to the *Hong Kong Standard*, said, "The staff shouted at Zuni saying it was inciting the audience and that if the play was not stopped immediately, they would summon fire services personnel and use *violence*, as a last resort, to evacuate the theatre" (E. Chan 1984). The fire curtain was then dropped onstage, stopping about a meter from the ground only when it hit someone's head, to which audience members shouted, "The Arts Centre is attempting murder!" The lights and sound system were also cut off, leaving Zuni to continue the performance in the auditorium in very dim house lights and with "a portable cassette to play the sound track." Verbal abuse between Zuni, the audience, and the management ensued (E. Chan 1984; L. Yu 2006, 204). Eventually, after Zuni had invited the audience to return to their original seats, in view

FIGURE 4. Scene in performance of *Opium War: Four Letters to Deng Xiaoping*, August 16–19, 1984, Shouson Theatre, Hong Kong Arts Centre. Photo credit © Zuni Icosahedron.

of the authorities' brash behavior in the matter, some audience members refused and remained onstage. When the Arts Centre inquired who they were, one responded, "I've already been invited by Zuni to participate in this play and hence I am an actor!" The staff further queried if they were Zuni members, another riposted in Cantonese, "Ngo hai Zunggwokjan!" (in Mandarin: Wo xi Zhongguoren) 我係中國人 (I am a Chinese), which yielded rave applause from other audience members. Yet another said he refused to sit beside Mao in the audience (Yuan 1984). Amid all this commotion, Zuni actors focused on performing the play. Interestingly, during the heated exchange with the authorities, the lines the actors recited were "keep calm," "change your point of view," "try to think from a different angle" (L. Yu 2006, 204)—the performance appeared to have spilled over into and merged with real life. In the final minutes of the performance, the fire curtain was raised but still without proper lighting (You 1984, 6).

The fiasco saw multiple media exchanges between Zuni and the Arts Centre as well as members of the public who wrote in to express their opinion. General manager of the Arts Centre Nicholas James criticized Zuni for "deliberately provoking the incident and creating a confrontation with the management and the audience," whereas Zuni retorted that the management's use of fire regulations was "an instrument of power" and their lowering of the fire curtain and cutting off the stage lights were "overbearing" ("Row" 1984). Some felt that Zuni performers running hurriedly up and down the narrow aisles of the auditorium was dangerous, and while respecting the need for art to push boundaries, Zuni had disregarded safety regulations (Zhang C. 1984). Others expressed disappointment with the haughty attitude the Arts Centre displayed in handling the entire affair; when contrasted with Zuni's seemingly going its own way in exploring the boundaries of the arts, they felt that instead of intentionally challenging the establishment, the artists were merely interpreting the regulations "differently" from the Arts Centre (Lau 1984; Yuan 1984).

While the play might not be Zuni's most ambitious work to date, it certainly sent ripples through the general public and the arts community on the questions raised regarding public interests, accountability, censorship, sponsorship, and not least safety regulations. Zuni showed that as a collective of individuals it would not bow down to authoritarian dogma and would be willing to confront the authorities when pushed into a corner. They were not afraid because they had been very conscious of documentation, and therefore in a series of follow-up media inquiries, interviews, and commentaries (Lilley 1998, 117), they could provide their side of the story with documented evidence to demonstrate that they were not troublemakers—an unfortunate stereotype with which many artists have been branded. As *South China Morning Post* reported, "It was perhaps the first time in Hongkong that audiences attending a performance were involved in a fiery debate with theatre personnel on such a scale" ("Row" 1984).[7] The fact that members of the audience were willing to stand up to the authorities alongside Zuni during the night of the confrontation at Shouson Theatre and that the general public wrote in to show their support gained it credibility.

This affair achieved significance in at least three areas. Zuni exhibited its uncompromising artistic position and courage to stand up to the authorities. The Shouson controversy provided a chance for the artistic community and bureaucracy to dialogue and clarified the ambiguities in regulations governing artistic practice. The general public also came to be educated in these realms and learn of Zuni's efforts to seek clarity. While detractors considered the theater company as troublemakers who were purposely being confrontational and political, supporters saw them as serious artists committed to pushing for greater artistic space. This really was an important case study in exploring the definition of theater experimentation and the problem of communication between bureaucrats and artists. Had this incident taken place not in Hong Kong but New York, Yung quipped, it would already have been recorded into contemporary art history and become part of the teaching curricula (L. Yu 2006, 204). Hence, the most plausible explanation on why a "relatively minor" event became "so overblown" was 1997 (Lilley 1998, 117). After all, the barriers dividing audience and performance were already broken during HKREP's *The Road*, which Gus Wong and Yung codirected in 1981. What's more, when Seals staged *Stockerlock and Millipilli* 火車歷險記 earlier in December 1980, groups of children were already running up onto the stage at the Shouson Theatre (Ling 1984b). In the words of Rozanna Lilley, "Without the fear that 'One Country, Two Systems' [would] fail to live up to its promise, without the concerns over curtailment of freedom of speech in the SAR, the potential ramifications of every action would not [have been] taken so seriously" (1998, 117).

---

7. The heated exchange on the final night of the performance surrounding the controversy between Zuni and the Hong Kong Arts Centre staff is reproduced in Ling 1984a and You 1984.

Given the current ebb in Sino-Hong Kong relations that has all but hit rock bottom, the comment "I am a Chinese" from an audience member on the final evening of the performance might today raise more than a few eyebrows. I would assume that really was a member of the audience rather than one planted by Zuni to stage this confrontational spectacle. On the one hand, the Arts Centre's handling of the matter, as represented by its general manager Nicholas James, seems to reconstitute the uncomfortable impression of the old colonial hierarchy. The Arts Centre's adamant refusal to negotiate was certainly looked upon disapprovingly in the eyes of the public. In fact, after these media exchanges, this confrontation appeared to convey the image of an all-powerful Arts Centre picking on a resource-strapped independent theater company trying to make an artistic point—very much in the David vs. Goliath fashion. On the other hand, what the audience member said in that exchange would have been taken to mean an identification not with the Chinese Communist Party per se but with Chinese culture at large. In her study of identity in Hong Kong translated theater, Shelby Chan describes a discernible Hong Kong identity surging in the last decade of colonial rule that embraced the Chinese *nation*—and not the Chinese *state*—one that desired "an alternative, better Chinese nation than that proffered by the Chinese state" (2015, 49). This analysis can be just as aptly applied here: identification of being Chinese rests with the individual's affinity with cultural bonds that exceed political representation of any particular state. At the same time, this could also be taken as a critical epiphany moment of decolonization of the arts in Hong Kong.

Repositioning Hong Kong in the Global Chinese Context

As the 1984 Sino-British Joint Declaration announced the impending return of Hong Kong to the People's Republic, sending shock waves across the city, the '97 plays among other artistic and cultural expression sought to locate Hong Kong's identity on the "imminence of its disappearance" (Abbas 1997, 7). Although modern drama in Hong Kong goes beyond the '97 plays, these works were indispensable in defining a local voice at a critical moment of the territory's history. Danny Yung's avant-garde theater played a vital role in spearheading this identity-seeking movement by problematizing the triangulation of the Sino-British-Hong Kong dynamics. After the controversy at the Arts Centre's Shouson Theatre, critics remember Yung as "the man who brought the establishment down on his neck in 1984 with his production of the *Opium War: Four Letters to Deng Xiaoping*" and a trailblazer of "creative theatre in Hongkong, a litmus test as to whether dissent will have a respected, and respectable, place in our future society" (Ram 1988).

The '97 plays sought to investigate an emotionally burdened political problem. In examining their dilemma with the impending return to China, Yung did not merely foreground Hong Kong's plight as a voiceless child sandwiched between two overarching parents pleading to be heard on the international scene. On the contrary, he reversed this power dynamics by placing China in the position of the observed and scrutinizing it from Hong Kong's position, effectively overturning the hierarchy frequently assumed between China and Hong Kong, imputing much subjective agency to the territory. Audiences who attend Zuni plays are thus encouraged in turn to acquire this agency by being challenged to contemplate critically on the questions that require them to fill in the narrative instead of being fed ready-made answers. By doing so, they become active participants in Yung's artmaking process and acquire subjective positions in deciding their own fates. Artist Kurt Chan Yuk-keung 陳育強 considers Yung to be

> a very good initiator who makes us discover the problems in the surroundings and reflect on the framework of one's thinking process. If art is the renovation of all kinds of experiences, which become numb or tired, Danny's works undoubtedly achieve the end result of enlightening their audience. Indeed, sometimes he really needs some very active audiences.
>
> (2003, 22)

This creative aesthetics is clearly influenced by the Brazilian dramatist Augusto Boal, who advocates that "everything is subject to criticism, to rectification" in the theater (1979, 134). Stating in no uncertain terms that "we are also the directors who stage our own actions," Boal champions a theater "where everyone is involved" (1997, 32), a strategy that is evident in *Opium War*.

By making the familiar strange one can develop a new angle of consideration, perhaps explaining Yung's emphasis on Brechtian distanciation in his dramatic praxis. In an interview he mentioned, "Many things and events around us probably deserve to be reevaluated, but we assume them to be natural. If we alter our point of view with which we are familiar to reexamine them, we might be able to see even more" (You 1984, 6). Often when probed Yung's response has never been to provide direct answers but to ask more questions that dig deeper into the issue. Like all of Yung's works, Kurt Chan suggests the way Yung's "discourse takes place is in a form of questions, putting forward his various opinions. Most of his works are in fact posing questions rather than conveying concrete messages" (2003, 22). Similarly, in "Theatre of the Oppressed," in place of expounding "a message or a revealed truth," Boal tries "to ask the right questions instead of" providing what are considered "the right answers" (1997, 36). In offering questions and not answers, therefore, Yung helps the respondent to contemplate more deeply, ruminate from greater angles, and discern other possibilities, hence opening up more alternatives.

In foregrounding Hong Kong's subjective agency, Yung also connects it to a larger perspective. The 1989 Tiananmen Square Incident in particular prompted a considerable shift in Yung's notion of Chineseness, pushing him henceforth to foster connections between Hong Kong and global artistic communities more acutely (W. Lim 2021, 53). For instance, he saw the One Country, Two Systems policy, which guarantees the capitalist economic system and the rights and freedoms of the Hong Kong people to remain unchanged for at least fifty years beyond the 1997 handover, as an unrivaled opportunity for artistic innovation as the city-state entered into a bifurcated political structure yet unrealized in the world. In the *Cultural Perspective Hong Kong 1997* 香港九七文化視野文件集 policy study Zuni compiled, the proposal recommended that just as Hongkongers attempt to understand China, Hong Kong culture must be introduced to the mainland to achieve greater mutual understanding (Woo and Leung (1996a) 1997, 2). In stark contrast to many Hongkongers madly rushing to learn Mandarin to make up for their deficiency in their soon-to-be national language, Yung's plays as well as his policy proposals have always sought to come up with alternative viewpoints and foreground Hong Kong's agency.

On the one hand, Yung ardently advocates Hong Kong art and subjectivity and promotes the visibility of Hong Kong on the global scene; on the other, he also displays great concern for Chinese and global culture. For example, contrary to the widespread apprehension that Hong Kong culture would be subsumed under the sheer mass of its mammoth neighbor in post-'97, Zuni has proposed that "Hong Kong should take up the responsibility of building the new Chinese culture, for Hong Kong is a part of China and Chinese culture has never been unchanging" (Woo and Leung (1996b) 1997, 4), distinctly identifying the major contribution Hong Kong can make in this new nexus. At the invitation of the Japanese government to direct the main show of the Japan Pavilion for the 2010 Shanghai World Expo, Yung proposed that he would do so only with the inclusion of cultural workers from Nanjing. This again demonstrates Yung's willingness to play the bridge-building role in his attempt to dissolve "the emotional hang-ups behind the blind spot" in Sino-Japanese relations. Yung was invoking the painful trauma of Japan's wartime atrocities in Nanjing (specifically, the Nanjing Massacre of 1937) during the Second World War and the intense yet unresolved prejudices between China and Japan in a bid "to tackle the affective barriers that still divide the two societies" (Ferrari 2017, 147) and "help establish a meaningful and strategic communication platform to face the scars left behind by history" (Yung 2011, 24). As I have attempted to demonstrate, Yung is an intellectual who would not cohere to simplistic binaries but rather raises the level of discussion to a much higher plane, contemplating complex issues of politics and identity from a longer historical perspective. As he states, matter-of-factly, "This is what artists can, and should, do" (Yung 2011, 24).

Yung's disregard for boundaries is evidenced in his work to not only cross the genres of theater, installation, music, dance, and film, but also transcend national borders and establish cross-cultural interactions with artists from different parts of the world. For instance, his experimental films, videos, and installations have also been shown in festivals in Europe, Asia, and the United States (Amranand 2008). Many of his collaborations with foreign artists also cross the traditional-contemporary temporal divide; for example, in *Lu gui bu* 錄鬼簿 (Book of ghosts, 2009), he worked with four Asian traditional performing arts masters from Bangkok, Jakarta, Nanjing, and Taipei to devise experimental performances on the theme of "'Ghosts' to reconnect the past with present," as described at the Zuni website (http://www.zuni.org.hk). He staunchly believes in the vital role artistic exchange plays in cultural development. Artists are able to exercise greater freedom during cultural exchange "to comment on other countries' situations" from an "outsider's perspective" as they "dialogue with artists from different countries" and regions (Amranand 2008). In Yung's own words:

> I don't see boundaries in arts . . . when you talk about cultural exchange, you're talking about two parties. So it's a concern of both parties on both sides. If I'm not from Hong Kong, should I take Hong Kong taxpayers' money to do this and to do that?

Come on, this is old-fashioned talking. Don't think that way. There's a regional identity. There's a global identity. There's a local identity. Cultural practitioners should be global citizens and should initiate global citizen responsibility.

(Amranand 2008)

With regard to "Zuni's attempt to speak to the theatrical and cultural hegemony of Hong Kong throughout the 1980's and beyond," Stephen Chan surmises that the group's "avant-gardist strategy has been organized primarily to examine the extent of boundaries (of the stage, of theatre, of politics, of love, of sex) and explore the possibilities of retracing the very logic of boundary itself" (1992, 37). Breaking down boundaries between disciplines and institutions is important because, says Yung, "artists and business people, critics and the general public, can all feel they are part of a joint enterprise. We need global culture advocates. All of us have to pick up the responsibility to help global culture develop" (K. Wong 2006).

Beyond 1997, Yung proposed with great ambition during the preparation phases of the West Kowloon Cultural District 西九龍文化區 that it should be developed as the arts center of the region. Initially, this forty-hectare megasite was proposed to become a conglomeration of arts and culture, fashion, consumerism, leisure, and mass entertainment. Yung was one of the few artists who sat on the West Kowloon Cultural District Authority Board from 2008 to 2014, after which he resigned citing as reasons the board directors' and management's lacking cultural vision, research and development, on top of their overly bureaucratic style of management ("Xijiu" 2014). During its planning stages, Yung highlighted all of Hong Kong's preexisting strengths over its regional cities and proposed that by hiring the best arts think-tanks and artistes, the city could become the Chinese Cultural Experimental Centre 中華文化實驗中心 and Global Cultural Centre 世界文化中心. When asked if Hong Kong has a population huge enough to consume the voluminous arts that will inevitably be produced by the cultural district, Yung responded in his customary rhetorical style: that depends on whether one has enough cultural vision and will to situate and transform Hong Kong into a regional cultural hub encompassing the Pearl River Delta, Macau, and Taiwan (Zhang Z. 2004, 44), squarely underscoring the centrality of Hong Kong yet simultaneously connecting it to a wider expanse beyond its immediate shores.

CHAPTER 4

Diaspora within China
Gao Xingjian and the Theater of Exile

On October 12, 2000, when the Swedish Academy announced Gao Xingjian 高行健 as the Nobel Literature laureate—and hence the first Chinese winner of the coveted prize—readers in both the Chinese- and English-speaking worlds were shocked. At the time of the award not many in China were familiar with Gao's name (Lovell 2006, 7), as he had basically become a persona non grata in his country of birth since his self-imposed exile to France in 1987. A de facto ban had been imposed on his works after he tore up his passport on international television denouncing the Chinese authorities' clampdown in the 1989 Tiananmen Square Incident (M. Lee 2006, 11). In the English-speaking world many were equally puzzled. Jennifer Ruark remarked that "American readers looking for books by Gao Xingjian ... wondered if they were banned in the United States as well as in China" when they failed to locate copies of his work in bookstores, following the hype of Gao's winning of the coveted prize (2000, A18). In Taiwan and Hong Kong, however, Gao was generally celebrated as a *Chinese* writer who had broken the century-long wait for the Nobel Prize in Literature (Lovell 2006, 7). Importantly, he is one who uses the *fangkuai zi* 方塊字, Chinese-squared characters, the writing system unique to the Chinese that has become a symbol of cultural pride and continuity in the long history of its unbroken civilization, in his creative writing. Of those who knew of Gao, they recognized him to be a pioneering figure in the early 1980s experimental drama scene in China. Sinologists learned of his reputation as an avant-garde writer having expounded treatises on experimenting with techniques of fiction writing as well as plays that got him into trouble with the authorities that later forced him to take flight from his home country. At the same time, some Chinese intellectuals and writers also felt bitter about the Nobel Committee's decision, wondering why the coveted prize was awarded to "an exile writer whose very 'Chineseness' was somehow in question" since he had "abandoned the homeland" and taken up French citizenship (Denton 2002, iii).

Prior to Gao's self-imposed exile to France, he was already a known entity outside the mainland. As early as 1982, the production of his first play by the Beijing People's Art Theatre (BPAT), *Alarm Signal* (1982), was hailed by the French newspaper *Cosmopolitan* as "the birth of avant-garde theatre in Beijing" (Gao (1991) 2006, 143).¹ Since the early 1990s scholars in Europe had been studying, discussing, and translating his works (Moran 2013, 67): he has been invited to guest lecture in Germany and France, his ink paintings exhibited in Austria, Denmark, Germany, and France, and his works staged, radio broadcasted, and translated in Yugoslavia, Hungary, Hong Kong, London, and France (Shelby Chan 2010). Julia Lovell's analysis of the Chinese quest for the Nobel Prize in Literature demonstrates the paradoxical nature of such a "complex" (*Nuobei'er qingjie* 諾貝爾情結). She finds that the anxious need for China's "belief to be affirmed by the West" reveals two contradictory elements: on the one hand is an "insecurity about Chinese national identity and the obsession with a diseased Chinese culture," and on the other is a self-aggrandizing "cultural machismo, angrily sensitive to slights and humiliations, [and one] that asserts China's cultural uniqueness" (2006, 7). Many historical factors account for this complex.

This chapter examines the Chinese state's hegemonic attempts at cultural definition and the critical responses of its artists in the 1980s. I focus on the example of Gao Xingjian, a pioneering figure who came to prominence in the avant-garde dramatic scene with his *Alarm Signal*, and whose reputation reached its acme with his second experimental play *Chezhan* 車站 (Bus stop, 1983). Labelled "anti-Party," "antisocialist" (Quah 2004b, 10–11), and at the same time a "great leap forward"

---

1. Luo Liang's (2014) study traces avant-garde drama on mainland China to Tian Han and his contemporaries as early as the 1920s.

for its "striking departure from the play-writing and theatrical convention of the past forty years" (Tay 1990, 113; S. Yu 1997, 18), the artistic merits and political contentions *Bus Stop* has simultaneously evoked are enough to distinguish it as a piece worthy of closer examination in its historicity. Scholars have studied various aspects of Western modernist influences in the play, comparing it to *Waiting for Godot*, with some even calling it a Chinese version of Samuel Beckett's seminal play. For instance, while Yu Shiao-ling argues that both plays are about the futility of waiting (1997, 17), Yan Haiping suggests that Gao's play is "no mere imitation of European modernism": Godot suspends any possibility for change, but the protagonist in *Bus Stop* is one "who tropes humanistic enlightenment and an individual search for direction in life at a moment of social transformation and political uncertainty" (2001, 22–23). William Tay too supposes that "the Silent Man is ultimately an allegorical representation of determination and hope" (1990, 117). For its technical innovations and philosophical treatment of waiting, Tam Kwok-kan argues that the play is "the most important milestone" in breaking away from the Ibsenian dramatic tradition and introducing absurdist theater to the Chinese stage (2001b, 65). Indeed, what distinguished the play was its formal qualities, Quah Sy Ren adds, instead of content, which in turn attracted it criticism (2004b, 64). Others like Jessica Yeung Wai-yee have approached the play through the paradigm of cultural translation, considering it as Gao's effort in "translating Modernism into China" to address issues that are manifested on the Chinese stage (2008, 60). My analysis builds on the illuminating insights of these previous studies and focuses on identity and diaspora, arguing that the play is Gao's attempt at deviating from the state-sanctioned narrative of selfhood and wresting the right of cultural definition away from the political center.

Wang Jing's study of high culture in politics, aesthetics, and ideology in the post-Mao era reminds us of how the Chinese postrevolutionary literature is inseparable from the 1980s' intellectual and cultural history, with its literature corresponding "intimately to the succession of ideas that swept over the ideological field" (1996, 4). Gao's rise to fame in the theatrical world of that decade must be understood in the context of the broader literary and cultural movements amid the political changes in that era. The central feature of this period was Deng Xiaoping's reform policies instituted in the wake of the Cultural Revolution of 1966 to 1976. The brainchild of the last years of Mao Zedong, this had in theory given top priority to class struggle but in practice thrown the country into turmoil, set back the economy, and in particular harmed the intellectual and artistic classes through clamping down on any free expression, driving many to suicide.

Gao's innovations in theater predated the *gaige wenxue* 改革文學 (reform literature), *shanghen wenxue* 傷痕文學 (scar literature), and *xungen wenxue* 尋根文學 (roots-seeking literature) (Quah 2004b, 74), yet the central position these movements occupied in Chinese literary history paint the broader scenario from which he emerged. Although Gao might not have claimed allegiance to any of these literary movements that engaged in a nationwide fever in experimenting with cultural traditions, these writers were all responding to the same political and social issues. Writers of these movements were in turn using their own modes of literary expression to respond to the changes occurring in the state that had had a totalizing impact on the individual. In this sense, despite Gao's insistence on "his independence, his desire for unlimited creative freedom and his right to transgress the borders of art," he remains, in the words of Izabella Łabędzka, "to a certain extent the 'child of his times'" (2008, 5). Drama of the new period, following other forms of art and literature of the same era, began as a critical response to the Cultural Revolution (Yan 1998, ix). As an aftermath of this "crisis of faith" (S. Yu 1997, 5-6), many looked to a past prior to the history of the People's Republic by seeking ancient myths that defined an earlier beginning of what it means to be Chinese. Therefore, an alternative Chineseness was sought not just across Singapore, Taiwan, and Hong Kong, but also within China. As I have discussed in the preceding examples, China's coming out of the Cultural Revolution ignited an identity crisis in the other three regions with a majority of ethnic Chinese, and likewise within mainland China, intellectuals/artists too were seeking what it means to be Chinese beyond the state's endorsement. Therefore, I propose the term "diaspora within China" to describe Gao's example: one who was born and bred in China and chose to reside on society's periphery for critique and reflection.

For the longest time because the function of modern Chinese drama had been didactic, drama reformers wanted to seek alternative forms of aesthetics to "break away from the existing dramatic dogma," which served such ideological purposes and had pervaded the contemporary Chinese theater scene (Quah 2004b, 46). The purpose of art, for Gao, was different. Neither to moralize nor champion anyone else's cause, Gao envisioned a theatrical aesthetics that would encourage proactive thinkers in both his actors and audience. He is unwilling to be in the servitude of the state or a spokesman of the revolutionaries. His lack of interest in creating work that champions the democracy movement is evident, for example, in *Taowang* 逃亡 (Escape, 1989), a play he had written based on the 1989 Tiananmen Square massacre, where he does not appear to be sympathetic to the cause of the student protestors and has in several instances even criticized them for being childish and unrealistic. Emotionally, Gao might be with the student demonstrators, but rationally, he would be failing his "intellectual consciousness" if he does not condemn the acts of the demonstrators as idealistic and naïve (Quah 2004b, 180). He sees that man is like a little bug, powerless against the state, and art's only (critical) function is to set oneself free. From Gao's experiences with the Chinese Communist Party (CCP), he sees fleeing as his way of survival: When a person is faced with a powerful institution such as the State, what choice does he have besides fleeing (Quah 2004b, 7)? Indeed, in his Nobel address, Gao advocates, "If the writer sought to win intellectual freedom the choice was either to fall silent or to flee. . . . This is the inevitable fate of the poet and the writer who continues to seek to preserve his own voice" (2001, 595). Commenting on Gao's act of fleeing, the critic Liu Zaifu states that the earliest examples of self-imposed literary exiles in Chinese history are Bo Yi 伯夷 and Shu Qi 叔齊, who did so as a rejection to the dynastic change from Shang to Zhou (c. 1046 BC). More importantly, their action is a continuation of the humanitarian spirit of nonviolence, and Gao's abscondence should be understood in this light (Liu Z. 2000, 8–9). Writing was considered an extremely dangerous act under Mao's dictatorship, even if done covertly, and one could not trust talking to anyone but him- or herself to maintain one's intellectual autonomy (M. Lee 2002a, 36). Only during the height of the Cultural Revolution, "when it was utterly impossible for literature," did Gao come to appreciate why creative writing was "so essential": because "literature allows a person to preserve a human consciousness" (Gao 2001, 595). Consequently, Gao has always sought to be on the peripheries of society, silently contemplating and critically reflecting on the fervor in the center, without having to be "swallowed up by fads or social establishments" (Fong 2005, viii). Long before he took off for France, his quest for an alternative aesthetics had already deviated from the mode of expression of the majority, making him a diasporic figure within his own country. And that is exactly what the protagonist, the Silent Man, in his play *Bus Stop* did.

The Cultural Revolution and Its Aftermath

After the 1949 Communist Revolution, fundamental changes shook up China's social fabric and reshaped all aspects of social life, challenging traditions and cultural legacies, and instituting Marxism-Leninism-Maoism as the official creed. This transformation permeated all levels of society and reached its calamitous peak during the Cultural Revolution, where a wave of uncontrollable fury and social turbulence swept the entire country. Discernibly, this period was when

> a new *selfhood* based on socialist ethics and epistemology came into existence. [And] it was not until the early 1980s, with the reinstatement of the "Open Door" policy that the authoritarian rule of the Communist Party was considerably shaken. For a short period of time there was a sense of expectancy among the people, who anticipated the emergence of a more liberal society. . . . Needless to say, these powerful and far-reaching social convulsions had a tremendous impact on the *shaping and reshaping of personhood* on the Chinese mainland.
> (Tam, Yip, and Dissanayake 1999, xii; italics mine)

Originating as an internal purging of dissident voices within the CCP, the Cultural Revolution erupted into a decade-long disorder that saw a massive wastage of human and material resources. For most of these ten years, up until at least the announcement of US president Richard Nixon's visit in July 1971, China's relations with the rest of the world were very sparse. All cultural creativity was stifled, and the eight model revolutionary operas promoted by Mao's wife Jiang Qing and the Gang of Four became the blueprint for all cultural production (Mackerras 1989, 100).[2] The saying of the times was "eight plays for eight hundred million people," with the dramatic stage almost barren otherwise (Ye 2008, 179). Ironically, Jiang Qing and the Gang of Four and their associates, who were largely ideologists, literary critics, and theatrical performers, were the very "literary" people who "virtually destroyed the Chinese theater; their obsessive concern about the power of theater led them to seek absolute control of that 'powerful' weapon" (Tung 1987, 5). Mabel Lee surmises that the mental rigid conformity of the period created "symptoms of spiritual deprivation" that yielded "a voracious appetite for the rations of personal freedom" (1996, 98). Thus, a wide

---

2. For studies of the model revolutionary operas, see X. Chen 2002 and Roberts 2010.

vacuum for artistic innovation and experimental work opened up in the immediate post–Cultural Revolution period for a Chinese audience starved of artistic nourishment.

Even though the decade of the 1980s was considered as a period of relative political openness and relaxation, the atmosphere at large did not herald a predictable constant. The Cultural Revolution ended with Mao's demise in 1976, propelling China into a new developmental phase with ramifications in all spheres of society. In literature and the arts, this was known as the *Xin shiqi* 新時期 (New era), which was characterized with movements spearheaded by artists known as the "reform literature," "scar literature," and "roots-seeking literature" that reflected on that catastrophic decade. On the one hand, this signaled the state's seemingly increased tolerance for criticism. Attempting to interpret the shocking violence and buzzing confusion of recent Chinese history, writers asked: Why do we Chinese do such things to one another? What went wrong? Because China had by then been almost entirely isolated from the free world for three decades, an intense curiosity to explore the West to see what people in China had been missing arose (Link 1984, 22–23). These young writers documented and protested problems in society that questioned state authority, engaging in heated literary debates that pitted realism against modernism 「現實主義還是現代主義」的批判 (Gao (1993) 2001, 4). On the other hand, state-sanctioned movements such as the Anti-Bourgeois Liberalization Campaign 反對資產階級自由化運動 (1981) and the Anti-Spiritual Pollution Campaign (1983) simultaneously clamped down further dialogue with civil society. Gao Xingjian himself was a victim of such attacks. In its attempt to introduce novel techniques of fiction writing from the West, his handbook *Xiandai xiaoshuo jiqiao chutan* 現代小說技巧初探 (Preliminary explorations on the art of fiction, 1981) sparked the debate on modernism in Chinese literary circles (M. Lee 1996, 103). Even after the book received praise from respected writers such as Wang Meng 王蒙 (b. 1934), who would soon become China's minister of culture, urging Gao to "continue exploring" (Gao (1991) 2006, 142), it was still banned during its reprint the year after "for promoting the Modernism of decadent bourgeois capitalist Western literature." This calamitous event seemed to become a recurrent episode in Gao's continued struggles with the state: despite the attention *Bus Stop* generated in the following year—or perhaps, because of it—the play was shut down after a few performances. Fearing the possibility of being locked away in one of the notorious prison farms in

Qinghai province, Gao escaped by fleeing to the western and southwestern parts of China, returning only when desire for his arrest had cooled in Beijing (M. Lee 2002a, 33–34).

Referring to this fluctuation as the "national literature weather," Perry Link pinpoints this phenomenon customary in socialist China to derive from "the amount and type of pressure or interference that the national political leadership applied to the literary scene." Good weather meant a broader freedom of expression, bad weather less, but

> how much freedom any given writer enjoyed at any particular moment was determined by more than the general weather ... and everyone's limits tended to shift when the weather changed. ... Because political leaders sometimes used literary outlets to broach purely political moves, the literary weather could have significance not just for stories and poems but for all of society.
>
> (Link 2000, 14)

Scholars have argued that the reason this type of "literature of lament and recrimination" could be propagated in the new era was because it found use to Deng Xiaoping "as an integral part of a controlled expression of discontent." However, since this new literary mode "hardly differed from the establishment's old model," it was first allowed and then even encouraged by the state because it "challenged little in terms of the politics of aesthetics" (G. Lee 2012, 109). Scar literature was launched with Liu Xinwu's 劉心武 (b. 1942) "Ban zhuren" 班主任 (Homeroom teacher, 1977) and got its name from Lu Xinhua's 盧新華 (b. 1954) short story "Shanghen" 傷痕 (Scar, 1978). While "Homeroom Teacher" tells of a juvenile delinquent who cuts class and a young woman whose model leftist characteristics turn her into an ignorant and insensitive bigot, suggesting the flaws of both characters to spring from the madness of the Cultural Revolution, "Scar" describes the mindless zealotry in the young female protagonist's environment that destroyed relations with her parents as well as boyfriend for no good reason (Link 2000, 17). Characterized by its strong denunciation of "the excesses of the Cultural Revolution" and the unspeakable misery the intellectual class experienced in the decade (G. Lee 2012, 109), Gao Xingjian applauds the genre for having revived literature's ability to critique reality ((1992) 2001, 120).

In the sphere of poetry, the work of the *menglong* 朦朧 ("obscure" or "misty") poets such as Bei Dao 北島 (b. 1949) and Yang Lian 楊煉 (b. 1955) espouse a kind of poetic sensibility "detached from clear-cut political messages" (X. Chen 1991, 143). In no way does this suggest that their poetry was apolitical, however. Quite the contrary, by responding to hymnal poetry, the dominant mode of poetic expression in praise of Mao and the CCP, misty poetry in fact conveyed disappointment with the CCP's lost idealism, corruption, and bureaucracy (X. Chen 1991, 144). Therefore, *menglong* poetry could be taken to embody the mood of disillusionment then pervasive in China that defied existing norms and conventions in a bid to strive for "new approaches to literature and art" (Yeh 2003, 523).

Leo Lee Ou-fan considers the 1980s' "roots-seeking literature" to be primarily an "anticenter" movement launched by young writers who were exploring the source of their own cultural origins in areas other than the political center. The younger generation felt severed from their cultural roots because the ideological campaigns of recent decades, and the Cultural Revolution in particular, had so deeply ruptured Chinese culture that they "must go in search of them" at the political peripheries (L. Lee 1991, 207–8). The roots these authors were searching for were less personal and familial and more cultural and historical (L. Lee 1989, xiii). As part of a cultural interrogation of Chineseness, the roots-seeking writers, such as novelists Han Shaogong 韓少功 (b. 1953) and winner of the 2012 Nobel Prize in Literature Mo Yan 莫言 (b. 1955), reexamined the central elite Han cultural hegemony shared by both Confucianism and communism to seek "an alternative basis for Chinese identity on the margins of China" in geographically remote regions like Tibet or parallel philosophical traditions like Taoism (G. Lee 2012, 166). Almost all these young writers had been sent to the countryside as *zhiqing* 知青 (educated youths) during the Cultural Revolution, spending a large part of their formative years living among the rural population. That they would look to the remote rural and minority areas for inspiration is therefore of little surprise. Imagined somehow as preserves of cultures "untouched by the homogenizing influence of modernization, westernization, and even Chinese revolution" (Leenhouts 2003, 534), roots writers considered the political peripheries to be "culturally richer than the center," hence divesting Beijing further of its political authority (L. Lee 1991, 207–8).

Several of these avant-garde fictions have, in addition, been successfully adapted onto the silver screen, such as Xie Jin's 謝晉 (1923–2008) *Furong zhen* 芙蓉鎮 (Hibiscus town, 1986) and Zhang Yimou's 張藝謀 (b. 1951) *Hong gaoliang* 紅高粱 (Red sorghum, 1987) and *Dahong denglong gaogaogua* 大紅燈籠高高掛 (Raise the red lantern, 1991), reaching a far wider audience beyond the traditional readership, which marked their acclaimed status as the third and fifth generation of Chinese filmmakers respectively. Chen Kaige's 陳凱歌 (b. 1952) *Huang tudi* 黃土地 (Yellow earth, 1984), for example, pioneered the avant-garde film genre to address the issue of state legitimacy by raising "the question of the Other voice—a true voice of the people that seems muffled and suppressed by the sound and the fury of the Communist Revolution" (L. Lee 1991, 210). Importantly, according to Zhang Xudong, this was a movement that "redefined the field of Chinese filmmaking visually as well as politically." The genre developed "a cinematic language disassociated from" the official discourse of socialist realism that hence created "a space of representation for an emergent public" to reflect on and consider "the cultural perplexity, ideological dilemma, and political ambivalence of China at the crossroads of its revolutionary past and its unknown future" (X. Zhang 1997, 5). Collectively, these avant-garde films focused on the repercussions of the Cultural Revolution, the ills of Chinese society, and the inadequacy of the CCP. At the same time, these cinematic representations share an interest with the fictional form from which they were adapted in their attention to regional customs and the conflict between tradition and modernity, magic realism, ethnic minorities, and nature that presented "marginal cultures as alternatives to the mainstream" (Leenhouts 2003, 536). The intellectual impetus of this literary movement has also given rise to a broader movement of "cultural self-reflection," which, as Leo Lee surmises, is

> a critical reexamination of all aspects of Chinese culture and history. [And] the dissatisfaction stems directly from a profound sense of disillusionment with the Cultural Revolution which ironically reduced Chinese culture to rubble. It is out of this sense of void that these writers, artists, and intellectuals feel compelled to redefine their own culture as they seek to redefine themselves: How to find a meaning of being Chinese other than what the Party has defined for them?
>
> (1991, 208)

Emergence of Gao Xingjian

From his experience growing up under the Maoist dictatorship, Gao Xingjian has developed a natural opposition to hegemony and any claim to orthodoxy—not just political but cultural and artistic as well.

Gao's response to the "vehement and feverish literature of the Cultural Revolution" where the maddening and fanatical roaring of the blind collective had so engulfed the individual, causing him/her to lose his/her senses, is his notion of "Cold Literature" (Fong 2005, xx). This type of literary expression proposes the writer to coldly observe the spectacle around him/her and write with an emotionally distanced and critical mind, which is "literature at its most fundamental." However, Gao states categorically that

> a writer should not totally disassociate himself from society. While refraining from active intervention in social and political issues, he should "exile" himself but at the same time take a position on the margin of society, thus facilitating his undisturbed observations on life and the self. . . . "Cold literature" survives by means of exile, and it strived to escape from the strangulation of society to conserve itself.
>
> (Fong 1999, xvi)

In his Nobel lecture, he notes that contemporary Chinese intellectual history has witnessed an era where literature was "deeply scarred by politics and power," and therefore the writer has no choice but to flee in order to preserve his artistic independence (Gao 2001, 594–95). To be sure, as a continuation of the long tradition of Chinese literary ethics, emerging playwrights in the early 1980s saw themselves as "speakers for the common folk" and "authors of social conscience and cultural change" (Yan 2001, 21). Enshrined since the beginning of China's modern literature, this "mentality of self-sacrifice for the nation" is something of which Gao is extremely wary (M. Lee 2002a, 38). He cautions that the call for patriotism and nationalist impulses are the "most reactionary of watchwords" utilized by the Nazis of the past and the CCP of today to "trick people." In his view, Chinese intellectuals keep going down the same old path of constantly engaging in revolution because they are not "mature enough" and would require a detached and independent attitude to learn that there is really no need to speak for the collective (Lee and Dutrait 2001, 743–44). While Gao might have publicly expressed his notion of cold literature in writing only in 1990,[3] as

---

3. These views were first expressed in writing in the essay "Wo zhuzhang yizhong leng de wenxue" 我主張一種冷的文學 (I advocate a kind of cold literature) completed in Paris on July 30, 1990, and published in the supplementary section *Shidai wenxue* 時代文學 of the Taiwan newspaper *Zhongshi wanbao* 中時晚報 (Aug. 12, 1990).

will be made clear in my analysis below, these ideas were germinating long before and evidenced in his plays as early as *Bus Stop*.

As the site of power, for Gao, the center "represents constraints, manipulation and repression leading to the loss of freedom" (Fong 2005, xl). Consequently he has retreated to the margins of society, taking refuge there as a diasporic member within his own state. Deviating from the mainstream, Gao's critical sensibilities drove him to explore other sources of Chinese heritage and experiment with a new theatrical aesthetics. He is of the view that contemporary Chinese thought has hitherto been dominated by Confucianism and Han culture from the northern central plains. Therefore, Gao has attempted to draw creative resources from the pre-Confucian, non-Han cultures, Taoism, and Zen Buddhism, as well as the folk, ritualistic, and tribal materials as represented by Qiang, Miao, and Yi districts located on the fringes of Han Chinese civilization (M. Lee 2000, viii). These either prioritize the primitive and peripheral nonliterati cultures 非文人文化 of the Yangtze south over the northern Han literati culture (Gao (1987) 2001, 116; Quah 2004b, 74) or challenge a singular dogmatic hegemony, and are adequately manifested in many of his later works such as *The Other Shore* (1986), *Soul Mountain* (1989), *Duihua yu fanjie* 對話與反詰 (Dialogue and rebuttal, 1992), and *Bayue xue* 八月雪 (Snow in August, 1997), among others.

Meiyou zhuyi 沒有主義 (Without isms), Gao's famous dictum, perhaps most aptly sums up his position. Despite being labeled as "avant-garde," "modernist," "absurdist," "roots-seeking," and even "counter revolutionary," Gao rejects labeling onto him any particular school of thought or "ism" (Gao (1993) 2001, 4). When asked during his exile days in France if he misses China or would have a problem writing for Chinese audiences since he has been living abroad for so long (Yeung 2000, 188), Gao responded that he is neither interested in writing specifically for a Chinese audience nor does he need geopolitical China since "the cultural traditions of China naturally reside within [him]" (Gao 2001, 596). In other words, his consistent refusal to be branded, stereotyped, or claimed by any doctrine or affiliation is an outright statement that he chooses to go his own way and rejects being told how to *be Chinese*.[4] Gao's artistic expression alternative to the status quo is motivated by a broader cultural reflection of the times: his is also "a

---

4. I am grateful to Wang Chun-yen for this insight.

quest for identities," and by implication, to apply Leo Lee's observation of the avant-garde writers onto Gao, "raise new and profound questions about what it means to be a Chinese even *inside* China" (1991, 209–11). Positioning himself on the diaspora of Chinese culture allowed Gao to constantly *dis*identify with the state's definition of Chineseness and chart his own path.

As with the realms of poetry, film, and fiction, at the end of the Cultural Revolution, Chinese dramatists similarly began searching for new ways of expression to liberate theater from the restrictions of the previous decades (S. Yu 2007, 821). On the one hand are plays that had been extremely popular but denounced during the Cultural Revolution being brought back to the stage, indicating "the ending of an era in the nation's cultural and political life and the beginning of what has been called 'a dramatic renaissance'"; on the other are works that condemned the massive political persecution enforced during those devastating ten years, such as Zong Fuxian's 宗福先 (b. 1947) *Yu wusheng chu* 於無聲處 (From the depth of silence, 1978) and Xing Yixun's 邢益勳 (b. 1941) *Quan yu fa* 權與法 (Power versus law, 1979). While these works still accounted for a nostalgic longing for the early years of the People's Republic of China, later dramas attempted to reevaluate "some of the most critical and complex experiences of the nation since 1949" (Yan 1998, ix–xii), such as Li Longyun's 李龍雲 (1948–2012) *Xiaojing hutong* 小井胡同 (Small well alley, 1981), which is notable for its strong element of social criticism and "sense of historical depth" (Cheung and Lai 1997, xv).

Another direction in which this dramatic renaissance headed was the spirit of experimentation that began to flourish in art and also influenced everyday life. What emerged on the dramatic stage known as *tansuo ju* 探索劇 (exploratory drama), *shiyan ju* 實驗劇 (experimental drama), and *xianfeng ju* 先鋒劇 (avant-garde drama) "generated some of the most interesting and perhaps most valuable phenomena in China's cultural heritage" (Łabędzka 2008, 9). This new dramaturgy delved into "private concerns and humanistic values" instead of "collective and class-based themes" that reflected on the nation's culture and history. Rather than adhering to behavioral models and providing straightforward answers to socioexistential questions, these dramatic explorations veered off from didacticism yet imbedded in them humanistic and modernist tropes that were "not entirely apolitical or devoid of subversive connotations" (Ferrari 2012, 16). Many notable experimental plays emerged in the period, including Liu Shugang's 劉樹綱

(1940–2022) *Yige sizhe dui shengzhe de fangwen* 一個死者對生者的訪問 (A dead man's interview of the living, 1985) and Wang Peigong's 王培公 (b. 1943) *WM women* WM我們 (We, 1985), pushing the reform of drama to a high point with the explosion of experimental works in the mid-1980s (S. Yu 1997, 6).

Artistically the most successful of the satirical plays written and in circulation soon after the end of the Maoist era that dealt with corruption and "backdoorism" in official practice, which tested "the limits of censorship," was *Jiaru wo shi zhende* 假如我是真的 (What if I really were?, 1979) by playwright Sha Yexin 沙葉新 (1939–2018) and actors Li Shoucheng 李守成 and Yao Mingde 姚明德 (Gunn 2013). Bearing a certain semblance to Nikolai Gogol's *The Inspector-General*, in this play, a working-class young man without any connection to the powerful and privileged impersonates the son of an important party official so as to obtain permission to return to his home city to marry his pregnant girlfriend before the child's delivery (X. Chen 2003, 443), only to find himself at the receiving end of bribes and favor-currying by high-ranking officials in the hope of gaining bigger ignoble favors. By placing its focus on "negative and morally flawed characters" (Gunn 1983b, 198), *What If I Really Were?* affords sympathy to this hooligan-protagonist, blurring the distinction between good and bad characters "for the first in a long time" in a play that attempts to earnestly explore current social issues (DiBello 1996, 25–26). What was even bolder perhaps was the timing of the play's setting—two years after the Cultural Revolution has concluded—suggesting that party corruption did not end with the fall of the Gang of Four, who were no longer in power (X. Chen 2003, 443). The fault, therefore, must lie somewhere else: perhaps the current regime or the socialist system in general (DiBello 1996, 26).

While the "wounded" and exposé plays of the late 1970s did indeed break down certain subject matters that were until then deemed off-limits, Yu Shiao-ling points out that with the exception of *What If I Really Were?*, these exploratory works did "not differ very much from those produced in the previous thirty years" (1997, 4). Hence, although experimental works like *Wo weishenme si le* 我為甚麼死了 (Why have I died?, 1979) by Xie Min 謝民 and *Wuwai you reliu* 屋外有熱流 (Hot springs outside, 1980) by Ma Zhongjun 馬中竣 (b. 1957), Jia Hongyuan 賈鴻源 (b. 1951), and Qu Xinhua 瞿新華 (b. 1955) predated *Alarm Signal*, nevertheless, critics are in general agreement that it was not until Gao Xingjian's first play to be staged by BPAT that experimental drama had achieved a significant impact, marking the emergence of China's "little theater movement" (Tian and Song 1999, 93; Chen Jide 2004, 250–51). As Martha Cheung Pui-Yiu and Jane Lai point out, the movement was of enormous significance in the history of modern Chinese theater "for its liberating effect on the dramatists and audience alike," getting them to seriously reconsider the "fundamental assumptions about the function and purpose of spoken drama," which for the past seven decades had been to educate the masses and serve the country's needs. Instead, the little theater now became a congregating space where actors and audience shared full and exciting experiences, which liberated the imagination and established a vital alternative theater (1997, xviii). Employing techniques such as flashbacks and changes in perspective with an emphasis on character psychology, *Alarm Signal*, shocked its audience because its presentation mode deviated significantly from established theater practice in the country (M. Lee 2006, 5). The young protagonist Heizi has been jobless for three years and is driven by financial reasons to join in a train robbery so that he can marry his girlfriend. At the crucial moment, Heizi redeems himself by turning against his fellow train robber, and is rewarded for this action with the promise of employment on the train. In selecting a would-be criminal as the play's protagonist, *Alarm Signal* therefore continues the trend begun in *What If I Really Were?* (S. Yu 1997, 15). Gao's collaboration with the then young director Lin Zhaohua 林兆華 (b. 1936) earned such success that the play went on to over a hundred performances with more than ten major drama companies across China producing it soon after (Quah 2004b, 9), on top of spawning many other little theaters in different parts of the country (M. Lu 2002, 45). Cao Yu, the foremost Chinese playwright and honorary president of BPAT, sent a telegram to congratulate the creative team in Beijing on its success when he heard about it from Shanghai (Gao (1991) 2006, 143).

Gao's bilingual abilities distinguished him in important ways from his peers. In their attempts to reform Chinese drama, some turned to the West for inspiration while others looked back to traditional Chinese theater to relocate their roots and transplant aspects of classical art forms onto the modern stage. Long-time president of the Shanghai People's Art Theatre 上海人民藝術劇院, the Cambridge-educated Huang Zuolin famously hailed Konstantin Stanislavsky, Bertolt Brecht, and Mei Lanfang as three of the greatest dramatists in the world and held that "the combination of these three techniques in a style of cohesive integrity may turn out to be the Chinese contribution to international art" (1994, 21). Going further than Huang, experimenting not only with Brecht and traditional Chinese theater, Gao also read and drew inspiration from Vsevolod Meyerhold, Antonin Artaud, Samuel Beckett, Eugène Ionesco, and Jean Genet, to mention only some of the European dramatists and practitioners with which he engaged, to explore different possibilities and expand the expressivity of theater, envisioning what he coins as a "modern Eastern theater" (Quah 2004b, 77). To be sure, his exposure to these Western theater theorists and practitioners was greatly enabled by his skills as a linguist. As a French major in the Beijing Foreign Languages Institute, and later working as editor and translator at the Foreign Languages Press in Beijing, he had direct access to the works of these major Western theater theorists and practitioners before most others in China had even heard of them (Quah 2004b, 166–67). After the Communist takeover in 1949, China remained relatively insular for the next few decades, and although Gao grew up at a time when foreign works were gradually being translated and imported into the country, censorship was much more prevalent in the case of English works. It was, however, not as strict for works in French (Quah 2004b, 6), and therefore Gao had the advantage of being able to access these alternative theatrical theories in their original languages. In contrast were the *menglong* poets who borrowed heavily from Western sources, despite none having proficiency in Western languages. Deprived of a high school education during the Cultural Revolution, which limited their exposure to both traditional Chinese and world literature, the misty poets could only look to Western translations. Unfortunately, since their access to translations was haphazard, the foreign works they ingested were done hastily and "often without an adequate understanding of the cultural context" in which they were written (Yeh 2003, 524). Gao's mastery of the French language therefore earned the praise of his contemporary, playwright Li Longyun, lauding him as having "an unprecedented advantage" in becoming "the leader of the 'second wave' of literary renaissance in the post-Mao period" (1993, 330; qtd. in X. Chen 2010, 28). On top of Gao's extraordinary tenacity to survive in adverse conditions, his departure from the mainland, and continued self-imposed exile in France, finding expression as an artist writing for both a Chinese and European readership was without doubt complemented by his linguistic skills (Lee and Dutrait 2001, 742).

Play Analysis: *Bus Stop*

The direction of the experimentation in the late 1970s to mid-1980s to reform the Chinese theater was heavily influenced by the political structures in China. In line with Gao's observation that the "fear of not being one of the masses (and the terrible consequences) had cowed individuals to obey the masters who controlled the masses" (M. Lee 2002a, 38), this direction clearly conforms to the collective identity to which the Chinese state had heretofore subjected its people. In a postscript discussion of *Alarm Signal* with director Lin Zhaohua, for instance, Gao expressed his view against an overly prescriptive theater, warning that in a play, "if the wordings are too polished, there is nothing for the actors to perform. They can then only recite their lines to be manipulated by directors like puppets" (Gao 1988, 119). Keenly aware of the need for drama to be given room for "experimentation and innovation" (Tam 2001a, 8), Gao contemplated on a theater that would stimulate his performers and audience alike to think for themselves and be reflective of their own conditions. Gao's creative input in the early 1980s dramatic scene has been celebrated as

> a striking departure from outdated theatrical convention, stereotyped characterization and acting, as well as unimaginative and unpopular playwriting . . . [that] positively enriched the range of expression open to artists involved in all forms of the performing arts in China, and have encouraged people to look into their own cultural heritage and literature to see what positive contributions it can make to the contemporary arts scene.
>
> (Barmé 1983, 377)

Alarm Signal, which heralded the emergence of experimental theater in China (Zou 1994, 46), was one of the works that began to fill the wide vacuum for artistic innovation and experimental work that the immediate post–Cultural Revolution period ushered in. By the time Gao left China, the sensational impact of his plays in the 1980s, *Alarm Signal* (1982), *Bus Stop* (1983), and *Wildman* (1985), had earned him the title "undisputed leader of Chinese experimental theatre" (Zou 1994, 54). That Gao's plays "attracted a wave of attention" in such a short span of time was inseparable from the "fundamentally changing atmosphere" in the early 1980s Chinese theater they reflected (Hsiung 2013, 16).

I will devote my discussion to Gao's second play, *Bus Stop*, a work that seriously treats identity and identification from the position of diaspora within China. Staged at the banquet hall on the third floor of the Capital Theatre in Beijing in 1983, the play opens with a group of people waiting in an unspecified locale for a bus into the city. As they wait, buses pass by but never stop, until the passengers are shocked to realize that ten years have passed. It is only then that they notice that one person—the Silent Man—has left the bus stop already, traveling to the city on foot. In a panic, those that remain begin to self-reflect. They wonder aloud—even addressing the audience directly—whether they might have reached the city by now if they, too, had left with the Silent Man.

Neither the passengers nor the audience ever learn whether the Silent Man has successfully made his way into the city. More importantly, the Silent Man's demonstration of breaking away and going his own way raises the *possibility* in the minds of the audience that they too have the potential of making unique decisions and doing things that differ from the collective. We could assume that he has reached the city, just as we could assume the crowd, having agreed to march to the city, will actualize this collective action. One character in the play, Director Ma, undermines this assumption at the end of the play by calling everyone to wait for him while he bends down to tie his shoelace (S. Yu 1997, 17). The play's ambiguity is one of its strengths, frustrating the state's desire for predictability and surety.

What made *Bus Stop* so controversial? Why was it described as "more *Hai Rui is Dismissed from Office* than *Hai Rui is Dismissed from Office*" and "the most poisonous play written since the founding of the People's Republic of China" (Gao (1991) 2006, 146–47)?[5] Despite gaining BPAT honorary president Cao Yu's tacit approval,[6] as well as the audience's enthusiastic reception, the play met with the onset of the Anti-Spiritual Pollution Campaign and was thus discontinued after only ten closed-door performances (Quah 2004b, 9–10). Furthermore, the Central Propaganda Department instructed two extra stagings of *Bus Stop*, issuing "specific work units" tickets to "write criticisms" to attack the play (Gao (1991) 2006, 148) and barring Gao from publication for one year (Fong 1999, xiii). Perhaps *Bus Stop*'s form and inherent messages

---

5. He Jingzhi 賀敬之, then in charge of literature in the Central Propaganda Department, made these allegations without even having watched the play (Gao (1991) 2006, 147). Widely considered as "the opening shot of the Cultural Revolution," *Hai Rui baguan* 海瑞罷官 (Hai Rui is dismissed from office, 1959) is a play written by Wu Han 吳晗 (1909-69) depicting the dismissal of a morally upright official in the Ming dynasty, satirizing Mao's dismissal of his long-time ally Peng Dehuai (Wagner 1990, 236).

6. When Gao Xingjian and director Lin Zhaohua were making rehearsal plans for *Bus Stop*, they visited Cao Yu and told him about the play, who replied, "It's a global subject, why can't you stage it?" After watching the dress rehearsal, no one in the theater dared to speak except Cao Yu, who raised his walking stick high in the air and shouted "Bravo!" (Gao (1991) 2006, 145–46).

proved to be such a formidable formula that the authorities had to prohibit further performances. In the words of Peter Brook:

> No tribute to the latent power of the theatre is as telling as that paid to it by censorship.... Instinctively, governments know that the living event could create a dangerous electricity—even if we see this happen all too seldom. But this ancient fear is recognition of an ancient potential. The theatre is the arena where a living confrontation can take place. The focus of a large group of people creates a unique intensity. Owing to this, forces that operate at all times and rule each person's daily life can be isolated and perceived more clearly.
>
> (1996, 122)

Two years later, Wang Peigong's *We* was to meet with a similar fate. The play was forced to stop after a few "internal" showings, and its director Wang Gui 王貴 (b. 1932) dismissed from his official post in the air force. Considered in this historical perspective, perhaps as an acknowledgement of their "latent power" (Brook 1996, 122), *Bus Stop* and *We* are among a small group of dramatic works "banned for their political contents in the post-Mao era" (S. Yu 1997, 21).

Scholars have remarked that *Bus Stop* contains many references to social problems in contemporary China, with the embedded critique accentuating the need for political reform. For instance, Yan Haiping recognizes "an unmistakably Chinese quality" in the play (1998, xx), while Yu Shiao-ling supposes that the act of waiting in the play is "a clear metaphor for life in China" (1997, 16). In Harry Kuoshu's analysis, "nothing was more familiar in ones' life than the bus"; since private cars were yet to be readily owned en masse at the time of the play's production, he identifies the relationships between the people and the bus, and among the passengers, therefore, to be a stark social critique on contemporary China. For instance, when the bus becomes too full for everyone to board, the order of the queue is completely disregarded and replaced by the prevalence of "'backdoorism' (favoritism)" in interpersonal relationships (1998, 463). This "backdoorism" Kuoshu describes has become an ingrained issue in China: instead of respecting the law that applies equally to all and everyone waiting their turn, people skip through formal channels to get their personal privileges because of private connections with those in power, reminding us of the acts committed by the high-ranking officials in *What If I Really Were?* In *Bus Stop*, Director Ma grumbles that he has bribed powerful people multiple times, and yet he still cannot board the bus. Even though his actions were clearly unethical, he somehow feels righteous complaining about the system's failure to make things more convenient for him. Other passengers who do not possess the financial means to bribe their way onto a bus, even if one were to stop in front of them, are naturally agitated.

The play also hints at other issues and events in recent Chinese history, such as the Cultural Revolution and the failure of the state's planned economy. The number of years the passengers spend waiting at the figurative bus stop coincides with the length of time of the Cultural Revolution. Having newly emerged from the decade-long disaster, the avid Chinese audience in the early 1980s would all too readily interpret the semiotics as expounded. Furthermore, exposure to winds and rains have left the faded sign at the bus stop barely legible. Although the two Chinese characters *feng yu* 風雨, literally "winds and rains," indicate the sign's deterioration by the elements of nature, Kuoshu suggests they also could imply "political campaigns" in Chinese idiomatic expression (1998, 466), reminding one of the cruelty of the persecutions made in the name of political campaigns in the recent past. If so, the play's final scene might serve as Gao's implicit call: if the people are tired of endlessly waiting for the state to change and desire to avoid the emergence of yet another bloody political campaign, they should rise up collectively against it. Gao denies that his works are explicit social criticism directed at specific locales, but as Constantine Tung reminds us:

> Allegorical interpretation has a long tradition in Chinese criticism. The distance of the time of the event in a historical play from the present does not prevent an interpretation in the contemporary context, and, indeed, a playwright's treatment of dramatic characters, plot and language in his play on a historical theme does often betray his stand and view on analogous current political and social issues. Furthermore, the playwright's intention to be ambiguous and indirect is often compromised by the level of conflict in his play.
>
> (1987, 17)

The buses' refusal to stop would be interpreted as an allegory of the state's failure to deliver its promises to the Chinese people, resulting in their endless wait and wastage of their youth (S. Yu 1997, 17; Yan 1998, xvi). Extending this reading, the people would inevitably be reminded that when it is tax filing season, time to pay a fine, whenever the state makes demands on its people, the "bus" would always be on time; in contrast, it never stops whenever its services are required. Can the "bus," therefore, ever be relied upon? What do we make of the relationship between the bus and its supposed passengers? In part perhaps because, among other perennial issues, the audience witnessing the performance spectacle in the early 1980s would realize just how huge the population in China has become, coupled with the concern that "the planned economy cannot provide enough jobs" and would pose "a serious social problem" (Kuoshu 1998, 464), the timing of the play became all too sensitive.

Form over Content

While scholars have sought to explain why *Bus Stop* landed in serious trouble with the authorities by examining its content, few have attempted to understand this from its form of presentation. If Geremie Barmé is right in surmising that *Bus Stop* is "the first play to introduce elements of the Theatre of the Absurd to a Chinese audience" (1983, 373), then the form of the play could pose a direct challenge to the existing party line and practices allowed within the theater. As Quah Sy Ren points out, "To be labeled as an 'absurdist' was tantamount to being called a 'reactionary.'" Gao understood the potential danger and "cautiously rejected any suggestion" of absurdist influence (2004b, 64).

Gao was steering himself clear of the play's presentational form rather than its content. Taken at face value, the play's alleged controversial content might appear tepid by today's standards. *Alarm Signal*, a play considerably less critical of the state, could not obtain approval at first due to its proposed form of representation, which deviated from BPAT's socialist realist tradition (Quah 2004b, 62). Quoting Terry Eagleton's statement that "in the modern aesthetic form becomes its content," Quah argues that form indeed "became a motif in the representation of modernity" for Chinese dramatists in the 1980s. And it was by the "appropriation of these forms" that a clearer picture of the Chinese dramatists' "ideological intentions and intellectual consciousness" has emerged (2004b, 60–61). As I will illustrate further below, *Bus Stop*'s presentational form served as Gao's critical mode of resistance.

Throughout the history of modern Chinese drama, despite serious efforts to experiment with various forms of expression to establish alternatives to realism by the dramatists, realism "survived and even underwent self-adjustment and transformation to remain the most all-embracing and multifaceted mode" in the post–Cultural Revolution era (Quah 2004b, 57). Thus, before the 1980s, the formal modes of presentation in modern Chinese drama were dominated by realism and naturalism, mostly represented by Ibsen and Stanislavsky. Despite Gao's denials, his influence from absurdism is obvious. Brecht, Artaud, Beckett, Genet, and Ionesco, from whom Gao borrowed heavily, had also rebelled against conventional styles of Western performance. By deviating from the norm, Gao's borrowing from these alternative dramatic theorists can both be interpreted as a mode of resistance performance against the political status quo as well as provide a subversive agenda in his commitment to seek the alternative. In *Bus Stop*, Gao had appropriated techniques from the theater of the absurd and Brecht's *Verfremdungseffekt* "to reveal human subjectivity, a quality previously repressed in conventional realist theater" (Quah 2004b, 62). Toward the end of the play, as the people realize that bus service at the stop may have been discontinued long ago, they begin to despair, lamenting the time past and the many opportunities lost in the intervening period. The performers then suddenly step out of their dramatis personae to address the audience directly, with Actor D drawing a comparison with the overbearing parental role of the CCP:

> ACTOR B *PLAYING* DIRECTOR MA: There are times in your life when you really have to wait.... Then you must have lined up to wait for the bus? Lining up is waiting.... Didn't you stand in line all that time for nothing? You can't help but be boiling mad.... If you line up and line up, and wait in vain for half your lifetime, or perhaps your whole lifetime, aren't you just playing a big joke on yourself? ...
>
> ACTOR D *PLAYING* MOTHER: The mother says to her son: walk, darling, walk! But the child can never learn. You might as well let him crawl on his own. Of course, sometimes you can support him.... You also have to allow him to fall.... A child can't learn to walk without tripping. To be a mother you have to be patient about this. Otherwise you're not qualified. No, you don't know how to be a mother.
>
> (Gao (1983) 1998, 57–58)

Brecht's *Verfremdungseffekt* seeks to prevent his audience from being wholly absorbed in the theatrical spectacle by interrupting the flow of the performance. In turn, this disruption alienates the audience from the mise-en-scène, emotionally distancing from and allowing them to critically reflect on the performance from different positions offered by the performers. Brechtian performers therefore underscore that the performance in the theater is not a real but a staged event. According to Peter Brook:

> Alienation is above all an appeal to the spectator to work for himself, so to become more and more responsible for accepting what he sees only if it is convincing to him in an adult way. . . . Brecht believed that, in making an audience take stock of the elements in a situation, the theatre was serving the purpose of leading its audience to a juster understanding of the society in which it lived, and so to learning in what ways that society was capable of change.
> (1996, 87–88)

By having his performers step out of their characters' personae to critique the performance and directly address the audience, Gao aims to alienate his audience in the Brechtian sense. In searching for a different type of contact with the audience, the 1980s new experimental Chinese theater "attaches considerable importance to the interaction between actor and spectator within a physical space" (Łabędzka 2008, 12). In their performers' personae, Actor B emphasizes the disappointment and futility of waiting in vain while Actor D insinuates and criticizes the paternalistic style of the state's governance. Confronted by this defamiliarized mode of presentation where the actors talk directly to them, the audience is thus shocked into contemplating the messages evoked.

Furthermore, the departure of the actors from their roles not only contradicts realist space-time logic, the audience is also directly confronted with a dialogic sequence that does not match the dramatic progression in the play. Similarly transgressed is the spatial-temporal linearity when the passengers suddenly realize an entire decade has passed upon learning of the Silent Man's departure. Gao appears to have designed this as a climactic moment in the performance: releasing the actors from their roles, they speak directly to the audience in their performers' personae in a manner that does not always follow the logic of rational language. Here, the actress playing the Young Woman breaks out of character. She delivers her lines at the same time as two other characters, Spectacles and Gramps. The three simultaneous speakers do not interact, and their utterances are incoherent when read in context with one another. Clearly, they are delivering three pieces of monologue:

> YOUNG WOMAN: To waste time like this, will we keep on wasting it forever?
> SPECTACLES: It is raining, it will rain?
> GRAMPS: Pawn six across to five, chariot five forward to one.
> . . .
> YOUNG WOMAN: Will you keep on suffering forever, as you wait forever?
> SPECTACLES: It is snowing it will snow.
> GRAMPS: Chariot three forward to five—assistant five retreat to six!
> . . .
> YOUNG WOMAN: Are you going to keep waiting like this, grumbling your whole life?
> SPECTACLES: Rain isn't snow snow isn't rain!
> GRAMPS: Elephant seven retreat to five, chariot three forward to seven, checkmate!
>
> (Gao (1983) 1998, 52–53)

Action and dialogue appear to be out of sync in this moment. Although the three are speaking simultaneously, the Young Woman who has stepped out of her dramatis persona appears to be directly addressing the audience while the two characters are each immersed in their own situations, giving the appearance of a myopic entity, detached from the concerns of the audience. She uses the second-person pronoun *you* in a confrontational manner, clearly addressing the audience, while Spectacles and Gramps are in no way reciprocating, one preoccupied with the weather and the other with the moves in a chess game. Furthermore, the questions she elicits are responses that would require her listeners to critically evaluate and reflect upon their present situations.

Gao's appropriated techniques from the theater of the absurd mark an important departure from the familiar theatrical conventions on the Chinese stage. Not only does it challenge the audience to see and imagine reality differently from ways they have erstwhile been conditioned by the state, importantly it also demonstrates his will to follow his own path. So often in absurdist theater "dialogue becomes divorced from the real happenings in the play and is even put into direct contradiction with the action." In exposing the limitations of rational language and hence its inadequacy in conveying reality, absurdist theater attempts "to penetrate to deeper layers of meaning" and provide a truer and more complex picture of reality, which includes "all the undertones, overtones, and inherent absurdities and contradictions of any human situation" (Esslin 1960, 11–13). As Martin Esslin describes in his now-classic essay "The Theatre of the Absurd":

> In the conventional drama every word means what it says, the situations are clearcut, and at the end all conflicts are tidily resolved. But reality . . . is multiple, complex, many-dimensional and exists on a number of different levels at one and the same time. Language is far too straightforward an instrument to express all this by itself. Reality can only be conveyed by being acted out in all its complexity.
>
> (1960, 13)

Because the world in Absurdist drama is devoid of "a clear-cut purpose or design," the audience are "invited to school their critical faculties" at an infinite number of possible readings and "attempt their own interpretation." In this way, the illogicality of the stage dialogue knocks the audience out of their otherwise "known framework of accepted values and a rational view of life," and while puzzling out the meaning of what they have just witnessed, pushes them to postulate a critical, detached position "to sharpen their wits on the play and be stimulated by it to think for themselves" (Esslin 1960, 13–14).

At the play's outset, the setting that greets the audience upon their entrance into the performance space already suggests a nonrealistic staging. The only prop onstage in this theater-in-the-round is the bus stop, represented by an asymmetrical cross. While Gao had meant the shape as "symbolic of a crossroads, or a fork in the road on the journey of life, or a way station in the lives of the characters," Izabella Łabędzka suggests this symbolism could take on further meanings of "a meeting point for the accidental, for would-be passengers; a crossroad for the barely interesting but particularly human fates of those wanderers who travel around the world" (2008, 126–27). Be it the intersection of life, an unplanned meeting point for people from all walks of life or different parts of the world, or the nation at a crossroad, the audience witnessing this spectacle in 1983 would be induced into thinking about choosing a path to follow, considering their future options, or pondering over their identity. The play's staging, coupled with Gao's use of polyphonic dialogue, the theater-in-the-round, among various other stage effects employed, could "shake the audience and have a cathartic effect on them" because these were postwar Western theater conventions that departed from the naturalist-realist presentation of life, with which the Chinese audiences were until then vaguely familiar (Barmé 1983, 376). These techniques aim to prompt the audience into reflecting about the issues embedded in the production in relation to their own situations, which echo Brecht's rejection of "the romantic notion that in the theatre we all become children again" (Brook 1996, 87).

Gao envisioned a theatrical aesthetics that would encourage proactive thinkers and condition a reflective audience. Symptomatic of the 1980s nonrealist plays, these cross-dialogues between characters and audiences "break from the belief in the hero as an authority" and are "critical, skeptical and self-reflexive in nature," thereby serving "as oppositional discourse" (Tam 2002, 52). This directly calls into question the patriarchy of the empire: since ancient times, the Chinese emperor has been referred to as the Son of Heaven, and these traditional familial ties extend to his citizens. Chinese political culture has always rested on the family analogy, with top leaders functioning in many ways as paternalistic authority figures for citizens of all ages (Link 1983, 2–3). Despite claiming to be a staunch eradicator of its imperial past, the CCP has expediently manipulated such tactics of control to its own advantage. Asking the people to take charge of their own lives as adults, therefore, amounts to sedition, abandoning the party line, provoking revolution. Although Gao has never publicly acknowledged it, the censors' reading of *Bus Stop*'s ending is the group's collective departure for the city, interpreted as a call to arms, stirring the people to advocate for themselves and champion their own causes. Only by Gao's choice of the play's form of presentation are these evidenced. The formal qualities of Brechtian and absurdist theater worked, in fact, to subvert the Chinese regime.

In calling upon the people to make up their own minds about choosing whether to stay or go, as the asymmetrical cross, the characters stepping out of their dramatis personae, and the play's ambiguous ending suggest, Gao's notion of "diaspora within China" is most evidently displayed in making the audience see themselves as individuated beings. By having the character step out of his/her dramatis persona and talk directly to the audience in a reflective mode, Gao is revealing that behind the veil of the character is a living, thinking actor, capable of deeper introspection and decision-making. Even if the characters eventually rise up and leave together with the rest of the collective, these decisions to be made are individual choices. Encouraging proactive thinkers and conditioning a reflective audience are, in effect, getting people to make choices individuated from the rest and be responsible to themselves. One needs to have the courage to be different from the majority and contemplate his/her own condition to make the best decision for him/herself, instead of comply with the state, in order to be a diasporic member within China. Nowhere in the play do we find this more obvious than in the figure of the Silent Man.

The "Ghost" of Lu Xun

Given the multiple layers of complexity in the possible interpretation of *Bus Stop*, what preparations did the producers make to stage the play? When Gao staged *Alarm Signal*, it was already labeled with having "blurred characterization" (Zhao 2000, 185), which strayed from the CCP's norms and raised the authorities' concerns. Gao had composed *Bus Stop* earlier, but he was advised by BPAT's then vice-president Yu Shizhi 于是之 (1927-2013) to shelve the production plan because the play was too avant-garde and could be weaponized against Gao in the highly volatile political climate of the early 1980s. As a result, Gao wrote *Alarm Signal*, and only after its success did he and Lin Zhaohua find the courage to stage *Bus Stop* without obtaining permission from the CCP (Gao (1991) 2006, 145–46).

To overcome the issue of censorship, Gao's resistance act could be considered as an appropriation of what Marvin Carlson terms "ghosting." Carlson describes the "ghosting" process as "using the memory of previous encounters to understand and interpret encounters with new and somewhat different but apparently similar phenomena" (2001, 6). *Bus Stop*'s staging was designed as a two-part sequel, with Gao's play immediately following the performance of Lu Xun's 鲁迅 (1881-1936) *Guoke* 過客 (Passerby, 1925).[7] Published as part of the collection in Lu Xun's anthology of prose-poetry entitled *Yecao* 野草 (Wild grass, 1927), *Passerby*, his only play, is about a nameless wayfarer who forges ahead toward his uncertain destiny without looking back. Significantly, in this 1983 BPAT production, the actor who plays the protagonist role in the preceding *Passerby* doubles up as the Silent Man in *Bus Stop*. As Carlson explicates on his notion of the "haunted body":

> The most familiar example of this phenomenon is the appearance of an actor, remembered from previous roles, in a new

---

7. For comparative studies of Gao and Lu Xun, see M. Lee 2002b; 2013.

characterization. The recycled body of an actor, already a complex bearer of semiotic messages, will almost inevitably in a new role evoke the ghost or ghosts of previous roles if they have made any impression whatever on the audience, a phenomenon that often colors and indeed may dominate the reception process.

(2001, 8)

Taking Carlson's theory of ghosting into account, Gao's resistance act reminds one of the Chinese axiom "using the past to refer to the present" 借古喻今. If, as Carlson suggests, "the expectations an audience brings to a new reception experience are the residue of memory of previous such experiences" (5), then Gao's well-considered choice of the same actor reappearing in both plays threads the common theme from the former play into the latter. As such, "Lu Xun's image of the wayfarer . . . who proceeds with his journey regardless of uncertainty," would resurface as the Silent Man and continue the message of traversing unfamiliar ground regardless of confronting uncertainty, which is "in stark contrast to the other characters who hesitate" (Quah 2004b, 65) in the latter play. The Chinese audience would have little trouble in getting the semiotic messages expounded on the Silent Man's body recycled from *Passerby*.

Significantly, more than recasting the actor into a new role, what Gao is doing here is to capitalize on the cultural authority of *Passerby*'s author. Lu Xun is hailed as the "father of modern Chinese literature," whose preeminence has yet to be surpassed by any writer in modern China, earning praises from even Chairman Mao who extolled him posthumously as "not only a great writer, but a great thinker and revolutionary as well" (Mao (1940) 1983, 372). By conjuring the memory of Lu Xun and playing up the connections between *Bus Stop* and *Passerby*, Gao was making efforts to circumvent the restrictions on his play. Indeed as Carlson suggests, theater is "the art most closely related to memory" because of its close association with evoking the past, uncannily restoring "the histories and legends of the culture" to a mysterious half-life (2001, 142). While the two plays might possess similarities, the political implications Gao has taken into consideration in the matter far outweigh its artistic concerns: drawing on the memories of a venerated literary figure, the ghost of Lu Xun, and the cultural credence he brings to mind, Gao's resistance act sought to ward off potential attack by the authorities. William Tay's reading of this doubling extends this complication even further: "although nearly sixty years have elapsed" between the two appearances of the lonely Passerby, his resurfacing in *Bus Stop* might "also suggest that the struggle and the journey are not yet over" (1990, 116).

Unfortunately, evoking the ghost of Lu Xun in *Bus Stop* failed to prevent Gao from getting into trouble with the censors then or later. In December 1983, Gao, along with four other modernist writers, were singled out for criticism by the Central Committee on charges for indulging in commercialism but whose actual basis, according to Wendy Larson, "is their acceptance of modernism and rejection of realism," and the accompanying "implicit rejection of certain aspects of Chinese society that their work contains" (1989, 60–61). Gao's handbook *Preliminary Explorations on the Art of Fiction* had in fact placed him "under surveillance since 1981." *Bus Stop* was brought to the stage in the immediate aftermath of the Cultural Revolution, and then shut down in this context of anxiety and uncertainty. As the play came under severe criticism and was abruptly halted after ten performances in the midst of the Anti-Spiritual Pollution Campaign, Gao absconded for a ten-month odyssey from Beijing into the wilderness in southwestern China, hence escaping the venomous attacks unleashed on him then (M. Lee 1996, 103). Reflecting on this and his experience in the Cultural Revolution, Gao realized that self-censorship was not enough to steer him away from political oppression and "fleeing was the best way of protecting himself" (Quah 2004b, 10).

Two years later, while the production of Gao's third play, *Wildman*, had been "very favourably received" (Fong 1999, xiv) and "acknowledged by dramatists and critics alike as a bold attempt to push the performing arts of China into a new realm" (Roubicek 1990, 186), the actors rehearsing in his fourth play, *The Other Shore*, BPAT students under Lin Zhaohua's direction, were halted after only one month (Fong 1999, xiv) and warned not to collaborate with Gao again. Thenceforth, Gao postulated that his dramatic experimentations could no longer continue in China without fear of being arrested, nor would his plays be performed without facing heavy censorship. Finally, in 1987, he took up residence in France during his invitation as a visiting artist in Germany. Enraged by the 1989 Tiananmen Square military crackdown on students, Gao publicly condemned the Beijing authorities, declaring that he would not return to China as long as they remained in power (Quah 2004b, 11–12). The state responded by actively erasing Gao's name from collective memory: when Gao was announced the winner of the 2000 Nobel Prize for Literature, few in mainland China had any recollection of him because a nationwide ban on all his works had been imposed for more than a decade.

Diaspora within China

In his theatrical experimentations, Gao has exemplified his radical departure from the state-endorsed collective identity. He decries the tragedy of modern Chinese literature to be in the servitude of politics ((1992) 2001, 121) and seeks to set it free from ideological constraints. Like the roots-seeking writers, Gao draws his creative expression from primitive and peripheral nonliterati cultures. At least three of his plays, *Wildman*, *Mingcheng* 冥城 (City of the dead, 1987), and *Shanhaijing zhuan* 山海經傳 (Of mountains and seas, 1989), for instance, give expression to cultural elements from regions, ethnicities, periods, and ideological systems that are nonmainstream and hence challenge the cultural hegemony and orthodoxy of the *zhongyuan* central plains 中原 as represented by the political center (Quah 2004b, 16–17), leading Henry Zhao Yiheng to go even as far as to call Gao's dramatic plays "modern Zen theatre" 現代中國禪劇 (2000). Assimilating elements from Brecht, Beckett, and Genet in his theatrical aesthetics is further evidence of Gao's anticenter stance: these Western dramatists had revolted in their own time from the conventions of realism, which incidentally also dominated the modern Chinese stage, out of which Gao and his peers were breaking, since its founding. This privileging of the periphery over the mainstream is in line with Gao's "cold literature," which he was developing at this time. Retreating to the margins of society, or what I call "diaspora within China," affords Gao the necessary distance to offer reflection, contemplation, and critique of the center, a position where he places "himself on the outside, a stranger to his own community" (Fong 1999, xvi–xvii).

This coldness was a reflection especially in stark contrast to the madness that engulfed the entire Chinese state during the Cultural Revolution and a deterrent to the modern Chinese literary tradition of becoming self-sacrificial lambs in order to save the nation. In his interview with Gregory Lee and Noël Dutrait, Gao expresses the view that

> politicos who aim to achieve a certain objective often speak in the name of the People. I think Chinese intellectuals should no longer use these concepts to express themselves. An intellectual only

represents himself; he's better off avoiding speaking for the collectivity, representing the People, representing the motherland, saving the nation. I think nobody can save anybody. I personally don't think I can save anybody. If I still write it's to show that I exist.

(Lee and Dutrait 2001, 744)

Therefore, Gao is especially critical toward the call for patriotism and nationalism, cautioning others against being made use of by the state, too often in the name of the collective. His play *The Other Shore* depicts how the masses are manipulated by the state in glamorously disguised deceit. These are personal experiences he gleaned from his purges during the Cultural Revolution as well as the Anti-Spiritual Pollution Campaign. What the modern Chinese intellectual needs, in Gao's view, is to "shake off this kind of blind nationalism, patriotism, jingoism, chauvinism" and adopt "a detached, independent attitude" (Lee and Dutrait 2001, 744).

Paradoxically, even if *Bus Stop* has been labeled as an absurdist play, the state might be extremely wary because of its appeal to realism. Gao himself has said that there is a very "realistic character in the absurd" ((1993) 2001, 8) and his "experimental plays often draw (their resources) from reality" (10). Indeed, as has been exemplified, much of the play's content draws immediate references to the sociopolitical situation in China at the time of its staging. On one level, *Bus Stop* exposes both the corrupt nature and ills of Chinese society: the ten-year wait and "backdoorism" allude to the wasted decade of the Cultural Revolution, political in-fighting, and the state's lack of direction. Furthermore, realization of the Silent Man's having entered the city on his own that prompted the rest of the passengers to rise collectively to the occasion is a direct challenge to the state's legitimacy, stating one's obvious distrust with the CCP's governance and hence the wish to rise up—implying either to leave or revolt.

Not forgetting the 1980s was a period of great social change that "had a tremendous impact on the shaping and reshaping of personhood on the Chinese mainland" (Tam, Yip, and Dissanayake 1999, xii), Gao's intervention in this postrevolutionary identity crisis from a diasporic perspective was pushing the audience to adopt a position, giving them a say in the matter on where they would like to go, and by extension who they want to be and what their identity is. But to where does Gao lead his audience? Does he indicate a particular direction in which they should go? Gao does not even clarify whether Director Ma would follow the crowd, having him bend down to tie his shoelace when they were taking off at the end of the play, much less point to a definitive destination for his audience. Critics like Geremie Barmé have asserted that despite not having explicitly stated so, the ending of the play is unambiguous: people rising and going to the city was obvious (1983, 375). My reading, however, is that by *not* plainly stating whether the people have actually gone to the city, this ambiguity is a strategy Gao purposely employed. What is absent is sometimes more present: hinting at the *possibility* of the people going to the city might be more powerful than declaring it outright. Rather than specifically instructing them on what to do—a treatment no different from the CCP, which the people would have been sick of—this ambiguous ending prompts the audience to consider the likelihood of going into the city. Instead of being prescriptive, the trope of the passerby and the symbolism of the cross present the option of choice to the audience, which thus invite them to reexamine their own meanings of personhood. As has been discussed of Danny Yung's empty chairs in the previous chapter, allowing the people to exercise their preference and planting the seed of possibility in their minds is a more latently subversive tool than outright instruction. And regardless of how one chooses, even contemplating the prospect of determining his/her own future is a bold step that deviated from the erstwhile state-sanctioned prescriptive art. In this way, hence, the Chinese audience members are exercising their choice of identity and identification that veered from the state's doctrine. No wonder Tam Kwok-kan considers the controversy *Bus Stop* aroused to chiefly be "on its ideological inclination and challenge to the socialist doctrines of literature and art" (2001b, 45).

Chen Xiaomei appraises *Bus Stop* as "one of the most astonishing achievements of early post-Mao theater," having accomplished "formalist and aesthetic innovations, which dramatically changed the landscape of modern spoken drama" (2010, 27-28). These experimentations with form and modes of presentation might perhaps have been considered as a greater threat to the state. Gao's continued search for an alternative aesthetics was part of an ongoing innovation that Chinese dramatists were exploring. Artists who were discontented with the existing state of affairs sought to challenge the orthodox dogma in the arts by attempting to find "an effective means to express divergent points of view" (Quah 2004b, 38-39). In portraying a dramatic representation that broke "away from the rather monolithic mode of realist theater that had dominated the Chinese stage" (X. Chen 2010, 27), Gao was essentially deviating from the CCP's portrayal of reality and thus defying the state's notion of being Chinese. Employing a mode of presentation that contradicted the state-sanctioned aesthetics is to pose a direct challenge to its singular claim of historical narrative. As with the avant-garde writers and filmmakers in the 1980s contesting the right of historical interpretation, Gao's intervention too wrested the meaning of being Chinese away from that defined by the CCP. Like the Silent Man in *Bus Stop*, Gao trod his own path against the collective, as well as against the collective will imposed by the Chinese state. His search for an alternative aesthetics is also "a quest for identities" and indeed "raise[s] new and profound questions about what it means to be a Chinese even *inside* China" (L. Lee 1991, 209–11).

Conclusion

By tracing the theater histories of these four locales with a majority of ethnic Chinese, this book has attempted to map the transnational geopolitical influences on the region that accounted for the rise of identities in each site in the 1980s. Only through examining the transnational histories of these individual sites together in a single study do we have a clearer sense, echoing Rey Chow's (2000, 24) and Wang Gungwu's (1999, 169) insights, of a pluralistic notion of Chineseness and diasporicity that defies uniformity. The interconnectedness of the entire region as well as the continued tensions and influences between China and the diaspora have also been illuminated as a result.

My study demonstrates that the resistance performance the intellectual dramatists created were not merely local responses to internal situations. While the way each locale defines its own contested sense of Chineseness is unique to the particular site's connected history with Chinese tradition and culture, a comparative analysis has illuminated a more holistic understanding of the transnational geopolitical impact on the region. Their alternative theaters have not only challenged the uncritical patriotic call of their home governments in imposing state-sanctioned identities onto their citizens, but they have also simultaneously resisted "the ways successive governments in the mainland have used the issue of national identity to claim the commitment of 'Chinese' populations" overseas (Siu 1996, 179). This bears particular significance with forming new alliances and identifying different possibilities for further exploration in related fields of study.

In part, Kuo Pao Kun's invitation to these dramatists in that historic Second Chinese-language Drama Camp meeting in 1987 was initiated to explore what models these similarly cultured sites have to offer. Newly released from state detention, not only did Kuo understand that his world had changed, but he was also keen to learn how *the world* had changed and impacted other Chinese-speaking sites. That Gao Xingjian, Danny Yung, and Stan Lai among others responded in kind suggested that Singapore was not alone in confronting the effects of regional geopolitics on suturing identity; these intellectual artists were keen, also, to observe the external impact in other Chinese-speaking sites and acquire strategies to cope with and respond to one another. Although this was not the first time all four dramatists had met, it certainly represented a significant exchange among a series of important fluid transnational flows of ideas that took place between them and other important Chinese dramatists in the 1980s. As a result of these meetings, the entire region became much more interconnected: an exchange of ideas, resources, and personnel increased, bringing about transnational artistic collaborations that greatly dynamized the scene. In retrospect, therefore, Rosella Ferrari views these meetings in the 1980s to

> have acquired almost mythical significance in the theatrical historiography of the region as the sites of seminal encounters between the founding fathers of contemporary Sinophone dramaturgy and experimental performance, and de facto cornerstones in the formation of transnational Chinese theatres.
>
> (2020, 213)

Not only have these exchanges enabled productive comparisons across the various locales that were particularly useful in resisting a homogeneous identity, thus debunking the notion of a unified, undifferentiated Chineseness, these increased interactions have simultaneously affirmed the uniqueness of their individual identities.

In the years following the Second Chinese-language Drama Camp, these four director-playwrights continued to participate actively in one another's artistic practice, directing one another's works and collaborating with artists from one another's sites. Below I flesh out several examples of how these dramatists continue to collaborate with and draw inspiration from one another, instill influence, and impact these other sites before drawing some concluding remarks.

Apart from the invitations to Singapore that Kuo Pao Kun extended to artists and their theater troupes for collaborations with him and to stage their works that I have detailed in chapter 1, his plays have also been directed by these other dramatists or staged at these various locales. Kuo's first play to premiere in China was *The Coffin Is Too Big for the Hole*. Performed in Mandarin at China's inaugural "Little Theater Festival" in Nanjing on March 22–24, 1989, the monodrama was directed by the eighty-three-year-old theater veteran, Shanghai People's Art Theatre's president Huang Zuolin (Kuo 1984c, 31), displaying extremely high regard for a foreign artist whose work was staged for the first time on the Chinese stage.

After completing the script for *Lingxi* 靈戲 (The spirits play, 1998), Kuo discovered that he needed to undergo surgery. He telephoned Stan Lai in Taipei to invite him to direct the play, and Lai accepted the request without having even read the script (Kuo 2000, 403). In the play's Chinese-language premiere, apart from Johnny Ng 黃家強, Goh Guat Kian, and Leanne Ong Teck Lian 王德亮, seasoned local theater actors who regularly perform in The Theatre Practice's (TTP) productions, the cast also consisted of Beijing People's Art Theatre's (BPAT) veteran Lin Liankun as well as Singapore's highly acclaimed television actor Xie Shaoguang 謝韶光, which resulted in a transmedia and transnational collaboration between artists in theater and television across Singapore, Taiwan, and China. The following year, Kuo created the multilingual play *Xiyang wuxian* 夕陽無限 (Sunset rise, 1999) after getting inspired by Stan Lai's *Red Sky* and brought it to Taipei in 2000 for the third biannual Chinese Drama Festival 華文戲劇節—the oldest platform showcasing the convergence of theory and praxis in the Chinese-speaking world.

Among these sites Kuo's relationship with Hong Kong might have been the closest, in part perhaps because he had spent time there in his youth. The first time *The Coffin Is Too Big for the Hole* was performed outside of Singapore was in none other than Hong Kong. Kuo brought the play to the 1986 Hong Kong Fringe Festival and directed the English version. The monodrama was translated into Cantonese as *Guncoi daaigwo lung* (in Mandarin: *Guancai daguo long*) 棺材大過窿 (literally: The coffin is bigger than the hole) and performed by one of Chung

FIGURE 5. Rehearsal of *The Spirits Play* (1998), in Singapore. Veteran Chinese theater actor Lin Liankun, Taiwanese director Stan Lai, and Singaporean playwright Kuo Pao Kun, in a rehearsal discussion of the upcoming play, which marks the increasing transnational collaborations in the Chinese-speaking theater world. Courtesy of The Theatre Practice.

Ying Theatre Company's principle actors, Lee Chun Chow 李鎮洲, and directed by its artistic director, Bernard Goss (February 14–18, 1986), at the Hong Kong Fringe Club. The following year Kuo brought its twin piece, *No Parking on Odd Days*, again to the Hong Kong Fringe Festival, which was performed in English by T. Sasitharan (February 5–6, 1987). A month later, Chung Ying staged these two monodramas as a double bill entitled "A City's Pressures" 城市壓力, which Goss directed and Lee performed in Cantonese at the Hong Kong Arts Centre (March 12–15, 1987) ("Plays" 1987, 17; H. Tsoi 2007, 134). The Hong Kong Fringe Club was also where Kuo sought inspiration for setting up The Substation—A Home for the Arts 電力站——藝術之家 in 1990 ("Kuo" 2012, 56), which became an interdisciplinary, multicultural incubation site for nurturing Singaporean artists that privileges works in progress over finished products. Subsequently, in 1991, he invited Chung Ying's veteran artist May Wong Mei Lan 黃美蘭 over to Singapore to serve as TTP's resident director and later long-time associate artistic director. In 1998, the Hong Kong Arts Development Council further invited Kuo to help assess the professional theater companies in the territory. In the same year, Kuo also brought *The Spirits Play* to Hong Kong to participate in the second biannual Chinese Drama Festival. His amicable relationship with the Hong Kong performing arts scene can be exemplified by the many essays written by Hong Kong dramatists to mourn his untimely demise in 2002.[1]

To commemorate Kuo's passing on September 10, 2002, six theater directors from the region—Stan Lai, Danny Yung, Hardy Tsoi (Hong Kong), Krishen Jit (Kuala Lumpur), Lin Kehuan (Beijing), and Xiong Yuanwei 熊源偉 (Shenzhen)—got together within one hundred days of his demise and presented *Chuanqi weiliao—xian gei Baokun de zuopin* 傳奇未了――獻給寶崑的作品 (Works for Pao Kun: Legend alive) to reinterpret "selections from Kuo's works to honour the recently deceased dramatist" from December 13 to 15, 2002 (Ferrari 2020, 221). Yung's piece was *Xunzhao xin Zhongguo (Taijian)* 尋找新中國（太監） (In search of modern China—Eunuch) and Lai's was entitled *Xinjiapo jixing* 新加坡即興 (Singapore impromptu). Originally planned by Vivien Ku Hwai-chun 辜懷群, managing director of Taipei's Novel Hall for Performing Arts 新舞臺表演廳, to wish Kuo a speedy recovery when his cancer relapsed, unfortunately this event had to be presented as a commemoration instead. That artists from different states came together so quickly to stage an artistic event for Kuo not only demonstrates "how much the Asian Chinese drama circles respect Pao Kun as well as treasure his friendship" (Kwok 2002), but also how integrated the regional artistic network has become.

Since gaining critical and popular acclaim in Taiwan, Stan Lai has been venturing overseas into other Chinese-speaking worlds. Besides having his plays tour internationally, Lai's cultural influence outside of Taiwan also lies in his extensive collaboration with foreign artists and cultural troupes. Owing to the invitation of the then Hong Kong Repertory Theatre (HKREP) artistic director Daniel Yang, *Red Sky* became Lai's first play to be staged by a theater company other than Performance Workshop ("Lai" 1998), being performed in Hong Kong prior to making its way to Beijing in December 1998. In March 2000, Danny Yung invited Lai to Hong Kong to collaborate in the project *Shiyan Shashibiya—Li'er wang* 實驗莎士比亞――李爾王 (Experimental Shakespeare: King Lear), along with avant-garde Chinese theater director Meng Jinghui 孟京輝 (b. 1964) and Taiwanese film director Edward Yang, to each devise a separate piece to "investigate connections between

---

1. For these commemorative essays by Hong Kong theater practitioners on the loss of the Singapore drama doyen, see Cheung and Fong 2003, Sim 2003, and Yung 2009, 456–57.

Shakespeare and the socio-historical developments of the three 'Chinas'" (Ferrari 2008, 60). Merging excerpts from *King Lear* and the Buddhist text *The Thirty-Seven-Fold Practice of a Bodhisattva*, Lai devised the contemplative piece *Pusa zhi sanshiqi zhong xiuxing zhi Li'er wang* 菩薩之三十七種修行之李爾王 (The King Lear of the thirty-seven-fold practice of a Bodhisattva) (Ferrari 2008, 62).

Earlier in the year, Lai had begun workshopping *A Dream Like a Dream* with UC Berkeley students, creating a three-and-a-half-hour English version in February and subsequently a full eight-hour Chinese version with the National Institute of the Arts (NIA) students on their Taipei campus in May (Lai 2011). Among the audience at the NIA performance was Fredric Mao Chun Fai 毛俊輝 (b. 1947), who would assume HKREP's artistic directorship the following year. Mao was determined, after watching the play, to convince the HKREP board to utilize the strength and resources of Hong Kong's flagship professional theater company to mount this theatrical epic in the territory, which was up until then perceived to be unstageable at any of the professional theater spaces in Taiwan due to its sheer magnitude and accompanying technical and logistical complications ("Rumeng" 2013). In celebration of HKREP's silver jubilee in 2002, when Lai was invited to be director-in-residence at the troupe, he brought the play to be performed by HKREP cast members under his direction. Thus, the inaugural staging of *A Dream Like a Dream* by a professional theater company took place in Hong Kong in Cantonese, starring Fredric Mao and television actress, singer, and Cantonese opera diva Liza Wang Ming-chun 汪明荃 (b. 1947) in its leading roles ("Rumeng" 2019). Only upon the success of this Hong Kong production did the staff of Taipei's National Theatre and Concert Hall 兩廳院, who had flown in to watch the play, discuss with Performance Workshop the possibility of staging this monumental production at the National Theatre, which finally materialized in 2005 ("Rumeng" 2013).

Lai has since moved his creative base to Shanghai. The thought of setting up a work center in China first dawned on him after the successful collaboration with BPAT actors on *Red Sky*. However, his early attempt at establishing the North Theater 北京北兵馬司劇場 in 2002, his own performance venue in Beijing run by local partners there, failed and wrapped up in September 2005 (Shui 2007, 141; Cecily Huang 2011). Learning from this experience, he founded the Theatre Above 上劇場 a decade later in 2015, a 699-seat venue in Shanghai dedicated to the performance of Lai's works among others. In addition, Lai cofounded the Wuzhen Theatre Festival 烏鎮戲劇節 in 2013, which has quickly become one of the top festivals in China and Asia annually.

Although his plays are still performed in Taiwan, none of his new works has premiered there in the past decade—until 2021, when he created a prequel to *Secret Love in Peach Blossom Land* (C. Wang 2021). Entitled *Jiang/Yun · zhi/jian* 江／雲·之／間 (River/cloud), this prequel fills in the missing forty-year gap between the two protagonists, Jiang Binliu and Yun Zhifan, what happened to them after their separation at the park in Shanghai until their reunion in Taipei. Significantly, the gap between the missing histories across the Taiwan Strait when denizens on both shores could not communicate with each other is explained. The play details the struggles of both Jiang and Yun, the different routes they took—and the difficulties each (representing the *waisheng* émigrés as well as the Chinese diaspora) had to endure—to make their way to Taiwan. The title of this prequel is taken from the surnames of the two protagonists: Jiang meaning "River" and Yun "Cloud." In some ways, thirty-five years after the sensational hit of *Secret Love*, the story has come full circle, wandering to other parts of China, the Chinese-speaking world, and the diaspora, and made a complete journey with the premiere of this prequel at the National Theatre in Taipei on April 2, 2021.

Danny Yung's transnational endeavors began even earlier. Thrice in the 1980s Zuni Icosahedron was invited to perform in Taipei, markedly impacting the experimental theater scene in Taiwan each time. Yung realized from the 1989 Tiananmen Square Incident that they do not quite understand China enough, and he has since proactively gone into the Chinese hinterland to work directly with performers of traditional art forms there, as well as seek cross-cultural collaborations with artists regionally and globally (W. Lim 2021, 53). These have manifested in many of Zuni's performance series, some of which focus on the theme of Chineseness, such as *One Hundred Years of Solitude* and *Journey to the East*. Taking the latter as an example, the 1997 rendition of the series, which was staged in January 1997 at the Hong Kong Arts Centre, saw seven ethnic Chinese theater and film director participants that included Taiwanese New Cinema and Hong Kong New Wave Cinema filmmakers Edward Yang and Stanley Kwan, and avant-garde theater directors Lin Zhaohua (Beijing), Li Liuyi 李六乙 (Beijing), Hugh Lee Kuo-shiu (Taipei), Edward Lam Yik-wah (Hong Kong), and Yung himself. The 1998 version, which was performed in January 1998 at the Hong Kong Arts Centre, went even further to invite collaborators beyond East Asia to involve ethnic Chinese auteurs from North America and Southeast Asia. Participants in this performance included multimedia artist Paul Wong 黃柏武 (Vancouver), visual artist Wong Shun Kit 王純杰 (Hong Kong), theater directors Ping Chong 張平 (New York), Stan Lai, Wei Ying Chuan 魏瑛娟 (Taipei), Zhang Xian 張獻 (Shanghai), and Ong Keng Sen (Singapore), as well as filmmakers Tsai Ming-liang (Taipei/Malaysia) and Eric Khoo 邱金海 (Singapore).[2] If Kuo started this network in the 1980s by inviting the then most prolific aspiring theater directors to Singapore, Yung most actively extended it.

With Kuo's demise, Yung's continued presence in the Singapore Chinese-language drama scene provided somewhat of a mentoring figure for younger artists in the city-state. Yung's invitation to conduct drama workshops in Singapore grew into a collaboration between Zuni and Singaporean Chinese theater company Drama Box. Thus, *Bainian zhi guji 10.0—Wenhua dageming* 百年之孤寂10.0—文化大革命 (One hundred years of solitude 10.0—Cultural revolution, 2011) was spawned with the main cast consisting of Singaporean actors (Ng 2021, 76). Furthermore, on the tenth anniversary of Kuo's passing, in 2012, Yung codirected with Sato Makoto 佐藤信 (b. 1943) of Tokyo's Za-Koenji Public Theatre 座・高円寺 a Kun-Noh intercultural collaboration of Kuo's *Spirits Play*.[3] A year later, Yung returned to the city-state to participate in *Xiang Baokun zhijing* 向寶崑致敬 (Salute to Pao Kun) with three other artists from Taiwan, China, and Macau to honor Kuo's legacy. Yung also serves as artistic advisor to the local theater company Emergency Stairs 避難階段 (f. 2017), participating annually in their theater festival "Southernmost" 最南階段 2017–19 that explored inter-Asian cultural interactions (W. Lim 2021, 60). Additionally, since the founding of the Huayi Festival—Chinese Festival of the Arts 華藝節 in Singapore in 2003, Zuni Icosahedron as well as Performance Workshop have been staging their works there regularly during the Lunar New Year holiday period (Quah 2013, 229), maintaining an active presence in the city-state. In the absence of a senior figure, Yung certainly contributed to nurturing the growth of Chinese-language theater in Singapore.

Despite the Chinese government's efforts to eradicate Gao Xingjian from public memory, he has earned celebrity status and his plays have

---

2. On intercity exchanges and collaborations emanating from Hong Kong and Singapore, see the recently published volume Ferrari and Thorpe 2021.

3. For detailed analyses of this Kun-Noh collaboration, see Uchino 2013 and Ferrari 2020, 207–79.

performed to critical acclaim in Singapore, Taiwan, and Hong Kong, among many other cities in the world. Endeavors by and collaborations with artists in these sites beyond China have become important in articulating, circulating, and promoting the thoughts and ideas of an artist whose writings continue to remain banned in China today. Since departing China, Gao's playscripts, novels, and essays are published in Chinese almost exclusively in Hong Kong and Taiwan. In addition, many of these works and especially his plays are translated and published in English by the Chinese University of Hong Kong Press, most notably by the translator of his plays Professor Gilbert Fong Chee Fun. Gao's first play to be performed in the Chinese-speaking world outside the mainland was in Hong Kong. *Bus Stop* was staged by the theater group Horizonte 第四綫劇社 (f. 1985) in 1986 (Shelby Chan 2010, 200) and directed by Ko Tin Lung, who would become Chung Ying's first Chinese artistic director. While the cast for *The Other Shore* was disbanded during its rehearsals at BPAT in Beijing in 1986, the play was staged at NIA in Taipei in 1990. Stan Lai, who was then head of its theater department, recommended Gao's play for production and even assumed the producer's role (Chiu and Lee 1997, 95–102). In 1995, Gao himself directed the play at the Hong Kong Academy for Performing Arts.

Significantly, the world premieres of Gao's several dramas and films took place in these alternative Chinese-speaking sites. In 1997, the Taiwanese theater troupe GuoGuang Opera Company 國光劇團 (f. 1995) commissioned Gao to write *Snow in August*, based on the story of the sixth patriarch of Zen Buddhism, Huineng 禪宗六祖慧能. The play was directed by Gao himself, starring Wu Hsing-kuo 吳興國 (b. 1953), Taiwan's preeminent performer of experimental Peking opera and artistic director of the Contemporary Legend Theatre 當代傳奇劇場 (f. 1986), in the leading role, and staged at the National Theatre in Taipei from December 19 to 22, 2002. The world premiere of Gao's *Of Mountains and Seas: A Tragicomedy of the Gods in Three Acts* opened at the Chinese University of Hong Kong. Hardy Tsoi directed the play in Cantonese as part of the "Gao Xingjian Arts Festival" 高行健藝術節 in May 2008. In 2013, Singapore hosted the premiere screening of Gao's third film, or what he calls "cinematic poetry" 電影詩, *Mei de zangli* 美的葬禮 (Requiem for beauty).[4] Gao has been bestowed honorary degrees by universities

---

4. For a study of *Requiem for Beauty* (2013) in English, see W. Lim 2018.

worldwide, several of which are in Taiwan and Hong Kong. Permanent Gao Xingjian collections have now been established at the Chinese University of Hong Kong as well as National Taiwan Normal University.

Multilingualism and Multicultural Experiences

As Diana Looser reminds us, whereas many plays have scripts, "the performance itself generates a range of meanings that exceed the boundaries of the written text" (2014, 15). Indeed, the dramatic works I have chosen to discuss are still being performed and find continued relevance in time periods and contexts beyond the moments when they were created. Yet the importance of historicizing them cannot be overstated. Historicizing these works and their producers prevents us from falling into the trap of blind hero worship. Undoubtedly these are among the most important artists in our contemporary times who have created, to use Martin Esslin's definition of absurdist theater, "the most demanding, the most intellectual theatre" (1960, 14). Nevertheless, it is crucial to recognize the historical contexts from which they arose and identify the specific sociopolitical issues to which they were responding that elevated them to their current eminent status. These four director-playwrights who are today celebrated as grandmasters 大師 did not simply appear out of nowhere. They had to confront the state, challenge accepted mainstream modes of representation, and even risk the possibility of incarceration. Like Diana Looser's analysis of new Oceanic theater, the works of these Chinese dramatists were extremely valuable "in their exposure of the dominant ideological and political maneuvers that regulate national and regional histories and affect present identities" (2014, 27). As the Chinese saying goes: does the hero make the times 英雄造時勢, or do the times make the hero 時勢造英雄? This book has demonstrated the latter.

The challenging yet rewarding task of weaving together four theater histories into a single coherent narrative has allowed me to discover significant features distinguishing these four dramatists from their contemporaries. Their rise to prominence in the 1980s was inseparable from the geopolitical conditions in the region; their heightened sensitivities to the changes in their immediate societies and the region propelled them to continue creating works that are highly relevant to their immediate societies well beyond the 1980s. Apart from Gao, their theater companies are still the most prominent ones in their locales. Not many artistic troupes can boast of having been in existence for four decades; at the time of this book's publication in early 2024, Performance Workshop will be in its fortieth year, Zuni Icosahedron its forty-second, and The Theatre Practice its fifty-ninth.

An important factor that distinguishes these dramatists from their peers is their multilingual abilities and transnational life experiences. A command of different languages gives them access to more diversified and complex life narratives, allowing them to tap into cultural recesses not immediately accessible to those who are monolingual. These four dramatists are at least bicultural and bilingual, if not multilingual. Yung and Lai were schooled in the United States, Kuo in Australia, while Gao majored in French language and literature. Their multilingual edge and multicultural sensibilities allow them to make connections with and draw on cultural resources from beyond the Chinese-speaking world, thus enriching their creative repertoire.

Among the generation of artists born in the 1940s–1950s in the Chinese-speaking world, many might speak at least one regional language as well as Mandarin; far fewer, however, had good command of a European language, especially at the level of fluency of these four dramatists. While the dramatists' knowledge of European languages did not determine their enviable legacies, it certainly allowed them significant advantages that contributed to their success. First, it provided them with cultural capital that represented the First World. Accompanying the military might of the West, especially just after the immediate postwar years, was its technological and economic superiority and social progressiveness that translated into cultural capital. Their experience and training in the most authoritative cultural institutions of the West, on top of the linguistic ability to collaborate directly with master artists from the West, gave these dramatists immense professional standing in the artistic circles of their respective home regions. My intention is less to privilege an Amero-Eurocentric point of view than to draw our attention to the unequal power relations that have asserted themselves, defined the modern era, and continue to shape our contemporary realities. Even if these most important ethnic Chinese intellectual dramatists are highly influenced by the West, this study on them is an attempt to raise voices from sites outside the West in a bid to begin the process of decolonization.

Second, having spent considerable time outside their home states afforded these dramatists lived experience in other styles of governance and power paradigms that might only be vaguely familiar to those who have led insular lives. These corporeal experiences that continually displaced them from their comfort zones took place during their early formative years, leaving an indelible imprint that shaped the dramatists' outlook on art and life. Having acquired other points of view for comparison with their home conditions might in part explain why their critical dramatic praxis always called for ways of scrutiny and contemplation that deviated from the mainstream. Not only have these early in-transit experiences unsettled them from their comfort zones, at the same time they have also seemingly opened up a "third eye" for these dramatists with which to view the world afresh. All of them created works that challenged the status quo from different perspectives, presenting reflections of alternative realities to the ones backed by the governments of their individual states. This might also account for why these dramatists have expressed that they find most comfortable residing on the margins of society, the in-between spaces of different cultures, affording them the necessary distance and space to critically reflect on the center.

Significantly, these transnational experiences developed in these dramatists a critical eye with which to view geopolitics. Their foreign language abilities and transnational experiences act almost like a mirror that gives them a reflection of themselves. This reflective mirroring enables them to become trailblazers, finding a unique path each for their own sites by examining and borrowing from similarities and differences of others between East and West. Cognizant of the fact that the problems confronting their homelands were not unique to but a result of the greater geopolitical reality, their theatrical works tended to reflect on issues that were simultaneously symptomatic of situations both domestic and abroad, instead of merely mired in narrow critique of their home governments. This might also explain why their works found a ready audience beyond their immediate shores, making them the most performed dramatists outside their home regions.

Writing in the special issue "The Living Tree: The Changing Meaning of Being Chinese Today" of the journal *Daedalus* in 1991, it must have been impossible for Leo Lee then to imagine a Chinese Joseph Brodsky, the Soviet poet in exile and winner of the 1987 Nobel Prize in Literature, someone "who writes in both his native language and the language of his adopted country in order to create an art that transcends national boundaries." The reason Lee fears this cul-de-sac is twofold: on the one hand is the omniscient Chinese government's legitimization of itself at the center, which has "dominated the literary imaginations of modern Chinese everywhere"; on the other is the artist's "misplaced obsession" that privileges the motherland's problems as "uniquely Chinese which lay absolute claim to the loyalty of Chinese in all parts of the world" (1991, 218). This "misplaced obsession" that Lee mentions is conceivably an even more salient problem in contemporary times. In Sylvia Lin Li-chun's interview with Gao Xingjian, she expressed the concerning view that "nationality is becoming increasingly important in the age of globalization," to which Gao responded:

> Nationality doesn't mean anything. For a writer, his or her work is what is most important and what readers want to see. I consider myself to be a global citizen without borders. Since leaving China, I always write, first and foremost, for myself; my ideal readers are also not restricted by borders. Getting reactions from readers from different countries pleases me; I consider that a confirmation of my creativity.
>
> (S. Lin 2008, 14)

Indeed, not only do these dramatists I study constantly *dis*identify with the notion of Chineseness imposed by their individual states, they also write with a distinctive awareness that rises above their national identities. Already they write with native linguistic flair in more than one language, and through translation their works have been staged in various parts of the world well beyond their immediate shores to audiences of different cultural traditions. To address Leo Lee's concerns, we have found not just one but four Chinese Joseph Brodskys in these dramatists in the diaspora. Indeed, even before Gao's winning of the coveted prize, Gilbert Fong had already gone as far as to say that Gao is "the first Chinese playwright" to have entered "world theatre" (1999, x). My book has demonstrated that all four dramatists are deserving of admission into the illustrious hall of world theater.

Future Directions

In terms of researching the Chinese diasporic performing arts, I have merely scratched the surface of this multifaceted field of inquiry. This book has only touched on the four most important figures in the 1980s. Apart from the one play I have analyzed in significant depth by each director-playwright, a treasure trove of works by these prolific artists are waiting to be examined in greater detail. Storytelling, film, television, painting, installation art, opera, musical, dance, fiction, and poetry, among other art forms in which these dramatists have also experimented, have yet to be given the attention they deserve. Their contemporaries, who inspired them, who they inspired, and the many other directors, playwrights, actors, theater companies, and theoreticians with whom they crossed paths and collaborated also warrant further study. The complex issues of language, identity, and politics that are discussed extensively in this book continue to be important themes in the performing arts well beyond the 1980s.

These grandmasters have inspired an entire generation of younger practitioners to take up the mantle, come forth, and become practitioners of theater or other art forms. Many who did so gave up their original professions with more lucrative salaries. And many indeed have since become leading artists in their immediate regions and beyond. What were the collective memories imprinted in these artists of a younger generation? What was the missionary zeal shared by their peers? In what ways had the influences of these gurus left a lasting impression on their works?

As we have seen, the dramatic scenes in each of the four states are anything but uniform. Even though all are ethnic Chinese majority states, their separate histories etched in them very different realities. How have the competing affiliations between Sinicization or localization affected dramatists who work in different languages? And how does this vary for those who work across languages? Surely the English-speaking, Western-cultured practitioner would have a different response and imagination of their postcolonial reality as compared to the Chinese-cultured artist, even if they both are ethnic Chinese. These are all heterogenous societies finding ways to connect and communicate, and language certainly has been a way for people to forge alliances. However, the latent hierarchical structure and power relations so embedded within the politics of language, as we have learned, can be as divisive and alienating as they are unifying. A comparative study of the diverse intracultural theaters within each site is long overdue.

A comparative locus allows us to see not just the distinctive features of these four dramatists but the region of the Chinese-speaking world more holistically. *Denationalizing Identities* contributes to global theater, transnational performance, and comparative drama studies and has the potential to reverse our implicit biases in at least three fields of inquiry. First, theater and performance studies has for too long had a very Western-centered orientation. Inclusion of Asian examples in drama anthologies or studies published in Western languages are mostly cursory, if they exist at all, and when they are mentioned traditional Asian theaters tend to be featured far more often than contemporary examples (X. Chen 2002, 20–21). This book contributes to shifting the dialogue to where it matters most: these four are the most significant and cutting-edge Chinese theater-makers of our times whose contributions to world theater can no longer be ignored.

Second, as in most subfields of Chinese studies, the focus of Chinese-language drama and performance is still very much on the mainland; some have included Taiwan, fewer have included Hong Kong.[5] The recent publications of the *Routledge Handbook of Asian Theatre* (S. Liu 2016) and *Transnational Chinese Theatres* (Ferrari 2020) are good examples that have begun to acknowledge the importance of Southeast Asia and the diaspora by including essays on Taiwan, Hong Kong, and the Southeast Asian region. My study addresses this imbalance not only by bringing out the significance and interconnectivity of the Chinese diaspora within the greater Chinese-speaking world, but also by underlining the central importance of the diaspora in the formation of alternative Chinese cultural identities. Only through the comparative vantage provided in the multiple frames of reference across various sites can we illuminate the issues in the region's postcoloniality, which are central to Cold War studies. Transnational comparative studies are still quite new in this field, and more of such work will be needed to better illuminate the transnational tensions and divergences in the Chinese-language theater world.

Third, although this study stems from the contestation of Chineseness, ironically none of these four diasporic dramatists claims to be at the center of Chinese culture. Instead, they are joined by their sense of marginality. The marginal spaces in between cultures are precisely where they borrow resources from, experiment with, and synthesize different cultural traditions. The distance on the periphery allows them to critically examine and reflect on the power hierarchy and resist the nationalistic impulses emitting from the political center. These illustrious figures who draw their creative resources from the margins

---

5. *Twentieth-Century Chinese Drama: An Anthology* (Gunn 1983a) is a pioneering example of an early anthology that has included Taiwan on top of examples from mainland China. Other anthologies and studies of drama that have included both Taiwan and Hong Kong are Cheung and Lai 1997, Joubin 2009, X. Chen 2010, Lei 2011, R. Li 2016, S. Liu 2016, and Ferrari 2020.

could serve as models of critical, intellectual theater-makers beyond the Chinese-speaking world. Because these dramatists have exhibited a vision that exceeds their cultural affiliations and transcends their national affinities, they could serve as useful examples in thinking about identity politics of the diaspora in theater and the arts that do not succumb to the call of Chineseness and ones that are not exclusively Chinese.

References

"A Life of Practice—Kuo Pao Kun." 2012-13. Exhibition at the National Museum of Singapore. September 14, 2012-February 24, 2013.

Abbas, M. Ackbar. 1997. *Hong Kong: Culture and the Politics of Disappearance*. Minneapolis: University of Minnesota Press.

Amranand, Amitha. 2008. "Looking Back and Beyond." *Bangkok Post*, March 26.

Anderson, Perry. 2004. "Stand-off in Taiwan." *London Review of Books* 26, no. 11: 12.

Ang, Ien. 2001. On Not Speaking Chinese: Living between Asia and the West. London: Routledge.

Atticus. 1960. "'The Good Woman of Szechuan' and 'Dido and Aeneas' Get the Vote of Dramatic, Musical Societies." *Singapore Free Press*, June 20, 6.

Barmé, Geremie. 1983. "A Touch of the Absurd—Introducing Gao Xingjian, and His Play *The Bus Stop*." *Renditions* 19-20 (Spring/Autumn): 373-78.

Benjamin, Geoffrey. 1975. "The Cultural Logic of Singapore's 'Multiracialism.'" [Working papers] Department of Sociology, University of Singapore, no. 44. Singapore: Department of Sociology, University of Singapore.

Birch, David. 1997. "Singapore English Drama: A Historical Overview, 1958-1985." In *Nine Lives: Ten Years of Singapore Theatre, 1987-1997*, edited by Sanjay Krishnan, 22-52. Singapore: Necessary Stage.

Boal, Augusto. 1979. *Theater of the Oppressed*. Translated by Charles A. Leal McBride and Maria-Odilia Leal McBride. New York: Urizen Books.

———. 1997. "The Theatre of the Oppressed." *Unesco Courier* 50, no. 11 (November): 32-36.

Bollen, Jonathan. 2020. *Touring Variety in the Asia Pacific Region, 1946-1975*. Cham: Palgrave Macmillan.

Bolling, Thomas E. "Danny Yung." Accessed March 13, 2008. http://faculty.washington.edu/kendo/yung.html.

Boon, Chan. 2013. "*Swallow* a Patriotic Song." *The Straits Times* (Singapore), August 9.

Braester, Yomi. 2008. "In Search of History Point Zero: Stan Lai's Drama and Taiwan's Doubled Identities." *Journal of Contemporary China* 17, no. 57: 689-98.

———. 2010. "Angel Sanctuaries: Taipei's Gentrification and the Erasure of Veterans' Villages." In *Painting the City Red: Chinese Cinema and the Urban Contract*, 187-223. Durham, NC: Duke University Press.

Brecht, Bertolt. 1964. *Brecht on Theatre: The Development of an Aesthetic*. Translated by John Willett. New York: Hill and Wang.

Brook, Peter. 1996. *The Empty Space*. New York: Touchstone.

Carlson, Marvin A. 2001. *The Haunted Stage: The Theatre as Memory Machine*. Ann Arbor: University of Michigan Press.

Chan, Evans. 1984. "A Fiery Row Engulfs Deng Show." *Hong Kong Standard*, August 21.

Chan, Felicia. 2008. "When Is a Foreign-Language Film Not a Foreign-Language Film? When It Has Too Much English in It: The Case of a Singapore Film and the Oscars." *Inter-Asia Cultural Studies* 9, no. 1: 97–105.

Chan, Johnny Koon-chung 陳冠中. 2001. "Xianggang ren de Xianggang?" 香港人的香港？ (A Hong Kong of the Hongkongers?). In *Xianggang wei wancheng de shiyan* 香港未完成的實驗 (Hong Kong's incomplete experiment), 60–64. Hong Kong: Zhinanzhen jituan youxian gongsi.

Chan, Kurt Yuk-keung 陳育強. 2003. "Re-reading 'Danny Yung's *The Deep Structure of Chinese Culture*'"「榮念曾的中國文化深層結構」的再閱讀. In *From Close From Afar: An Anthology on Danny Yung* 距離：拾話榮念曾, edited by May Fung 馮美華, 19–22. Hong Kong: 1a Space.

Chan, Shelby Kar-yan 陳嘉恩. 2010. "Gao Xingjian xiju yu dianying chuangzuo nianbiao" 高行健戲劇與電影創作年表 (Chronology of Gao Xingjian's dramatic and cinematic works). In *Lun xiju* 論戲劇 (On theater), by Gao Xingjian 高行健 and Gilbert Fong Chee Fun 方梓勳, 196–208. Taibei: Lianjing chuban shiye gufen youxian gongsi.

——. 2015. *Identity and Theatre Translation in Hong Kong*. Berlin: Springer.

Chan, Shelly. 2018. *Diaspora's Homeland: Modern China in the Age of Global Migration*. Durham, NC: Duke University Press.

Chan, Stephen Ching-kiu 陳清僑. 1987–88. "Temporality and the Modern Subject: Effects of Memory in Lai Sheng-ch'uan's *The Other Evening, We Put Up a Show of 'Hsiang-sheng.*'" *Tamkang Review* 淡江評論 18, nos. 1–4 (Autumn–Summer): 23–37.

——. 1992. "Speaking Politically of Zuni Speaking Politically." 政治的進念・進念的政治. In *Zuni 10th Anniversary Commemorative*, 36–38. Hong Kong: Zuni Icosahedron.

Chang, Bi-yu. 2002. "Cultural Change and Identity Shift in Relation to Cultural Policy in Post-war Taiwan, with Particular Reference to Theatre." PhD diss., City University London.

——. 2015. *Place, Identity, and National Imagination in Post-war Taiwan*. London: Routledge, Taylor & Francis Group.

Chang, Yvonne Sung-sheng. 1993. *Modernism and the Nativist Resistance: Contemporary Chinese Fiction from Taiwan*. Durham, NC: Duke University Press.

——. 2007. "Representing Taiwan: Shifting Geopolitical Frameworks." In *Writing Taiwan: A New Literary History*, edited by David Wang Der-wei and Carlos Rojas, 17–25. Durham, NC: Duke University Press.

Chen, Agnes. 1991. "Will a Hundred Flowers Bloom?" *The Straits Times* (Singapore), February 17.

Chen Jide 陳吉德. 2004. *Zhongguo dangdai xianfeng xiju, 1979–2000* 中國當代先鋒戲劇, 1979–2000 (Contemporary avant-garde theatre in China, 1979–2000). Beijing: Zhongguo xiju chubanshe.

Chen Juan 陳娟. 2013. "Rong Nianzeng: 'Xianggang wenhua jiaofu' meiyibu zuopin dou pingyi zhe shehui" 榮念曾："香港文化教父"每一部作品都

評議著社會 (Danny Yung: Every production of the "cultural godfather of Hong Kong" is a critique on society). *Guoji xianqu daobao* 國際先驅導報, July 26. http://cul.qq.com/a/20130723/012037.htm.

Chen, Letty Lingchei. 2006. *Writing Chinese: Reshaping Chinese Cultural Identity*. New York: Palgrave Macmillan.

Chen, Xiaomei. 1991. "'Misunderstanding' Western Modernism: The Menglong Movement in Post-Mao China." In "Monumental Histories," special issue, *Representations* 35 (Summer): 143–63.

———. 2002. *Acting the Right Part: Political Theater and Popular Drama in Contemporary China*. Honolulu: University of Hawai'i Press.

———. 2003. "Performing the Nation: Chinese Drama and Theater." In *Columbia Companion to Modern East Asian Literature*, edited by Joshua Mostow, Kirk Denton, and Bruce Fulton, 437–45. New York: Columbia University Press.

———, ed. 2010. *The Columbia Anthology of Modern Chinese Drama*, New York: Columbia University Press.

———. 2016. "Introduction: Propaganda Performance, History, Landscape." In *Staging Chinese Revolution: Theater, Film, and the Afterlives of Propaganda*, 1–55. New York: Columbia University Press.

Chen, Ya-Ping. 2018. "*Shen-ti Wen-hua*: Discourses on the Body in Avant-Garde Taiwanese Performance, 1980s–1990s." *Theatre Research International* 43, no. 3: 272–90.

Cheung, Martha Pui-Yiu. 2005. "Yung, Danny." In *The Oxford Encyclopedia of Theatre and Performance*, edited by Dennis Kennedy. Oxford: Oxford University Press. http://www.oxfordreference.com/views/ENTRY.html?subview=Main&entry=t177.e4308.

Cheung, Martha Pui-Yiu, and Jane Lai Chui-chun, eds. 1997. *An Oxford Anthology of Contemporary Chinese Drama*. Hong Kong: Oxford University Press.

Cheung Ping-kuen 張秉權 and Gilbert Fong Chee Fun 方梓勳, eds. 2003. "What Kinds of Drama Are We Staging" 我們演甚麼戲. Special issue, *Xianggang xiju xuekan* 香港戲劇學刊 (Hong Kong drama review) 4.

Chew Boon Leong 周文龍. 2008. "Wenti xijujia Rong Nianzeng" 問題戲劇家榮念曾 (Danny Yung, the dramatist who raises questions). *Lianhe zaobao* 聯合早報 (Singapore), August 5.

Chia, Helene. 1986. "'You Only Live Once': Some Reflections." *Performing Arts* (Singapore) 3 (August): 46–47.

Chia, Joshua Yeong Jia, and Loh Pei Ying. 2012. "Rediffusion." Singapore Infopedia. https://www.nlb.gov.sg/main/article-detail?cmsuuid=9d4b7199-fa91-417d-832d-b4160c7c9d59.

Ching, Leo T. S. 2001. *Becoming "Japanese": Colonial Taiwan and the Politics of Identity Formation*. Berkeley: University of California Press.

Chiu Kun-liang 邱坤良 and Lee Chiang 李強, eds. 1997. *Juchang jiashu: Guoli yishu xueyuan xijuxi yanchu shilu* 劇場家書：國立藝術學院戲劇系演出實錄 (Letters from the theater family: Performance records of the Department of Theatre Arts at the National institute of the arts). Taipei: Shulin, 1997.

Chong, Wing Hong 莊永康. 1988. "Feast for Drama Enthusiasts." *The Straits Times* (Singapore), January 5, 5.

Chou, Katherine Hui-ling. 2016. "Modern Theatre in Hong Kong, Taiwan, Korea and North Korea: Taiwan." In *Routledge Handbook of Asian Theatre*, edited by Steven Liu Siyuan, 333-39. London: Routledge, Taylor & Francis Group.

Chow, Rey. 1993. *Writing Diaspora: Tactics of Intervention in Contemporary Cultural Studies*. Bloomington: Indiana University Press.

———. 2000. "Introduction: On Chinese-ness as a Theoretical Problem." In *Modern Chinese Literary and Cultural Studies in the Age of Theory: Reimagining a Field*, edited by Rey Chow, 1-25. Durham, NC: Duke University Press.

Chow, Tse-tsung 周策縱. 1989. "Closing Remarks." In *Di'erjie Huawen wenxue datong shijie guoji huiyi: Dongnanya Huawen wenxue* 第二屆華文文學大同世界國際會議：東南亞華文文學 (Proceedings of the second international conference on the Commonwealth of Chinese literature: Chinese literature in Southeast Asia), edited by Wong Yoon Wah 王潤華 and Horst Pastoors 白豪士, 359-62. Singapore: Goethe-Institut and Singapore Association of Writers.

Chow Yung Ping 周勇平. 1983. "Jinnian · ershi mianti: Xiezai siyue yishu zhongxin yanchu 'Liang nüxing' zhi qian" 進念・二十面體：寫在四月藝術中心演出「兩女性」之前 (Zuni Icosahedron: Written before the staging of *One Woman/Two Stories* at the Hong Kong Arts Centre in April). *Sing Tao Weekly* 星島週刊 (Hong Kong), April.

Chu Tien-wen 朱天文. 1986. "You yichu Lai Shengchuan de xi" 又一齣賴聲川的戲 (Yet another Stan Lai play). In *Anlian taohuayuan* 暗戀桃花源 (Secret love in peach blossom land), by Lai Sheng-chuan, 12-15. Taibei: Huangguan.

Chua, Beng Huat. 2009. "Being Chinese under Official Multiculturalism in Singapore." *Asian Ethnicity* 10, no. 3: 239-50.

Chun, Allen. 1996. "Fuck Chinese-ness: On the Ambiguities of Ethnicity as Culture as Identity." *boundary 2* 23, no. 2 (Summer): 111-38.

Chung Ming-der 鍾明德. 1990. "Xiaojuchang fazhan zhi pinggu: Juchang shinin de huigu yu zhanwang" 小劇場發展之評估：劇場十年的回顧與展望 (Ten years of little theater: A review and a look at the future). *Dangdai* 當代 (Con-temporary monthly) 49: 64-83.

———. 1999. *Taiwan xiaojuchang yundongshi: Xunzhao linglei meixue yu zhengzhi* 臺灣小劇場運動史：尋找另類美學與政治 (History of the little theater movement of Taiwan: In search of alternative aesthetics and politics). Taibei: Yangzhi.

Chung Yi-huei 鐘羿惠. 2012. *Chuangyi Zhongguo: Rong Nianzeng yu Xianggang de yishu zhengzhi* 創意中國：榮念曾與香港的藝術政治 (A creative China: Danny Yung and the politics of art in Hong Kong). Taibei Shi: Guoli Taiwan daxue zhengzhi xuexi Zhongguo dalu ji liang'an guanxi jiaoxue yu yanjiu zhongxin.

Clarke, David. 1996. "Zuni Icosahedron in Context." In *Art & Place: Essays on Art from a Hong Kong Perspective*, 144-49. Hong Kong: Hong Kong University Press.

Dai Jinhua 戴錦華. 2012. "After Post-Cold War" 後冷戰以後 (lecture). Graduate School of Humanities and Social Sciences, National Chiao Tung University, Hsin-chu, Taiwan.

Davidson, Andrew P., and Kuah-Pearce Kuhn Eng. 2008. "Introduction: Diasporic Memories and Identities." In *At Home in the Chinese Diaspora: Memories, Identities and Belongings*, edited by Kuah-Pearce Kuhn Eng and Andrew P. Davidson, 1–11. Basingstoke, Hampshire; New York: Palgrave Macmillan.

Denton, Kirk. 2002. "Editor's Note." *Modern Chinese Literature and Culture* 14, no. 2 (Fall): iii–vi.

Devan, Janadas. 2000. "Kuo Pao Kun on Plays and Prison." *The Straits Times* (Singapore), May 19.

Di'erjie Huayu xijuying zhuanji bianweihui 第二屆華語戲劇營專輯編委會, ed. 1988. *Maixiang duoyuanhua xiju: Di'erjie Huayu xijuying zhuanji* 邁向多元化戲劇：第二屆華語戲劇營專輯 (Toward a multivalent theater: Proceedings of the Second Chinese-language Drama Camp). Singapore: Xinjiapo Chaozhou bayi huiguan wenjiao weiyuanhui chubanzu.

Diamond, Catherine. 1993. "The Role of Cross-Cultural Adaptation in the Little Theatre Movement in Taiwan." PhD diss., University of Washington.

Diamond, Elin, ed. 1996. *Performance and Cultural Politics*. London: Routledge.

DiBello, Michelle Leigh. 1996. "*The Other Shore*: The Search for a 'Spiritual Home' in Contemporary Chinese Drama." PhD diss., Stanford University.

Digital Collection of Originality in Theatre of Yi-Wei Yao, Chi-Mei Wang and Stan Lai 姚一葦、汪其楣、賴聲川戲劇創意典藏計畫. Accessed May 13, 2013. http://e-theatreen.teldap.tw/chi-mei-wang.

Dolan, Jill. 1988. *The Feminist Spectator as Critic*. Ann Arbor: UMI Research Press.

———. 2006. "The Polemics and Potential of Theatre Studies and Performance." In *The SAGE Handbook of Performance Studies*, edited by D. Soyini Madison and Judith Hamera, 508–26. Thousand Oaks: Sage.

Ee, Jaime. 2000. "The Father of Singapore Theatre." *Business Times* (Singapore), March 11.

Esslin, Martin. 1960. "The Theatre of the Absurd." *Tulane Drama Review* 4, no. 4 (May): 3–15.

"Experts to Stage Forum." 1987. *South China Morning Post* (Hong Kong), April 30, 16.

Fang Xiu 方修. 1979. *Ma Hua xin wenxue daxi (zhanhou) 4: Xiju yi ji* 馬華新文學大系（戰後）4：戲劇一集 (A comprehensive anthology of modern Malayan Chinese literature (post–World War II) 4: Drama volume one). Singapore: Shijie shuju.

Ferrari, Rossella. 2008. "Transnation/Transmedia/Transtext: Border-Crossing from Screen to Stage in Greater China." *Journal of Chinese Cinemas* 2, no. 1: 53–65.

———. 2012. *Pop Goes the Avant-Garde: Experimental Theatre in Contemporary China*. London: Seagull Books.

———. 2017. "Asian Theatre as Method: The Toki Experimental Project and Sino-Japanese Transnationalism in Performance." *TDR* 61, no. 3 (Fall): 141–64.

———. 2020. *Transnational Chinese Theatres: Intercultural Performance Networks in East Asia*. Cham: Palgrave Macmillan.

Ferrari, Rossella, and Ashley Thorpe, eds. 2021. *Asian City Crossings: Pathways of Performance through Hong Kong and Singapore*. London: Routledge.

REFERENCES

Fok Yit Wai 霍月偉. 1993. "Huayu juchang luohou le ma?" 華語劇場落後了嗎？ (Is Chinese-language theater outdated?). *Lianhe zaobao* 聯合早報 (Singapore), July 7.

Fong, Gilbert Chee Fun 方梓勳. 1992a. "Xu: Du ju tese de Xianggang huaju" 序：獨具特色的香港話劇 (Preface: The unique Hong Kong theater). In *Xianggang huaju lunwen ji* 香港話劇論文集 (Essays on Hong Kong theater), edited by Gilbert Fong Chee Fun 方梓勳 and Hardy Tsoi Sik Cheong 蔡錫昌, 3–11. Xianggang: Zhongtian zhizuo youxian gongsi.

———. 1992b. "Jia zai Xianggang: Xianggang huaju de bentu xingxiang" 家在香港：香港話劇的本土形象 (My home is Hong Kong: Self image in Hong Kong drama). In *Xianggang huaju lunwen ji* 香港話劇論文集 (Essays on Hong Kong theater), edited by Gilbert Fong Chee Fun 方梓勳 and Hardy Tsoi Sik Cheong 蔡錫昌, 99–117. Xianggang: Zhongtian zhizuo youxian gongsi.

———. 1994. "Xu" 序 (Preface). In *Xianggang huajuxuan* 香港話劇選 (Selected plays of Hong Kong), edited by Gilbert Fong Chee Fun 方梓勳 and Tian Benxiang 田本相, 8–34. Beijing: Wenhua yishu chubanshe.

———. 1999. Introduction to *The Other Shore: Plays by Gao Xingjian*, translated by Gilbert Fong Chee Fun, ix–xlii. Hong Kong: Chinese University Press.

———. 2000. "Huawen xiju yanjiu—Ye suan shi xu" 華文戲劇研究——也算是序 (Research on Chinese-language drama). In *Xinjiyuan de Huawen xiju: Di'erjie Huawen xijujie (Xianggang, 1998) xueshu yantaohui lunwenji* 新紀元的華文戲劇：第二屆華文戲劇節（香港·1998）學術研討會論文集 (Chinese drama in the new era), edited by Gilbert Fong Chee Fun 方梓勳, 9–11. Xianggang: Xianggang xiju xiehui, Xianggang Zhongwen daxue xiju gongcheng.

———. 2005. "Freedom and Marginality: The Life and Art of Gao Xingjian" 自由與邊緣性：高行健的生命與藝術. Translated into Chinese by Shelby Chan Kar-yan 陳嘉恩. In *Cold Literature: Selected Works by Gao Xingjian* 冷的文學：高行健著作選 (Chinese-English Bilingual Edition), translated by Gilbert Fong Chee Fun 方梓勳 and Mabel Lee 陳順妍, viii–xlvii. Hong Kong: Chinese University Press.

———. 2006. "Xunzhao xiju de gushi: Zhong Jinghui de yishu licheng" 尋找戲劇的故事：鍾景輝的藝術歷程 (A story of searching for drama: The artistic journey of Chung King Fai). In *Liang'an shengdian sidi xuange: Diwujie Huawen xijujie xueshu yantaohui lunwenji* 兩岸盛典四地弦歌：第五屆華文戲劇節學術研討會論文集 (Celebration across the strait, string songs from four places: The 5th Chinese drama festival academic conference), edited by Tian Benxiang 田本相, 138–60. Kunming: Yunnan daxue chubanshe.

Fong, Gilbert Chee Fun, and Shelby Chan Kar-yan. 2016. "Modern Theatre in Asia: Hong Kong." In *Routledge Handbook of Asian Theatre*, edited by Steven Liu Siyuan, 328–33. London: Routledge, Taylor & Francis Group.

Fung Wai-choi 馮偉才. 1988. "Xu" 序 (Prologue). In *Xianggang duanpian xiaoshuoxuan, 1984–1985* 香港短篇小說選，1984–1985 (Selected works of Hong Kong novels, 1984–1985), edited by Fung Wai-choi 馮偉才, 1–6. Xianggang: Sanlian shudian.

Gao, Xingjian 高行健. (1983) 1998. "*Bus Stop*: A Lyrical Comedy on Life in One Act." Translated by Kimberly Besio. In *Theater and Society: An Anthology of Contemporary Chinese Drama*, edited by Yan Haiping, 3–59. New York: M. E. Sharpe.

———. (1987) 2001. "Chidao de xiandai zhuyi yu dangjin Zhongguo wenxue" 遲到的現代主義與當今中國文學 (The belated modernism and contemporary Chinese literature). In *Meiyou zhuyi* 沒有主義 (Without isms), 108–19. Taipei: Lianjing.

———. 1988. *Dui yizhong xiandai xiju de zhuiqiu* 對一種現代戲劇的追求 (In pursuit of modern drama). Beijing: Zhongguo xiju chubanshe.

———. 1990. "Wo zhuzhang yizhong leng de wenxue" 我主張一種冷的文學 (I advocate a kind of cold literature). *Zhongshi wanbao·Shidai wenxue* 中時晚報 · 時代文學 (Taiwan), August 12.

———. (1991) 2006. "Wilted Chrysanthemums." *The Case for Literature*. Translated by Mabel Lee, 140–54. London: HarperCollins. Translation of "Geri huanghua" 隔日黃花.

———. (1992) 2001. "Zhongguo liuwang wenxue de kunjing" 中國流亡文學的困境 (The predicament of Chinese exile literature). In *Meiyou zhuyi* 沒有主義 (Without isms), 120–28. Taipei: Lianjing.

———. (1993) 2001. "Meiyou zhuyi" 沒有主義 (Without isms). In *Meiyou zhuyi* 沒有主義 (Without isms), 3–14. Taipei: Lianjing.

———. 2001. "The Case for Literature." Translated by Mabel Lee. *PMLA* 116, no. 3 (May): 594–608. Translation of "Wenxue de liyou" 文學的理由 (2000).

Gao Yin 高音. 2006. *Beijing xinshiqi xijushi* 北京新時期戲劇史 (Theater history of the new era in Beijing). Beijing Shi: Zhongguo xiju chubanshe.

George, Cherian. 2000. *Singapore: The Air-Conditioned Nation. Essays on the Politics of Comfort and Control, 1990–2000*. Singapore: Landmark Books.

Goh, Beng Choo. 1987. "Four-day Camp with Drama in Store." *The Straits Times* (Singapore), December 7, 5.

———. 1988. "Taiwan's Star Director Thrives on Improvisation." *The Straits Times* (Singapore), January 7, 3.

Gong Min 貢敏. 1996. "Nanyu chengshou de 'wangwo' zhi jing" 難於承受的「忘我」之境 (The unbearable state of "forgetting me"). In *Zhonghua minguo bashisi nian Biaoyan yishu nianjian* 中華民國八十四年 表演藝術年鑑 (Performing arts yearbook), edited by Lin Ching-yun 林靜芸, 26–33. Taibei shi: Zhongzheng wenhua.

Gunn, Edward Mansfield, Jr., ed. 1983a. *Twentieth-Century Chinese Drama: An Anthology*. Bloomington: Indiana University Press.

———. 1983b. "Introduction to *What If I Really Were?*" In *Stubborn Weeds: Popular and Controversial Chinese Literature after the Cultural Revolution*, edited by Perry Link, 198–200. Bloomington: Indiana University Press.

———. 2006. *Rendering the Regional: Local Language in Contemporary Chinese Media*. Honolulu: University of Hawai'i Press.

———. 2013. "Modern Chinese Drama." Oxford Bibliographies Online: Chinese Studies, edited by Timothy Wright. Last modified April 22. https://www.oxfordbibliographies.com/display/document/obo-9780199920082/obo-9780199920082-0011.xml?rskey=g9QhAV&result=119.

Hall, Stuart. 1996. "Introduction: Who Needs 'Identity'?" In *Questions of Cultural Identity*, edited by Stuart Hall and Paul Du Gay, 1-17. Thousand Oaks, Calif.: Sage.

Han Lao Da 韓勞達. 1986. "Quzhong ren weisan: *Xiaobaichuan* yanchu ganyan yishu" 曲終人未散：《小白船》演出感言一束 (*The Little White Sailing Boat* postproduction thoughts). In *Laoda juzuo: Xiju chuangzuo ji suibi* 勞達劇作：戲劇創作及隨筆 (Plays and essays by Han Lao Da), 128-32. Singapore: Xinjiapo Chaozhou bayi huiguan, wenjiao weiyuanhui chubanzu.

Haowai 號外 (City magazine). 2007a. "Notebook on City x Zuni" 進念：香港實驗. In "City x Zuni: School of Avant Garde" 進念‧香港實驗, special issue, 364 (January): 103-105.

———. 2007b. "Classroom: Music + Visual." In "City x Zuni: School of Avant Garde" 進念‧香港實驗, special issue, 364 (January): 108-113.

Hong Zicheng 洪子誠. 1999. *Zhongguo dangdai wenxueshi* 中國當代文學史 (History of contemporary Chinese literature). Beijing: Beijing daxue chubanshe.

Hsiung, Yuwen. 2013. *Expressionism and Its Deformation in Contemporary Chinese Theatre*. New York: Peter Lang AG.

Hsu, Amanda Yuk-kwan 許旭筠. 2009. "A Genealogy of Hong Kong Urban Literature and Cinema." In *Hong Kong Urban Culture & Urban Literature* 香港都市文化與都市文學, edited by Leung Ping-kwan 梁秉鈞, Amanda Hsu Yuk-kwan 許旭筠, and Caroline Lee Hoi-lam 李凱琳, 2-17. Hong Kong: Hong Kong Story Association.

Hsu Po-yun 許博允. 2018. *Jinghui yuanyun: Xu Boyun huiyilu* 境會元勻：許博允回憶錄 (Memoirs of Hsu Po-yun). With Liao Chien-hui 廖倩慧 and Lee Hui-na 李慧娜. Taibei Shi: Yuanliu chubanshe shiye gufen youxian gongsi.

Hu Xingliang 胡星亮. 2007. "Xianggang houxiandai xiju de tansuo yu kunhuo" 香港後現代戲劇的探索與困惑 (Study on post-modern drama in Hong Kong). *Shoudu shifan daxue xuebao (Shehui kexue ban)* 首都師範大學學報 (社會科學版) (Journal of Capital Normal University [Social sciences edition]) 3 T176: 90-96.

Huang, Cecily. 2011. "No Strings Attached: An Interview with Stan Lai." *That's Beijing* (Beijing), August 3. http://www.thatsmags.com/Beijing/index.php/article/detail/77/no-strings-attached.

Huang Chien-yeh 黃建業. 1988. "Yizhong qianwei de ganran: Xie zai 'Jinnian‧ershi mianti' *Shiritan* yanchu zhi qian" 一種前衛的感染：寫在「進念‧廿面體」《拾日譚》演出之前 (An infectious avant-garde: On Zuni Icosahedron's *Decameron*). *Minsheng bao* 民生報 (Taiwan), August 9.

Huang, Zuolin 黃佐臨. 1994. "Fusing of Revolutionary Realism with Revolutionary Romanticism." In "Tradition, Innovation, and Politics: Chinese and Overseas Chinese Theatre across the World," edited by William H. Sun, special section of *TDR* 38, no. 2 (Summer): 18-29.

Huawen xijujie (Di 6 jie) 華文戲劇節 (第6屆). 2007. *Xi, you Xianggang wutai Zhongguo qing zhanlan* 戲‧遊 香港舞台中國情展覽 (Play: Hong Theatre—Romance with China). Hong Kong: Hong Kong Federation of Drama Societies and Hong Kong Drama Project, Chinese Univ. of Hong Kong.

"Huayu huajutuan niandi ban xijuying huanying xuesheng baoming canjia" 華語話劇團年底辦戲劇營歡迎學生報名參加 (Year-end Chinese drama camp welcomes student registrations). 1987. *Lianhe zaobao* 聯合早報 (Singapore), November 16, 20.

Hwang, David Henry. 2001. "In Today's World, Who Represents the 'Real' China?" *New York Times*, April 1, 32.

Ingham, Mike. 2005. "Hong Kong–based English-language Theatre." In *City Stage: Hong Kong Playwriting in English*, edited by Mike Ingham and Xu Xi, 1–10. Hong Kong: Hong Kong University Press.

Ingham, Mike, and Xu Xi, eds. 2005. *City Stage: Hong Kong Playwriting in English*. Hong Kong: Hong Kong University Press.

Jeyaretnam, Phillip. 1990. "Let the Banquet Begin, Who Needs the Cook?" *The Straits Times* (Singapore), September 27.

"Jinnian zenyang tiaozhan juchang neiwai guiju?" 進念怎樣挑戰劇場內外規矩？ (How Zuni challenges regulations inside and outside the theatre). 1988. *Yazhou zhoukan* 亞洲週刊, September 4, 37.

Jit, Krishen. 1990. "Introduction: Kuo Pao Kun—The Man of the Future in Singapore Theatre." In *The Coffin Is Too Big for the Hole, and Other Plays*, by Kuo Pao Kun, 7–28. Singapore: Times Books International.

———. 2000. "No Parking on Odd Days." In *Images at the Margins: A Collection of Kuo Pao Kun's Plays*, 92–97. Singapore: Times Books International.

Joubin, Alexa Alice [a.k.a. Alexa Huang]. 2009. *Chinese Shakespeares: Two Centuries of Cultural Exchange*. New York: Columbia University Press.

Kershaw, Baz. 1992. *The Politics of Performance: Radical Theatre as Cultural Intervention*. London: Routledge.

Koh, Angeline. 2014. "Max Le Blond." Singapore Infopedia. http://eresources.nlb.gov.sg/infopedia/articles/SIP_2014-01-10_181943.html.

Koh, Siong Ling, ed. 1999. *Arts, Cultural & Media Scenes in Singapore*. Singapore: Ministry of Information and the Arts.

Kok, Heng Leun. 2016. "Chinese Theatre: Moving beyond a Century." In *Theatre*, by Robin Loon, Kok Heng Leun, Zizi Azah Binte Abdul Majid, and Vadivalagan Shanamuga, 43–57. Singapore: Institute of Policy Studies, Straits Times Press.

Kowallis, Jon Eugene von 寇致銘. 1997. "The Diaspora in Taiwan and Hong Kong Film: Framing Stan Lai's *The Peach Blossom Land* with Allen Fong's *Ah Ying*." In *Transnational Chinese Cinema: Identity, Nationhood, Gender*, edited by Sheldon Lu, 169–86. Honolulu: University of Hawai'i Press.

———. 2013. "Haixia liang'an de rentong wenti: Zhonghua Minguo yibai zhounian jinian yu Lai Shengchuan zuopin" 海峽兩岸的認同問題：中華民國一百週年紀念與賴聲川作品 (The question of identity on both sides of the Taiwan Straits: Lai Shengchuan's works and the 100th anniversary of the Republic of China). In *Kuawenhua qingjing: chayi he dongtai ronghe—Taiwan xiandangdai wenxue wenhua yanjiu* 跨文化情境：差異和動態融合—臺灣現當代文學文化研究 (The transcultural condition: Differences or dynamic fusion—Studies of modern and contemporary Taiwan literature and culture), edited by Peng Hsiao-yen 彭小妍, 121–37. Taibei Shi: Zhongyang yanjiuyuan Zhongguo wenzhe yanjiusuo.

———. 2018. "The Diaspora and the Nation: A Cultural Poetics of Re-Membering in Lai Shengchuan's Taiwan Trilogy." *Journal of Modern Literature in Chinese* 15, no. 2: 157–80.

Kubin, Wolfgang 顧彬. 2009. "Why Deal with Hong Kong Literature?" 為甚麼要談香港的文學？ In *Hong Kong Urban Culture & Urban Literature* 香港都市文化與都市文學, edited by Leung Ping-kwan 梁秉鈞, Amanda Hsu Yuk-kwan 許旭筠, and Caroline Lee Hoi-lam 李凱琳, 32–44. Hong Kong: Hong Kong Story Association.

Kuo, Pao Kun 郭寶崑. (1984) 2007. "Aidelei yishujie de chongji zhi san: *Dengdai Guotuo* de yinyu leguan" 艾德雷藝術節的衝擊之三：《等待果陀》的陰鬱樂觀 (Impact from the Adelaide arts festival (III): Melancholy and optimism in *Waiting for Godot*). In *The Complete Works of Kuo Pao Kun*, vol. 6: *Commentaries* 郭寶崑全集・第六卷・評論, ed. Tan Beng Luan 陳鳴鸞, 12–14. Singapore: Practice Performing Arts School and Global Pub.

———. 1984a. "Baba juyi de qishi—Kan *Xuan xifu*" 峇峇劇藝的啟示——看《選媳婦》 (Revelations from Peranakan theatrical arts: Watching *Choosing a Daughter-in-law*). *Lianhe zaobao* 聯合早報 (Singapore), June 22, 4.

———. 1984b. "People's Theatre?" *Singapore Monitor*, July 6, 26.

———. (1984) 1990. "The Coffin Is Too Big for the Hole." In *The Coffin Is Too Big for the Hole, and Other Plays*, 29–46. Singapore: Times Books International.

———. 1985. "The Newest 'Wave' in Hong Kong: Theatre Is Making Its Ripples Felt." *Singapore Monitor*, February 6, 16.

———. 1988. "MaMa Looking for Her Cat: The 'Mama' Process." Playwright's and Director's Message. *Mama Looking for Her Cat* house program.

———. (1988) 2012. "Mama Looking for Her Cat." In *The Complete Works of Kuo Pao Kun*, vol. 4: *Plays in English* 郭寶崑全集・第四卷・英文戲劇, edited by C. J. Wee Wan-ling, 81–97. Singapore: Practice Performing Arts School and Global Publishing.

———. 1996. "Gu'er qingjie Bianyuan xintai: Xinjiapo biaoyan yishu de dute xingge" 孤兒情結 邊緣心態：新加坡表演藝術的獨特性格 (Orphan complex, marginal mentality: Unique characteristics of the performing arts in Singapore). *Lianhe zaobao* 聯合早報 (Singapore), August 18.

———. 1997a. "Between Two Worlds: A Conversation with Kuo Pao Kun." In *Nine Lives: Ten Years of Singapore Theatre, 1987–1997*, edited by Sanjay Krishnan, 126–42. Singapore: Necessary Stage.

———. 1997b. "Playwright's Voice: A Forum on Playwriting." In *Nine Lives: Ten Years of Singapore Theatre, 1987–1997*, edited by Sanjay Krishnan, 54–71. Singapore: Necessary Stage.

———. 1998. "Dao Wang Sha" 悼王沙 (Mourning Wang Sha). *Lianhe zaobao* 聯合早報 (Singapore), January 20.

———. 1999. "Zheshi xumu, tahai nianqing" 這是序幕，他還年輕 (This is just prologue, he is still young). In *Lai Shengchuan: Juchang 1* 賴聲川：劇場 1 (Stan Lai: Theater 1), edited by Yang Shu-hui 楊淑慧, 13–14. Taipei: Yuanzun wenhua qiye gufen youxian gongsi.

———. 2000. *Images at the Margins: A Collection of Kuo Pao Kun's Plays*. Singapore: Times Books International.

———. 2001. "Kuo Pao Kun." In *Interlogue: Studies in Singapore Literature: Interviews*, edited by Ronald D. Klein, 4: 104–27. Singapore: Ethos Books.

———. 2020. "What Makes Theatre Modern? An Interview with Kuo Pao Kun by Quah Sy Ren." Translated by Wong Chee Meng. In "Kuo Pao Kun," special issue, *Inter-Asia Cultural Studies* 21, no. 2: 189–98.

"Kuo Pao Kun Festival 2012—In Search of Kuo Pao Kun" Festival Guide 《郭寶崑節——尋找郭寶崑》導覽手冊. Organized by The Theatre Practice.

Kuoshu, Harry H. 1998. "Will Godot Come by Bus or Through a Trace? Discussion of a Chinese Absurdist Play." *Modern Drama* 41, no. 3 (Fall): 461–73.

Kwok, Kenneth. 2002. "The Portrait of an Artist." *The Flying Inkpot Theatre Reviews* (Singapore), December 15. https://inkpotreviews.com/oldInkpot/02reviews/02revlegealiv.html.

Łabędzka, Izabella. 2008. *Gao Xingjian's Idea of Theatre: From the Word to the Image*. Leiden: Brill.

Lai Bojiang 賴伯疆. 1993. *Dongnanya Huawen xiju gaiguan* 東南亞華文戲劇概觀 (An overview of Chinese-language drama in Southeast Asia). Beijing: Zhongguo xiju chubanshe.

Lai, Chee Kien. 2013. "The Little Sparrow That Could" [English translation of Liang Wenfu's "Xiaoxiao maque dan zhuzhi"]. August 11. https://www.facebook.com/girlinpinafore/posts/490720354352798.

Lai, Jane Chui-chun 黎翠珍, and Vicki Ooi Cheng-har 黃清霞. 2017. "Xianggang xiju ziliaoku ji koushu lishi jihua (Diyiqi): Li Cuizhen, Huang Qingxia luyin fangwen (er) Haibao jutuan de chengli yuanqi" 香港戲劇資料庫暨口述歷史計劃（第一期）：黎翠珍、黃清霞錄音訪問（二）海豹劇團的成立緣起 (Hong Kong drama archive and oral history project (phase one): Interview with Jane Lai and Vicki Ooi (2) The origins of The Seals Players). Interviewed by William Chan 陳瑋鑫. International Association of Theatre Critics (Hong Kong) 國際演藝評論家協會（香港分會）, January 6. https://youtu.be/JYPZzpM_KVM.

Lai, Stan Sheng-chuan 賴聲川 (in collaboration with the cast). (1986) 2010. "Secret Love in Peach Blossom Land." Translated by Stan Lai. In *The Columbia Anthology of Modern Chinese Drama*, edited by Chen Xiaomei, 967–1025. New York: Columbia University Press.

———. (1986) 2014. "Something Out of Nothing: On Improvisation and Theater." Translated by Alexa Joubin (a.k.a. Alexa Huang). In *The Columbia Sourcebook of Literary Taiwan*, edited by Yvonne Chang Sung-sheng, Michelle Yeh, and Fan Ming-ju, 368–73. New York: Columbia University Press.

———. 1988. "Jielu yu shentou: Jinnian de juchang yishu" 揭露與滲透：進念的劇場藝術 (Disclosure and penetration: The theatrical art of Zuni). *Lianhe wanbao* 聯合晚報 (Taiwan), August 26.

———. (1989) 1999. "Zheyiye, sheilai shuo xiangsheng?" 這一夜，誰來說相聲？ (Look who's cross-talking tonight?). In *Lai Shengchuan: Juchang 3* 賴聲川：劇場3 (Stan Lai: Theater 3), edited by Yang Shu-hui 楊淑慧, 181–320. Taibei: Yuanzun wenhua qiye gufen youxian gongsi.

———. 1990. "The Structuring of Spontaneity: An Assessment and Documentation of Improvisational Creative Methods in the Modern Taiwan

Theatre." In *Studies in Chinese-Western Comparative Drama*, edited by Thomas Luk Yun-tong, 135–55. Hong Kong: Chinese University Press.

——. 1992a. "Wutaiju *Anlian taohuayuan* de dansheng" 舞台劇《暗戀桃花源》的誕生 (The birth of the play *Secret Love in Peach Blossom Land*). In *Wo anlian de taohuayuan* 我暗戀的桃花源 (The peach blossom land I am secretly in love with), edited by Hong Hong 鴻鴻 and Yue Hui 月惠, 15–29. Taibei Shi: Yuanliu chuban shiye gufen youxian gongsi.

——. 1992b. "Paipian qianzouqu" 拍片前奏曲 (Prelude to the film's shooting). In *Wo anlian de taohuayuan* 我暗戀的桃花源 (The peach blossom land I am secretly in love with), edited by Hong Hong 鴻鴻 and Yue Hui 月惠, 31–34. Taibei Shi: Yuanliu chuban shiye gufen youxian gongsi.

——. 1994. "Specifying the Universal." In "Tradition, Innovation, and Politics: Chinese and Overseas Chinese Theatre across the World," edited by William H. Sun, special section of *TDR* 38, no. 2 (Summer): 33–37.

——. (1998) 1999. "Zixu yi: Guanyu yige 'shichuan' de juben" 自序一：關於一個「失傳」的劇本 (Prologue 1: On a 'missing' play). In *Lai Shengchuan: Juchang 3* 賴聲川：劇場3 (Stan Lai: Theater 3), edited by Yang Shu-hui 楊淑慧, 11–14. Taibei: Yuanzun wenhua qiye gufen youxian gongsi.

——. 1999. "Lai Shengchuan nianbiao" 賴聲川年表 (Chronology of Stan Lai). In *Lai Shengchuan: Juchang 3* 賴聲川：劇場3 (Stan Lai: Theater 3), edited by Yang Shu-hui 楊淑慧, 397–99. Taibei: Yuanzun wenhua qiye gufen youxian gongsi.

——. 2008. "Luminosity in the Darkness: Remembering Edward Yang." *Inter-Asia Cultural Studies* 9, no. 1: 3–6.

——. 2010. "Lai Shengchuan—Juanlian zai zheyicun" 賴聲川——眷戀在這一村 (Stan Lai—Attachment to this village). *Mingren mianduimian* 名人面對面 (Star face). Interview by Xu Gehui 許戈輝. Phoenix Satellite Television Holdings Chinese Channel. February 21.

——. 2011. "Weaving Local Stories into Epic Theatre: On *The Village* and the Preservation of Collective Memory." Lecture at UC Berkeley, Institute of East Asian Studies, January 18. https://www.youtube.com/watch?v=5rXZW91wbM0.

——. 2021. *Selected Plays of Stan Lai: The Complete Set*. Edited by Lissa Tyler Renaud. 3 vols. Ann Arbor: University of Michigan Press.

Lai, Stan Sheng-chuan 賴聲川, et al. 2007. "'Lai Shengchuan juchang yishu guoji xueshu yantaohui': Lai Shengchuan yu yishuqun zuotan" 「賴聲川劇場藝術國際學術研討會」：賴聲川與藝術群座談 (A Panel Discussion: Stan Lai vs. Theater Artists). In "Stan Lai's Theatrical Works and Art" 賴聲川劇場藝術專輯, special issue, *Xiju xuekan* 戲劇學刊 (Taipei Theatre Journal) 5 (January): 99–119.

"Lai Shengchuan daoyan zuopin Shouci you Xianggang huajutuan yanchu" 賴聲川導演作品 首次由香港話劇團演出 (Stan Lai's directorial work to be performed by Hong Kong repertory theatre for the first time). 1998. *Xinwen gongbao* 新聞公報, September 12. https://www.info.gov.hk/gia/general/199809/12/0912137.htm.

"Lai Shengchuan dazao 'Modu zhuanshuban' *Anlian taohuayuan*" 賴聲川打造「魔都專屬版」《暗戀桃花源》 (Stan Lai creates an "exclusive

Shanghai rendition" of *Secret Love in Peach Blossom Land*). 2017. *Meiri toutiao* 每日頭條 (KK News), March 1. https://kknews.cc/entertainment/r9qxky4.html.

Lam, Edward Yik-wah 林奕華. 2006. "Jinnian bawu, yingchi fantang" 進念八五，影癡飯堂 (Zuni at 1985, canteen for the film addicts). In *Dianying haowai: Xianggang guoji dianyingjie sanshi zhounian tekan* 電影號外：香港國際電影節三十週年特刊 (Filming howwhy: Hong Kong Int'l Film Festival 30th anniversary), edited by Li Cheuk To 李焯桃, Zeng Fan 曾凡, and Bono Lee 李照興, 26-29. Xianggang: Xianggang guoji dianyingjie xiehui, "Haowai" zazhi.

Larson, Wendy. 1989. "Realism, Modernism, and the Anti-'Spiritual Pollution' Campaign in China." *Modern China* 15, no. 1 (January): 37-71.

Lau Shing Hon 劉成漢. 1984. "Jinnian—Ting buliao de zhanzheng" 進念——停不了的戰爭 (Zuni—The war that cannot be stopped). *Dianying shuangzhoukan* 電影雙週刊 (Film biweekly) 151, December 6.

Le Blond, Max. 1986. "Drama in Singapore: Towards an English Language Theatre." In *Discharging the Canon: Cross-Cultural Readings in Literature*, edited by Peter Hyland, 112-25. Singapore: Singapore University Press.

———. 2000. "Mama Looking for Her Cat." In *Images at the Margins: A Collection of Kuo Pao Kun's Plays*, 139-44. Singapore: Times Books International.

Lee, Bono 李照興. 2006. "Women kaishi jiao ziji: Xianggang ren—1976 de qianqian houhou" 我們開始叫自己：香港人——1976的前前後後 (We started to call ourselves Hongkongers—around 1976). In *Dianying haowai: Xianggang guoji dianyingjie sanshi zhounian tekan* 電影號外：香港國際電影節三十週年特刊 (Filming howwhy: Hong Kong Int'l Film Festival 30th anniversary), edited by Li Cheuk To 李焯桃, Zeng Fan 曾凡, and Bono Lee 李照興, 6-9. Xianggang: Xianggang guoji dianyingjie xiehui, "Haowai" zazhi.

Lee, Caroline Hoi-lam 李凱琳. 2009. "Xianggang dushi wenhua ji wenxue ganlan" 香港都市文化及文學概覽 (A genealogy of Hong Kong urban culture and literature). In *Hong Kong Urban Culture & Urban Literature* 香港都市文化與都市文學, edited by Leung Ping-kwan 梁秉鈞, Amanda Hsu Yuk-kwan 許旭筠, and Caroline Lee Hoi-lam 李凱琳, 18-31. Hong Kong: Hong Kong Story Association.

Lee, Gregory B. 2012. *China's Lost Decade: Cultural Politics and Poetics 1978–1990. In Place of History*. Brookline, Mass.: Zephyr Press; Lyon: Éditions Tigre de Papier.

Lee, Gregory, and Noël Dutrait. 2001. "Conversations with Gao Xingjian: The First 'Chinese' Winner of the Nobel Prize for Literature." *China Quarterly* 167 (September): 738-48.

Lee, Hugh Kuo-shiu 李國修, et al. 1988. "Jinnian wei juchang dailai jinbu de guannian" 進念為劇場帶來進步的觀念 (Zuni brings progressive concepts for the theater). *Zili wanbao* 自立晚報 (Taiwan), August 21, 13.

Lee, Leo Ou-fan. 1989. Introduction to *Spring Bamboo: A Collection of Contemporary Chinese Short Stories*, edited and translated by Jeanne Tai, xi-xvii. New York: Random House.

———. 1991. "On the Margins of the Chinese Discourse: Some Personal Thoughts on the Cultural Meaning of the Periphery." In "The Living

Tree: The Changing Meaning of Being Chinese Today," special issue, *Daedalus* 120, no. 2 (Spring): 207–26.

Lee, Mabel. 1996. "Walking out of Other People's Prisons: Liu Zaifu and Gao Xingjian on Chinese Literature in the 1990s." *Asian and African Studies* 5, no. 1: 98–112.

———. 2000. Introduction to *Soul Mountain*, by Gao Xingjian, translated from the Chinese by Mabel Lee, v–xi. New York: HarperCollins.

———. 2002a. "2000 Nobel Laureate Gao Xingjian and His Notion of Cold Literature." In *Sighs Too Deep for Tears: RLA Lectures 2001*, edited by Colette Rayment, 33–40. Sydney: RLA Press.

———. 2002b. "On Nietzsche and Modern Chinese Literature: From Lu Xun (1881–1936) to Gao Xingjian (b. 1940)." *Literature and Aesthetics* 11: 23–43.

———. 2006. "Introduction: Contextualising 2000 Nobel Laureate Gao Xingjian." In *The Case for Literature*, by Gao Xingjian, 1–24. London: HarperCollins.

———. 2012. "Introduction: Aesthetic Dimensions of Gao Xingjian's Fiction, Theatre, Art, and Filmmaking." In *Gao Xingjian: Aesthetics and Creation*, by Gao Xingjian, translated by Mabel Lee, vii–xxiii. Amherst, NY: Cambria Press.

———. 2013. "On the Position of the Writer: Lu Xun and Gao Xingjian." In *Talking Literature: Essays on Chinese and Biblical Writings and Their Interaction*, edited by Raoul David Findeisen and Martin Slobodnik, 179–92. Wiesbaden: Harrassowitz Verlag.

Lee, San Chouy. 1989. "Towards a Bilingual Theatre." *The Straits Times* (Singapore), May 22.

Lee Yu-lin 李玉玲. 2013. "Zishen yanyuan Gu Baoming Zouzai xiju yu beiju de zhongjian" 資深演員顧寶明 走在喜劇與悲劇的中間 (Traversing in-between comedy and tragedy: Veteran actor Ku Pao-ming). *Biaoyan yishu* 表演藝術 (Performing arts review) 252 (December). http://par.ntch.edu.tw/article/show/1385974863667935.

Lee Yu-lin 李玉玲 and Andy Yu Kuo-hwa 于國華. 2005. "*Xiangduilun* Lai Shengchuan, Ding Naizhu disheng miyu yi liao sanshi nian" 《相對論》賴聲川 丁乃竺 低聲密語 一聊30年 (*Theory of Relativity*: Soft whispers of Tibetan Buddhist wisdom between Stan Lai and Ting Nai-chu for 30 years). *Lianhe bao* 聯合報 (Unitas) (Taiwan), April 5. http://www.sulanteach.net/我的學習/賴聲川%20丁乃竺/相對論.htm.

Leenhouts, Mark. 2003. "Culture against Politics: Roots-Seeking Literature." In *Columbia Companion to Modern East Asian Literature*, edited by Joshua Mostow, Kirk Denton, and Bruce Fulton, 533–40. New York: Columbia University Press.

Lehmann, Hans-Thies. 2006. *Postdramatic Theatre*. Translated by Karen Jürs-Munby. London: Routledge.

Lei, Daphne Pi-Wei. 2006. *Operatic China: Staging Chinese Identity across the Pacific*. New York: Palgrave Macmillan.

———. 2011. *Alternative Chinese Opera in the Age of Globalization: Performing Zero*. Basingstoke: Palgrave Macmillan.

———. 2019. *Uncrossing the Borders: Performing Chinese in Gendered (Trans) Nationalism*. Ann Arbor: University of Michigan Press.

Leung Man-to 梁文道. 2009. "Rong Nianzeng—Haiyou henduo shiqing yaoxiang, haiyou henduo shiqing yaozuo" 榮念曾——還有很多事情要想，還有很多事情要做 (Danny Yung—Still much to think about, still much to be done). In *Fangwen: Shiwu ge you xiangfa de shuren* 訪問：十五個有想法的書人 (Interviews: Fifteen judicious people of belles-lettres), 90–105. Xianggang: Shang shuju.

Leung Ping-kwan 梁秉鈞. 2011. "'Gaibian' de wenhua shenfen: Yi wuling niandai Xianggang wenxue wei li" 「改編」的文化身份：以五零年代香港文學為例 (The cultural identity of "adaptation": The case of 1950s Hong Kong literature). In *Xianggang wenxue de chuancheng yu zhuanhua* 香港文學的傳承與轉化 (The continuation and transformation of Hong Kong literature), edited by Leung Ping-kwan 梁秉鈞, Chan Chi-tak 陳智德, and Mathew Cheng Ching-hang 鄭政恆, 107–31. Xianggang: Huizhi chuban.

Li Longyun 李龍雲. 1993. "Xiju wenxue duanxiang" 戲劇文學段想 (Random thoughts on dramatic literature). In *Huangyuan yu ren: Li Longyun juzuo xuan* 荒原與人：李龍雲劇作選 (Wilderness and man: Selected plays by Li Longyun), 318–77. Beijing: Zhongguo shehui kexue chubanshe.

Li, Ruru 李如茹, ed. 2016. *Staging China: New Theatres in the Twenty-First Century* 舞台中國：二十一世紀新戲劇. New York: Palgrave Macmillan.

Li Xiaoyang 李曉陽. 1995. "Chule yonggan, dadan, youmeiyou yuanchuang—80-90 niandai" 除了勇敢、大膽，有沒有原創——八〇～九〇年代 (Apart from courage and bravery, is there originality—the 1980s-90s). *Biaoyan yishu* 表演藝術 (Performing arts review) 33 (July): 50–57.

Li Yijun 李亦筠. 2013. "Zao jinbo 23 nian Liang Wenfu gequ *Maque xian zhuzhi* jiejin" 遭禁播23年 梁文福歌曲《麻雀銜竹枝》解禁 (After 23 years, ban lifted on Liang Wern Fook's song *Sparrow with Bamboo Twigs*). *Lianhe zaobao* 聯合早報 (Singapore), August 2.

Liang Wern Fook 梁文福. 2013. "Xiaoxiao maque dan zhuzhi" 小小麻雀擔竹枝 (The little sparrow that carried the bamboo twigs). *Lianhe zaobao* 聯合早報 (Singapore), August 10.

Lilley, Rozanna. 1998. *Staging Hong Kong: Gender and Performance in Transition*. Richmond, Surrey: Curzon.

Lim Soon Hock 林順福. 1995. "Lun zhanhou wunian minzu zizhu langchao sheng zhong de Xin Ma huaxiao xiju huodong" 論戰後五年民族自主浪潮聲中的新馬華校戲劇活動 (On Singaporean and Malayan Chinese-medium school activities in the first five years of the post–World War II period). In *Dongnanya Huaren wenxue yu wenhua* 東南亞華人文學與文化 (Southeast Asian Chinese literature and culture), edited by Yeo Song Nian 楊松年 and Wong Hong Teng 王慷鼎, 146–67. Singapore: Xinjiapo Yazhou yanjiu xuehui, Nanyang daxue biyesheng xiehui, Xinjiapo Zongxiang huiguan lianhe zonghui.

Lim Soon Lan 林春蘭, and Tan Beng Luan 陳鳴鸞, eds. 2012. *The Complete Works of Kuo Pao Kun*. Vol. 9: *Life and Work: A Pictorial Record* 郭寶崑全

集 · 第九卷 · 生活與創作圖片. Singapore: Practice Performing Arts School and Global Publishing.

Lim, Wah Guan. 2018. "From Theater to Cine-Poetry: Gao Xingjian's Performance Theories." In *Gao Xingjian and Transmedia Aesthetics*, edited by Mabel Lee and Liu Jianmei, 201-15. Amherst, New York: Cambria Press.

———. 2021. "From 1989 to 1997 and Beyond: Zuni Icosahedron's Transnational Explorations." In *Asian City Crossings: Pathways of Performance through Hong Kong and Singapore*, edited by Rossella Ferrari and Ashley Thorpe, 50-68. London: Routledge.

Lin Guosian 林果顯. 2011. "Chinese Culture Renaissance Movement" 中華文化復興運動. *Encyclopedia of Taiwan* 臺灣大百科全書. http://taiwanpedia.culture.tw/en/content?ID=3968.

Lin Kehuan 林克歡. 2007a. "Xianggang de shiyan xiju" 香港的實驗戲劇 (Hong Kong experimental drama). In *Xiaofei shidai de xiju* 消費時代的戲劇 (Theater in consumer society), 103-11. Taibei Shi: Shulin chuban youxian gongsi.

———. 2007b. *Xiju Xianggang, Xianggang xiju* 戲劇香港，香港戲劇 (Dramatizing Hong Kong, Hong Kong drama). Hong Kong: Oxford University Press.

Lin, Sylvia Li-chun. 2008. "Between Homeland and Heartland: An Interview with Nobel Laureate Gao Xingjian." *World Literature Today* 82, no. 3 (May/June): 12-14.

Ling Zi 凌諮. 1984a. "Yapian zhanzheng—Deconstruction of Theatre and Stage" 鴉片戰爭——Deconstruction of Theatre and Stage (Opium war—Deconstruction of theatre and stage), 60-63. Zuni Icosahedron Experimental Arts Archive https://drive.google.com/file/d/1lHQ77hIdU4dMocxjjYKIfg4l0IjWMCcy/view

———. 1984b. "Dui *Yapian zhanzheng* zhiyi de huida" 對「鴉片戰爭」質疑的回答 (Response to questions on *Opium War*). *Xinbao* 信報 (Hong Kong), August 25.

Link, Perry. 1983. "Introduction: On the Mechanics of the Control of Literature." In *Stubborn Weeds: Popular and Controversial Chinese Literature after the Cultural Revolution*, edited by Perry Link, 1-28. Bloomington: Indiana University Press.

———. 1984. Introduction to *Roses and Thorns: The Second Blooming of the Hundred Flowers in Chinese Fiction, 1979-80*, edited by Perry Link, 1-41. Berkeley: University of California Press.

———. 2000. *The Uses of Literature: Life in the Socialist Chinese Literary System*. Princeton, NJ: Princeton University Press.

———. 2007. "The Crocodile Bird: *Xiangsheng* in the Early 1950s." In *Dilemmas of Victory: The Early Years of the People's Republic of China*, edited by Jeremy Brown and Paul G. Pickowicz, 207-31. Cambridge, MA: Harvard University Press.

Liou, Liang-ya. 2011. "Taiwanese Postcolonial Fiction." *PMLA* 126, no. 3: 678-84.

Liu, Joyce Chi-hui. 1997. "Re-staging Cultural Memories in Contemporary Theatre in Taiwan: Wang Qimei, Stanley Lai, and Lin Huaimin."

http://www.srcs.nctu.edu.tw/joyceliu/mworks/mw-taiwantheatre/StageCulture/StageE.html.

Liu Kuang-neng 劉光能. 1986. "Liangchu taohuayuan, yiyang cuolian" 兩處桃花源，一樣錯戀 (Two peach blossom lands are both wrongly in love). In *Anlian taohuayuan* 暗戀桃花源 (Secret love in peach blossom land), by Stan Lai Sheng-chuan 賴聲川, 16-25. Taibei: Huangguan.

Liu, Petrus Yi-der. 2011. *Stateless Subjects: Chinese Martial Arts Literature and Postcolonial History*. Ithaca, NY: East Asia Program, Cornell University.

———. 2015. *Queer Marxism in Two Chinas*. Durham, NC: Duke University Press.

Liu, Steven Siyuan, ed. 2016. *Routledge Handbook of Asian Theatre*. London: Routledge, Taylor & Francis Group.

Liu Yichang 劉以鬯. 1985. "Wushi niandai chuqi de Xianggang wenxue—Yijiu bawu nian siyue ershiqi ri zai 'Xianggang wenxue yantaohui' shang de fayan" 五十年代初期的香港文學——一九八五年四月二十七日在「香港文學研討會」上的發言 (Early 1950s Hong Kong literature—Delivered at "Hong Kong literature conference" April 27, 1985). *Xianggang wenxue* 香港文學 (Hong Kong literature monthly) 6 (June 5): 13-18.

———. 1993. "Youren shuo Xianggang meiyou wenxue" 有人說香港沒有文學 (Some say Hong Kong has no literature). *Wenhuibao · wenyi* 文匯報·文藝 (Hong Kong), June 8.

Liu Zaifu 劉再復. 2000. *Lun Gao Xingjian zhuangtai* 論高行健狀態 (On the condition of Gao Xingjian). Hong Kong: Mingbao chubanshe.

Lo, Jacqueline May Lye. 2004. *Staging Nation: English Language Theatre in Malaysia and Singapore*. Hong Kong: Hong Kong University Press.

Looser, Diana. 2014. *Remaking Pacific Pasts: History, Memory, and Identity in Contemporary Theater from Oceania*. Honolulu: University of Hawai'i Press.

Lovell, Julia. 2006. *The Politics of Cultural Capital: China's Quest for a Nobel Prize in Literature*. Honolulu: University of Hawai'i Press.

Lu, Min 盧敏. 2002. "Chinese Modern Drama in the Past 20 Years" 中國話劇20年斷想. *Women of China English Monthly*, February, 43-45.

Lu, Sheldon Hsiao-peng. 1997. "Chinese Cinemas (1896-1996) and Transnational Film Studies." In *Transnational Chinese Cinema: Identity, Nationhood, Gender*, edited by Sheldon Lu, 1-31. Honolulu: University of Hawai'i Press.

Lü Sushang 呂訴上. 1961. *Taiwan dianying xiju shi* 臺灣電影戲劇史 (A history of cinema and drama in Taiwan). Taibei Shi: Yinhua chubanbu.

Luo, Liang. 2014. *The Avant-Garde and the Popular in Modern China: Tian Han and the Intersection of Performance and Politics*. Ann Arbor: University of Michigan Press.

Ma Baoshan 馬寶山. 1988. "Minzhu jingshen de tixian—'Jinnian · ershimianti' zouguo de daolu" 民主精神的體現——「進念·廿面體」走過的道路 (The embodiment of the democracy spirit—the path Zuni Icosahedron took). *Jiefang yuebao* 解放月報, May, 81-82.

Ma Sen 馬森. 1984a. "Cong ren de ganjue chufa: Xiandai xiju fazhan dawen" 從人的感覺出發：現代戲劇發展答問 (Starting from human emotions:

Questions and answers on the development of modern drama). *Lianhe bao* 聯合報 (Unitas) (Taiwan), February 15.

———. 1984b. "Yige xinxing juchang zai Zhongguo de dansheng—Ji Lai Shengchuan daoyan de *Women doushi zheyang zhangda de*" 一個新型劇場在中國的誕生——記賴聲川導演的《我們都是這樣長大的》 (The birth a new theater form on the Chinese stage—On Stan Lai's *We All Grew Up Like This*). *Zhongguo shibao* 中國時報 (China Times) (Taiwan), January 15.

———. 1985. *Ma Sen xiju lunji* 馬森戲劇論集 (Collected essays on drama by Ma Sen). Taibei Shi: Erya chubanshe.

———. 1991a. *Dangdai xiju* 當代戲劇 (Contemporary theater). Taipei: Shibao.

———. 1991b. *Zhongguo xiandai xiju de liangdu xichao* 中國現代戲劇的兩度西潮 (The two Western tides in modern Chinese drama). Tainan: Wenhua shenghuo xinzhi chubanshe.

———. 1996. "Baling nian yilai de Taiwan xiaojuchang yundong" 八〇年以來的台灣小劇場運動 (The little theater movement in Taiwan since the 1980s). In *Taiwan xiandai juchang yantaohui lunwenji: 1986–1995 Taiwan xiaojuchang* 台灣現代劇場研討會論文集：1986-1995台灣小劇場 (Modern Taiwanese theater conference proceedings: The little theater in Taiwan 1986-1995), edited by Wu Ch'üan-ch'eng 吳全成, 19-28. Taipei: Wenjianhui.

Ma Sen 馬森, et al. 1988. "'Dangdai juchang fazhan de fangxiang' zuotanhui" 「當代劇場發展的方向」座談會 (Symposium on "The direction of contemporary theater development"). In "The Direction of Contemporary Theater's Development" 戲劇專輯：當代劇場發展的方向, special issue, *Lianhe wenxue* 聯合文學 (Unitas literary monthly) 5 (T: 41) (March): 10–35.

Mackerras, Colin P. 1989. "Drama and Politics on the Chinese Mainland, 1976–89." *Issues and Studies* 25, no. 8 (August): 80–117.

Madhavan, Sangeetha. 2004. "Cutting-Edge Collaboration: Kun Opera, Zuni Style was an Enriching Experience." *The Business Times* (Singapore), January 30.

Mahoney, Dino. 2005. "Forward." In *City Stage: Hong Kong Playwriting in English*, edited by Mike Ingham and Xu Xi, vii–x. Hong Kong: Hong Kong University Press.

Mao Zedong 毛澤東. (1940) 1965. "On New Democracy" 新民主主義論. In *Selected Works of Mao Zedong*, 2: 339–84. Beijing: Foreign Languages Press.

Maulod, Adlina. 2009. "Lim Chor Pee." Singapore Infopedia. https://www.nlb.gov.sg/main/article-detail?cmsuuid=07934fbe-c7ba-45d5-aed3-b893ed424dc2.

Mo Xin 漠心. 1987. "Liu zhuanjia yu ni fenxiang xinde" 六專家與你分享心得 (Six experts offer their reflections). *Lianhe zaobao* 聯合早報 (Singapore), December 29, 28.

Mok, Augustine Chiu-yu 莫昭如. 1984. "Programme Notes for Performance of *1984/1997*" 民眾劇場街頭劇. The 70's Biweekly and People's Theatre, October. https://digital.lib.hkbu.edu.hk/mok/types/Performance/ids/MCY-002250/dates/[1984-10]/languages/en.

Moran, Thomas. 2013. "Gao Xingjian." In *Dictionary of Literary Biography*, vol. 370: *Chinese Fiction Writers, 1950–2000*, edited by Thomas Moran and Ye (Dianna) Xu, 65–80. Detroit: Gale Cengage Learning.

National Culture and Arts Foundation 財團法人國家文化藝術基金會. 2001. "Guojia wenyijiang diwujie huojiang yishujia: Lai Shengchuan" 國家文藝獎第5屆獲獎藝術家：賴聲川 (Winner of the 5th annual national award for arts: Stan Lai). https://www.ncafroc.org.tw/artist_detail.html?id=1227.

"Naye shuo xiangsheng shouru chuang jilu" 那夜說相聲收入創紀錄 (Revenue for *The Night We Became Cross-Talk Comedians* breaks record). 1985. *Lianhe bao* 聯合報 (Unitas) (Taiwan), June 9.

Ng, How Wee. 2021. "Dialectics as Creative Process and Decentring China: Zuni Icosahedron and Drama Box's *One Hundred Years of Solitude 10.0: Cultural Revolution*." In *Asian City Crossings: Pathways of Performance through Hong Kong and Singapore*, edited by Rossella Ferrari and Ashley Thorpe, 69–91. London: Routledge.

Ngui, Caroline. 1987. "A Break and a New Start: Agnes—Saint or Sinner?" *The Straits Times* (Singapore), February 14.

Ooi, Vicki Cheng-har 黃清霞. 1995. "The Best Cultural Policy Is No Cultural Policy: Cultural Policy in Hong Kong." *European Journal of Cultural Policy* 1, no. 2: 273–87.

———. 2005. "Seals: Twenty Years After" 海豹劇團：廿載回顧. In *Huigu dangnian: Haibao jutuan jijin youxian gongsi* 回顧當年：海豹劇團基金有限公司 (Reflections: Seals Players Foundation, 1979–1993), edited by Lynn Yau 邱歡智, 14–46. Hong Kong: Encounter Entreprise Hong Kong.

Oon, Clarissa. 2001. *Theatre Life! A History of English-Language Theatre in Singapore through the Straits Times, 1958–2000*. Singapore: Singapore Press Holdings.

Patsalidis, Savas. 2018. "'In China, Directors Are Considered More Highly than Playwrights': Interview with Stan Lai." *Critical Stages/Scènes critiques: The IATC Journal*, no. 18 (December). http://www.critical-stages.org/18/between-the-modern-and-the-traditional-in-contemporary-chinese-theatre-interview-with-stan-lai/.

Peterson, William. 2001. *Theater and the Politics of Culture in Contemporary Singapore*. Middleton, CT: Wesleyan University Press.

Phelan, Peggy. 1993. *Unmarked: The Politics of Performance*. London: Routledge.

"Plays about Pressure." 1987. *South China Morning Post* (Hong Kong), February 7, 17.

Poon Bik-wan 潘壁雲, ed. 2012. *Xianggang huajutuan 35 zhounian xiju yantaohui: "Xiju chuangzuo yu bentu wenhua" taolun shilu ji lunwenji* 香港話劇團35周年戲劇研討會：「戲劇創作與本土文化」討論實錄及論文集 (Proceedings & papers of the Hong Kong repertory theatre's 35th anniversary seminar on "Theatre creativity and local culture"). Xianggang: Xianggang huajutuan.

Quah, Sy Ren 柯思仁. 1994. "Xinjiapo juchang shiyan zhi lu" 新加坡劇場實驗之路 (The path of experimentation in Singapore theater). *Xiju yishu* 戲劇藝術 (Theatre arts) (Shanghai) 2: 120–21.

———. 1996. "Cong xiju fukan tantao zhanqian Xin Ma juyun de kunjing yu fangxiang" 從戲劇副刊探討戰前新馬劇運的困境與方向 (The study of the dilemma and direction of the prewar drama movement in Singapore and Malaya as reflected in the newspaper supplements). *Yazhou wenhua* 亞洲文化 (Asian Culture) 20 (June): 88–100.

———. 2002. "Evolving Multilingual Theatre in Singapore: The Case of Kuo Pao Kun." In *Ethnic Chinese in Singapore and Malaysia: A Dialogue between Tradition and Modernity*, edited by Leo Suryadinata, 377–88. Singapore: Times Academic Press.

———. 2004a. "Form as Ideology: Representing the Multicultural in Singapore Theatre." In *Ask Not: The Necessary Stage in Singapore Theatre*, edited by Tan Chong Kee and Tisa Ng, 27–42. Singapore: Times Edition.

———. 2004b. *Gao Xingjian and Transcultural Chinese Theater*. Honolulu: University of Hawai'i Press.

———. 2005. "Daolun: Guo Baokun de pipan xing juchang yu Xinjiapo rentong de jian'gou" 導論：郭寶崑的批判性劇場與新加坡認同的建構 (Introduction: The critical theatre of Kuo Pao Kun and the construction of a Singaporean identity). In *The Complete Works of Kuo Pao Kun*, vol. 2: *Plays in Chinese, the 1980s* 郭寶崑全集・第二卷・華文戲劇集 (2)：1980年代, edited by Quah Sy Ren 柯思仁 and Pan Cheng Lui 潘正鐳, xiii–xxviii. Singapore: Practice Performing Arts School and Global Publishing.

———. 2006. "'Chufa shi wo de huanxiang, piaopo shi wo de jiayuan': Xinjiapo dangdai wenhua jingguan de chuangzao zhe Guo Baokun" "出發是我的還鄉，漂泊是我的家園"：新加坡當代文化景觀的創造者郭寶崑 ("Departing is my arriving, wandering is my residence": The creator of contemporary Singaporean cultural landscape Kuo Pao Kun). *Dushu* 讀書 (Studies) 8 (August): 21–28.

———. 2010. "Representing Idealism and Activism: Kuo Pao Kun's Theatre in the 1960s and 1970s." In "Reviewing Singapore," special issue, *Moving Worlds: A Journal of Transcultural Writings* 10, no. 1: 148–61.

———. 2011. "Guo Baokun de juchang yu 1980 niandai Xinjiapo rentong de pipan xing jian'gou" 郭寶崑的劇場與1980年代新加坡認同的批判性建構 (Kuo Pao-Kun's theatre and critical construction of Singapore identity in the 1980s). *Zhongguo xiandai wenxue* 中國現代文學 (Modern Chinese literature) 20 (December): 71–95.

———. 2012. "Kuo Pao Kun's First Decade of Art and Social Activism (1965–1976): In the Context of Singapore Chinese-Language Theatre." Unpublished paper delivered at "Kuo Pao Kun International Conference," National Museum of Singapore, September 14–15.

———. 2013. *Xi ju bainian: Xinjiapo huawen xiju 1913–2013* 戲聚百年：新加坡華文戲劇1913-2013 (Scenes: A hundred years of Singapore Chinese-language theatre, 1913–2013). Singapore: Select Books.

Rajendran, Charlene. 2019. "Open Platforms for Dialogue and Difference: Critical Leadership in Singapore Theatre." In *The Routledge Companion to Theatre and Politics*, edited by Peter Eckersall and Helena Grehan, 329–32. Abingdon: Routledge.

Ram, Vernon. 1988. "Zuni's Leading Rabble-Rouser." *Hong Kong Standard*, June 18.

Renaud, Lissa Tyler. 2010. "Interview with Stan Lai (Lai Shengchuan): Director and Playwright." *Critical Stages/Scènes critiques: The IATC Journal*, no. 2 (Spring). http://www.critical-stages.org/2/interview-with-stan-lai-lai-shengchuan-director-and-playwright/.

Roberts, Rosemary A. 2010. *Maoist Model Theatre: The Semiotics of Gender and Sexuality in the Chinese Cultural Revolution (1966–1976)*. Leiden: Brill.

Rogers, Amanda. 2014. *Performing Asian Transnationalisms: Theatre, Identity, and the Geographies of Performance*. London: Routledge.

Roubicek, Bruno. 1990. "Translator's Introduction—*Wildman*: A Contemporary Spoken Drama." *Asian Theatre Journal* 7, no. 2 (Autumn): 184–91.

"Row over Staging of Play Hots Up." 1984. *South China Morning Post* (Hong Kong), August 22.

Ruark, Jennifer K. 2000. "Nobel Author's Works Prove Hard to Find in the U.S." *Chronicle of Higher Education* 47, no. 15 (December 8): A18.

"Rumeng zhi meng (2013)" 如夢之夢 (2013) (A dream like a dream [2013]). Performance Workshop Creative Culture. https://www.pwshop.com/portfolio-cht/zht-theater/如夢之夢/.

"Rumeng zhi meng" 如夢之夢 (A dream like a dream). 2019. Hong Kong Repertory · Main Stage Production. https://www.hkrep.com/event/19-3/.

Sakai, Naoki. 1997. *Translation and Subjectivity: On "Japan" and Cultural Nationalism*. Minneapolis: University of Minnesota Press.

Santayana, George. 1905. *Life of Reason; or, The Phases of Human Progress*. New York: Scribner's.

Sasitharan, Thirunalan. 1989. "Shallow Stage." *The Straits Times* (Singapore), December 29.

———. 2017. "The World Does Not Treat Us Unkindly or Forget Us in the Midst of Solitude . . ." The Esplanade Archives: Offstage Researchers, December 28. https://www.esplanade.com/offstage/researchers/explore/reflections-on-kuo-pao-kun-and-singapore-theatre-in-the-1980s.

Seet, K. K. [Khiam Keong]. 1994. "Cultural Untranslatability as Dramatic Strategy: A Speculative Look at the Different Language Versions of Kuo Pao Kun's Plays." In *Prize-Winning Plays*, vol. 6: *Beyond the Footlights New Play Scripts in Singapore Theatre*, edited by Thiru Kandiah, 243–55. Singapore: UniPress. NUS-Shell Short Plays Series.

Shen, Shiao-ying 沈曉茵. 1995. "Permutations of the Foreign/er: A Study of the Works of Edward Yang, Stan Lai, Chang Yi, and Hou Hsiao-Hsien." PhD diss., Cornell University.

———. 2020. "Cong xieshi dao mohuan—Lai Shengchuan de shenfen yanyi" 從寫實到魔幻——賴聲川的身分演繹 (From the real to the magical: Stan Lai's mutable identity). In *Guangying luoman shi: Taiwan dianying de yishu yu lishi* 光影羅曼史：台港電影的藝術與歷史 (The romance of light and shadow: Art and history of Taiwanese cinema), 229–41. Taipei: Yuanliu chuban.

"Shenghuo · juchang jiehe Xianggang huajutuan yanchu 'Dalu'" 生活 · 劇場結合 香港話劇團演出「大路」 (Life merges with theater—Hong Kong Repertory Theatre stages *The Road*). 1981. *Xin baoren* 新報人 12, no. 4 (November 22): 7.

Shenzhen shi xijujia xiehui 深圳市戲劇家協會 and Jinnian ershi mianshi 進念二十面體 (Zuni Icosahedron), eds. 1993. *Zhongguo dalu, Taiwan, Xianggang, Xinjiapo xijujia guanyu Huayi Huayu diqu xiju biaoyan yu wenhua biaoxiang de duihua* 中國大陸、台灣、香港、新加坡戲劇家關於華裔華語地區戲劇表演與文化表象的對話 (Dialogue among dramatists from China, Taiwan, Hong Kong, and Singapore, regarding theater performance and cultural representation in the Chinese-speaking regions). Shenzhen: Xijujia xiehui.

Shih Hsin-hui 施心慧. 1988. "Zhongguoren wutaishang chengxian de maodun: Biandao Rong Nianzeng" 中國人舞台上呈現的矛盾：編導榮念曾 (The dilemma the Chinese presents on stage: Director-playwright Danny Yung). *Zili zaobao* 自立早報 (Taiwan), September 8.

Shih, Shu-mei. 2007. *Visuality and Culture: Sinophone Articulations*. Berkeley: University of California Press.

———. 2013. "Against Diaspora: The Sinophone as Places of Cultural Production." In *Sinophone Studies: A Critical Reader*, edited by Shu-mei Shih, Chien-hsin Tsai, and Brian Bernards, 25–42. New York: Columbia University Press.

Shui Jing 水晶. 2007. "Zhujie: *Anlian* guanjianci suoyin" 注解：《暗戀》關鍵詞索引 (Footnote: Index to the keywords in *Secret Love*). In *Anlian taohuayuan · Hongse de tiankong* 暗戀桃花源 · 紅色的天空 (Secret love in peach blossom land · Red sky), by Stan Lai Sheng-chuan, 108–44. Beijing: Dongfang chubanshe.

Sim, Amy Kok Eng 沈幗英. 2003. "Xianggang he le zhimindi naishui bian de wuneng? Ji 'Xunzhao Xianggang xiju—Guo Baokun de qishi' yantaohui" 香港喝了殖民地奶水變得無能？記"尋找香港戲劇—郭寶崑的啟示"研討會 (Has drinking from the milk of colonialism turned Hong Kong theatre impotent? A record of the symposium 'Looking for Hong Kong theatre—Inspiration from Kuo Pao Kun'). *Lianhe zaobao* 聯合早報 (Singapore), February 26.

Singerman, Deborah. 1983. "Zuni's Work is 'Abstract': Productions Speak for Themselves." *South China Morning Post* (Hong Kong), September 4, 14.

Siu, Helen F. 1996. "Remade in Hong Kong: Weaving into the Chinese Cultural Tapestry." In *Unity and Diversity: Local Cultures and Identities in China*, edited by Liu Tao Tao and David Faure, 177–96. Hong Kong: Hong Kong University Press.

Souza, John de. 1985. "Coffin's English Debut." *The Straits Times* (Singapore), November 15, 19.

Su Xinqi. 2018. "Liu Yichang, Hong Kong Author Whose Works Inspired Wong Kar-wai Films, Dies at 99." *South China Morning Post* (Hong Kong), June 9.

Sze-Lorrain, Fiona. 2007. "Gao Xingjian: Who is *Xingjian Gao*?" In *Silhouette/Shadow: The Cinematic Art of Gao Xingjian*, edited by Fiona Sze-Lorrain, 181-90. Paris: Contours.

Tam, Kwok-kan. 2001a. "Introduction: Gao Xingjian, the Nobel Prize and the Politics of Recognition." In *Soul of Chaos: Critical Perspectives on Gao Xingjian*, edited by Tam Kwok-kan, 1-20. Hong Kong: Chinese University Press.

———. 2001b. "Drama of Dilemma: Waiting as Form and Motif in *The Bus Stop* and *Waiting for Godot*." In *Soul of Chaos: Critical Perspectives on Gao Xingjian*, edited by Tam Kwok-kan, 43-66. Hong Kong: Chinese University Press.

———. 2002. "The Politics of the Postmodernist Theatre in China." *Interlitteraria* 7: 39-57.

Tam, Kwok-kan, Terry Yip Siu-han, and Wimal Dissanayake. 1999. "Introduction—Self in Four Chinese Communities: China, Taiwan, Hong Kong and Singapore." In *A Place of One's Own: Stories of Self in China, Taiwan, Hong Kong and Singapore*, edited by Tam Kwok-kan, Terry Yip Siu-han, and Wimal Dissanayake, xi-xxii. Oxford: Oxford University Press.

Tan, Alvin. 2012. Remarks made on "Roundtable 2 (In English)." "Kuo Pao Kun International Conference," National Museum of Singapore, September 14-15.

Tan, Chee-Beng. 2013. Introduction to *Routledge Handbook of the Chinese Diaspora*, 1-12. Hoboken: Taylor and Francis.

Tan, E. K. [Eng Kiong]. 2013. *Rethinking Chineseness: Translational Sinophone Identities in the Nanyang Literary World*. Amherst, NY: Cambria Press.

Tan, Eugene Kheng Boon. 2003. "Re-Engaging Chineseness: Political, Economic and Cultural Imperatives of Nation-Building in Singapore." *China Quarterly* 175 (September): 751-74.

Tang Shu Wing 鄧樹榮. 2009. "Meiyou jiuqi, wo rengshi lüshi" 沒有九七，我仍是律師 (Were it not for 1997, I might still be a lawyer). In *Hezi jing: Xianggang wenhua biezhuan* 盒子經：香港文化別傳 (Box book: The beauty and the beast of Hong Kong culture 1987-2007), vol. 3: *Duihua* 對話 (Conversations), edited by Kung Chi Shing 龔志成, 128-36. Hong Kong: MCCM Creations.

Tao Qingmei 陶慶梅 and Hou Shuyi 侯淑儀. 2003. *Cha'na zhong—Lai Shengchuan de juchang yishu* 剎那中——賴聲川的劇場藝術 (Flash of a moment: Stan Lai's theater art). Taipei: Shibao wenhua.

Tay Bin Wee 鄭民威 et al. 1982. "Xinjiapo huayu huaju de guoqu・xianzai・weilai" 新加坡華語話劇的過去・現在・未來 (The past, present, and future of Singapore Chinese-language drama). *Xingzhou ribao* 星洲日報 (Sin Chew Jit Poh) (Singapore), November 4, 18 and November 6, 38.

Tay, William Shu Sam. 1990. "Avant-garde Theater in Post-Mao China: *The Bus-Stop* by Gao Xingjian." In *Worlds Apart: Recent Chinese Writing and Its Audiences*, edited by Howard Goldblatt, 111-18. Armonk, New York; London: M. E. Sharpe.

Tian Benxiang 田本相 and Gilbert Fong Chee Fun 方梓勳, eds. 2009. *Xianggang huaju shigao* 香港話劇史稿 (History of Hong Kong spoken drama essays). Shenyang: Liaoning jiaoyu chubanshe.

Tian Benxing 田本相 and Song Baozhen 宋寶珍. 1997. "Qing huigui, Xianggang huaju yipie (liang ti)" 慶回歸, 香港話劇一瞥(兩題) (Celebrating the handover, a glance at Hong Kong drama). *Da wutai yishu shuangyuekan* 大舞台藝術雙月刊 4: 10–16.

———. 1999. "Cong xiandai xing dao minzu xing—Zhongguo huaju jiushi nian" 從現代性到民族性—中國話劇九十年 (From modernism to nationalism–90 years of Chinese spoken drama). *CUHK Journal of Humanities* 中大人文學報 3 (January): 40–106.

Tsao, Chip 陶傑. 2008. "Tao Jie" 陶傑 (Tsao Chip). In *Dialogue with*, edited by Ni 尼 (Gary), 148–59. Xianggang: Zhu Dawei.

Tsoi, Grace. 2012. "Danny Yung." *HK Magazine*, November 15. http://hk-magazine.com/city-living/article/danny-yung.

Tsoi, Hardy Sik Cheong 蔡錫昌. 1992. "'Keneng de' yu 'yinggai de' Xianggang huaju weilai shunian de fazhan" 「可能的」與「應當的」：香港話劇未來數年的發展 ("Could be" and "should be": Hong Kong drama's development in the next few years). In *Xianggang huaju lunwen ji* 香港話劇論文集 (Essays on Hong Kong theater), edited by Gilbert Fong Chee Fun 方梓勳 and Hardy Tsoi Sik Cheong 蔡錫昌, 77–82. Xianggang: Zhongtian zhizuo youxian gongsi.

———. 2007. "Gao Benna de Zhong Ying ji qi hou" 高本納的中英及其後 (Bernard Goss's Chung Ying and others). *Xianggang xiju xuekan* 香港戲劇學刊 (Hong Kong drama review) 6: 131–34.

Tsu, Jing. 2010. *Sound and Script in the Chinese Diaspora*. Cambridge, MA: Harvard University Press.

Tu, Wei-ming. 1991. "Cultural China: The Periphery as the Center." In "The Living Tree: The Changing Meaning of Being Chinese Today," special issue, *Daedalus* 120, no. 2 (Spring): 1–32.

Tung, Constantine. 1987. "Introduction: Tradition and Experience of the Drama of the People's Republic of China." In *Drama in the People's Republic of China*, edited by Constantine Tung and Colin Mackerras, 1–27. New York: State University of New York Press.

Uchino, Tadashi 內野儀. 2013. "After Three Years of the ICH Project: In Search of Ways for Restoring the Power of Theatre to Speak with the Dead." 非物資文化遺產計劃三年之後：尋找回復劇場與亡靈對話力量的途徑. In *Yazhou biaoyan yishu: Cong chuantong dao dangdai* 亞洲表演藝術：從傳統到當代 (Asia performing arts: From the traditional to the contemporary), edited by Jessica Yeung Wai-yee 楊慧儀 and Wong Yue-wai 王裕偉 (editor-in-chief: Danny Yung 榮念曾), 295–99. Xianggang: Jinnian ershi mianti.

Wagner, Rudolf G. 1990. *The Contemporary Chinese Historical Drama: Four Studies*. Berkeley: University of California Press.

Wang An-ch'i 王安祈. 2012. "THEA 2015 Selected Readings from Classics of Chinese drama: The Contemporary" THEA 2015 中國戲劇名著選讀：現代 (classroom notes). Taipei: National Taiwan University, Department of Drama and Theatre. Spring.

Wang, Chun-yen 汪俊彥. 2004. "Xiju lishi, biaoyan Taiwan: 1984–2000 Lai Shengchuan xiju zhi xiju changyu yu Taiwan/Zhongguo tuxiang yanjiu"

戲劇歷史、表演台灣：1984-2000 賴聲川戲劇之戲劇場域與台灣/中國圖像研究 (Dramatizing history, performing Taiwan: A study of the theatre field and the Taiwanese/Chinese image in Stan Lai Sheng-chuan's drama 1984-2000). MA thesis, National Taiwan University, Department of Drama and Theatre.

——. 2014. "Fanyi 'Zhongguo': Lai Shengchuan de xiangshengju" 翻譯「中國」：賴聲川的相聲劇 (Translating China: Identity politics in Stan Lai's *xiangsheng* plays). *Zhongwai wenxue* 中外文學 (Chung-wai literary monthly) 43, no. 3 (September): 77-106.

——. 2018. "What Does 'An Open Body' Say: The Body and the Cold War in the Early 1980s Theatre of Taiwan." *Inter-Asia Cultural Studies* 19, no. 4: 568-77.

——. 2021. "'Yanqian daoling' Wang Junyan jingcai jiexi *Jiang/yun·zhi/jian*"【演前導聆】汪俊彥精彩解析《江／雲·之／間》(Preshow introduction to *River/Cloud* by Wang Chunyen). Taipei, National Theatre. April 2. https://www.youtube.com/watch?v=VFZJv0dzl9Y.

Wang, David Der-wei 王德威. 2006. "Huayu yuxi wenxue: Bianjie xiangxiang yu yuejie jian'gou" 華語語系文學：邊界想像與越界建構 (Sinophone literature: Imagined boundaries and constructed transcendence). *Zhongshan daxue xuebao (Shehui kexue ban)* 中山大學學報 (社會科學版) (Journal of Sun Yatsen University [social science edition]) 46, no. 5: 1-4.

Wang, Gungwu. (1999) 2004. "A Single Chinese Diaspora? Some Historical Reflections." In *Diasporic Chinese Ventures: The Life and Work of Wang Gungwu*, edited by Gregor Benton and Liu Hong, 157-77. Abingdon, Oxon: Taylor and Francis.

Wang, Jing. 1996. *High Culture Fever: Politics, Aesthetics, and Ideology in Deng's China*. Berkeley: University of California Press.

Wang Mo-lin 王墨林. (1987) 1992. "1987 Taiwan・Xianggang xiaojuchang de duihua zhi er" 1987 臺灣・香港小劇場的對話之二 (Conversation between the little theaters of Taiwan and Hong Kong in 1987, part 2). In *Dushi juchang yu shenti* 都市劇場與身體 (Urban theater and the body), 301-7. Taibei: Daoxiang chubanshe.

——. 1996. "Xiaojuchang de chengzhang yu xiaoshi—Xiaojuchangshi shi yichang 'biaoyan' huoshi yichang 'yundong'?" 小劇場的成長與消失——小劇場史是一場「表演」或是一場「運動」？(The growth and disappearance of the little theater—is the history of the little theater a "performance" or a "movement"?). In *Taiwan xiandai juchang yantaohui lunwenji: 1986-1995 Taiwan xiaojuchang* 台灣現代劇場研討會論文集：1986-1995 台灣小劇場 (Modern Taiwanese theater conference proceedings: The little theater in Taiwan 1986-1995), edited by Wu Ch'üan-ch'eng 吳全成, 101-17. Taipei: Wenjianhui.

Wang Yu-hui 王友輝. 1996. "Pinglun" 評論 (Commentary). In *Taiwan xiandai juchang yantaohui lunwenji: 1986-1995 Taiwan xiaojuchang* 台灣現代劇場研討會論文集：1986-1995台灣小劇場 (Modern Taiwanese theater conference proceedings: The little theater in Taiwan 1986-1995), edited by Wu Ch'üan-ch'eng, 70-75. Taipei: Wenjianhui.

———. 2000. "Taiwan shiyan juzhan yanjiu (1980-1984)" 臺灣實驗劇展研究 (1980-1984) (The festival of Taiwan experimental theater [1980-1984]). *Yishu pinglun* 藝術評論 (Arts review) 11: 197-220.

Wang Yumin 王毓敏. 1988. "Faxian xiju xin tiandi" 發現戲劇新天地 (Discovering the new world of drama). *Lianhe zaobao* 聯合早報 (Singapore), January 7, 27.

Wang Zun 王樽. 2010. "Lai Shengchuan—Xingzou zai wutai yu yingxiang de bianyuan" 賴聲川——行走在舞台與影像的邊緣 (Stan Lai—Walking on the peripheries of stage and film). In *Yigeren de dianying, 2008-2009* 一个人的電影，2008-2009 (One (wo)man's film, 2008-2009), 262-83. Shanghai: Shanghai wenyi chubanshe.

Watson, Amanda. 2002. "I Learnt to Mambo and Cha-cha with Famous Movie Stars." *South China Morning Post* (Hong Kong), July 27, 4.

Wee, C. J. Wan-ling. 2012. "Introduction: Kuo Pao Kun's Contemporary Theatre." In *The Complete Works of Kuo Pao Kun*, vol. 4: *Plays in English* 郭寶崑全集·第四卷·英文戲劇, edited by C. J. Wee Wan-ling, xi-xxx. Singapore: Practice Performing Arts School and Global Publishing.

Weinstein, John. 2015. "Introduction: Community Theater in the Taiwanese Context." In *Voices of Taiwanese Women Three Contemporary Plays*, edited by John Weinstein, 1-18. Ithaca: Cornell University East Asia Program.

Welsh, Frank. 1993. *A Borrowed Place: The History of Hong Kong*. New York: Kodansha International.

Wong, Jacob Hing-cheung 黃慶鏘. 1982. "The Quest for a Hong Kong Theatre." *Tamkang Review* 淡江評論 12, no. 3: 259-65.

Wong, Kim Hoh. 2006. "Renaissance Man—At 63, Danny Yung Either Heads or Sits on the Boards of at Least a Dozen Arts and Cultural Bodies." *The Sunday Times* (Singapore), September 24.

Wong Meng Voon 黃孟文, and Xu Naixiang 徐迺翔, eds. 2002. *Xinjiapo Huawen wenxueshi chugao* 新加坡華文文學史初稿 (A preliminary study of the history of Singapore Chinese literature). Singapore: Xinjiapo guoli daxue zhongwenxi; River Edge, NJ: Bafang wenhua qiye gongsi.

Wong, Souk Yee. 2005. "Destabilising Nationalist Discourse in Kuo Pao Kun's *Mama Looking for Her Cat*." In *Beyond Good and Evil? Essays on Literature and Culture of the Asia-Pacific Region*, edited by Dennis Haskell, Megan McKinlay, and Pamina Rich, 79-94. Crawley: University of Western Australia Press [for] the Westerly Centre.

Wong, Yoon Wah 王潤華. 1989a. "A Critical Assessment of Writing in Chinese." *Singa: Literature and the Arts in Singapore* 18 (June): 72-76.

———. 1989b. "Lun Xinjiapo Huawen wenxue fazhan jieduan yu fangxiang" 論新加坡華文文學發展階段與方向 (The origins and developments of Singapore Chinese literature). In *Di'erjie Huawen wenxue datong shijie guoji huiyi: Dongnanya Huawen wenxue* 第二屆華文文學大同世界國際會議：東南亞華文文學 (Proceedings of the second international conference on the Commonwealth of Chinese literature: Chinese literature in Southeast Asia), edited by Wong Yoon Wah 王潤華 and Horst Pastoors 白豪士, 56-66. Singapore: Goethe-Institut and Singapore Association of Writers.

——. 1995. "Obsession with China: Chinese Literature in Singapore and Malaysia." In *Crossing Borders: Transmigration in Asia Pacific*, edited by Ong Jin Hui, Chan Kwok Bun, and Chew Soon Beng, 359–77. Singapore; New York: Prentice Hall.

Woo, Mathias Yan Wai 胡恩威. 2007. "Yige shehui zong xuyao you yixie ren zai zuo yixie shiyan de shi" 一個社會總需要有一些人在做一些實驗的事 (Every society needs some people doing some experimental work). In "City x Zuni: School of Avant Garde" 進念・香港實驗, special issue, *Haowai* 號外 (City Magazine) 364 (January): 106–7.

Woo, Mathias Yan Wai 胡恩威, and Leung Man-to 梁文道. (1996a) 1997. "Yu teshou canxuanren lun wenhua shiye: Yiguo liangzhi de wenhua wenti" 與特首參選人論文化視野：一國兩制的文化問題 (Debating with the chief executive candidates on cultural perspective: On the problem of culture for One Country, Two Systems). In *Xianggang jiuqi wenhua shiye wenjian ji* 香港九七文化視野文件集 (Cultural perspective Hong Kong 1997), 1–2. Hong Kong: Hong Kong Cultural Sector Joint Conference, International Association of Theatre Critics (HK), and Zuni Icosahedron.

——. (1996b) 1997. "Yu teshou canxuanren lun wenhua shiye: Rentong Zhongguo haishi jianzao Zhongguo" 與特首參選人論文化視野：認同中國還是建造中國 (Debating with the chief executive candidates on cultural perspective: To identify with or to build China). In *Xianggang jiuqi wenhua shiye wenjian ji* 香港九七文化視野文件集 (Cultural perspective Hong Kong 1997), 3–4. Hong Kong: Hong Kong Cultural Sector Joint Conference, International Association of Theatre Critics (HK), and Zuni Icosahedron.

Wu Jing-jyi 吳靜吉. 1996. "Pinglun: Shiwu ge wenti—Huiying Ma Sen jiaoshou 'Baling nian yilai de Taiwan xiaojuchang yundong'" 評論：十五個問題——回應馬森教授〈八〇年以來的台灣小劇場運動〉 (Commentary: Fifteen questions in response to Professor Ma Sen's "The little theater movement in Taiwan since the 1980s"). In *Taiwan xiandai juchang yantaohui lunwenji: 1986–1995 Taiwan xiaojuchang* 台灣現代劇場研討會論文集：1986–1995台灣小劇場 (Modern Taiwanese theater conference proceedings: The little theater in Taiwan 1986–1995), edited by Wu Ch'üan-ch'eng 吳全成, 29–34. Taipei: Wenjianhui.

Wu Muqing 吳牧青. 2008. "Ruzhen sijia, jixing jiting—Lai Shengchuan" 如真似假，即行即停——賴聲川 (Appearing real, seemingly false, going to proceed yet stopping—Stan Lai). *Pobao* 破報 (Taiwan), January 14.

Wu Sufen 吳素芬, and Lan Linghan 藍羚涵. 2009. "Taiwan dangdai de wudao, xiju, juchang ji biaoyan tuanti" 台灣當代的舞蹈、戲劇、劇場及表演團體 (Dance, drama, theater, and performing arts groups in contemporary Taiwan). In *Yishu shenghuo: biaoyan yishu* 藝術生活：表演藝術 (Applied performing art), edited by Wu Sufen et al., 196–224. Taibei shi: Guoli Taiwan yishu jiaoyuguan.

"Xijiu dongshiju huanban Rong Nianzeng chuzou" 西九董事局換班 榮念曾出走 (Danny Yung departs after change of board at West Kowloon Cultural District). 2014. *Sing Tao Daily* 星島日報 (Hong Kong), May 27.

Xinjiapo Huayu huaju tuanti, 1983 nian xijuying lianhe gongweihui 新加坡華語話劇團體，1983年戲劇營聯合工委會, ed. 1983. *Jiwang kailai: 60 nian Huayu huaju shiliao zhan; Diyijie xijuying* 繼往開來：60年華語話劇史料展；第一屆戲劇營 (Inheriting tradition and moving forward: An exhibition of 60 years of history of Chinese-language theater; the first drama camp). Singapore: Xijuying lianhe gongweihui.

Xin she·Xin Ma Huawen wenxue daxi bianji weiyuanhui 新社·新馬華文文學大系編輯委員會, eds. 1971. *Xin Ma Huawen wenxue daxi · diqi ji · juben* 新馬華文文學大系·第七集·劇本 (A comprehensive anthology of Singapore and Malayan Chinese-language literature, vol. 7, plays). Singapore: Jiaoyu chubanshe.

Xu Jin 徐瑾. 2010. "Xianggang wenhua jiaofu Rong Nianzeng: Wutai meiyou bianyuan" 香港文化教父荣念曾：舞台没有边缘 (The cultural godfather in Hong Kong, Danny Yung: The stage has no boundaries). *Zhongguo jingyingbao* 中國經營報 (China business journal), November 1, D08.

Xu Lanjun 徐蘭君. 2012. "Zou Nanyang: Zhongyi gewutuan de kuaguo lüxing ji biaoyan zhengzhi (1946–1948)" 走南洋：中藝歌舞團的跨國旅行及表演政治 (1946–1948) (Traveling the southern seas: China traveling dancing and singing troupe's transnational expedition and the politics of performance [1946–1948]). Unpublished paper presented at the Department of Chinese Literature, National Taiwan University, Taipei. December 20.

Yan, Haiping. 1998. "Theater and Society: An Introduction to Contemporary Chinese Drama." In *Theater and Society: An Anthology of Contemporary Chinese Drama*, edited by Yan Haiping, ix–xlvi. New York: M. E. Sharpe.

———. 2001. "Theatrical Impulse and Posthumanism: Gao Xingjian's 'Another Kind of Drama.'" *World Literature Today* 75, no. 1 (Winter): 20–29.

Yang Bishan 楊碧珊. 1993. *Xinjiapo xijushi lun* 新加坡戲劇史論 (On the history of Singaporean drama). Singapore: Haitian wenhua qiye siren youxian gongsi.

Yang, Dominic Meng-hsuan. 2020. *The Great Exodus from China: Trauma, Memory, and Identity in Modern Taiwan*. Cambridge: Cambridge University Press.

Ye Changhai 葉長海. 2008. "Shanghai xiju wutai sanshi nian" 上海戲劇舞臺三十年 (Shanghai theatrical stage in thirty years: From 1970s to the present). *Xiju yanjiu* 戲劇研究 (Journal of theater studies) 1 (January): 179–94.

Yeh, Michelle. 2003. "Misty Poetry." In *Columbia Companion to Modern East Asian Literature*, edited by Joshua Mostow, Kirk Denton, and Bruce Fulton, 520–26. New York: Columbia University Press.

———. 2010. "Literature as Identity Formation: Reading Chinese Literature in Translation." In *Literature in Translation: Teaching Issues and Reading Practices*, edited by Carol Maier and Françoise Massardier-Kenney, 117–35. Kent, OH: Kent State University Press.

Yeo, Robert Cheng Chuan. 2012. "Kuo Pao Kun and the Making of the English-language Canon of Plays." Unpublished paper delivered at "Kuo Pao Kun International Conference," National Museum of Singapore, September 14–15.

Yeo Song Nian 楊松年, and Jian Wenzhi 簡文志, eds. 2004. *Lixin de bianzheng: Shi Hua xiaoshuo pingxi* 離心的辯證：世華小說評析 (Centrifugal dialectics: Readings in world Chinese fiction). Taipei: Tangshan.

Yeung, Jessica Wai-yee 楊慧儀. 2000. "Gao Xingjian de 'Zhongguo qingyijie'" 高行健的「中國情意結」 (The "China complex" in Gao Xingjian). In *Jiedu Gao Xingjian* 解讀高行健 (Reading Gao Xingjian), edited by Lin Manshu 林曼叔, 182–89. Hong Kong: Mingbao chubanshe.

———. 2008. *Ink Dances in Limbo: Gao Xingjian's Writing as Cultural Translation*. Hong Kong: Hong Kong University Press.

———. 2021. "Augustine Mok Chiu-yu's Intercultural Asian People's Theatre: Imagining 'the Third Way' for Hong Kong." In *Asian City Crossings: Pathways of Performance through Hong Kong and Singapore*, edited by Rossella Ferrari and Ashley Thorpe, 113–30. London: Routledge.

"Ying Xianggang xijujie yaoqing Guo Baokun Guan Xingbo jiang canjia Yazhou huaren juzuojia huiyi" 應香港戲劇界邀請郭寶崑官星波將參加亞洲華人劇作家會議 (Kuo Pao Kun and Stella Kon to attend Asian Chinese playwright conference at the invitation of the Hong Kong theater circle). 1987. *Lianhe zaobao* 聯合早報 (Singapore), March 23, 4.

Yip, June Chun. 2004. *Envisioning Taiwan: Fiction, Cinema, and the Nation in the Cultural Imaginary*. Durham, NC: Duke University Press.

You Chongsheng 尤冲繩. 1984. "Juchang: Shijie de suoying—Fang *Yapian zhanzheng* biandao Rong Nianzeng" 劇場：世界的縮影——訪『鴉片戰爭』編導榮念曾 (Theater: Microcosm of the world—Interview with *Opium War* director-playwright Danny Yung). *Dianying shuangzhoukan* 電影雙週刊 (Film biweekly) 144, August 30, 5–8.

Yu, Louis Kwok-lit 茹國烈. 2006. "Rong Nianzeng: Jinnian yishu shiyan lücheng" 榮念曾：進念藝術實驗旅程 (Danny Yung: The journey of Zuni's artistic experiment). *Haowai* 號外 (City Magazine) 363 (December): 203–4.

Yu, Shiao-ling. 1997. "Introduction: Chinese Drama after the Cultural Revolution, 1978–1989." In *Chinese Drama after the Cultural Revolution, 1979–1989: An Anthology*, edited and translated by Yu Shiao-ling, 1–34. Lewiston, NY: Edwin Mellen.

———. 2007. "Li Longyun." In *The Columbia Encyclopedia of Modern Drama*, edited by Gabrielle H. Cody and Evert Sprinchorn, 820–21. New York: Columbia University Press.

———. 2019. "Tradition and Modernity: Two Modern Adaptations of the Chinese Opera *Hezhu's Match*." *Asian Theatre Journal* 36, no. 2 (Fall): 416–38.

Yuan Qunying 袁羣英. 1984. "*Yapian zhanzheng* yanchu shi qi fengbo—Jinnian chengyuan poubai zhenxiang" 「鴉片戰爭」演出時起風波——進念成員剖白真相 (*Opium War* performance stirs controversy—Zuni members reveal the truth). *Economic Journal* (Hong Kong), August 23.

Yung, Danny Ning Tsun 榮念曾. 1997. "Chronicle of Women—Liu Sola in Concert." In *An Oxford Anthology of Contemporary Chinese Drama*, edited by Martha Cheung Pui-Yiu and Jane Lai Chui-chun, 825–73. Hong Kong: Oxford University Press.

———. 2005. "Guanyu Haibao ersanshi" 關於海豹二三事 (Two or three things about the Seals). In *Huigu dangnian: Haibao jutuan jijin youxian gongsi* 回顧當年：海豹劇團基金有限公司 (Reflections: Seals Players Foundation, 1979–1993), edited by Lynn Yau 邱歡智, 98–100. Hong Kong: Encounter Entreprise Hong Kong.

———. 2007. "Chuchu douxiang wutai, chuchu dou keyi shi wutai" 處處都像舞台，處處都可以是舞台 (Everywhere is like a stage, anywhere can be a stage). *Jinnian yanshen yuedu* 進念延伸閱讀 (Zuni extended reading resources). https://zuni.org.hk/education/resource/延伸閱讀-3-處處都像舞台/.

———. 2009. *Zhongguo shi ge da huayuan: Rong Nianzeng juchang yishu 1984–2008* 中國是個大花園：榮念曾劇場藝術 1984–2008 (China is a big garden: Danny Yung's theatrical art 1984–2008). Hong Kong: E+E Jinnian ershi mianti.

———. 2011. "Rong Nianzeng: Chuangzuo yinggai baiwujinji" 榮念曾：創作應該百無禁忌 (Danny Yung: Creativity should be free from taboos) (bilingual). *Jinnian · ershimianti 2010 zhi 2011 niandu baogao* 進念·二十面體 2010-11 年度報告 (Zuni Icosahedron annual report 2010/11), 22–25.

———. 2013. "Rong Nianzeng" 榮念曾 (Danny Yung). Xianggang: Xianggang diantai. Video. Interview by Radio Televsion Hong Kong (RTHK). https://youtu.be/P_kH1u-aweE?si=Bp3OuLSHVaCSJdpU.

Zhan Daoyu 詹道玉. 2001. *Zhanhou chuqi de Xinjiapo Huawen xiju, 1945–1959* 戰后初期的新加坡華文戲劇 (1945–1959) (Singapore Chinese-language drama in the early post–World War II period [1945–1959]). Singapore: Xinjiapo guoli daxue Zhongwenxi; Bafang wenhua qiye gongsi.

Zhang Chuyong 張楚勇. 1984. "'Yapian zhanzheng' yanchu fasheng yiwai: Anquan wenti yinqi zhenglun" 「鴉片戰爭」演出發生意外：安全問題引起爭論 (Accident during *Opium War* performance: Sparks debate about question of safety). *Economic Journal* (Hong Kong), August 22.

Zhang Liuzu 張劉足. 2010. "World Theater Exhibition" 世界劇展. *Encyclopedia of Taiwan* 臺灣大百科全書. http://taiwanpedia.culture.tw/web/content?ID=13669.

Zhang Lixuan 張俐璇. 2009. "Yao Yiwei" 姚一葦. *Encyclopedia of Taiwan* 臺灣大百科全書. http://taiwanpedia.culture.tw/web/content?ID=2254.

Zhang, Xudong 張旭東. 1997. Chinese Modernism in the Era of Reforms: Cultural Fever, Avant-garde Fiction, and the New Chinese Cinema. Durham, NC: Duke University Press.

Zhang Zilan 張紫蘭. 2004. "Xi Jiulong: Wenhua daduhui de jiyuan—Zhuanfang: Jinnian ershi mianti yishu zongjian Rong Nianzeng" 西九龍：文化大都會的機緣—專訪：進念二十面體藝術總監榮念曾 (West Kowloon: The opportunity for a cultural metropolis—Interviewing Zuni Icosahedron artistic director Danny Yung). *Yazhou zhoukan* 亞洲週刊, July 4, 44–45.

Zhao, Henry Yiheng 趙毅衡. *Towards a Modern Zen Theatre: Gao Xingjian and Chinese Theatre Experimentalism*. London: School of Oriental and African Studies, University of London.

Zou, Jiping. 1994. "Gao Xingjian and Chinese Experimental Theatre." PhD diss. University of Illinois at Urbana-Champaign.

Index

absurdist theater, 88, 92, 98, 99, 132, 161, 170, 179, 180, 182–183, 189, 201. *see also individual plays and authors*
Action Theatre, 59
Alarm Signal (*Juedui xinhao*; Gao), 31, 160, 172–173, 175, 179, 185
alienation, 29, 63, 65, 66–67, 109, 137, 144, 180–181, 205
All in This Family Are Human (*Women yijia doushi ren*; Lai), 75–76
All in Two Families Are Human (*Women liangjia doushi ren*; Lai), 75–76
allegory, 58, 99, 100, 105, 140, 161, 178
alternative theater/aesthetics/cultural identities, 5, 9, 15–18, 21, 26–28, 37, 65, 72, 119, 146, 162–163, 170, 173–174, 190–192
American House (*Dawu*; Chan), 136
Anti-Bourgeois Liberalization Campaign, 165
Anticommunist/Russian Resistance plays (*Fangong kang'e ju*), 86–87, 90
Anti-Spiritual Pollution Campaign, 31, 165, 176, 187, 189
Are You There Singapore? (Yeo), 50
Artaud, Antonin, 174, 180
Asia in Theatre Research Circus (later Centre), 59
"Asian Chinese Playwrights' Conference," 17n7
Asian Theatre Festival and Conference, 91, 122
avant-garde drama/theater (*xianfeng ju*), 5, 10, 89, 121–122, 171

Ba Jin, 31
Baau Hon Lam, 130, 132
Bach Variations (*Bianzou Baha*; Lai), 91
backdoorism, 172, 177–178, 189
Bamboo Curtain, 4
Basement Workshop, 119

Be My Sushi Tonight (TheatreWorks), 51
Beauty of Xi Shi, The (*Xi Shi*; Yao), 131
Beckett, Samuel, 102–103, 161, 174, 180, 188
Bei Dao, 166–167
Beijing Foreign Languages Institute, 30, 174
Beijing People's Art Theatre (BPAT), 18, 24, 31, 56, 75, 173, 176, 179, 185, 194, 197, 200
bensheng/benshengren, 82–83, 86, 112
"Big Hong Kong, Little China and Britain," 136
bilingualism
   directing workshops and, 58–59
   education policy and, 63–64, 72
   staging attempts and, 52, 53
   see also multilingualism/bilingualism
Boal, Augusto, 142–143, 149, 155–156
Book of Ghosts (*Lu gui bu*; Yung), 157
Brecht, Bertolt, 10, 56, 88, 134, 144, 173–174, 180–181, 184, 188
Brechtian, 57, 68, 137, 148, 155
Bridge: The Magazine of Asians in America, 120
Broken Record #1 (*Pojilu yihao*; Yung), 120
Brook, Peter, 177, 181
"Bubbles" Conceptual Comics exhibition, 120
Bus Stop (*Chezhan*; Gao), 9, 18–19, 31, 160–161, 163, 165, 170, 174–187, 189–190, 200
Byakko Sha (White tiger club), 91

Cao Yu, 85, 131, 173, 176
Caucasian Chalk Circle (Brecht), 56, 57n16
censorship, 43, 80, 86, 108n14, 117, 125, 172, 174, 176–177, 185, 187
Chan, Margaret, 47n10, 52
Chan Koon-chung, Johnny, 140–141
Chan Maw Woh, 45n9

239

INDEX

Chang Hsiao-feng, 88, 90, 92
Chang Hsiao-yen, 74
Chekhov, Anton, 87, 134
Chen Baichen, 131
Chen Kaige, 168
Chen Zhenya, 41, 48
Chiang Ching-kuo, 82, 93
Chin Shih-chieh, 89, 94
China Traveling Theater Company, 131
Chinese Civil War, 80, 101, 109, 112, 128
Chinese Communist Party (CCP), 45, 102, 128, 163, 164, 167, 168, 185, 191. *see also* communism
Chinese Cultural Experimental Centre, 158
Chinese Culture Renaissance Movement, 80
Chinese diaspora, 6, 17–20, 33, 77, 111, 162–163, 184, 206–207
Chinese Drama Centre, 87
Chinese Drama Festival, 194, 196
Chinese Music, Dance, and Drama Society, 40, 41, 42, 131
Chinese Playwriting Studio, 59n19
Chineseness
　challenges to, 5, 192–193, 198, 204, 207
　China and, 160, 162, 167, 171
　as framework, 4, 6, 8–9
　Hong Kong and, 120, 124, 129, 136, 156
　performing in Cold War, 10–17
　Singapore and, 73
　Taiwan and, 78–83, 113–116
Chong Ping, 199
Choo Woon Hock, 53
Chronicle of Three Women (*Lienü zhuan*), 146–149
Chu Hak, 56n15, 130
Chua Soo Pong, 52
Chung Cheng High School Drama Club, 41, 42
Chung King Fai, 130–131, 132–133
Chung Ying Theatre Company, 135, 137, 194–195
Circular Ruins Theater, 89
City of the Dead (*Mingcheng*; Gao), 188
Cloud Gate Dance Theatre, 91, 93
Coffee Shop (*Kopitiam*; Kuo), 57, 58
Coffin Is Too Big for the Hole, The (*Guancai taida dong taixiao*; Kuo), 51, 53, 71, 194–195
cold literature (*Leng de wenxue*), 22, 169–170, 188
Cold War, 4, 6, 7–8, 10–17, 44–45, 80–81, 92

collective improvisation, 97, 114–115
colonialization/colonialism, 7, 21, 37, 42, 50, 128–129, 145, 154
Colorado Shakespeare Festival, 135
Committee for Chinese Drama Appreciation, 87
communism, 80n4, 81, 86–87, 101–102, 167. *see also* Chinese Communist Party (CCP)
Confucianism, 81, 167, 170
Contemporary Legend Theatre, 200
corruption, 172, 177–178, 189
Council for Cultural Affairs, 93
Council for the Performing Arts, 135
Critical Point Theater Phenomenon, 89
Cultural China, 10
cultural fever debate, 8
cultural orphans, 55
Cultural Revolution, 6–9, 24, 26, 30, 80, 82–83, 127, 132, 134, 161–169, 171, 178, 189
culture of the body, 91–92

"Da Xianggang, xiao Zhong Ying," 136
Dead Man's Interview of the Living, A (*Yige sizhe dui shengzhe de fangwen*; Liu), 171–172
Deng Xiaoping, 30, 117, 139, 145, 161, 166
Dialogue and Rebuttal (*Duihua yu fanjie*; Gao), 170
diaspora, marginal consciousness in, 17–33
Dim Sum: A Little Bit of Heart (Wang), 119
Dragon Dance (*Longwu*; Wong), 91
Drama Box, 63n21, 72, 199
drama camps, 1–3, 17, 56, 193
Dream Like a Dream, A (*Rumeng zhi meng*; Lai), 76, 197
Dream of the Red Chamber (*Honglongmeng*; Lai), 76
Dreamers (*Mengxiang jia*; Lai), 76

Edward Lam Dance Theater, 125
1841 (Chan), 136
Elizabeth II, Queen, 141
Emergency Stairs, 199
Emily of Emerald Hill (Kon), 51, 52–53
empty chair, motif of, 142–145, 149, 190
epic theater, 88, 144
Escape (*Taowang*; Gao), 163
Esslin, Martin, 183, 201
ETCeteras, The, 3n1, 63n21

Evening Climb, The (*Huanghun shangshan*; Kuo), 47n10
exile, self-imposed, 10, 163, 169–170
Experimental Shakespeare: King Lear (*Shiyan Shashibiya—Li'er wang*), 196–197
Experimental Theater Exhibition, 88, 90, 92
experimental theater/drama (*shiyan ju*), 122–124, 171–175, 181
Experimental Theatre Club (ETC), 51–52
experimentation, spirit of, 89, 171
exploratory drama (*tansu ju*), 10, 171, 173

Fan Man-nung, 90
Fangong kang'e ju (Anticommunist/Russian Resistance plays), 86–87, 90
Fangyuan Theater, 89
Fate of Three Miles Village, The (*Fengyu Santiaoshi*; Yue), 40
First Chinese-language Drama Camp, 56
folklore storytelling (*jianggu*), 47
Foreman, Richard, 123
From the Depth of Silence (*Yu wusheng chu*; Zong), 171

Gang of Four, 164, 172
Gao Xingjian
  background of, 30–31
  collaboration and, 199–201
  concept of diaspora and, 18–19
  critical appraisals of, 3–4
  cultural fever debate and, 8
  Cultural Revolution and, 164–168
  diaspora within China and, 188–191
  drama camps and, 56, 193
  emergence of, 168–174
  form over content and, 179–185
  generational context and, 6
  little theater movement and, 9
  Lu Xun and, 185–188
  marginal consciousness and, 22
  multilingualism and, 173, 202
  on nationality, 204
  play analysis and, 174–179
  political circumstances affecting, 24
  published corpus of, 25
  sociohistorical context and, 159–163
Garrison Players, 132, 133
gender, power dynamics and, 146–148
Genet, Jean, 174, 180, 188
getai, 42
gezai xi, 98

ghosting, 185–186
Glass Menagerie, The (Williams), 132
Global Cultural Centre, 158
Godot Theatre Company, 96
Goh Boon Teck, 63n21
Goh Guat Kian, 59, 194
Goh Lay Kuan, 28, 49
Goh Poh Seng, 50
Gone with the Sea (*Shi hai*; Tsang), 136
Goss, Bernard, 137, 195
Grotowski, Jerzy, 56, 57
GuoGuang Opera Company, 200

Hai Rui Is Dismissed from Office (*Hai Rui baguan*; Wu), 176
Han Lao Da, 66
He Zhu's New Match (*He Zhu xinpei*; Chin), 56, 88–89, 90, 92, 94, 114
Heng, Ivan, 59
Hey, Wake Up! (*Wei, xingxing!*; Kuo), 43
Ho, Pia, 91, 121, 146
Hong Kong
  Chinese diaspora and, 18
  film industry in, 118–119
  history of control of, 127–128
  immigrants and, 129–130
  linguistic variations and, 5
  migration waves to, 124–125
  return of, 4, 7, 30, 117, 130, 135–136, 138
  Umbrella Revolution in, 17
Hong Kong Academy for Performing Art (HKAPA), 135, 138, 200
Hong Kong Arts Centre, 120, 126, 135, 139, 146, 150, 151*fig*, 152–155, 195, 198
Hong Kong Arts Development Council, 195
Hong Kong Drama Project, 136
Hong Kong Dream (*Xianggang meng*; Cheung and Tsoi), 136
Hong Kong Federation of Drama Societies, 126
Hong Kong Fringe Club, 195
Hong Kong Fringe Festival, 194–195
Hong Kong New Wave Cinema, 118–119, 198
Hong Kong Repertory Theatre (HKREP), 98, 121, 135, 153, 196, 197
Hong Kong Stage Club, 132
"Hong Kong trilogy," 136
Hong Kong University Drama Lab, 121
Hong Shen, 10

INDEX

Hot Springs Outside (*Wuwai you reliu*; Ma, Jia, and Qu), 172
Hou Hsiao-hsien, 84
Hsiung Shih-I, 131
Hsu Po-yun, 90
huaju, 85–87, 130, 133
Huang Zuolin, 10, 57, 173, 194
Huayi Festival—Chinese Festival of the Arts, 199
Hui, Ann, 118
Hui Koon-kit, Samuel, 124–125
Huineng, 200
Hundred Years of Cultivating People, The (*Bainian shuren*; Low), 43
Hwang Mei-shu, 88, 92

I Am Hong Kong (*Wo xi Xianggangren*; To and Tsoi), 136, 137
Ibsen, Henrik, 180
identity
  of becoming, 5–10, 16, 21, 26
  collective, 123–124
  as construction, 13
  doubled, 77
In Search of Modern China—Eunuch (*Xunzhao xin Zhongguo [Taijian]*; Yung), 196
independence movement, Taiwanese, 78

Jit, Krishen, 3, 20, 57n16, 60–61, 196
Journey to the East (*Zhongguo lücheng*), 121, 198
Journey to the West (*Xiyouji*; Lai), 76
juancun, 115

King Lear of the Thirty-seven-fold Practice of a Bodhisattva, The (*Pusa zhi sanshiqi zhong xiuxing zhi Li'er wang*; Lai), 197
Ko Tin Lung, 135, 200
Kok Heng Leun, 59n18, 63n21
Kon, Stella, 51
Ku Hwai-chun, Vivien, 196
Ku Pao-ming, 87, 94
Kuo Jian Hong, 49
Kuo Pao Kun
  background of, 27–28
  bridging language streams and, 54–61
  collaboration and, 194–196
  critical appraisals of, 3–4
  detention of, 23–24, 28, 45
  diaspora and, 20
  drama camps and, 193
  on ethnic identities, 54–55
  generational context and, 6
  on *Godot*, 103
  influence of, 8
  on Lai, 106
  language policy and, 70–73
  local consciousness and, 39–49
  localization of English-language theater and, 49–53
  marginal consciousness and, 22–23
  multilingualism and, 202
  photograph of, 32*fig*, 195*fig*
  play analysis and, 61–70
  published corpus of, 25
  SAP and, 42–43
  sociohistorical context and, 34–39
  on theater in Hong Kong, 135
Kuomintang (KMT; Nationalist Party), 80, 82, 86–87, 91, 100, 101–102, 112
Kwan, Stanley, 118, 198

La MaMa Experimental Theatre Club, 88
Lai Chui-chun, Jane, 133, 173
Lai Kok Bun, 131
Lai Sheng-chuan, Stan
  background of, 28–29
  Chinese-Taiwanese identification and, 106–113
  collaboration and, 194, 196–198, 199, 200
  critical appraisals of, 3–4
  cross-strait divide and, 6–7
  drama camps and, 56, 193
  on experimental theatre, 123
  generational context and, 6, 23
  Kuo's passing and, 196
  marginal consciousness and, 22
  multilingualism and, 202
  multiple perspectives and, 113–116
  photographs of, 32*fig*, 195*fig*
  play analysis and, 95–106
  political history and, 79–84
  published corpus of, 25
  on roots, 115
  sociohistorical context and, 74–79
  Taiwan theater history and, 85–95
Lam Yik-wah, Edward, 121, 125, 146, 198
Lan Ling Theatre Workshop, 56, 88–89, 92, 93, 94, 95, 114
language
  ethnicity and, 10
  linguistic pluralism, 35–36
  linguistic variations, 5, 8
  multilingualism, 202
  policy, 8, 36, 45, 46, 61, 63–64, 67–68, 70–73, 83
  power and, 10–11
  see also multilingualism/bilingualism
Lao She, 85

INDEX 243

Le Blond, Max, 50–51, 52, 61
Lee, Chris, 74
Lee Chun Chow, 195
Lee Dai Sor, 47
Lee Kuo-shiu, Hugh, 75n1, 91n8, 94, 95–96, 198
Lee Li-chun, 94, 95–96
Lee Woon-wah, 56n15, 130–131, 132
Leung Man-to, 119
Li Ang (Shih Shu-tuan), 88, 120n1
Li Huan-hsiun, 89
Li Lien Fung, 50
Li Liuyi, 198
Li Longyun, 171, 174
Li Man-kuei, 85, 87–88
Liang Chi-ming, James, 96
Liang Qichao, 10
Liang Wern Fook, 34–35, 47n10
Lim Beng Chew (Shi Keyang), 43
Lim Chor Pee, 50, 52n13
Lim Hai Yen, 3n1, 59n18, 63n21
Lim Jen Erh, 59
Lim Kay Tong, 53
Lin Chen, 27, 43
Lin Ching-hsia, Brigitte, 74, 110
Lin Kehuan, 125, 196
Lin Liankun, 75, 194, 195*fig*
Lin Zexu, 140
Lin Zhaohua, 31, 173, 175, 176n6, 185, 187, 198
Lingam, Chandran K., 52
linguistic pluralism, 35–36
linguistic variations, 5, 8
listening, importance of, 114–115
little theater movement, 9, 88–93, 95–96, 173
Little White Sailing Boat, The (*Xiaobaichuan*), 48, 57–58
Liu Ching-min, 57, 94
Liu Ts'un-yan, 130
Look Who's Cross-Talking Tonight? (*Zheyiye, sheilai shuo xiangsheng?*; Lai), 6, 56, 79
Lord Meng Chang (*Meng Chang jun*; Lee), 131
Low Ing Sing, 27, 41, 43, 48
Lu Dun, 130
Lu Xun, 185–187

Ma Sen, 88, 90, 92, 94, 95
Makoto, Sato, 199
Mama Looking for Her Cat (*Xunzhao xiaomao de mama*; Kuo), 8, 35, 36, 46, 57, 60–70, 62*fig*, 71, 73
Mao Chun Fai, Fredric, 197
marginal consciousness, 18–19, 21–23, 206–207

martial arts novels (*wuxia xiaoshuo*), 47, 128
martial law, 82, 94, 108, 109–110
May Fourth Movement, 39, 40, 43, 45, 128
Mei Lanfang, 2, 173
Meng Jinghui, 196
Millennium Teahouse (*Qianxiye, women shuo xiangsheng*; Lai), 75
Mimi Fan (Lim), 50
Ming Hwa Yuan, 98
Mishima (*Jiamian—Sandao youjifu de gushi*), 121
misty (*menglong*) poetry, 166–167, 174
Modernist literary movement, 83–84, 92–93, 95, 97, 114
Mok Chiu Yu, Augustine, 137–138
Moths, The (*Kapai-Kapai*; Noer), 45n9, 57
multicultural experiences, 201–204
multilingualism/bilingualism, 33, 52–53, 55, 58–61, 63–64, 71–72, 173, 201–204. *see also* language; *Mama Looking for Her Cat* (*Xunzhao xiaomao de mama*; Kuo)
multiracial model/multiracialism, 35, 37–39, 68–69, 72

Nanyang University, 45
Nanyang University (Nantah) Drama Club, 43
National Establishment Council, 90
National Institute of Dramatic Art (NIDA), 28, 49
National Institute of the Arts (NIA; later Taipei National University of the Arts), 29, 93, 197, 200
National Theatre and Concert Hall, Taipei, 76, 197
National Theatre of China, 98
National Youth Theatre, 75
Nativist literary movement, 83–84, 92–93, 95, 97, 114
naturalist realism, 40, 56, 180, 184
Necessary Stage, The, 59
Nepotism (*Quandai feng*), 41
New Aspect Arts Centre, 90–91, 122
Ng, Johnny, 194
Ng Chia Kheng, 47
Night We Became Cross-Talk Comedians, The (*Nayiye, women shuo xiangsheng*; Lai), 6, 23, 74–75, 96, 106
1984/1997 (Mok and Yuen), 137
1997 plays, 7, 127, 154–155
Nirvana (*Nie pan*; Liu), 131
No Parking on Odd Days (*Danri buke tingche*; Kuo), 53, 60, 195
Nobel Prize in Literature, 4, 159–160, 167, 169, 188

INDEX

North Theater, 197
Notebook Theater, 89
Nurse Angamuthu's Romance (Le Blond), 51

Of Mountains and Seas (*Shanhaijing zhuan*; Gao), 188, 200
On the Hong Kong Stage (*Xianggang wutaishang*), 136
One Hundred Years of Solitude (*Bainian zhi guji*), 123, 140, 198, 199
One-China policy, 82, 101
Ong Keng Sen, 59, 199
Ong Teck Lian, Leanne, 194
Ong Toh, 47
Ooi Cheng-har, Vicki, 133
Oolah World, The (*Wula shijie*), 57
Opium War, 127, 138, 145
Opium War: Four Letters to Deng Xioaping (*Yapian zhanzheng: Zhi Deng Xiaoping de sifeng xin*; Yung), 7, 118, 126, 137, 138–154, 151*fig*
Orphan of Zhao, The (*Zhaoshi gu'er*; Lai), 131
Other Shore, The (*Bi'an*; Gao), 31, 170, 187, 189, 200
Our Town (Wilder), 132
Ouyang Yuqian, 10
Overflow of Life, The (*Shengming de juedi*; Tan), 43

Pai Hsien-yung, 90
Passerby, The (*Guoke*; Lu Xun), 95, 185–187
Peking Opera, 88–89
People's Action Party (PAP), 37, 44, 47
People's Republic of China (PRC), 6, 45, 80, 82, 100–101, 117, 127
Performance Workshop, 23, 56, 74–75, 79, 92–93, 95–96, 98, 106, 114, 125, 197, 199
Ping-fong Acting Troupe, 75n1, 91n8, 96
Plucking Stars (*Zhaixing*; Lai), 94
poor theater, 57, 92
Portraits of Women (*Lienü zhuan*), 126, 146
Power Versus Law (*Quan yu fa*; Xing), 171
Practice Performing Arts School (PPAS), 49, 61
Practice Theatre Ensemble/School, 49
Preliminary Explorations on the Art of Fiction (*Xiandai xiaoshuo jiqiao chutan*; Gao), 165, 187
Pun Tak Shu, 121

Qing government/dynasty, 10, 127, 140

radio broadcasters, 47
realism, 95, 132, 179–180, 188, 190–191
Recreation and Music Research Group, 43
Red Lotus Society (*Feixia A Da*; Lai), 75
Red Nose (*Hong bizi*; Yao), 75n1
Red Sky (*Hongse de tiankong*; Lai), 75, 194, 197
Rediffusion, 47
Rediffusion Mandarin Drama Group, 27
Rediffusion Mandarin Play Group, 43
Reform and Opening Up period, 8–9, 129
reform literature (*gaige wenxue*), 162, 165
Republic of China (ROC), 6, 80, 82, 85–86, 100–101
Requiem for Beauty (*Mei de zangli*; Gao), 200
Rhythm of Life (*Shenghuo de xuanlü*; Lim), 43
Rive-Gauche Theater Group, 89
River/Cloud (*Jiang/Yun · zhi/jian*; Lai), 198
Road, The (*Dalu*; Wong and Yung), 121, 153
Romance of the Rock (*Shitou ji*), 140
Romance of the Western Chamber (*Xixiang ji*; Hsiung), 131
Room with Paper Flowers (Goh), 50
roots-seeking literature (*xungen wenxue*), 162, 165, 167–168
Rosary Hill School Drama Club alumni, 121–122

Salute to Pao Kun (*Xiang Baokun zhijing*), 199
Samseng and the Chettiar's Daughter, The (Le Blond), 51
Sasitharan, Thirunalan, 59, 71, 73, 195
scar literature (*shanghen wenxue*), 162, 165, 166
Seals Theatre Company, 121, 133, 134, 135, 136, 153
Secret Love in Peach Blossom Land (*Anlian taohuayuan*; Lai), 7, 23, 75, 77, 95–106, 107*fig*, 109–113, 198
Selantan Arts Ensemble, 43
self-determination, 42, 78
Sha Yexin, 172
Shakespeare, William, 15, 134, 196–197
Sham, John, 120
Shamlet (*Shamuleite*; Lee), 75n1
Shanghai People's Art Theatre, 173, 194
Shanghai Theatre Academy (STA), 56n15, 59n19
Shouson Theatre, 139, 146, 151*fig*, 153, 154
Shum Sing-tak, Jim, 122
Silly Little Girl and the Funny Old Tree, The (*Sha guniang yu guai laoshu*; Liu), 57

INDEX

Singapore
  Cold War and, 7–8
  drama camp in, 1–3
  English, primacy of in, 44, 45–46
  linguistic divide in, 8
  linguistic variations and, 5
  Red Scare in, 4
Singapore Amateur Players (SAP), 41, 42–43
Singapore Federation of Chinese Drama Associations, 54, 57
Singapore Festival of Art, 45n9, 57
Singapore I-Lien Dramatic Society, 43
Singapore Impromptu (*Xinjiapo jixing*; Lai), 196
Singapore Performing Arts Studio (SPAS), 23, 28, 43, 49
Singapore's Chinatown: A Changing Scene (*Fengyu Niucheshui*; Yue), 40
Singlish, 50, 51
Sino-British Joint Declaration, 7, 30, 117, 126, 135, 137, 138, 148–149, 154
Small Well Alley (*Xiaojing hutong*; Li), 171
Snow in August (*Bayue xue*; Gao), 170, 200
socialist realism, 9, 168, 179
Soul Mountain (*Lingshan*; Gao), 31, 170
Sparrow with Bamboo Twigs (Liang), 34–35, 47n10
Speak Mandarin Campaign, 35
Spirits Play, The (*Lingxi*; Kuo), 194, 195fig, 199
Stage Club, The, 52n13
Stanislavsky, Konstantin, 56, 173, 180
Stockerlock and Millipilli, 153
street operas, 27, 47–48
street theater, 137–138
Strooker, Shireen, 97
Substation—A Home for the Arts, The, 195
Sun Zuping, 59n19
Sunrise (*Richu*; Cao Yu), 131
Sunset Rise (*Xiyang wuxian*; Kuo), 194
surtitles/translation, absence of, 64–65, 67–68
Sword Has Two Edges, The (Li), 50

taboo, 29, 108, 125, 126
Taiwan
  Chinese diaspora and, 18
  Chineseness and, 79–83
  Lai's work and, 6–7
  linguistic variations and, 5
  return of, 85–86
  Sunflower movements in, 17
  "two Chinas" and, 6
Taiwanese New Cinema, 75, 84, 198

Tan, Alvin, 59
Tan Poh Han, 43, 50
Tang Shu Wing, 138
Tao Yuanming, 99, 100
Tay Bin Wee, 48
Teahouse (*Chaguan*), 56
Teo, William, 59, 65
Thatcher, Margaret, 29–30, 117, 145
Theatre Above, 197
"Theatre of the Oppressed" (Boal), 142–143, 148, 156
Theatre Practice, The, 49, 125, 194, 202
TheatreWorks, 51, 59
Third Stage, 59
Thunderstorm (*Leiyu*; Cao Yu), 131
Tian Han, 10
Tiananmen Square Incident, 31n11, 156, 159, 163, 187, 198
T'ien Experimental Drama Club, 88
Ting Nai-chu, 96
To Kwok-Wai, Raymond, 136
Touch Base policy, 129
Toy Factory Theatre Ensemble, 63n21
Tsai Ming-liang, 89, 199
Tsoi Sik Cheong, Hardy, 136, 137, 196, 200
2.28 Incident, 82, 86

Uekrongtham, Ekachai, 59
Umbrella Revolution, 17
United Nations, 42, 80–81, 82, 101
U-Theatre, 94
utopia, 99, 100, 105, 108–109, 111, 113

Verfremdungseffekt, 56, 144, 180–181
Village, The (*Baodao yicun*), 115

waisheng/waishengren, 18, 79, 82–83, 86, 109, 111–112, 114, 116, 198
Waiting for Godot (Beckett), 102–103, 133, 161
Wandering in the Garden, Waking from a Dream (*Youyuan jingmeng*; Pai), 90
Wang, Wayne, 119
Wang Chi-mei, 94
Wang Gui, 177
Wang Meng, 165
Wang Ming-chun, Liza, 197
Wang Mo-lin, 91–92
Wang Peigong, 172, 177
Wang Qiutian, 27, 43, 48
Wang Sa, 47
We (*WM women WM*; Wang), 172, 177

INDEX

We All Grew Up This Way (*Women doushi zheyang zhangda de*; Lai), 94, 95
Wei Ying Chuan, 199
West Kowlooon Cultural District, 158
What If I Really Were? (*Jiaru wo shi zhende*; Sha, Li and Yao), 172, 173, 177
When Smiles Are Done (Goh), 50
White Terror, 82, 83, 91
Why Have I Died? (*Wo weishenme si le*; Xie), 172
Wildman (*Yeren*; Gao), 31, 175, 187, 188
Wilson, Robert, 123
Without Isms (*Meiyou zhuyi*; Gao), 170
W!ld Rice, 59
Woman Who Broke the Mirror, The (*Dapo jingzi de nren*; Lin), 43
Wong, Gus, 91, 121, 153
Wong Hing-cheung, Jacob, 122
Wong Jim, James, 134n5
Wong Mei Lan, May, 195
Wong Souk Yee, 36, 59, 63
Woo Yan Wai, Mathias, 125
Works for Pao Kun: Legend Alive (*Chuanqi weiliao—xian gei Baokun de zuopin*), 196
World Theater Exhibition, 87–88
Wu Hsing-kuo, 200
Wu Jing-jyi, 56, 88, 90, 95
Wuzhen Theatre Festival, 198

Xia Yan, 85, 131
xiangsheng play series (Lai), 6, 74, 79, 95–96, 106, 108n14
Xiao Wu Theater, 89
Xie Shaoguang, 194
xinyao (ballads composed by young Singaporeans, or Singaporean ballads), 34–35
Xiong Yuanwei, 196
xiqu, 10, 85

Ya Xian, 85
Yang, Edward, 84, 196, 198
Yang Lian, 166–167
Yang Shih-peng, Daniel, 56, 135

Yao Ke (Yao Xinnong), 130
Yao Yi-wei, 29, 75n1, 85, 88, 92, 94
Ye Fong, 47
Yeo Cheng Chuan, Robert, 50
Yeung Wing-Tak, David, 121
Yu Qiuyu, 3, 56
Yu Shizhi, 185
Yu Yun, 59n19
Yue Ye, 40
Yuen Che Hung, 137
Yung Ning Tsun, Danny
    background of, 29–30
    blueprints used by, 25
    collaboration and, 196–197, 198–199
    critical appraisals of, 3–4
    drama camps and, 56, 193
    establishment of reputation of, 24
    generational context and, 6
    Hong Kong and, 7
    Hong Kong in global Chinese context and, 154–158
    Kuo's passing and, 196
    on Lai, 97
    localization and, 126–138
    marginal consciousness and, 22
    multilingualism and, 202
    photograph of, 32*fig*
    play analysis and, 138–154
    possibility and, 190
    sociohistorical context and, 117–126

Za-Koenji Public Theatre, 199
Zha Lifang, 59n18
Zhang Xian, 199
Zhang Yimou, 167
Zhao Rulin, 41, 42
zhiqing, 167
Zhou Yu, 88
Zhu Xu, 27, 48
Zuni Icosahedron, 24, 29–30, 91, 117–119, 121–123, 125–126, 138–140, 142, 146, 150, 152–158, 198–199, 202

www.ingramcontent.com/pod-product-compliance
Lightning Source LLC
Chambersburg PA
CBHW032146230426
43672CB00011B/2460